FIRE & DESOLATION

FIRE & DESOLATION

*The Revolutionary War's 1778 Campaign
as Waged from Quebec and Niagara Against
the American Frontiers*

GAVIN K. WATT

DUNDURN
TORONTO

Copyright © Gavin K. Watt, 2017

All rights reserved. No part of this publication may be reproduced, stored in a retrieval system, or transmitted in any form or by any means, electronic, mechanical, photocopying, recording, or otherwise (except for brief passages for purpose of review) without the prior permission of Dundurn Press. Permission to photocopy should be requested from Access Copyright.

Cover image: Chris Armstrong
Printer: Webcom

Library and Archives Canada Cataloguing in Publication

Watt, Gavin K., author
    Fire and desolation : the Revolutionary War's 1778 campaign as waged from Quebec and Niagara against the American frontiers / Gavin K. Watt.

Includes bibliographical references and index.
Issued in print and electronic formats.
ISBN 978-1-4597-3858-4 (softcover).--ISBN 978-1-4597-3859-1 (PDF).--ISBN 978-1-4597-3860-7 (EPUB)

    1. United States--History--Revolution, 1775-1783--Participation, Canadian. 2. United States--History--Revolution, 1775-1783--Campaigns. 3. United States--History--Revolution, 1775-1783--Indians. 4. Canada--History--1775-1783. 5. Northern boundary of the United States--History--18th century. 6. Iroquois Indians--Wars--History--18th century. 7. Indians of North America--Wars--1750-1815. I. Title.

FC420.W3825 2017	971.02'4	C2017-900756-4
		C2017-900757-2

1 2 3 4 5   21 20 19 18 17

 Conseil des Arts du Canada   Canada Council for the Arts       ONTARIO ARTS COUNCIL CONSEIL DES ARTS DE L'ONTARIO an Ontario government agency un organisme du gouvernement de l'Ontario

We acknowledge the support of the **Canada Council for the Arts** and the **Ontario Arts Council** for our publishing program. We also acknowledge the financial support of the **Government of Ontario**, through the **Ontario Book Publishing Tax Credit** and the **Ontario Media Development Corporation**, and the **Government of Canada.**

Care has been taken to trace the ownership of copyright material used in this book. The author and the publisher welcome any information enabling them to rectify any references or credits in subsequent editions.
— *J. Kirk Howard, President*

The publisher is not responsible for websites or their content unless they are owned by the publisher.

VISIT US AT

 dundurn.com | @dundurnpress | dundurnpress | dundurnpress

Dundurn
3 Church Street, Suite 500
Toronto, Ontario, Canada
M5E 1M2

Contents

Acknowledgements	7
Comparative Timetable of the 1778 Campaign	9
List of Abbreviations	13

Chapter One — 15
Lake Champlain, Upper Hudson River, and Lower Quebec
"Lakes full of the Enemy's boats"

Chapter Two — 93
Mohawk Region
"Victims to the Rage of their savage Neighbours"

Chapter Three — 163
The Wyoming and Wyalusing Campaigns
"Stand firm and the day is ours!"

Chapter Four — 218
New York's Midwestern Frontier
Hostile Designs of the Indians and Tories

Chapter Five — 248
Back in the Mohawk Region
"A shocking sight … of savage and brutal barbarity"

Notes	321
Bibliography	364
Image Credits	377
Index	379

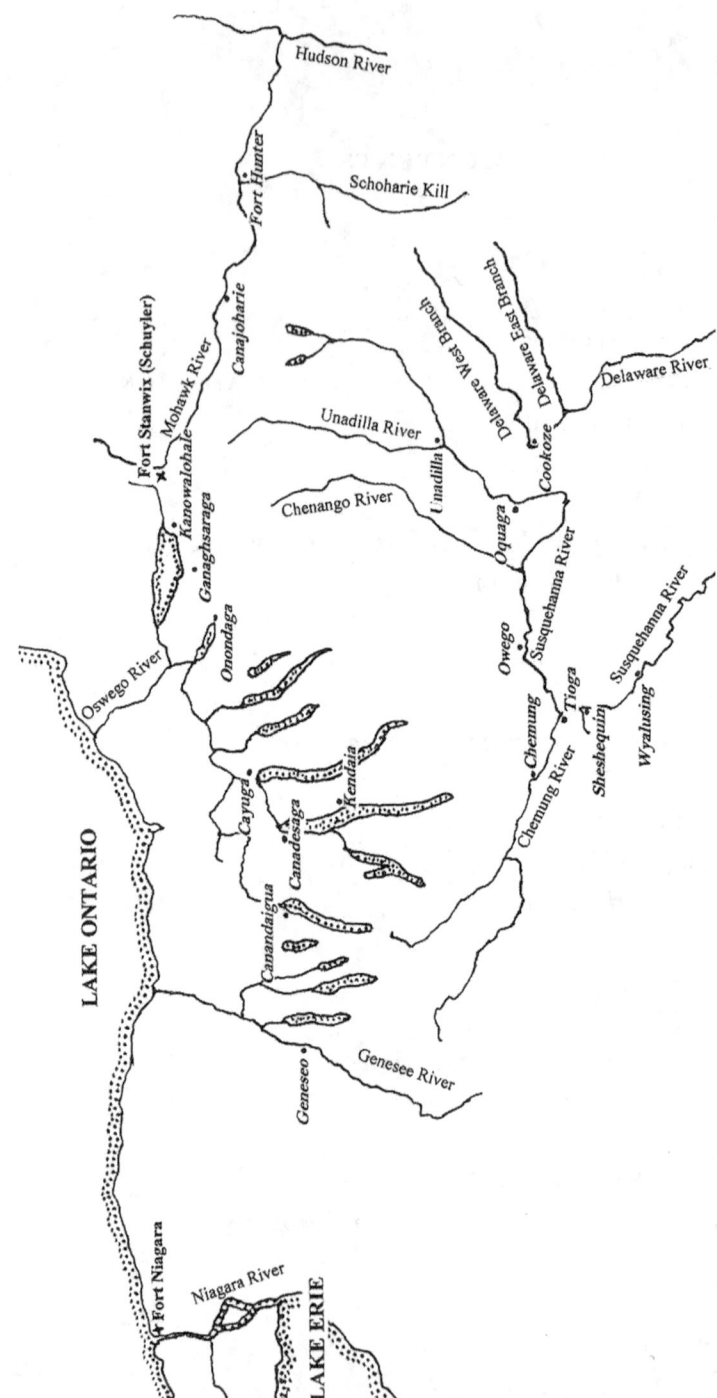

Locations of major "Indian Castles" and primary Native assembly points.

Acknowledgements

Once again, I must give thanks to the noted northern New York historian Jim Morrison of Gloversville, who over the decades has shared a wealth of meticulously gathered historical information.

I am greatly indebted to Bill Smy, who provided me with his gigantic collection of personally prepared transcripts relating to Butler's Rangers' history.

My thanks to Michael Barbieri, a historian and re-enactor, for his strong support and preparation of a detailed map of Major Carleton's expedition against the Otter Creek settlements.

My great thanks to my friend Professor Carl Benn of Ryerson University, who specializes in the history of the Six Nations. His guidance on several complex issues has been most appreciated.

The late Paul L. Stevens's superb study of the Natives' relationship to both the British and the Congressional administrations has added substantially to this work.

My thanks to historian/re-enactor Nathan Hoffmann, who saved me from the gaffe of incorrectly designating Alden's Massachusetts Regiment.

My thanks also to Don Glickstein, author of *After Yorktown*, who offered help with some difficult issues, and to my online correspondent, Picky Parnell, who has supplied useful references.

I also wish to acknowledge contributions from Dr. John A. Houlding, Kim Stacy, and Ken D. Johnson.

Lastly, to my friend and fellow Royal Yorker re-enactor Christopher Armstrong, my great thanks for his extensive assistance with preparing images for this book, and for the cover design.

Other than in quotations from primary sources, my use of the term "Canadien" refers exclusively to Franco Canadians. When I employ "Canadian," I am referring to both Anglo and Franco Canadians.

COMPARATIVE TIMETABLE OF THE 1778 CAMPAIGN

CHAMPLAIN AND UPPER HUDSON	THE MOHAWK AND SCHOHARIE REGIONS	PENNSYLVANIA	NEW YORK'S MID-WESTERN FRONTIER
		Jan 3 Butler's Rangers' detachment captured on PA/NY border	
		Feb–Apr Senecas & Cayugas extensively raid western PA	
Feb 17 Lafayette arrives in Albany to command invasion of Canada			
	Mar 7 Schuyler holds 6Ntns council at Johnstown		
Mar 12 Natives attack Shelburne, VT			
Mar 13 Congress cancels Lafayette's invasion	**Mar 15** Tories & Natives destroy Fairfield		
	Mar 29 Natives destroy Snydersbush		
			Apr Natives raid Cochecton

CHAMPLAIN AND UPPER HUDSON	THE MOHAWK AND SCHOHARIE REGIONS	PENNSYLVANIA	NEW YORK'S MID-WESTERN FRONTIER
	Apr 1 Fort Plank construction begins		
	Apr 15 Walter Butler escapes		
	Apr 20 Tories & Natives attack Ephratah	**May** Major council of 6Ntns & affiliates at Tioga Second council of 6Ntns with Major Butler	
	May 30 Skirmish at Cobleskill	**May 20** Oneidas skirmish at Barren Hill	
	Jun 2–6 Tories & Natives strike Mayfield, Philadelphia & Fonda's Bushes, Fish House, Tilleborough		
	Jun 18 Native war party in Schoharie	**Jul 2** Wyoming actions begin	
	Jul 5 The Great Runaway		
	Jul 18 Natives destroy Springfield & Andrewstown		
Jun 26 General Haldimand takes command			**Aug mid** Militia confront war party near Pepacton

CHAMPLAIN AND UPPER HUDSON	THE MOHAWK AND SCHOHARIE REGIONS	PENNSYLVANIA	NEW YORK'S MID-WESTERN FRONTIER
Aug mid Peters's Onion River	**July 24** Alden's 6MA arrives Cherry Valley		**Aug 20** War party raids Peenpack
	Aug 9 Brant hits Schoharie		**Aug 26** Continentals at Pakatakan
	Aug 10 Continentals raid Butternuts		**Sep 5** Natives & Tories raid Lackawack
	Sep 17 Large raid on Fort Dayton & German Flatts		
	Sep 19 Rebel Oneidas destroy Butternuts & part of Unadilla	**Sep late** Hartley's Expedn	
Oct 13 Lafayette proposes new plan to attack Quebec	**Oct 9** Continentals destroy Oquaga & Unadilla	**Oct 29** Wyoming corpses buried	
Oct 29–Nov 10 Major Carleton's Lake Champlain & Otter Creek Raid			
Nov d'Estaing's Proclamation to the Canadiens			

CHAMPLAIN AND UPPER HUDSON

THE MOHAWK AND SCHOHARIE REGIONS

Oct mid Royal Yorkers & Kanehsatakes at Johnson Hall

Nov 11 Cherry Valley attack

PENNSYLVANIA

NEW YORK'S MID-WESTERN FRONTIER

List of Abbreviations

1Lieutenant — First Lieutenant
2Lieutenant — Second Lieutenant
1Major — First Major
2-I-C — Second-in-Command
6NID — Six Nations Indian Department
ACM — Albany County Militia
2ACM — 2nd Albany County Militia Regt; 1ACM, 3ACM, et cetera
Capt — Captain
C-in-C — Commander-in-Chief
CO — commanding officer
Col — Colonel
LCol — Lieutenant-Colonel
ContLine — Continental Line
2MA — 2nd Massachusetts ContLine; 6MA, et cetera
1NH — 1st New Hampshire ContLine
1NY — 1st New York ContLine; 2NY, 3NY, et cetera
4PA — 4th Pennsylvania ContLine; 8PA, et cetera
DQMG — Deputy Quartermaster General
HQ — Headquarters

IT — Indian Territory
KRR — King's Royal Regiment of New York/King's Royal Yorkers
Lt/Lieut — Lieutenant
MA — Massachusetts
NH — New Hampshire
NY — New York
OC — officer commanding
OCM — Orange County Militia
4OCM — 4th Orange County Militia Regt; 3OCM, et cetera
Pdr — pounder, the designation for the weight of solid shot fired by an artillery piece
QID — Quebec Indian Department
QM — Quartermaster
QMG — Quartermaster General
QLR — Queen's Loyal Rangers
RHE — Royal Highland Emigrants
RO — Regimental Orders
TCM — Tryon County Militia
1TCM — 1st Tryon County Militia Regt; 2TCM, 3TCM, et cetera
UCM — Ulster County Militia
1UCM — 1st Ulster County Militia Regt; 2UCM, 3UCM, et cetera
VMR — Vermont Militia Regiment
1VMR — 1st Vermont Militia Regt; 2VMR, 3VMR, et cetera
VT — Vermont

Chapter One

Lake Champlain, Upper Hudson River, and Lower Quebec

"Lakes full of the Enemy's boats"

Disasters of the 1777 Campaign

The 1777 campaign had been an outstanding success for the Continental Army and its militia auxiliaries in the northern theatre. Two British expeditions out of Canada had been soundly defeated — first, a subordinate venture under St. Leger was thwarted and compelled to retreat, and then a major thrust led by Burgoyne was forced into an ignominious surrender at Saratoga. Despite these victories, there were unresolved issues that the American Congress needed to address in the north. Notably, Quebec Province remained British, and was a potential base for future operations against the young republic. Because Quebec stretched from the Atlantic Ocean to the Mississippi River, it loomed like a dark cloud above the United States. While Britain's army had been defeated, her navy still dominated Lake Champlain and kept that traditional invasion route open.

As long as the British controlled Quebec, there would be a threat of renewed invasion attempts. As well, the British maintained military alliances with many northern Native tribes, encouraging them to wage war against the republic and supplying them with the means to do so, which meant that frontier settlements were at continuous risk and westward expansion was blocked.

A New Invasion of Canada

A few weeks before the tail end of Burgoyne's straggling, defeated columns reached the Atlantic coast, Major-General Horatio Gates, the victor of Saratoga, made a plan to attack St. John's, Quebec. On November 15, he instructed the Continental ranger captain, Benjamin Whitcomb, to deliver a message to Colonel Timothy Bedel at Haverhill, in New Hampshire's Cöos region. Without delay, Bedel was to raise three hundred volunteers for an attack on Canada, placing himself in command, with Whitcomb as his major.[1]

Bedel had seen extensive service as a New Hampshire Provincial lieutenant at the reduction of Fortress Louisbourg and the capture of Havana, Cuba, during the Seven Years' War. He was a member of New Hampshire's provincial assembly and, in May 1775, had been appointed to command a company of rangers for service in the invasion of Canada, and simultaneously to act as the northern army's de facto Indian agent. In 1776, he was promoted to colonel and ordered to return home to recruit his rangers to regimental strength. Once this was accomplished, he went back to Quebec, where his regiment was assigned an advanced position at The Cedars up the St. Lawrence River from Montreal. Bedel was absent at the Native settlement of Kahnawake when the British attacked The Cedars, forced his regiment to surrender, and defeated a relieving force. As a result, he was dismissed in disgrace. As Gates was pleased to appoint Bedel to the key role in this new venture into Canada, it seems that cooler heads had prevailed, and his explanations for being absent from The Cedars had been investigated and accepted.[2]

Massachusetts-born Whitcomb was one of the most successful partisan leaders of the northern war. He also was a Seven Years' War veteran of several campaigns in a Massachusetts Provincial regiment.

At war's end, he moved his family about — to New Hampshire, the Grants, and the Cöos region. When the new war broke out, he took his family back to southern New Hampshire and accepted a lieutenant's commission and the recruiting officer's role in Young's company of Bedel's Rangers. He served throughout the Canadian invasion, and during the retreat made his way back to Ticonderoga, where he volunteered for the hazardous assignment of scouting the British lines as far north as Montreal. According to one of his contemporaries, he was well-suited to this task. "Whitcomb was a presumptuous fellow, entirely devoid of fear, of more than common strength, equal to an Indian for enduring hardship or privation, drank to excess even when in the greatest peril, balls whistling around his head." During one of his long-range scouts, he garnered lasting notoriety by sniping and mortally wounding a British brigadier from the cover of woods. This act earned him a death sentence from Quebec's governor, Guy Carleton. Whitcomb was unmoved by this threat, and his skills as a scout and leader were recognized when he was promoted to captain and instructed to raise a two-company corps of Continental rangers. His rangers performed yeoman's duty during the 1777 campaign, fighting as light infantry in the first battle of Saratoga.

A second invasion of Canada had been in Gates's mind even before he succeeded in defeating Burgoyne. Based on information gathered from Canadian Native spies, Colonel Moses Hazen of Congress's Own Second Canadian Regiment had convinced the general that the majority of Quebeckers were pro-rebel and that the marginally garrisoned forts at St. John's and Chambly were vulnerable to attack. In mid-September, he instructed Colonel Bedel to recruit a body of Abenaki warriors and, as noted, two months later, to raise three hundred New Hampshire and Vermont troops. This force was to launch an attack on St. John's beginning February 1. Gates planned that Bedel's raid would be followed in the spring by a full-scale expedition against Montreal employing Hazen's two-hundred-man Canadien Regiment and five hundred volunteers to unite with Bedel. At least, that was Gates's plan.

So, he must have had a rude surprise when he discovered on December 3, 1777, that Congress had already made its own plans to mount a secret raid to destroy the British shipping locked in the winter's ice at St. John's and nearby ports on the Richelieu River, which in a stroke would remove the naval threat on Lake Champlain. Brigadier-General John Stark of New Hampshire, who had commanded the stunning defeat of Burgoyne's unwise adventure near Bennington, was chosen to command this new strike into Quebec from his headquarters at Saratoga.

Congress's decision to give Stark the command of the opening strike had the potential to be awkward, as he and Bedel were at odds. To ensure a prominent say in the venture, Gates, the perpetual plotter, contrived to get himself placed on the newly created Board of War.

About this same time, Congress decided upon a full-blown "irruption into Canada" under the command of the young French adventurer, the Marquis de Lafayette. Following Stark's initial attack to reduce shipping, a 2,500-man expedition would be mounted from Albany under Lafayette's command, with Conway as his second and Stark his third; Bedel would be entirely sidelined. Lafayette was to occupy Montreal and wait there for reinforcements — presumably to be led by Gates — for the ultimate reduction of Quebec City, which would add a second major feather in the latter's ambitious cap.[3]

Congress believed that Lafayette's selection would be well-received by Quebec's predominantly francophone population and calm any residual fears and resentments left over from the disastrous 1775 invasion. Six French gentlemen were appointed to attend Lafayette and serve as officers for the bodies of Canadiens to be raised in Canada. As the vast majority of Franco-Quebeckers had stubbornly resisted being co-opted by either side of the conflict during the three previous campaigns, this measure was undoubtedly optimistic.[4]

On January 24, Gates informed Stark of Congress's plan to mount a major expedition against Canada with Lafayette in command, and that the Irish-born French Army career officer Major-General Thomas Conway, who was at the time the United States' army's

Marie-Joseph Paul Yves Roch Gilbert du Motier, Marquis de Lafayette (1757–1834), Major-General, United States Army.

inspector-general, had been appointed second-in-command. Stark was instructed to act in concert with Lafayette and Conway to promote "the interest and political views of the United States in Canada." It is interesting that Gates was the one to reveal the news of Conway's appointment, as the pair of them had earlier toyed with the idea of Gates replacing General George Washington as supreme commander.[5]

Washington had been kept in the dark about Congress's plan to invade Canada, and when the details came to his attention, he was anything but impressed, styling the venture a "child of folly." Nor was Lafayette eager to accept the commission; Washington, however, persuaded him to take the role, while privately thinking the expedition would never materialize. The young Frenchman was enthused by the idea of a conquest, but, as an intimate of Washington's, he undoubtedly knew of Gates's and Conway's manoeuvring, and unsuccessfully demanded that Conway be replaced by his personal friend Major General Baron Johann de Kalb, a German-born French officer.[6]

The Board of War's instructions to the marquis were over Gates's signature as its president. They detailed the troops assigned to the expedition: Brigadier John Nixon's Massachusetts Brigade; Colonel Goose Van Schaick's 1st New York Regiment; Colonel Seth Warner's Additional Regiment; Colonel James Livingston's

1st Canadian Regiment; Colonel Moses Hazen's 2nd Canadian; Colonel Timothy Bedel's New Hampshire Regiment; and Captain Benjamin Whitcomb's Rangers. The board reasoned, "As most of the Troops ordered for this Service have been upon Duty in Canada, there will be no want of any other Guides than such as may be chosen from among them — Genl Stark, Colo Warner and Col Bedel, with the Assistant Deputy Quarter Master General Colonel Hazen, know every Road, Pass and Post in the Country — You have only to consult with them as you advance, and if absolutely necessary upon your Retreat."

The QM general, the commissary general, and the commander of artillery were instructed to provide ammunition, provisions, stores, and carriages "requisite for the intended Service," and Hazen was sent forward to expedite these orders. Lafayette was told, "You need therefore be under no concern for Supplies," and that as the expedition's "[s]uccess will depend principally upon the vigour, and alertness with which the Enterprise is conducted, the Board recommend it to you to lose no time — the rapidity of your motions and the consternation of the enemy will do the business."

As a nod to the inclemency of the season, Lafayette was advised that the commissary of clothing at Albany had been ordered "to furnish all the Woollens, and every Comfort his Stores can afford." Tentage was considered unnecessary, as his troops would be constantly in the woods at night and were "[well-]acquainted with the mode of covering themselves." He was instructed, "Upon your gaining possession of St. Johns or Montreal, you will publish a Declaration of your Intentions to the Canadians, and invite them to join the army of the United States — Colonel Hazen's Regiment of four Battalions is to be first completed to the Establishment and the Officers and Soldiers who inlist are to be allowed the Bounty and Reward offer'd them by Congress."

Lafayette was given the latitude to judge the "political complexion of the Inhabitants." If he thought it unwise or unnecessary to have the Canadians take "an open Part with these States," he was to publish a Manifesto requiring their strict neutrality. If he discovered "a general disinclination of the Natives [i.e., the Canadiens] to join the American Standard," he was to destroy all the works and vessels at St. John's, Chambly, and Île-aux-Noix and retire to the settlements below, and then to Saratoga.

> If on the contrary the Canadians are ardently desirous of assisting to establish the Freedom and Independence of America, you will inform them that when they embark in the common cause, they must determine to receive the Resolves of Congress and the Currency of America, with that Reverence and Alacrity, which have ever been manifested in the Acts and Dealing of the Subjects of the United States. They are then to be requested to send Delegates to represent their State in the Congress of the United States and to conform in all Political Respects to the Union and Confederation established in them.

When he managed to take possession of Montreal, Lafayette was to seize for the use of the public all arms, ammunition, and warlike stores, linens, woollens, and Indian goods, "making such allowance for the private Property so secured as you shall think most consistent with Justice and sound Policy and the Merits of the respective individuals — In transacting this business, you will take effectual Care to prevent every Species of Plunder, and embezzlement as these may tend to raise Suspicions in the minds of the Canadians that may be both dishonorable and prejudicial to the Interest of the United States."[7]

Raise suspicions! Such understatement! Surely Canadien memories were not so short as to forget the rebel occupation of two years before — the passing of worthless Continental currency and bogus promissory notes, the plundering of Montreal's commercial storehouses, and threats of general arson.[8]

And What of Quebec?

In contrast, little was happening in Quebec. Burgoyne's failure had dealt a major blow, and it was extremely difficult to compensate for the loss of so many fine troops. London had no grand plans in the offing to reassume a northern offensive, and no reinforcements were destined for the province. Carleton continued to sulk over his removal as the Northern Army commander, and waited impatiently for his replacement. He declined to take any responsibility for his Native allies, as their management had been taken from his hands by the British government's American secretary, Lord George Germain. This left the Indian Department's agents in lower Quebec, Niagara, and Detroit floundering with weak financial support and no fresh instructions.

Although Burgoyne's reports of Native failures and defections were a recurring theme in his correspondence, he could not claim that the Quebec Indian Department's European officers had shirked their duties. Historian Paul Stevens notes, "Burgoyne's misadventures had gutted the Canada Indian Department and seriously endangered British Indian policy throughout the northern district." Of the department's four British resident officers, one was badly wounded and recuperating in Montreal; another was killed in the Walloomscoick battle; one was a prisoner of the rebels; and another had taken refuge in New York City. Three British supernumerary officers attached to the department were in a similar state. The Canadien officers faired only marginally better — two were disabled by wounds, another was dead, and two were prisoners of the rebels. To meet the immediate needs of the new year, only a handful of Canadiens were on duty with Major Campbell and his deputy, Captain Fraser, both of whom had escaped Gates's notice after the surrender as being responsible for his feared and detested Native foes.[9]

Carleton understood that his major responsibility was to protect Canada from another rebel invasion. He needed an early warning system, and knew that Provincial and Native scouts were his best method for gaining intelligence in the depth of winter. While he deplored Native warfare, the governor in no way rejected their superb skills as deep-penetration agents. He established a system of patrols, beginning in December, that emanated from the St. Lawrence and Richelieu posts. The first patrol was led by one of Campbell's most active department officers, Jean-Claude-Chamilly de Lorimier, who was able to persuade some loyal Kahnawakes to attend. On January 12, Carleton instructed Sir John Johnson, the loyalist managing the Secret Service, to coordinate efforts with Colonel Campbell to send out a series of long-range patrols, which began on February 3.

Lieutenant Wills Crofts, 34th Regiment, who shared responsibility for oversight of the fractious Abenaki community of Odanak with Canadien militia captain Jean-Baptiste-Melchior Hertel de Rouville, was successful in dispatching a patrol to the St. Francis River. A second Abenaki patrol was sent out ten days later, but rebel influence in this settlement was so strong that raising men for these scouts was difficult, and de Rouville augmented the Natives' efforts with Canadien patrols to examine the nearby Yamaska and Nicolet Rivers.

Jean-Baptiste-Melchior Hertel de Rouville (1748–1817), Capitaine, Milice de Québec.

Parties crawled across Vermont and upstate New York. Similarly, Native, and Ranger scouts were dispatched from Niagara to scour the Mohawk region and northern Pennsylvania. Needless to say, the rebels were active in this same pursuit, and their scouts haunted lower Quebec, Oswegatchie, and Niagara.[10]

While King George III and the British parliament were shocked over the loss of Burgoyne's army, there had been considerable satisfaction over Howe's capture of Philadelphia. Any contentment over this accomplishment was due to fade quickly, however, as King Louis XVI of France viewed Burgoyne's decisive defeat as proof that the rebels were capable of achieving independence from Britain, and on December 6, he authorized the negotiation of an alliance with the United States, which was finalized on February 6. One month later, France declared war on its ancient enemy. Suddenly, the American war had expanded into a worldwide conflict.

Vermont Takes Action

The minutes of Vermont's governing council for February 10, 1778, noted a request from Colonel Hazen, the commander of the Continental troops in Albany, to raise as many volunteers as possible to serve in an expedition against Canada. The council resolved to raise three hundred volunteers for a regiment to be commanded by Lieutenant-Colonel Commandant Samuel Herrick. They were to continue in service till the end of April. Benjamin Wait was to be major, and the captains were to be Ebenezer Allen, Jesse Sawyer, Parmelee Allen, Ebenezer Wood, Abner Sealey, and Josiah Boyden. Subalterns who had served in the 1777 campaign were to be offered the opportunity to serve again. If any chose not to, the captains were directed to appoint such men as would be most likely to raise their quota of men. This instruction was expanded on February 15 to award each volunteer a ten-dollar bounty, plus wages and a right to plunder similar to that received by "Volunteers from the other free

& Independent States of America." Those without shoes, stockings, or blankets would have them provided from Continental stores. Recruiting officers would receive a dollar for each recruit. The goal was to have the men ready for service by March 1.

Because Stark's three-man scout dispatched north on Lake Champlain had been taken by British Provincials operating from Pointe-au-Fer, the council recommended that Hazen mount a guard at a proper post on the lake to secure the hay and forage deposited there for the army, noting that their loss would be very detrimental to the northern expedition.[11]

Lafayette Arrives

Lafayette arrived in Albany on February 17, where he met with New York's governor, George Clinton, whom he discovered was not at all enthusiastic about the invasion. Lafayette found that Generals Schuyler, Lincoln, and Arnold were of the same mind. It was said that there were neither funds, provisions, nor men to guarantee success. Indeed, there was widespread disgust that the Board of War would contemplate such a campaign in the middle of the winter. Two days later, Lafayette reported to Washington.

> Why am I so far from you, and what business had the board of war to hurry me through the ice and snow without knowing what I should do, neither what they were doing themselves? You have thought, perhaps, that their project would be attended with some difficulty, that some means had been neglected, that I could not obtain all the success and that immensity of laurels which they had promised to me; but I defy your excellency to conceive any idea of what I have seen since I left the place where I was quiet and near my friends, to run myself through all the blunders of madness or treachery (God knows what).

Lafayette met with General Conway, who had preceded him by three days, and was pleased to find him very active and displaying the best of intentions. Conway's first words were that the expedition was impossible. He advised the young Frenchman that Schuyler, Lincoln, and Arnold were against the enterprise, as were many other important officers. Even Hazen said the States were not strong enough to launch this attack, although the soldiers of his regiment were eager to proceed. Lafayette noted that "Everybody answers me that it would be madness to undertake this operation."

> I have been deceived by the board of war; they have, by the strongest expressions, promised to me one thousand, and (what is more to be depended upon) they have assured to me in writing, *two thousand and five hundred combatants, at a low estimate.* Now, Sir, I do not believe I can find, *in all,* twelve hundred fit for duty, and most part of those very men are naked, even for a summer's campaign. I was to find General Stark with a large body, and indeed General Gates had told to me, *General* Stark *will have burnt the fleet before your arrival.* Well, the first letter I receive in Albany is from General Stark, who wishes to know *what number of men, from whence, for what time, for what rendezvous, I desire him to raise.* Colonel [Bedel], who was to rise too, would have done something *had he received money.* One asks, what encouragement his people will have, the other has no clothes; not one of them has received a dollar of what was due to them. I have applied to every body, I have begged at every door I could these two days, and I see that I could do something were the expedition to be begun in five weeks. But you know we have not an hour to lose, and indeed it is now rather too late, had we every thing in readiness.

> There is a spirit of dissatisfaction prevailing among the soldiers, and even the officers, which is owing to their not being paid for some time since. This department is much indebted, and as near as I can ascertain, for so short a time, I have already discovered near eight hundred thousand dollars due to the continental troops, some militia, the quarter-master's department, &.c. &c. &c. It was with four hundred thousand dollars, only the half of which is arrived to day, that I was to undertake the operation, and satisfy the men under my commands. I send to Congress the account of those debts. Some clothes, by Colonel Hazen's activity, are arrived from Boston, but not enough by far, and the greatest part is cut off.
>
> We have had intelligence from a deserter, who makes the enemy stronger than I thought. There is no such thing as straw on board the [St. John's] vessels to burn them. I have sent to Congress a full account of the matter; I hope it will open their eyes. What they will resolve upon I do not know, but I think I must wait here for their answer. I have enclosed to the president, copies of the most important letters I had received. It would be tedious for your excellency, were I to undertake the minutest detail of everything; it will be sufficient to say that the want of men, clothes, money, and the want of time, deprives me of all hopes as to this excursion....

The marquis's closing comments reflected a rich young aristocrat's concern over his personal prestige, a personality characteristic that many rebellious Americans found deplorable in British noblemen.

> Your excellency may judge that I am very distressed by this disappointment. My being appointed to the command of the expedition is known through the

continent, it will be soon known in Europe, as I have been desired by members of Congress, to write to my friends; my being at the head of an army, people will be in great expectations, and what shall I answer?

I am afraid it will reflect on my reputation, and I shall be laughed at. My fears upon that subject are so strong, that I would choose to become again only a volunteer, unless Congress offers the means of mending this ugly business by some glorious operation; but I am very far from giving to them the least notice upon that matter. General Arnold seems very fond of a diversion against New York, and he is too sick to take the field before four or five months. I should be happy if something was proposed to me in that way, but I will never ask, nor even seem desirous of anything directly from Congress; for you, dear general, I know very well, that you will do every thing to procure me the only thing I am ambitious of — glory.

Three days later, he wrote a petulant letter to Washington.

I have written lately to you my distressing, ridiculous, foolish, and indeed, nameless situation. I am sent with a great noise, at the head of an army for doing great things; the whole continent, France and Europe herself, and what is the worst, the British army, are in great expectations. How far they will be deceived, how far we shall be ridiculed, you may judge by the candid account you have got of the state of our affairs.... The want of money, the dissatisfaction among the soldiers, the disinclination of every one (except the Canadians who mean to stay at [i.e., return] home) for this expedition, are as conspicuous as possible; however, I am sure I will

> become very ridiculous, and laughed at.... I confess, my dear general, that I find myself of very quick feelings whenever my reputation and glory are concerned in anything. It is very hard indeed that such a part of my happiness, without which I cannot live, should depend upon schemes which I never knew of but when there was no time to put them into execution. I assure you, my most dear and respected friend, that I am more unhappy than I ever was.

Despite Lafayette's concerns about lost reputation, a great many efforts had been made to support the expedition; however, in light of what Lafayette saw as larger issues, he ignored them. To his credit, the marquis addressed some of the more egregious problems in the north.

> [T]wo hundred thousand dollars are arrived, I have taken upon myself to pay the most necessary part of the debts we are involved in. I am about sending provisions to Fort Schuyler; I will go see the fort. I will try to get some clothes for the troops, to buy some articles for the next campaign. I have directed some money to be borrowed upon my credit to satisfy the troops, who are much discontented. In all I endeavor to do for the best, though I have no particular authority or instructions; and I will come as near as I can to General Gates' intentions, but I want much to get an answer to my letters.[12]

On March 13, Congress finally recognized that the mounting of a Canadian invasion was impossible and cancelled the operation. Concerned that Lafayette's reputation may have been undermined, they passed the following resolution. "That Congress entertain a high sense of his prudence, activity, and zeal and that they are fully persuaded nothing has or would have been wanting on his part, or on the part of the officers who accompanied him, to give the expedition the utmost possible effect." The marquis returned to Valley Forge early in April.

Vermont's Defensive Arrangements

On February 25, the Vermont Council advised Major Benjamin Wait of Herrick's regiment that the intended expedition to Canada had been cancelled. Wait was instructed to give immediate orders to his several officers on the east side of the Green Mountains to desist from engaging any more men until further orders. Those already recruited were needed to defend the frontiers and Wait was to ask them if they were willing to do so for a short tour. They would receive ten dollars per month wages. Similar instructions were given to Captain Isaac Clark and Lieutenant Bradley, who were likely recruiting on the west side of the mountains.[13]

It is apparent that Captain Clark remained on active service, as he was instructed at the turn of the month to convey the families of four notorious Tories — Samuel Adams, Isaac Brisco, Caleb Henderson, and Philo Hard — to the enemy's lines. A list of goods that Mrs. Adams was permitted to remove was provided and proved surprisingly generous, considering her husband was wanted for murder.[14]

In the full expectation of statehood, the New Hampshire Grants had declared their independence from Britain shortly after Congress's Declaration of Independence on July 4, 1776, but it was not to be. The thorny issue of New York's claims to the Grants was too complex to be dealt with by congressmen already weighted down by funding, supplying, and waging the war. To say the Grants' leadership was disappointed would be an understatement. They organized themselves as an independent state and adopted the name Vermont, but continued to support the war effort. For the first year, the new state was administered by a council of safety; however, the citizens agitated for a governing body, and in March 1778, a governor's council was formed, which assumed the duties of a council of safety and Board of War. Thomas Chittenden was governor; Ira Allen, a councillor and state treasurer; Nathan Clark, speaker of the General Assembly; Jonas Fay, secretary of state; Joseph Fay, secretary of the governor and the council; and the councillors appointed were Jeremiah Clark, Benjamin Carpenter, Paul Spooner, Jacob Bayley, and Moses Robinson. Matthew Lyon acted as deputy secretary to the governor and council. A General Assembly was created on the 12th, and one of its first acts was to appoint Seth Warner to the rank of brigadier general in recognition of his outstanding service during the Canadian invasion and occupation, and throughout the Burgoyne expedition.[15]

When the raid against St. John's was abandoned, Major Whitcomb's ranging companies took station at the falls in Rutland, Vermont. During the spring, his rangers, assisted by men of Warren's Vermont militia and Warner's Continentals, took over a sawmill, and incorporated it with an existing blockhouse and new barracks into a stockade fort, which was christened Fort Ranger. By mid-year, Whitcomb was post commandant and had some five hundred troops at his disposal, including Captain Thomas Lee's Independent Company of Continental Rangers.[16]

Fort Ranger was located east of the falls, built with untrimmed hemlock logs sunk in a trench five feet deep. The pickets rose fifteen feet, inclined slightly outwards, and were sharpened atop. Between each outer picket was an inner row eight feet high. Loopholes were cut six feet apart. The overall shape of the fort was elliptical, and enclosed about two acres. On the east and west sides there were large gates to admit teams, and on the south wall, a wicket gate for collecting water from Otter Creek. A blockhouse of hewn logs stood in the north-west of the fort, and its outer walls formed part of the stockade. Along the north side were officers' barracks, with roofs sloping up toward the pickets, and troop barracks were along the south wall. There was a single nine-pdr gun, but its emplacement is unknown.[17]

Quebec Alarmed

On March 2, a Native patrol arrived in Montreal with two prisoners from the Albany neighbourhood, who reported that a rebel army was on the march against Canada. Brigadier Henry Watson Powell, who commanded Montreal district, called out the city's and Trois Rivières's militia. The province's Indian Department commander, Lieutenant-Colonel John Campbell, put the Native villages on alert. Powell sent an express to Carleton, which brought him from Quebec City to Montreal. The governor later reported to Germain that Lake Champlain had frozen over early and the ice had been fine, increasing the threat of invasion. When a second Native party brought in new prisoners who reported that the rebel army had retired, the alarm ended.[18]

On March 2, a mixed patrol of Royal Yorkers under the command of Ensign William Redford Crawford and a party of Akwesasnes set out. Iroquois from that community were generally more reliable and more committed than those from Kahnawake. The patrol prowled about the Mohawk Valley for several weeks before returning to Montreal on April 19.[19]

The Shelburne Raid

In January, the residents of the small Vermont community of Shelburne, located a few miles south of the Onion River, had heard rumours about a likely enemy attack, presumably aimed at destroying a substantial storehouse of wheat owned by Moses Pierson, who had abandoned his holdings the previous autumn in fear of enemy action. Assistance was requested from the Vermont Council, and that month Captain Thomas Sawyer of Clarendon and a detachment of fourteen militiamen of the 5th Regiment (5VMR) accompanied Pierson to the village in a seventy-mile march through deep snow and bitter cold. Over the next two months, they worked at reinforcing Pierson's house with logs and turned the place into a blockhouse.

The council's minutes of March 5 noted that the Commander-in-Chief at Albany had been contacted either to supply troops for the protection of the inhabitants of the Onion River and Lake Champlain areas, or to supply provisions for one hundred men and officers to be raised by Vermont. Stark opted for the latter, gave his approbation for raising the men, and sent orders to the commissary at Bennington to furnish Continental provisions. Consequently, two companies of fifty able-bodied, effective men, each commanded by a captain and two lieutenants, were ordered to be raised by a ten-dollar bounty for every NCO and private and four pounds per month wages for two months' service.

During the council meeting of March 6, instructions were issued to Captain Ebenezer Allen, one of the company commanders. His primary mission was to protect the inhabitants near Lake Champlain and along Otter Creek. Once his company was raised, he was to take post at New Haven Fort, where he would send scouts out to watch the enemy's movements. He was to confine any disaffected inhabitants from north of the fort and secure their estates for use of the state.

Three days later, the council wrote again to Captain Allen: "You are hereby directed to March the men already enlisted by virtue of Commission or Warrant from Lt. Colo Herrick for the Intended Expedition into Canada, & you & the other officers (who have enlisted any such Soldier) may be hereby assured that any reasonable encouragement heretofore offered shall be paid [to] them." They promised Allen supplies of everything necessary for the comfort of his camp.[20]

An Imminent Attack

In early March, two men came to Shelburne to purchase wheat, and about this time, several residents who were known Tory sympathizers left the settlement, causing the others to brace for a possible attack.

On March 12, fifty-seven Native warriors, accompanied by Chamilly de Lorimier, came to Shelburne, guided by a Tory named

Philo who had skated up the lake to fetch them. The two wheat buyers were asleep beside the blockhouse's open window and were killed in the opening volley. The raiders concentrated their efforts on Pierson's reinforced house, twice setting it afire. On the first occasion, militia lieutenant Barnabas Barnum, a Monkton man, was killed while putting out the fire. On the second occasion, Captain Sawyer offered his watch to the volunteer who would douse the flames. Joseph Williams rose to the challenge, cut a hole in the roof, and poured Mrs. Pierson's barrel of beer onto the flames while arrows and balls flew about him. After a two-hour fight, the attackers withdrew, leaving Lorimier and a senior warrior dead in a nearby field. The defenders believed that other bodies had been sunk in a hole cut in the ice.

The Native skirmishers were immediately pursued, and two who had fallen behind and were likely wounded were taken. The militiamen believed twelve warriors had been killed, which would have represented a great loss indeed for their community, although the only corpses found were those of Lorimier and the war captain. The Council's congratulatory letter to Captain Sawyer indicated that he had lost some other men besides Barnum and the two wheat buyers.

The question arises: Was the wheat really the attackers' target, or was it the blockhouse? Whichever the case, the stroke failed, and neither was destroyed. Worse, one of the Quebec Indian Department's most active and determined officers had been lost. As the council feared that the British would make another attempt on Shelburne, Sawyer was ordered to retreat to the blockhouse at New Haven, as he could more readily be reinforced there. He was to bring off all the "friendly" inhabitants, but was ordered not to destroy any of Shelburne's buildings or grain.[21]

Rebel Natives' Mission

After a mid-March council with elements of the Six Nations, rebel Indian Commissioner General Philip Schuyler initiated a bold plan to employ the Kahnawake, Louis Atayataghronghta, and three Oneidas. They were to infiltrate the British post at Oswegatchie and burn all the British vessels and boats wintering there, and any others found along the St. Lawrence shore as they travelled downriver to Kahnawake. If Atayataghronghta failed in that task, he was to burn the shipping at St. John's. Schuyler had promised a reward of $1,000 "in hard species" if either mission were accomplished, which he hoped Congress would approve. Although the party found nothing to sabotage, they were successful in visiting Kahnawake and spreading Schuyler's propaganda. Atayataghronghta was able to set up a spy network and a system of couriers to carry information regularly to Schuyler about British preparations.[22]

Schuyler noted in his report to Congress that during the British regime a successful measure had been to grant several reliable Six Nations senior warriors captains' commissions, which the Indian commissioners recommended be adopted for the rebels' allies.[23]

Activities in Vermont and New York

The Vermont Council sent orders to Captains Ebenezer Allen and Isaac Clark on March 19, first noting Sawyer's "Signal Victory over the enemy at Shelburne," then instructing the captains to march to his relief without loss of time and take post at Fort William on Otter Creek. They were to send out scouts to protect the inhabitants, harass the enemy, and secure the wheat stored at Shelburne, but not burn or destroy any buildings or other effects. Any inhabitants that they were unable to protect were to be urged and assisted to move within their lines soonest. Those who refused "such kind invitations" were to be treated as enemies of Vermont and the United States.[24]

On March 24, Vermont's assembly addressed the ownership of a parcel of land in Hartford Township that had been granted to the Tory, Whitehead Hicks, former mayor of New York City. In flagrant violation of the king's order-in-council, Hicks had been granted fifty thousand acres near Otter Creek by Lord Dunmore when he was governor of New York Province. This was one of several excessively large grants that infuriated New Hampshire grantees. When Dunmore moved to his new assignment in Virginia, Hicks transferred ownership of the lands to him, which proved the transaction had been fraudulent. The lands were forfeited to the United States, and Congress recommended they be immediately sold. William Gallup had applied to make the sale "to Good Inhabitants," and his request was approved.[25]

Two days later, this decision was followed by another ruling dealing with Tory lands. The Council set up a court to confiscate and order the sale of real and personal estates belonging to enemies of the United States in Cumberland County. The court was empowered to confiscate and sell all lands and estates that were deemed forfeit, and to appoint commissioners to settle the accounts of all creditors of said estates. The council then voted to send Joseph Marsh and Jonas Fay as delegates to the Continental Congress to announce officially the formation of the Vermont state. They were to be accompanied by Colonel Elisha Payne, a farmer, lawyer, judge, and mill owner, who lived in Cardigan, a New Hampshire town leaning toward a union with Vermont; this visit, however, never took place.[26]

Vermont's council was sitting at Arlington on April 10 when it instructed Captain Ebenezer Wallace of the Arlington company of 2VMR to take two able-bodied men north to search the woods "critically & diligently" for persons who had gone over to the enemy and were in Vermont as spies, or for anyone who might be an enemy. They were to seize such persons and bring them before the board. Wallace was authorized to call out militiamen to assist in this mission as required. Further, he was empowered to administer an oath of secrecy to all persons who gave him assistance in this matter.[27]

On April 22, the council addressed a petition from the inhabitants along Otter Creek north of Pittsford in Vermont, who believed they were extremely vulnerable to attack. As the state was unable to protect people's holdings north of Pittsford and Castleton, they instructed the petitioners and the inhabitants of Bridport, Addison, and Panton to remove to safety (presumably to Rutland.) Those who chose not to do so were warned they would be considered Vermont's enemies. Residents around Pittsford chose to build Fort Mott on the east side of Otter Creek.

Captain Ebenezer Allen was advised that a militia reinforcement was on its way to assist him, bringing a supply of medicines, dressings, and one hundred cartridges. Allen was to assist the above-mentioned citizens and protect them "against the fury & Rage of Savages and Diabolical Tories."[28]

On April 24, Vermont's governor, Thomas Chittenden, issued a flurry of orders. He instructed that all troops raised for Colonel Warner's Regiment from the Cumberland County militia regiment and the two Bennington regiments were to march without delay to Rutland, where they would be mustered and given ammunition. This urgency was prompted by the imminent expiry of the enlistments of Allen's and Clark's companies, and the intelligence that British armed vessels were at and about Crown Point and Ticonderoga. Incomplete

Thomas Chittenden (1730–1797), Governor of the Republic of Vermont.

companies were to march with their officers, and the men required to complete them were to be raised expeditiously and dispatched.

As Warner's Regiment had been called to Albany, and because of Allen's and Clark's expiring enlistments, Colonel Herrick, 2VMR, and Colonel Warren, 5VMR, were to raise fifty-seven and sixty men respectively and march them to Rutland as quickly as possible.

Captain Nathan Smith of Bridport, a former lieutenant in Warner's and currently in the 5VMR, was instructed to march his company to assist Ebenezer Allen in removing families from the exposed frontier, taking care to keep people as compact and as safe as possible. Smith's company was to continue in duty for twelve days from the April 22nd instant or longer, unless counter orders were received from the council.[29]

Chittenden was in council on April 29 when he wrote to his lieutenant governor, Major-General Joseph Marsh, who commanded the militia east of the mountains, replying to his letter of April 3. He had delayed answering until he received clarification from Gates about the necessity for raising the quota of three hundred men to augment Warner's Regiment. Gates had "earnestly request[ed] me to Draft three hundred men to Recruit Colo Warner's Regiment, & that nothing might retard their immeadiate joining him when they would receive General Starks orders who Commands in this department under the Direction of General Gates." The governor noted that those men had already been raised and were in service with part of Warner's regiment at Fort Ranger in Rutland under the command of Captain Gideon Brownson.

Further, Chittenden advised that Colonel Peter Olcott of Norwich had written that, if he attempted to draft the number ordered from his regiment, the men would engage instead with Colonel Bedel; however, the governor postulated that both Olcott and Bedel must realize that the drafted men should do as ordered and that Bedel had no right to countenance such disobedience. That Bedel's regiment was being raised on the Continental establishment further complicated the issue. Another of Chittenden's letters, written on May 22, clarified this rather murky issue; apparently, the addressee is unknown.

The day before, the governor had received a letter from General Gates at the Continental depot in Fishkill, once again requesting that Vermont raise three hundred men to augment Warner's Continental Regiment. Chittenden called his council together to discuss the issue. He reported that in March, Vermont's General Assembly had ordered three hundred men to join Colonel Seth Warner's regiment, and that on the west side of the mountain, 115 had been raised and were already serving with forty men of Warner's under Captain Gideon Brownson at Rutland; however, fulfilling the quota on the mountain's east side had been retarded by Lafayette's contradictory orders to Colonel Bedel, under which the latter had enlisted 399 men.

Nonetheless, Bedel advised Chittenden that his regiment was prepared "on the shortest notice to assist you against any force that may come from the Lake against you, as some of my scouts have discovered parties on the Lake & in the Woods." Chittenden noted that, if Gates ordered the troops already raised to march to Albany, the inhabitants of Vermont's northern frontiers would abandon their settlements and create much expense and uneasiness, and prevent the raising of provisions for their own and the public's consumption. He added a postscript: "I am informed that Colo Beedels [Bedel's] men are not in actual Service for Want of Provisions, except some small Scouts."[30]

Altered Troop Dispositions

May saw a flurry of activity concerning troop dispositions in the U.S. Army's northern department. General Conway was ordered to take Greaton's 3rd Massachusetts (3MA) and Alden's 6MA regiments, and Stevens's artillery, ammunition, and stores from Albany to Fishkill.[31] As noted above, the Vermont Committee was requested to supply three hundred recruits for Warner's Additional Regiment, which would be employed in the defence of Albany and the upper Hudson against possible sabotage by Tories and to discourage British scouting activities. A few rangers were recruited in

Albany County to "secure such persons who going at large may be dangerous to the liberties of America."[32] Albany mayor John Barclay was very concerned about the Continentals being sent to Fishkill, as he had only 150 militiamen, many of whom were employed on public duties, to guard stores, provisions, the hospital, vessels, and prisoners, of whom there were one hundred. Ten of these had been sentenced to death, and if any were able to get loose, could greatly distress the city. The city's council requested that a regiment at least 150 strong be left behind. Stark responded by retaining Alden's regiment, and advised General Gates of his action, explaining that no dependence could be placed on the militia.[33]

On May 24, Stark wrote to Gates to advise that Governor Chittenden had complained to him about having to supply three hundred men to Albany as Vermont expected an invasion from Canada. British vessels had been observed cruising off Crown Point and about the lake. Stark ordered Bedel to place scouts along the Onion River and near St. John's to warn of enemy movements, and recommended that the request for three hundred men be rescinded. Gates replied six days later that, if the reinforcement could not be expected from Vermont, Stark was to apply to the militia commanders in Massachusetts's Hampshire and Berkshire counties for a similar number and forward Alden's regiment to Fishkill.[34]

From Albany on May 31, Stark sent an urgent report to Gates about a raid on Cobleskill, and advised that he had requested assistance from Albany County militia general Abraham Ten Broeck, who had received Stark's plea while at a church service and promised to help after church was over, as he could not "do any business before, for fear of frightening the town into fits," such was the extreme anxiety of the county's residents. Stark pled for a few field pieces and a regiment of Continentals. The next day, Stark advised Ten Broeck that Gates had ordered one hundred men from the county's militia brigade to garrison the city and guard its stores, again noting that the city's militia could not be depended upon. He also reported that Natives and Tories had destroyed part of Cobleskill and that a mixed detachment of Continentals and Schoharie militia had sortied to attack them, but other than six men, the militia stood by while the Continentals did their duty.[35]

Stark confirmed to Gates on June 2 that the British hospital in Albany, which was caring for Burgoyne's casualties, would be removed south, and Alden's regiment would depart for Fishkill as soon as the wind permitted. He reminded Gates that he had recommended that Bedel's New Hampshire Regiment be mustered by a Continental muster master, and, as those troops had been at home doing nothing, they should be employed elsewhere, such as along the Onion River, which would free up Warner's Regiment to come to Albany. He confirmed that he had sent orders to the brigadiers of Hampshire and Berkshire Counties to send two hundred men to garrison Albany and nearby places.[36]

Two days later, Stark reported that Vermont's Colonel Herrick had applied for the pay for the men of his regiment raised for the cancelled Canadian expedition. Stark commended Herrick's bravery and good conduct and believed him to be a suitable officer to

Ethan Allen (1730–1789), the bold founder of the Green Mountain Boys and key member of the Vermont Council.

scourge the Natives and Tories. Further, he recommended Colonel Ethan Allen to command the Continental Army in the Grants and deal with Tories and other such villains, and noted that Bedel had reported that his regiment was complete and would be ready for the field as soon as provisions arrived.[37]

Gates sent two letters by express to Stark to forward to Ethan Allen and Bedel. He explained that he had ordered Bedel to send without delay one hundred men of his regiment to reinforce Stark, which he believed would constitute a good reinforcement when coupled with the Massachusetts militia. Stark was instructed to have Colonel Richard Varick, deputy muster master, send a deputy to muster Bedel's regiment. As to that regiment's deployment, it was suggested that Stark consult with Ethan Allen, whom Gates had ordered Bedel to obey.[38] It seems that everyone doubted Bedel, as later became obvious.

Bolton Reports about Lafayette

Lieutenant-Colonel Mason Bolton, 8th Regiment, the commander of the British post of Fort Niagara, wrote to Governor Carleton on April 6 with details of the rebels' intended invasion of lower Quebec, led by Lafayette. Two days later, Major John Butler of the Rangers and Six Nations Indian Department contributed further observations in a letter to the governor. In summation, the two officers reported that there were few troops at Albany, but a considerable number had been sent to Lake George with quantities of hand sleighs and ice creepers. It was said the invaders would bypass Île-aux-Noix and St. John's, and surprise Montreal. Bolton doubted the news, as the British army in Quebec was stronger than it had been when the rebels invaded in 1775, which he thought would supply sufficient discouragement.[39]

A short report published in the *Quebec Gazette* of June 4 gave quite accurate details of the cancelled invasion, and bogus information about Ticonderoga. "The so much talked of Northern expedition against Canada is knock'd up; the Marquis de Fyate [Lafayette] and Mr. Conway were to be the commanders and were promised by the Congress an army of 5000 men with their own regiments; but on their arrival at the Lakes, half the number could not be mustered, and the project, of course, was laid aside; however the rebels have taken post at Ticonderoga, and intend to throw up fortifications at that place."[40]

A Tory Hanging

On June 9, the Vermont Council chose a two-man committee to prepare a congratulatory letter to Ethan Allen on his safe return from imprisonment in England. The same day, Allen was appointed state attorney for the negotiations between the United States and Vermont, and also to represent the Tory David Redding, a private in John Peters's Queen's Loyal Rangers who had been captured while on a foraging patrol almost a month after the Walloomscoick battle of August 16, 1777. Redding was to be tried that day for inimical conduct against Vermont and the United States. His crime was to have taken arms on behalf of the Crown against the rebels, during which service he foraged for supplies, like all soldiers on either side of the conflict; however ordinary his actions, they were deemed sufficient grounds to hang him, and he swung for his sins on June 11. Clearly, Allen's intercession had been perfunctory.[41]

Vermont's Eastern Union

As noted, the firm grip on Vermont's affairs depended on a small cabinet council, which had begun its life as the council of safety. The state's assembly convened infrequently for short sessions, but the council met almost every day, and, although the constitution vested legislative power entirely in the assembly, political decisions had to be made, and the council filled the gap. Despite the Allens' autocratic stance, many Vermonters were grateful to their faction for defying New York and avoiding taxes — but not everyone shared this admiration. The humbling of the Allen cabal became the ambition of Jacob Bayley, the most energetic leader east of the Green Mountains and west of the Connecticut River, where sentiments favouring New York were more prevalent. Bayley had agreed to Vermont's independence as a last resort, and there was little love between his supporters and those of the Allens' "Bennington mob." Ira Allen's disposal of many large properties confiscated from loyalists raised concern among Bayley's associates, as none of the proceeds went to the Continental treasury. One method of undermining the power of the Allen faction was to increase opposing representation in the Vermont Assembly by incorporating New Hampshire's towns on the Connecticut River's east bank, which were estranged from the state's seaboard majority. At a moment when the Allens' attention was diverted, the assembly outraged New Hampshire by voting on June 11 to admit sixteen of her towns into what became known as the Eastern Union, an action that did nothing to enhance Vermont's chances at statehood.

As a result, Bedel's regiment fell under Vermont's sway. As it was the major defence force along the northern reaches of the Connecticut River, the assembly resolved on June 12 to empower the colonel to take as much grain, meat, and other provisions from anywhere in the state, paying a reasonable price for all goods. At the same time, the assembly ordered that one hundred from Bedel's regiment be sent to the west side of the mountains to guard the frontiers. How the assembly expected to control the movement of Continental troops when Stark could not is a mystery.[42]

Accordingly, Governor Chittenden wrote to Colonel Bedel that same day, advising that General Gates had ordered all the Continental Troops at Albany to Fishkill, and that they had already marched. This left Vermont's frontier "very thinly Guarded." Warner's Regiment was the only other Continental regiment left in the north, and Chittenden worried that the enemy would distress the frontiers with scouting parties, "and [as] the connection between this State & a number of Towns on the East side of Connecticut river is compleated, [I] should think it would be for the General Good that a part of your regiment be sent to Rutland to join those raised here for the present to be under my direction in Council, and accordingly, should take it as a favour, that after you have sent an hundred men to Albany ... you would send over such a part of the Remains of your Regiment as you can spare." The Council hoped that he could spare a hundred men. He added in a postscript that the men should be sent "by Onion river, & so on to Rutland, which will serve as a Scout, & guard not only this, but your frontiers."[43]

The Shelburne raid had disturbed the council. On the 13th, Chittenden ordered Colonel Samuel Herrick's 2VMR to draft one hundred men (one-sixth of his command), properly officered and supplied each with a half-pound of powder and two pounds of lead. Herrick, or his lieutenant-colonel, was to march to Rutland with all speed to join Captain Brownson's detachment for the immediate defence of the frontiers. Twenty-seven men of Gideon Warren's 5VMR (again, one-sixth of his command) were to be taken under command, and all were to remain in the area for twenty days.

Colonel Samuel Fletcher, who commanded one of the two Cumberland County militia regiments, was advised by Chittenden "that a Scout of 500 of the Enemy are now at Crown Point, who have Just returned from a Scalping Tour in Tryon County who have brought with them a Considerable number of prisoners." He was ordered to draft seventy-three men "without the least delay," have them properly officered and equipped, and then march to Rutland.

The governor ordered the commissary of issues in Bennington to supply Samuel Robinson, the captain of Bennington's 1st company, 2VMR, twenty-seven pounds of powder and 108 pounds of lead. Timothy Moss of Wells was ordered to supply twelve pounds of powder, twenty-one of lead, and twenty-four flints to the Bennington commissary. Robinson, who guarded the stores with fifteen militiamen at Rutland, was authorized to draw seventeen-and-a-half pounds of powder and thirty pounds of bullets.[44]

Bedel's Regiment

The militia brigadiers of Hampshire and Berkshire Counties in Massachusetts had agreed to supply two hundred militiamen for Albany's defence. Gates presumed that, with Ethan Allen's assistance and the reinforcement from Bedel's, the frontier would be secured. He advised Stark that a recent meeting with the neutralist faction of the Seneca nation revealed that there was little to fear about "real alarms in his district."[45] Of course, neutralists currying favour might be expected to offer such an opinion, but that Gates naively accepted it as reality is amazing.

When Ethan Allen responded positively to Stark's request, he stroked the old soldier's ego by commenting on his "reputation, and the hatred and fear" felt for him by the Tories. "The tories, and the friends of tories, give us some trouble yet. Their management in a great measure keeps alive the anarchy which has heretofore disturbed the peace of Vermont.... I am of opinion that we shall never be at peace while one of the traitors is suffered to remain in the country. I hear you are doing well with some of them," a euphemism referring to the hangings that had taken place in Albany. Stark happily replied that he looked forward to a visit "from a man whose fame has been so extensive," and that the Vermonter could "rely upon my cooperating with you in purging the land of freedom from such most infamous and diabolical villains." He added, "In response to rumours about Bedel's regiment, if any iniquity has been practiced upon the public, I hope in a few days to discover it," and requested that Allen use his "best endeavours to ascertain their numbers and employments."[46]

Stark was justifiably feared by the Tories. His predilection for hanging continued into 1781 when, contrary to the accepted conventions of war, after a mock trial, he lynched a loyalist officer who had been taken in military uniform. On the other hand, once Vermont was denied statehood by Congress, Allen took a moderate view of Tories to the point of opening negotiations with the British to rejoin the empire. Thereafter, his independent state became a safe haven for loyalists.[47]

Whether Allen was able to shed any light on Bedel's regiment is unknown, but on June 20, Stark reported to Gates that he doubted Bedel had half the number that his returns stated, and urged sending for the whole regiment, which would uncover any false statements. He claimed that Bedel had drawn double pay and rations for a full regiment the previous winter for the St. John's raid, but none of his men had left their homes, and he doubted they were actually enlisted. "I think it the duty of every lover of his country to endeavor to find out such people, which, without ordering them some where else, is impossible; for he can muster all the inhabitants, and as soon as they are mustered, they go to their own business again, and cheat the continent of their wages and provisions."

Like a dog with a bone, Stark refused to give up his angst over Bedel. He wrote to Gates on July 7, noting that some sixty of Bedel's troops were due to arrive in Albany that day, but he was convinced that the bulk had only been raised for home service, so he had ordered Bedel to bring the remainder to the city so that the truth of the matter would be revealed.[48]

A collection of Bedel's papers reveals that those "one hundred" men at Albany were very keen to return to the regiment's headquarters at Haverhill and that, despite Stark's and Gates's orders, he was unwilling to march the rest of his men hundreds of miles simply to satisfy Stark's nagging doubts. The upper Connecticut valley committees of safety were concerned about local security and supported Bedel's stand, allowing him to fend off Gates's and Stark's demands; however, New Hampshire's president, Meshech Weare, displayed considerable aggravation when writing to the state's congressional delegates months later about the towns on the east bank of the Connecticut, which had joined Vermont's Eastern Union:

> You know, that Col. Timothy Bedel, who has received great sums of money from Congress, and their generals, under pretence of keeping some companies, last winter, and now a regiment, for the defence of that northern frontier, or to be in readiness for marching into Canada, (though very little service has been done, as I am informed) by influence of the money and his command, has occasioned a great share in the disorders in those towns. 'Tis wished by the more sober, solid people in that quarter, he could be removed for some other command, if he must be kept in pay and employed.[49]

Despite the doubts and accusations leveled at Bedel, his efforts were invaluable to the United States. His immense influence with the Algonkian tribes in Quebec, Maine, and Nova Scotia (Abenaki, Mi'kmaq, Maliseet) was instrumental in preventing the British from being able to rely on their loyalty and services. Pressure from British agents had forced many families to leave Odanak and live in the woods in the Cöos region, where they were supported by Bedel and the rebel Indian commissioner, James Dean. Their warriors were able to move back and forth across the border to gather and deliver intelligence, to the great discomfort of Quebec's administration.[50]

Stark's Zone of Responsibility

On June 23, Stark wrote to Hampshire County's militia brigadier, advising him that his counterpart in Berkshire County had supplied one hundred men and requesting that Hampshire meet their promise to do the same. Stark's zone of responsibility had been defined by Gates on May 30 as the state of New York north and west of Albany and as far south as Livingston Manor on the Hudson, which explains the concerns he next addressed. "The western frontiers are in great distress, and unless speedily relieved, the settlement must be broken up, which will be a great injury to the United States of America. As it is the best country for bread in America, which is much wanted for the use of the army, I hope you will succeed in sending the men, so that I shall rest assured of your vigilance and good wishes toward the welfare of your country and the common cause."[51]

Stark was vigilant in reporting all misuses of funds and abuses of public trust. He had earlier told Gates about many officers in and about Albany who were underemployed and "devouring the children's bread." He listed a colonel, a major, twelve captains, four clerks, and fourteen junior officers, all being compensated more than captains of battalions. He took care to define how many assistant quartermasters were required and where they should be stationed; he complained of a lack of wagons for public use, and that a great many carpenters were at work erecting storehouses that he thought were excess to requirements. He supposed the craftsmen could be employed more fruitfully elsewhere. Then, he noted that many soldiers had been removed from their regiments to work as clerks and were paid more than any regimental officer, which he noted made the troops uneasy, since "the soldier, who is despised, must run all risks for nothing, while these others are devouring the fat of the land."[52]

Quebec's New Governor

The *Quebec Gazette* of June 27 announced that General Frederick Haldimand and his suite had arrived in the frigate *Montreal*. "On this occasion the streets from the landing place to the Chateau were lined by the British and Canadian militia and the troops of the garrison. Upon leaving the frigate, the General was saluted by the ships in the river, and by the garrison when he landed. When he arrived at the Chateau he was met by the members of the Legislative Council and by them conducted to the council chamber where his Commission was read and the usual oaths administered to him."

Frederick Haldimand (1718–1791), Captain-General and Governor of Quebec, by John Francis Rigaud.

At long last Governor Carleton's replacement had arrived. The two men had much to discuss, in particular the recent treaty between France and the United States and its implications for Quebec. Lafayette's cancelled invasion was an obvious example of what could have occurred, and the threat of Hazen's Road in upper Vermont must have been a topic. After several weeks of affable consultation, on August 6, Carleton boarded the *Montreal*, no doubt with great relief and little remorse, and sailed for Britain.[53]

Stark Vents

Stark wrote to New Hampshire's president on June 28 asking him to take charge of the Tory prisoner Zadock Wright, whom he styled "an arrant poltroon." Wright was the major of John Peters's

Queen's Loyal Rangers and had been captured earlier in the year on a scout from Quebec. The people of No. 4 township refused to harbour the man, and Stark hoped Weare would take him. The brigadier took the opportunity to deride Albany City's militia battalion, again using one of his favourite words to describe ne'er-do-wells. "I could place no dependence upon the militia; such a set of poltroons is not to be found on the face of the earth. When their all is at stake, they rather choose to see it destroyed than to hazard any thing it its defence." Stark was in full flood describing the Schoharie militiamen's conduct at Cobleskill:

> a party of Cont troops ... being informed that a party of the enemy were advancing ... marched out, but could not induce the militia to follow them, except seven or eight; and in a short time were engaged with a party of the enemy, in which action the captain, and the lieutenant, and fifteen men were killed, while the militia coldly looked on, but did not go to their assistance. Such is their conduct; and when I applied to them for a guard for their State prisoners, they told me there were so many tories among them that they could not be depended upon.

Stark offered a solution for these problems. "The people do very well in the hanging way. They hanged nine on the 16th of May; on the 5th of June, nine; and have 120 in jail of which I believe more than one half will go the same way."[54]

Vermont's Fort Rutland

The fort at Rutland was in part garrisoned by Warner's Regiment during the early summer, and patrols went out frequently to scour the woods. On one occasion, Private David Welch was on the flank of a patrol when he came across a column of smoke. He crept forward and spotted two Natives seated at a fire, presumably using the smoke to fend off mosquitoes. Welch sank to the ground to watch for others. Satisfied there were none, he eased his firelock forward and shot one fellow, then leapt up to run down the second. The warrior whirled and fired, but missed, tossed aside his gun, and came at Welch with his tomahawk, which the Vermonter warded off with his empty piece, hooking the axe from the man's hand. It fell to the ground and Welch lunged for it. Stooping to pick it up, he took a knife wound on his hand. Welch struck the warrior with the tomahawk, driving him to the ground, where he killed him with a second blow. Thinking swiftly, the Continental reloaded his own firelock, and those of his victims. His patrol mates, who had heard the gunfire, then appeared. The corporal ordered an immediate retirement to the fort. Upon reporting the events, the patrollers were, as was usual, ordered not to mention any details of the patrol to the other soldiers, and Welch was cautioned to disguise the cause of his wound — presumably to avoid any panic in the garrison and surrounding community.[55]

No one appears to have considered that the two victims may have been friendly Natives simply out hunting, proving that, to the military around them, Indians were simply Indians.

An Alarm from Fort Stanwix

Colonel Peter Gansevoort, 3NY, who commanded at Fort Stanwix, reported to Stark that he had received intelligence from Oswegatchie of a likely enemy attack, and the brigadier ordered Alden's 6MA to reinforce him, which left him with no troops in Albany other than the thoroughly distrusted city militia and the Berkshire militiamen. On July 9, he asked Gates to send him some Continentals, ideally more than one company. As well, he wrote to Colonel Seth Warner to come to Albany to command the militia, as he lacked a Regular field officer to do so.[56]

Gates wrote from White Plains five days later. He referred to a letter Stark had written on June 10, mysteriously complaining about

Alden: "Colonel Alden's behavior is exactly what it was last year. Be assured that he shall be made to answer for his conduct." The shoes and stockings that were "so much wanted by that regiment" were on the way.

Stark must have indicated concern about "another Canada expedition being heedlessly undertaken," because Gates predicted that "the period is not far distant when that province must join the great confederation, without any force being raised to effect it; or if any, such only as is merely necessary to take possession." This statement was not entirely inane, as the French fleet commanded by Vice-Admiral Charles-Hector Comte d'Estaing had just arrived off New York City.[57]

Stark had been badgering Gates to send additional artillery, and was informed on the 18th that two brass field pieces would very soon be in Albany. Further, the Continental artillery officer, Lieutenant-Colonel Ebenezer Stevens of the artillery maintenance

Vice-Admiral Charles-Hector, Comte d'Estaing (1721–1794).

company, reported that Stark already had two good iron guns, a fact that Stark had been quietly ignoring. Gates reasoned that, with the brass pieces, Stark should be entirely satisfied in that department, although whether Stark had sufficient gunners, powder, and shot was not addressed.

If the alarm of a coming attack from Oswegatchie on Fort Stanwix continued to obtain credit, Stark was to apply immediately to Hampshire and Berkshire Counties for more militia, and to inform Colonel Allen that it was Gates's request that he march out all the militia possible to collect at Albany.

Stark advised Gates that he was forwarding under guard eight "tories, who have been found so inimical to their country that the council of our good friends at Bennington have thought proper to send them as a present to their friends, to obey their laws and worship their gods in future. I would to God every State on the continent would follow their example. If this meets your approbation, you will send them to the enemy's lines, where they will be received."[58] This action stirred a pot, as will be seen later.

The Vermont council did not make a great number of loyalist estate confiscations — only 158 by April 1778; however, the Allens saw fit to persecute individuals with New York land grants who wished to remain neutral, not only in the conflict between Vermont and New York, but also in the war between Britain and the United States. In Ethan's view, even worse were Yorker-Vermonters who took sides with New York against Vermont while espousing the causes of the rebellion; as he reasoned, one could not oppose Vermont without being a Tory. In July, Ethan sent another "seventeen wicked Tories" of Bennington to Albany to have them thrown into jail or banished to within the British lines at New York City. Five of their number petitioned Governor Clinton on the 15th of July that they had "never in any instance acted unfriendly to the American Cause, altho' it is alleged or expressed in the Sentence of banishment, that they stand charged with inimical Conduct against the United States of America." They contended that the true cause of "their severe and unparalleled Treatment" was owing to their "acknowledging

George Clinton (1730–1812), Governor of New York.

themselves to be subjects of the State of New York, and not recognizing the validity and existence of the State of Vermont."[59] This was grist to Clinton's mill, and he continued his practice of denying Vermont's existence by making military and civil appointments in the Grants. These issues would continue to simmer.

A Fumbled Expedition from Quebec

In early July, General Haldimand ordered his first offensive action since taking command. Lieutenant-Colonel John Peters had met the new governor in Quebec City, and received instructions to mount an expedition of two hundred loyalist soldiers and one hundred Native warriors to march through Vermont to the Cöos country and destroy the region.⁶⁰ Peters commanded a remnant of the Queen's Loyal Rangers, one of Burgoyne's regiments that had taken a horrific beating during the expedition. Although he employed the title of lieutenant-colonel, his small unit of some eighty men hardly warranted that rank, and he was being paid as a captain and was officially referred to as such. Of course, he entertained hopes of rebuilding his unit and earning field rank and pay. As a New Hampshireman who had firmly established himself in Cöos, he appeared the logical choice to lead this effort.

By July 16, Haldimand had altered the plan to the less-ambitious goal of destroying the harvest along the Onion River valley. He instructed Sir John Johnson to select one hundred volunteers and appropriate officers from the different parties of loyalists from Burgoyne's army, whose knowledge of the country would render them capable of service. They were to set out in bateaux on the twenty-first.

In Peters's new orders of July 25, Haldimand noted that a small body of Natives "for the purpose of scouring the woods and securing your march" would be added to the detachment of "one hundred men with officers from the different bodies of Royalists attached to the Corps of Sir John Johnson...." Instructions were given for the Natives' supervision, to prevent "every act of cruelty or inhumanity from being committed by them."

Peters was to draw boats at Montreal from the DQMG and firearms from Brigadier Powell. At Chambly, the commissary officer there would furnish him with provisions and ammunition.⁶¹

After Peters set out, the governor received fresh intelligence from reliable sources that Colonel Moses Hazen, commander of Congress's Own 2nd Canadian regiment, had left Albany on July 9 with four Natives and the Canadien renegade, Joseph Langlois dit Traversy of Saint-François du Lac. Traversy was Congress's accomplished secret agent who had already visited his family at his home parish on three separate occasions in 1778 while gathering intelligence, despite a watch being set to prevent him. Haldimand wrote to the American secretary that Traversy's infiltrations proved the high degree of disaffection among many Canadiens who either assisted him or chose to keep mum about his presence. The governor's informant advised that Hazen intended to extend the road started by Jacob Bayley in 1777.

Bayley, the founder of the Cöos settlement of Newbury on the Vermont side of the Connecticut River, had been instructed to create a road by cutting through twenty miles of forest to the tiny hamlet of Peacham. If Hazen could continue the road through a notch in the mountain chain, it would provide an alternative to the Lake Champlain invasion corridor and have the advantage of being on internal lines within Vermont until it crossed the Quebec border.[62]

On July 26, additional orders were dispatched to Peters to "press his march" and capture Hazen's party. A reward of two hundred dollars each was offered for the capture of Hazen or Traversy.[63] Peters remembered the timing of the change to his orders as follows: "Having arrived at Lake Champlain, on my way to Cohos General Haldimand's letter overtook me, which gave leave to all my party to return that chose to do so, but permitted me to pay a visit to Onion River." Likely his memory was at fault, and the orders had been altered before he set out.

Meanwhile, Hazen was already at Bayley's in Newbury. The latter wrote to General Gates on July 13, mentioning Hazen's arrival the evening before to make inquiries about the road's state. Bayley believed a "landroad very practicable"; he had surveyed a route from his place to St. John's, and it was marked and cleared for ninety-five miles, and blazed for a further thirty miles. He had also surveyed to the south end of Lake Memphremagog and from hence to Missisquoi Bay. Water carriage on the river was good from Hartford, except for five or six short rapids around which there were good cart roads. As to provisions, between six and ten thousand bushels of wheat were available, abundant beef, and one hundred tons of hay. If an expedition was contemplated on the road, Bayley claimed he could raise 1,500 men, and offered to serve personally.[64]

The Expedition Unhinged

Peters's expedition went awry even before it reached the Onion River. In a contemporary report, he wrote that the Natives had expressed doubts about executing Haldimand's orders, and, when some misfortune occurred with their bateaux, they insisted upon a council during which they declared they would go home. Peters reported that a Captain Horton intervened, which was most likely Lieutenant Richard Houghton, 53rd Regiment, who was seconded to the Quebec Indian Department. He "used Every exertion to Shame them out of such Dastardly Conduct and on my Declaring by the Advice of my Officers that we Should Proceed If they Left us — they all Agreed to Go on Except fourteen Mohawks [if] we would Return to Missisque Bay — and that I would Procure them a Supply of Rum to be at that Place on their Return." Accordingly, Peters applied to the governor for a supply of rum and provisions to be deposited at Missisquoi Bay and continued forward on August 12.

In his postwar recollections, Peters claimed that some of his Provincials became discouraged and turned back when the rest of the Natives suddenly left, and that only thirty-four men proceeded to the Onion River. If he had actually started with one hundred loyalists, then over sixty had returned. Nonetheless, his party was able to destroy a "Block-house and all the buildings on [the river] for about thirty miles," and returned to St. John's on August 23. His report made no mention of Hazen's party.[65]

The results of this little expedition were disappointing, and Hazen's party was neither intercepted nor captured. Questions arose: Why had the Natives abandoned Peters? If his memories were correct, all of them turned back before reaching the Onion River. As Houghton was the resident British officer at Kahnawake, the men were likely from that settlement, and notoriously difficult to manage. If Peters had decided to "come the old soldier" and lecture them about how to behave in the manner of Burgoyne the year before, they could easily have spurned him. What of the loyalists who left the expedition? Their "discouragement" could have been the result of the decades-old angst between New Englanders and Yorkers. Any officers and men recruited for the expedition from Burgoyne's other remnant units — Jessup's, McAlpin's, or Leake's — would have been Yorkers, and none too keen to be commanded by a Vermonter from New Hampshire, which Peters might have anticipated. Moreover, if this was a source of the problem, Sir John Johnson also should have foreseen that possibility and made a better selection.

These incidents pointed to questionable leadership, which registered with Haldimand, as he did not employ Peters again in any ventures requiring complex management.

A KEY DECISION

In August, Haldimand made an interesting decision that proved very useful for the defence of Quebec. Rather than driving off the New York Mohawks to Niagara, which appears to have been Carleton's goal, Haldimand decided to encourage those who had taken refuge at Lachine. At their request, he appointed Daniel Claus as their agent in the role of a deputy superintendent for the Six Nations. This gave Guy Johnson's department an official role in lower Quebec and kept Claus from having to deal with John Butler at Niagara, for whom he held an irrational aversion. The appointment further blurred Native management, as Claus had been Sir William's manager of the Seven Nations of Canada for decades, and his presence meant their nations' delegates often circumvented Lieutenant-Colonel Campbell and his Quebec Department officers.

Although the appointment represented a minor role, it came as a most pleasant surprise to Claus after his years of battling with Carleton over his responsibilities and remuneration. He was well-known to the Fort Hunters, as he had mastered both spoken and written Mohawk. They had revered his father-in-law, Sir William Johnson, and this loyalty accrued to Claus, who set up his headquarters close to Lachine in Montreal, near his favourite brother-in-law, Sir John Johnson. As a former Royal Americans officer, Claus related well to Haldimand, and his Native charges provided essential services as reliable, hardy scouts and raiders.

An additional benefit to having the Fort Hunters in lower Quebec was their positive influence on the Canada Indians. While there was little intercourse between their communities, the example of a confederacy's elder brother who was eager for the war and in full support of the British was invaluable.[66]

Continued Angst in the Rebels' Northern Department

Stark wrote to Washington complaining that he and his officers were substantially out of pocket due to the expense of raising men for the abandoned expedition against St. John's and requesting compensation. He observed that a number of state prisoners in the city were drawing Continental provisions that should be supplied by New York, and there were a number of soldiers' wives in residence who were starving and being refused assistance by the city's politicians.[67] Gates had not looked with favour upon Stark's message that Tories were to be sent to him from Bennington. He wrote to Governor Chittenden explaining that they would be prime spies for the British if sent to New York City, and if sent to Canada, would provide intelligence about the defenseless state of the frontiers. If Stark accepted these Tories, he would be obliged to confine them in Albany's city hall, where they would be under the inspection of the city committee, which, he pointed out, was not well-inclined toward Vermont. He recommended that Chittenden retain them until the end of the season, when they could be sent to Canada if they continued to be untrustworthy. How Vermont's governor received these offerings is unknown;[68] however, the issue erupted three months later when Governor Clinton wrote to Congress in deep anger: "The unwarrantable Conduct of the usurped Government of the People on the Grants, in sentencing to Banishment a number of

Brigadier-General John Stark (1728–1822), controversial commander of the U.S. Northern Department at Albany.

the Subjects of this State and of Genl. Starke, in attempting to carry the same into Execution, calls upon me again to Trouble Congress with the Copies of several Letters & papers on the Occasion which are of themselves so intelligible as not to require any Explanation of mine." Gates enclosed a copy of General Washington's letter revealing the situation, as well as

> [c]opies of three other Papers which I have since received tending to prove the true Charecters of the Persons attempted to be banished.... I have no Reason to believe that Genl. Starke has been punished or even reproved for his Offence which you will readily perceive is no less than having imployed the Authority & Arms of the Continent against the Liberties of the Subjects of this State — that the

> Silence of Congress on this Occasion after the Matter was referred to their Decission by his Excellency Genl. Washington may be considered as countenancing these unwarrantable Measures.[69]

Stark may have been cautioned over this issue by his superiors, but that did nothing to deter him from supporting Vermonters until late in 1781, when their promises to help him repel invasions from Montreal and Oswego proved insincere.

British Dominate Lake Champlain

The British controlled Lake Champlain and their ships were on constant patrol, which greatly alarmed the rebels. At times, naval ratings went ashore and fell into the hands of Major Whitcomb's Continental rangers. At other times, deserters were taken, who chirped like songbirds, offering details of British preparations and rumours of coming actions. The truth was difficult to sift.[70]

In a typical burst of outrage, on September 28 Stark directed a communication to the "British Commander at Crown Point" railing against the master of a vessel who had detained a rebel captain carrying a flag of truce while he was conducting "a number of people in your interest." The master claimed to be acting under orders from the "Commander at Crown Point." Stark frothed that the "laws of humanity" forbade such an action and threatened to "make retaliation" against British prisoners in his custody, stating he would "not let that piece of broken faith pass unnoticed." Anyone who knew Stark would recognize the threat was very real.

A letter of the same date from Stark to Governor Chittenden clarifies that a prisoner exchange was underway at Crown Point; the "commander" must therefore have meant the senior British officer there, as there was no permanent garrison. As the exchange included a number of Vermonters, Stark sent four Canadien prisoners to the governor with instructions to keep them until he was given a like number in return. The flag captain's detention must have been temporary, as there is no record of any man of any rank being taken at Crown Point in September 1778 and held prisoner in Quebec.

Ominously, Stark added that the enemy would come against Vermont in the fall and the governor should reinforce his posts. "Otherwise, your frontiers might share the same fate as German flats," which had just been thoroughly destroyed. Referring to Yorker politicians who opposed Vermont's aspirations, he added, "I know that you have enemies here, which induces me to give it [a warning], as your own exertions must be your salvation."[71] The Vermont Council took quick action. On the 30th, Major General Marsh was ordered to muster the Cumberland County militia immediately and provide a return on the state of the men, arms, ammunition, and accoutrements to the governor. One hundred men were to be raised from Bennington County to defend the northern frontiers, and were to remain in service until December 1. That same day, Chittenden ordered Colonel Herrick to raise seventy well-armed, fully equipped, able-bodied, effective men and officers from his regiment also to serve till December 1. Colonel Warren was similarly ordered to raise thirty men from the towns of Sandgate, Manchester, Dorset, Rupert, and Danby for the same purpose.[72]

A Major Strike from Quebec

On October 15, Haldimand reported to Lord Germain the results of Peters's Onion River raid, noting that, while the effort had not been entirely successful, many barns and two mills had been destroyed and the settlers along the lower river had been forced to abandon their holdings, all accomplished at no cost to the detachment. However, there were a number of settlements remaining on the shores of Lake Champlain, along Otter Creek, and around Ticonderoga and Crown Point that could support an invading army, and he intended to mount another expedition to neutralize them. "I propose to send a respectable party, which will be covered by some of the ships and Gun Boats, and that it shall be as late as possible in going out as the Damage it may then do the enemy will be irreparable this season."[73]

Haldimand believed that a major failure of Peters's leadership had been the defection of his Native warriors, and reasoned that the commander of the new expedition would need their full confidence and co-operation. He likely had a preference for Regular officers, as he had the example of the successful June raid into the Mohawk Valley led by Captain John Ross, 34th Regiment, and selected Guy Carleton's nephew, Major Christopher Carleton, 29th Regiment. Not only was young Carleton an accomplished Regular officer, he had a great deal of experience with the Natives of Canada, having lived among them for several years, adopting their customs, such as tattooing and wearing a nose ring, and, most tellingly, marrying a Native woman — in his words, enjoying "the happiest [days] of his life." He learned to speak a Native dialect and became extremely well-regarded among the Seven Nations. Christopher was so thoroughly acculturated that his family had considerable difficulty wooing him back to his previous life. To make use of his experience and skills was a natural choice under the extreme demands of a civil war. Governor Carleton had employed his nephew as a commander of the Canada Nations' contingents during his 1776 campaign, and now Haldimand turned to him again.[74]

Orders were given to the 29th Regiment's companies "to cross the lake" in mid-October. On the 15th, Captain Alexander Fraser, deputy commander of the Quebec Indian Department, was assigned to the expedition. He sent an alarming report to Haldimand: "I am sorry to find that our destination (so far from being secret) is the public topic of conversation here in every Company & it is alleged by those who have lately been upon Scouts to the other side of Lake Champlaine that the rebels are informed that three hundred Indians were to be sent about this time to destroy the settlement along Otter Creek."[75]

Haldimand wrote to Captain William Chambers,[76] Lake Champlain's commodore, to advise about the coming movement up the lake and to request him to give directions to the various vessels under his command to aid and assist Christopher Carleton and to follow his orders. The same day, he instructed Colonel Forbes MacBean, commander of the Royal Artillery, to supply two 5.5" Royal mortars, a suitable quantity of ammunition, and some mantelets — musket-proof shields made of three-inch-thick planks about five feet tall that could be moved into place to give cover to the mortar crews.[77]

The various elements of Carleton's expedition embarked from locations near Île-aux-Noix on October 24. Lieutenant John Enys, 29th Rangers, reported that Captain Alex Fraser had overall command of the Natives, and that Lieutenant Houghton had charge of the Kahnawakes. The following table of participants is taken from Enys's diary.

	Maj	C	Lt	En	P
29Regt	1	2	5	1	120
31Regt		2	3	1	96
53Regt		1	0	2	50
KRR NY			1	0	30
Savages					80
	1	5	9	4	376[78]

Enys attended Eton College for over a decade before entering the 29th in 1775. His regiment was posted to Quebec City and arrived in time to participate in raising the rebels' siege in May 1776. During the clearance of the rebels from Canada, the 29th reoccupied Montreal. In 1777, Burgoyne chose to leave the regiment's line companies to defend the province and took its flank companies on his expedition. Consequently, as a line company ensign, Enys saw no action during the campaign, which at the very least saved him from captivity. His promotion to lieutenant occurred in February 1778.[79]

Major Carleton reported the expedition's composition somewhat differently, and presumably more accurately. He listed officers and men from the 29th, 31st, 53rd, the 29th Rangers, the Royal

Regiment of New York, and the Royal Artillery. Although both he and Enys reported Royal Yorkers on the expedition, these were men from Burgoyne's remnant units who were being administered by that regiment, and were not on the regiment's rolls.

There were one major, seven captains, ten lieutenants, three ensigns, one surgeon, fifteen corporals, seventeen serjeants, five drummers, four matrosses, and 291 privates, a total of 354 men. General Powell reported that seventy-two Natives left with the expedition, and the Canadien officer, M. Verneuil de Lorimier, noted that twenty-five Kahnawakes, who had been hunting, would join en route. This gave a grand total of 454 men, considerably larger than Enys's accounting.[80] Powell sent Carleton a former gunner named Smith who had been with him at Ticonderoga. Smith had "a perfect knowledge of the country, and will be found a very useful man." Carleton added fifty-nine men "to assist in working the Gun boats and guarding them and the bateaux after the Troops are landed."[81]

Carleton delayed at Île-la-Motte until eight o'clock on the morning of October 25, waiting for the last group of Natives out of concern that they would turn back if he left without them. When the elements of the expedition came together, they had two schooners, the *Carleton* and *Maria*, and a number of gunboats. A Mr. Campbell,[82] who was paddling a canoe up the lakeshore, saw the gunboats and joined Carleton. "He inform'd me that for certain I had been expected five weeks before at Rutland, that Whitcomb's post was Augmented to five hundred men, that Colonel Warner with two hundred was at Fort Edward, and that all the Militia was orderd to be ready at a Moment's warning."[83]

Carleton set off at two on Monday morning, October 26. The force sailed to Flat Rock Point and sheltered in the deep bay behind. The major ordered a departure before dusk, but strong winds prevented the launching of a canoe to gather fresh intelligence, which Campbell's information had rendered critical. The next day, Carleton ordered a field day "to practice … Wood fighting."

Enys wrote a humourous account of this activity.

During our Stay here our party went into the Woods a little way to practice tree[i]ng as they Call it, that is to Say the Manner of hiding ourselves Behind Trees S[t]umps &c. &c. &c. and at our return the Major was pleased to say the Men had exceeded his expectations tho I could See very plainly our Aukwardness diverted the Indians and Roialists who are by far better hands at this Work being bred in the Woods from the Infancy, and Accustomed to this Manner of hiding themselves in order to Shoot Deer, and other Wild Beasts.[84]

A Cautious Advance

After the exercises, Carleton assembled the Native headmen and advised them that he wanted to send scouts into the country to confirm the enemy's strength and postings. The chiefs approved of this precaution, and provided a canoe and five young men. The major chose Solomon Johns as the scout. He had been a loyalist volunteer under Burgoyne and hailed from the Otter Creek valley. In turn, he requested the assistance of a serjeant from Captain Sherwood's company of Queen's Loyal Rangers. To avoid observation, the two loyalists lay flat in the canoe, covered by a blanket. The warriors were instructed to paddle to the vessel at Crown Point, remain there till dusk, then land Johns and the serjeant where they thought best and return to Carleton. Johns expected to return to the drop-off in four days.[85]

Carleton had planned to move the expedition at dusk, but veering winds again prevented it. For five days, the expedition lay stalled, but remained undiscovered, despite the fact that the bay, as Enys observed, was a "very Indifferent Shellter for to hide our boats and fires." The wind abated by the morning of October 29, and Carleton ordered a second field day at ten o'clock. At 4:00 p.m., the canoe returned from putting the two scouts ashore with the news that a rebel canoe had been spotted and pursued, but, when it ran into Bulwagga Bay at Crown Point, the warriors thought best to let it go. Carleton was worried that the rebels were close by, and was concerned by his scouts' news that the schooner *Carleton* had left Crown Point and fallen down to the mouth of Otter Creek. The rebels were prevented from patrolling the lake in daylight hours, and his intention had been to have a vessel posted at Crown Point to check nighttime excursions, by which means the expedition might be discovered. He ordered the *Maria* to replace her sister and requested that the Native headman send two scouting parties up the lake — one to cover Johns's rendezvous point and prevent him from being taken, the second to find and take the rebel canoe.

On October 30, a carelessly cut-down tree fell on a wigwam, mortally wounding a soldier of the 29th and sending another back to Quebec. The expedition departed at dusk, and by two in the morning had travelled fifteen miles. After rounding Split Rock, the raiders put in at North-West Bay, where there was decent concealment. The next day, there was some excitement when a sail was spotted at the bay's mouth, but after some tense hours, it was identified as a ship's boat from the *Carleton*. That evening, both scouting parties returned without any new intelligence.

As the night was so clear, the expedition waited till past midnight to set out. The boats moved in such utter silence that they passed within half a mile of the *Maria* without being discovered, despite her crew expecting their movement and the moon waxing full. At four in the morning of November 1, the boats were at the bottom of Bulwagga Bay, from where Carleton sent a message to Lieutenant Alder on the *Maria* informing him of their arrival. Alder sent word that he had sent his boat to collect four Otter Creek men who had been spotted in a house on Chimney Point. When Carleton arrived at the schooner to interrogate them, they were most unco-operative. Convinced they had been sent to collect intelligence, he detained them.

The major later noted that one of the men, Daniel McIntosh, told him "Great untruths." One might ask, "What did he expect?"

Yet he did have reason to doubt McIntosh, who, as a newly-arrived Scottish immigrant, had come to Otter Creek in 1771 with the high-handed Yorker, Colonel Reid. Reid's settlement site already had a dozen occupants who held ten-year-old grants from New Hampshire, which the colonel chose to ignore. He ousted the settlers and appropriated their sawmill, and a large inventory of logs and boards for his own use. Much jousting followed, which culminated in the Green Mountain Boys driving off Reid and his people, except two — McIntosh and John Cameron — who threw in their lot with the rioters and remained on the creek. Men who readily switched allegiances were worthy of concern.[86]

Enys reported there was only a single house, occupied by an older couple, left standing at Crown Point. While some Regulars and Provincials were visiting there, another lake inhabitant, who had been hunting with his son, came to the house for refreshment. As a further precaution, both hunters were confined.

On Sunday, November 2, Carleton dispatched fresh scouting parties to various points, and at noon, one of the Native parties returned with a prisoner named Benjamin Everest, whom Enys noted was known to some of the loyalists, who warned he would escape if not heavily bound.

Everest was from Addison, Vermont, and had been at the taking of Ticonderoga and Crown Point in 1775, and the battles at Hubbardton and Bennington in 1777. He later claimed he had intentionally dressed out of uniform in order to spy.[87] Carleton ordered him taken to the main guard, and that no one was to come near him or speak to him. Yet, as predicted, he escaped while a rope was being fetched, running through the guard and past a great many bystanders, Enys included. Natives were ordered to pursue, but they delayed to fetch weapons, and the slippery, sprightly Everest got clean away, later to serve as a lieutenant in Warner's Regiment.

When Carleton's scouting party from the mountain opposite Crown Point returned, they reported seeing two rebels they were unable to capture. Carleton was worried. He immediately assembled a council with the headmen and told them that he feared the force's presence was no longer a secret, and that there was not a moment to be lost. Being unaware of the strength of Whitcomb's post at Rutland, he would not touch it, but would take the greatest part of his force up Otter Creek. Captain Alex Fraser, thirty rangers, and thirty young warriors would be sent forward to Pittsford to destroy everything in their path. If they had to retire, they could march faster than any pursuit, and be able to fall back on the main party. The chiefs gave their approval.

At midnight, Solomon Johns returned and explained that he had taken so long because his contact failed to show. He must have made other arrangements to collect intelligence, as he made a most detailed report. There were three hundred men at Rutland, and two hundred at Fort Edward; the arms of the inhabitants along Otter Creek were stored at the blockhouse at the falls, with three hundred and fifty pounds of powder, and ball in proportion. Although Johns had heard that Whitcomb had forty-four men out as scouts on various parts of the lake, he had not detected any alarm over Carleton's approach. This was fresh news, and Carleton called another council after daybreak the next morning to apprise the headmen of Johns's findings, which put them "in Great Spirits about the plan determin'd on the night before only they thought it most advisable, not to Sett off untill the dusk of the Evening."[88]

Again, events conspired to alter the plan. A Native patrol dispatched the day before returned at noon with the news that they had been pursued by two rebel boats containing some thirty men each. The Natives had landed and hid their canoe, then marched overland to camp. They had also seen "several large smokes" rising from the sawmill near Ticonderoga. Carleton postponed departure, and sent off Lieutenant Houghton with a party of warriors to take another count of the rebel boatmen and seize a prisoner if possible.

Houghton returned at one o'clock on the 4th to report that he had not seen any fire or people in or near Ticonderoga, but through his telescope had spied the stern of a bateau drawn into some bushes on the opposite shore of the bay to the point where the Natives had last seen them, and two armed men patrolling the beach. At four that afternoon, Carleton was informed by Lieutenant Alder that a canoe had been spotted at the house of a local man named Smyth on the lake's east shore, about two miles from Chimney Point. He had taken a boat to investigate, and Smyth had come running to the shore to warn him that a scouting party of Whitcomb's people had come from Ticonderoga and left the house just twenty minutes before. More scouts were dispatched with orders not to return until they had taken a prisoner, or determined there were no detachments lurking about.

An officer and thirty men were sent to fetch Smyth. They took post near Smyth's house to ambush any party that might arrive, and two gunboats were stationed offshore to prevent surprise. Before Smyth was sent to Carleton, he revealed where the rebels had hidden their boats and a canoe in a creek.

An Escaped Rebel Prisoner

One of the hunters captured at Lake George who then escaped arrived at Fort Edward on November 5 and reported that five hundred British were encamped at Crown Point, and that they would divide into three detachments to destroy the inhabitants. This information was sent to Colonel Alexander Webster of the Charlotte County Militia, who received it the next day and ordered his captains to hold themselves in readiness to march at a minute's warning.[89]

Smyth Interrogated

Smyth was brought to Carleton's camp at one in the morning of November 5. He said that a Lieutenant Crook with an ensign and twenty-five Whitcomb's Rangers had arrived the night before at his house from their camp near Ticonderoga in two boats, with a birch canoe taken that day from some Natives. They stayed until noon and, after hiding their vessels near the house, set off to patrol four miles down the lake, with the intention of returning that night.[90]

Carleton doubted Smyth's information. He was positive that the two boats were the same as those his Indian scouts had encountered, and because of their use of boats, he concluded they had come from Skenesborough, not Rutland. Did this mean that he thought they were a detachment from Fort Edward, rather than from Rutland? And, if so, what did it matter?

The Rebel Scouts

In fact, the scout's leader was William Crook, the lieutenant in Captain Jesse Safford's Company of Warner's Regiment. The company's payroll of November 30, 1778, shows a strength of thirty-three, including the captain. Major Whitcomb had sent Crook on a reconnaissance of the lake with a twenty-four-man party, which may have been a mix of able-bodied men drawn from Warner's, Whitcomb's, and Vermont militiamen, a common practice.[91]

Carleton immediately dispatched a pursuit "with the knowledge and cooperation of the Indians." Captain Hugh Dixon, 29th, took two subalterns and forty Regulars with Captain Alex Fraser and a like number of warriors. They were to patrol the shoreline between Smyth's and Chimney Point and bring off any men found there. Dixon set off at two in the morning. His detachment returned at two the next afternoon and reported they had gone seven miles down the lake, but could not overtake the rebels, as they had struck off into the woods towards Otter Creek. Dixon had taken fifteen inhabitants prisoner from along the lake, who said the rebels had a twelve-hour lead on the pursuers, which meant they had no intention of coming back to Smyth's, despite their claim.

The scouting party sent to Ticonderoga returned at dusk, having found no sign of tracks or fires. At 10:00 p.m., a second party that had been across at Mount Independence returned with a similar report. Carleton immediately called for a council of the chiefs and asked if they would agree to set off the next morning to follow the plan they had previously approved. They replied that they would

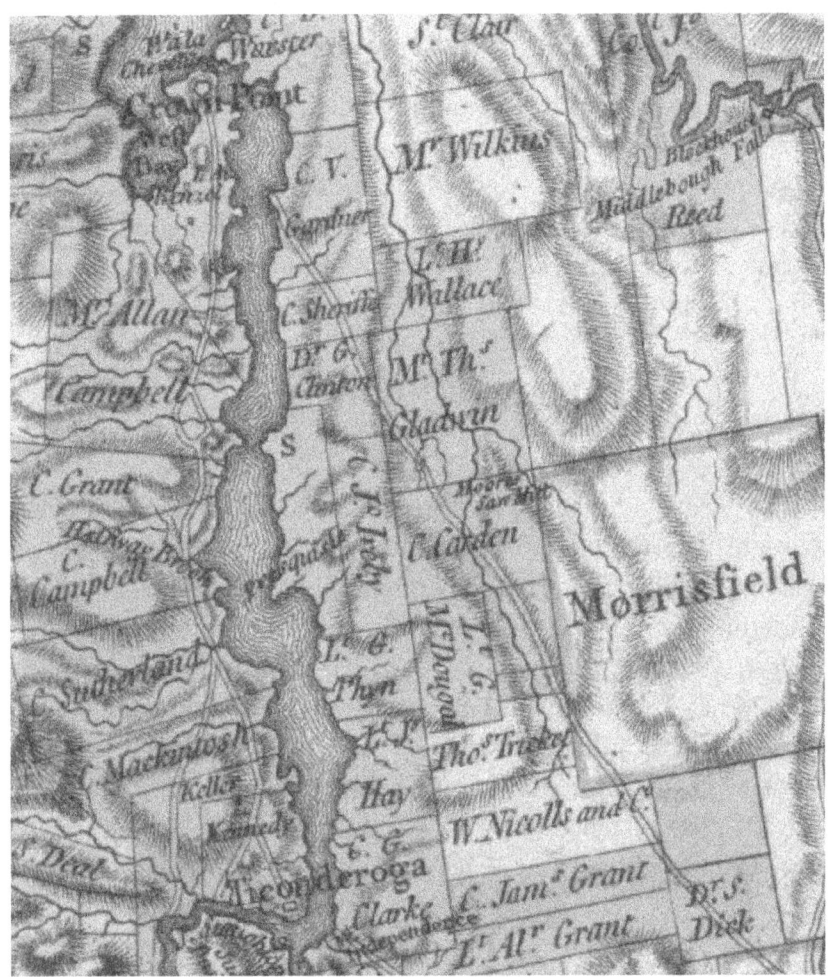

*Moore's Sawmill on the Crown Point Road
(detail from Claude Joseph Sauthier map, 1779).*

have to consult with their young men before giving an answer, and it was too late to do so. The night was marred by the desertion of two German recruits, one of the 31st, the other, the 53rd. Carleton ordered an immediate pursuit and offered a reward, but they "got clear off."

Fort Ranger Alerted

At Fort Ranger, Major Whitcomb reported, "On the 6th instant ... arrived two men from a party of 24 Men under command of Lt. Cook, whom I had sent to the lake several days before. They confirmed that the British were on the lake in force." Whitcomb called in Colonel Gideon Warren's 5VMR "to intercept the Enemy, & to cut off their communication with the Lake if possible."[92]

Carleton Moves

Carleton rose before dawn on the 6th and held a council. The chiefs thought it would be imprudent to strike higher on the creek than where the major had proposed going, but they would go that far if Carleton promised to take care of their horses — presumably, those collected from the habitations — to which he agreed. The chiefs asked what Carleton would pay for cattle; he advised eight dollars for large oxen, and in proportion for smaller ones, which he hoped "would prevent them from amusing themselves about other plunder." He recommended that they be sure to leave provisions for any women and children they turned out. With those details settled, the expedition got underway.

The major designated the expedition's senior captain, Andrew Ross, 31st, to command a detachment of two captains, five subalterns, and one hundred rankers, supported by twenty loyalist Provincials led by Captain Jonathon Jones of Jessup's King's Loyal Americans. Brothers William and Thomas Fraser, lieutenants in McAlpin's American Volunteers, joined Jones as Gentlemen Volunteers. Captain Alex Fraser and Lieutenants Richard Houghton and Richard Brown of the Quebec Indian Department accompanied the Natives, all of whom were to go, except six or so who remained with the major. Ross's force would make the major thrust up Otter Creek to destroy the settlements.[93] The expedition left Bulwagga Bay at eleven o'clock, and at two in the afternoon landed on the east side of the lake two miles above Chimney Point, and set off immediately.

Thirty minutes later, Carleton sent off Lieutenant William Farquhar, 29th, with thirty men guided by Captain Justus Sherwood of the Queen's Loyal Rangers. A matross was assigned to carry a fiercely burning incendiary device known as a fireball in case the detachment had trouble setting strong fires. Their mission was to destroy Moore's sawmill and some nearby houses. The initial approach would be by water until they arrived opposite Putnam's Creek where they would land and take a road about seven miles to the mill. Captain Hutchinson Dunlap, 53rd with a subaltern and thirty men was sent to secure Farquhar's route of retreat. He was to send a party along the road about half way to the mill, from where they could reinforce Farquhar if necessary.[94]

These precautions were sensible, as Paul Moore was an arch rebel whose mill and house were on the Crown Point Road, which had been laid out by John Stark in 1759 to connect the Fort at No.4 to Lake Champlain. Moore's Mill served not only as a supply depot, but a rendezvous for Warner's regiment and Whitcomb's Rangers, so there was every chance that rebel soldiers would be there when Farquhar arrived.

When nothing was heard from Dunlap or Farquhar by midnight, Carleton concluded they "had met no Obstruction" and dispatched Captain Dixon with twenty-four Regulars to destroy Raymond's Mills situated north of Crown Point at the mouth of Stacy Brook on the New York shore opposite to, and slightly south of Button Mould Bay.

Misinformation

On the morning of November 7, Colonel Webster of Charlotte County received a verbal report that "the Lakes was full of the Enemy's boats. I Imediatly sent of[f] a scout to Skenesborrough to know the Truth & ordred the militia to Embodie which they readly did at my Howse; my Scout returned & reportd that they

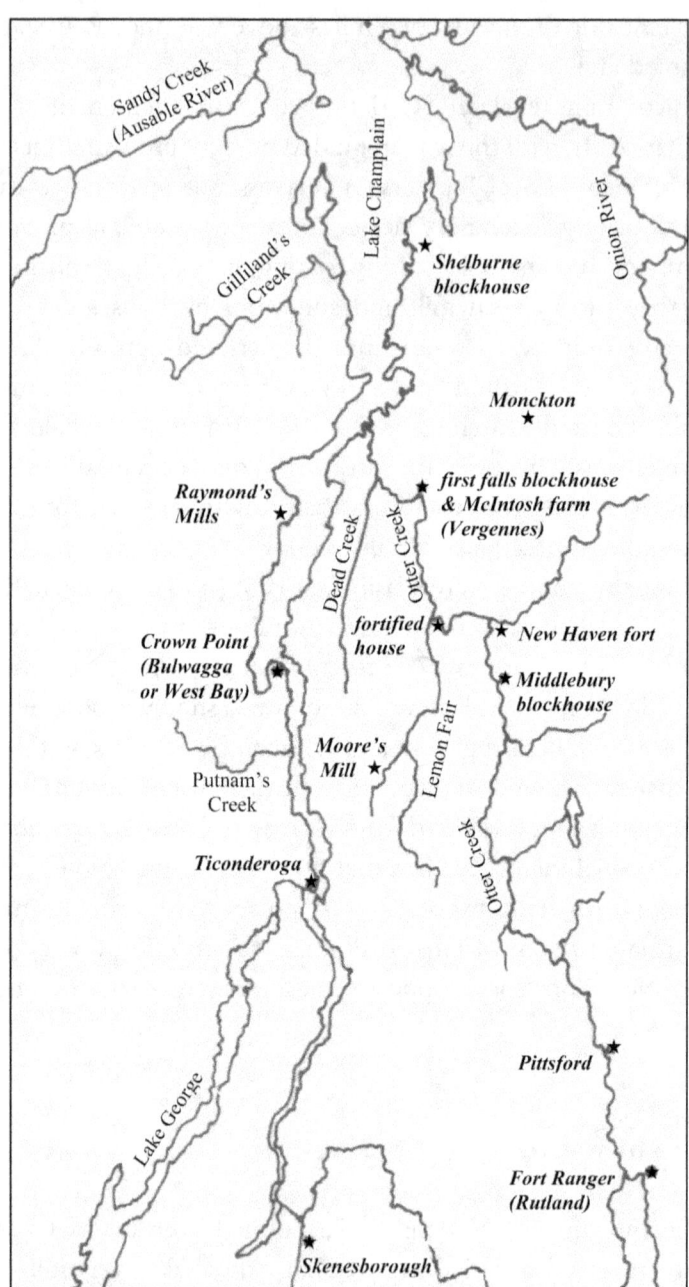

Scenes of Action, 1778.

Could not here of any Enemy." Webster ordered his men to return home with the caution to hold themselves ready to march on the shortest notice.[95]

The Expedition's Initial Results

At daylight on November 7, Carleton moved north on the lake's east side and destroyed buildings along the way. He was joined en route by Captain Dixon who brought news that he had found a large quantity of grain and flour in and about Raymond's Mill and destroyed the lot; however, the detachment sent to Moore's Mill had not fared so well.

Dunlap reported that he had personally accompanied Farquhar along the road to a house about five hundred yards from the mill. A rebel sentry posted at the house door challenged, and upon receiving no reply, gave fire and ducked back into the house. Dunlap took control and formed up the Regulars to return fire. Whitcomb's Lieutenant Crook had posted men in a small log building that flanked the house's door, which caused Dunlap to fear the loss of several men if he attempted an assault on the house. Crook reported that the attackers numbered thirty-six, which indicates that Dunlap did not call forward his 53rd detachment stationed half-way down the road. After a musketry exchange, during which a redcoat was wounded, the rebels ceased fire. Dunlap heard cries from inside the house. With wishful thinking, he concluded his opponents had many wounded. Dunlap assumed those in the house were an advanced guard for a larger party at the mill, and decided to withdraw. Night had fallen, and instead of leaving a detachment to prevent a sortie from the house and proceeding to destroy the mill, he returned to the boats in fear of being surrounded in the woods by superior numbers. Certainly not a sterling result!

Needless to say, Crook's report to Whitcomb about the incident presented things somewhat differently. He had recognized Dunlap's loyalist guide, Justus Sherwood, and credited him with leading the raiders. It would have been typical of Sherwood to be foremost in the action, which might have given Crook that impression. Crook claimed to have killed two of the British and wounded several more, while his men suffered only one man slightly wounded. When the redcoats were gone, his detachment marched to Rutland.[96] While Carleton's detachments were at work, his remaining troops destroyed the settlements on the east side of the lake until they arrived at Button Mould Bay and stopped for the night.[97]

Ross's Detachment

Captain Andrew Ross's force marched due east to a deep valley where the Natives agreed to spend the night, as the surrounding high hills would block the sight of their campfires. They resumed their march at daybreak, and after about five miles, came to a large, unfordable creek, which they crossed on a fallen tree. On the other side, they found a large, broken chest and four empty flour barrels. Four miles on, they came across two small deserted houses, one a blacksmith's shop, and a good supply of corn and a horse. After destroying the buildings, they marched another two miles and found a weaver's home with two large barns full of several sorts of grain, which they destroyed. About noon, they struck Otter Creek at Asa Blodget's tiny house and barn in Middlebury, but again, saw no inhabitants, and found only a little corn.[98]

Ross now formed two detachments, sending Lieutenant Houghton with Natives and Provincials to burn a farmhouse about two miles up the creek where they discovered a large quantity of grain, but no people or cattle. Indian Department officer, M. Joseph Marie LaMothe, along with six or seven "upper Country Indians," swam the creek and destroyed one or two farms on the other side, but found neither people nor cattle. As soon as these two detachments returned, the force burned a large number of houses and barns, and great quantities of hay, corn, and grains, but again no cattle or people were found.

After the detachment quit the settlement, their guide left the road and struck off through the woods. Some five miles later, they came across the house and blacksmith's shop they had destroyed in the morning. They continued a great distance through dense woods, and it was a long time before they struck the proper trail again. In the evening, just short of the ford where they would cross the creek, they stopped to camp.

On the morning of the 8th, the force rose early. Soon after seven o'clock, the Natives crossed the ford and opened such hot gunfire on the cattle and poultry found there that the soldiers thought the crossing was being contested. The troops rushed forward and crossed as fast as they came up. Once over, they discovered their first inhabitants — a family of a man, two women, and eight or nine small children who were very glad to see soldiers, as the Natives had "frightened them almost to death."

Enys was amazed at their equanimity, "You hardly suppose how quietly all these Yankees take any distresses, so much so that they appear to have lost all sort of feeling. They expressed no Sort of Surprize or Greif at our Coming and only Said very cooly they did not Suppose we Should come so far into their Country"; however, the man's wife was upset when she was told her husband would be taken to Canada, and that she must go to her friend's and not attempt to follow. The woman complained that this was very hard usage, as they had never done anything against the king's troops, but Enys thought this was a "d———d lie as … the house was fitted up as a place of defence to command the passage of the ford."

A great many cattle of all kinds were found, with large stores of hay, grain, corn, flax, and other crops. The inhabitants were allowed to take clothes, provisions, and a milk cow to supply their needs for the trip to the nearest settlement. Afterwards, the Natives were allowed to plunder the house, which Enys noted "they allways look upon as their undoubted right." In a display of humanity, a small building was left standing to shelter from the cold any folk who would pass that way to the ford.[99]

When everything else around the ford was destroyed, word came from some source that a party of rebels was in a house down the creek on the opposite bank. Lieutenant Robert Arbuthnot, 31st Regiment, was sent to investigate, with thirty men and some Natives. They re-crossed the ford and marched to the house, but found only a family in residence. Meanwhile, the rest of the detachment moved down the creek, driving the cattle until opposite Arbuthnot's party, which was at work destroying the house, and "burned another house while waiting for the detachment to finish and recross in a canoe." The detachment continued down the creek, destroying all that was found, and set up camp a mile or two from the lower falls, where an elderly woman calmly watched her worldly goods go up in smoke until she realized she had left her tobacco pipe inside, whereupon she gave a "dreadful outcry.... She was totally ruined and undone that she could never live two days." As to all her other property, "She said [it] was only the fortune of war and that the Rebels treated the Friends to Government much worse." Enys made an interesting observation about one of the upper country Indians, "who have very little intercourse with white people and are supposed to be more barbarous and Cruel than the Canadian Indians." The man was observed diligently stripping goods from a house that was about to be burned. Everyone thought he did so for himself, but he gave his loot to the woman of the house and would not allow his fellows to interfere.[100]

Webster Alerted Again

On the night of November 7, an express from Skenesborough arrived at Colonel Webster's house warning that the British were burning on both sides of the lake and begging his assistance. Webster ordered out his regiment and sent a warning message to Cambridge. Two hundred militiamen quickly turned out and marched to Skenesborough. Webster ordered the company from above Fort Edward to co-operate with Colonel Warner if needed, or join him at Skenesborough, then sent a scout to Crown Point for intelligence.[101]

Carleton at Otter Creek

On November 8, Major Carleton sent five Natives up Otter Creek to examine both sides and determine whether there were any troops in the blockhouse at the first falls. He was at the creek's mouth by 8:00 a.m., where he halted for an hour before continuing upstream with two gunboats and the bateaux. By three in the afternoon, his scouts rejoined with two prisoners, who said there were no rebel troops in that part of the country, nor had they heard any news of Captain Ross. Carleton continued up the creek till he was about four miles from the lake where Dead Creek joins at a little bluff and set up camp, ordering an abattis to be built. At seven o'clock, fires could be seen upstream; Carleton pointed them out to his warriors, postulating that they belonged to Captain Fraser, although the Natives had doubts. He persuaded them to send a scout, who returned at midnight to report the fires belonged to LaMothe's upper-country Ottawas, who said the rest of Ross's detachment was two miles higher up the creek.[102]

Fort Ranger Reacts

Presumably, Lieutenant Crook arrived at Fort Ranger in Rutland late on the 8th. The report about his observations on the lake and his skirmish at Moore's Mill prompted Colonel Warren to assemble a large detachment of militia. At the same time, Major Whitcomb sent seventy men under Captain Parmelee Allen of Herrick's regiment to East Bay at Skenesborough, where he was to gather boats and bring them to Crown Point so Warren's detachment could cross the lake if necessary. Warren set off down Otter Creek, probably on the 9th, and shortly after, Whitcomb followed with 130 men.[103]

Carleton's Expedition Reassembles

Early on the morning of November 9, Carleton sent the gunboats downriver with orders to make their best way to Île-aux-Noix. He started up the creek at 7:00 a.m. About this time, Ross had word that Carleton was at the creek's mouth and would come up to the falls, so he marched his detachment and soon arrived at the falls, where they were surprised to see the blockhouse had been burned. Ross discovered that LaMothe and his Ottawas, who had left the camp the night before without informing anyone, had found the building empty and set it afire. A very fine farm near the blockhouse belonged to the Scotsman Daniel McIntosh, who had been taken earlier by Lieutenant Alder at Crown Point. McIntosh had been considered a loyalist, but his name had been found on an incriminating document, so his excellent house, outbuildings, and an immense quantity of grain, cattle, and poultry were destroyed or removed. McIntosh's wife and her female friend were permitted to accompany him as prisoners, which Enys noted was "an Indulgence granted to no one else."[104]

At ten, Carleton arrived at the falls four miles upstream from Dead Creek. Ross advised him that he had detached Captain Jonathon Jones and his twenty Provincials with orders to destroy Monkton township, a remarkably rich "Nest of the Greatest Rebels in that part of the Country." The township was up the creek and about eight miles cross-country from Champlain. Jones's secondary, but equally important, mission was to capture Winthrop Hoyt, an interpreter who frequently conducted Congress's business with Quebec's Native peoples.

Jones rejoined just before dusk at 4:00 p.m. He had captured Hoyt and several others, and destroyed a considerable quantity of arms, ammunition, grain and forage, and brought off twenty-four head of cattle. Carleton sent the beeves overland to the lake and set off in the bateaux with the expedition, arriving at the lakeside camp at eleven o'clock, and the prisoners were sent aboard the shipping that lay off the creek's mouth.[105]

The next morning and early afternoon were spent ferrying the cattle to Split Rock. Carleton instructed Verneuil de Lorimier, Kahnawake's Canadien officer, to go to the Rock to determine whether the Natives' account of collecting sixty head was accurate.[106] The major reckoned that, including those brought in by Captain Jones, the count should be upwards of ninety. Orders were given to Ross's 31st detachment to remain at Gilliland's Creek for twenty-four hours, and once the oxen had passed by, to destroy the mills and other buildings there. They would be protected by the sloop *Lee*, a re-rigged rebel cutter captured at Valcour Island. As it transpired, Ross either misunderstood his orders, or they were unclear, as he missed burning the buildings along the creek.

After leaving provisions and a large bateau for the two old men, women, and children to use to go to Skenesborough, the force departed the mouth of Otter Creek by four o'clock. The *Maria* set sail for Pointe-au-Fer, while the rest of the force and the *Carleton* ran down the east shore to destroy the buildings on that side.

At 2:00 a.m. on the morning of November 11, the expedition was on the water when the wind blew so fresh that the boats were separated. Carleton had his sloop put in at Grande-Île with two boats and they waited there till one in the afternoon, when he saw five other boats and pushed off, landing at Pointe-au-Fer at dusk. The next day, the expedition sailed at 10:00 a.m. and reached Île-aux-Noix by one in the afternoon.[107]

The Rebel Pursuit

Warren's and Whitcomb's troops stopped several miles from Lake Champlain and dispatched a party to reconnoitre. To everyone's great surprise, they returned with the news "that all the houses, and other buildings on the Lake [and] forty miles up Otter Creek, were burnt, with all the Grain, Forage & effects, the men taken prisoners, all the living animals that could [not] be brought off killed, the Women & Children after being plundered were sent to

Skeensborough & the Enemy with shipping &c. have made their escape." Whitcomb immediately sent men to assist the families who had "escaped the general conflagration" and to make a further reconnaissance of the enemy. Upon their return, the news was the same: the enemy was gone. It was said that "one Frazier" — meaning Alexander Fraser — had commanded the expedition, and had sworn to kill Whitcomb before Christmas or lose his own life.[108]

Humanity

One could conclude from Carleton's and Enys's journals that the expedition had shown a great deal of humanity toward the inhabitants; however, when Webster's scouts arrived at Skenesborough, they reported that the women and children had been stripped and left without stockings and shoes in snow three to four inches deep. Horrifyingly, many of the beasts collected by the raiders were herded into the houses that were set afire. Other animals had chunks cut out of them and ran about bleeding to death.[109]

Carleton's Report

Carleton's report mentioned some unspecified misbehaviour of two Lake of Two Mountain Indians, blaming two unnamed "low fellows who live with them and having the Advantage of speaking their language persuades them to all sort of irregularities & wrong headedness." He commended Lieutenant Richard Brown, who had managed the Kanehsatakes to the great satisfaction of their headmen, and he estimated that four months' provisions for twelve thousand men had been destroyed.[110]

Carleton had proven a consummate practitioner of the *petit-guerre* — leading his disparate force with a sure hand; advancing with great care; and carefully collecting intelligence before acting. When he judged the time right, he struck decisively and swiftly.

Daniel Claus

Lieutenant-Colonel Claus was embarrassed about his reduced status, and tried valiantly to avoid interfering in Colonel Campbell's jurisdiction, which for decades had been his own. Yet his extensive experience had taught him the danger of spurning Native peoples. He complained to the governor that "when the Indians of Major Carleton's party came to Town, I had them all about me to hear the News. I endeavoured all in my power to disengage myself from [them], it being vastly troublesome to have them so often abt. oneself, but all to no purpose, and should one disoblidge them, they would say all the past Friendship & Regard towards them was but Hypocrisy & Self Interest, and throw the same Reflection upon their present Managers."[111]

A Change to the Rebel Command

During the time that Major Carleton was making his preparations for his raid, Brigadier Stark had been relieved as Northern Department commander by Brigadier Edward Hand, who arrived in Albany on October 24. Consequently, Stark's squabble with Bedel quietly disappeared. Hand was on the rebound from a difficult and frustrating assignment at Pittsburg in Pennsylvania, and he likely found Albany a relief by comparison, although he was only in place for one month before he was replaced by Brigadier James Clinton, brother of the New York's governor. Clinton was to retain the command until mid-1781, when he was replaced by the returning Stark.[112]

The Franco-American Invasion Threat

Governor Haldimand had little time to bask in Carleton's success, or to consider Claus's discomfiture. While still in London, he had been apprised of France's alliance with the United States and wrote that it could "scarcely be doubted that Canada will be the principal object of the design of the French as well as of the Rebels." At the time, he had requested substantial reinforcements for the army in Canada, but none had been forthcoming, and the possibility of a combined Franco-American invasion was always in the forefront of his thoughts.[113] No doubt the arrival on July 8 of a large French fleet of twelve ships of the line and fourteen frigates off Rhode Island with transports chock-a-block with Regulars raised his concerns.

Washington's young French protégé, the Marquis de Lafayette, appeared before Congress on October 13 with a new plan to invade Canada. The historian Max Mintz notes that Lafayette had become infatuated with the idea of an invasion, and was regretting his hasty rejection of the earlier scheme. He believed that, now that his homeland had entered the war and her naval and military assets were in America, a joint expedition could easily deliver Quebec to Congress and ensure his military reputation. It did not occur to him that Congress might not be eager to establish another monarchy on the northern border, as getting rid of the current one was proving challenging enough. Lafayette urged Congress to permit him to return to France to obtain support for a 12,600-man, two-pronged attack, one to strike through Niagara, and the other to move up Lake Champlain to Montreal, supported by a French squadron sailing up the St. Lawrence.

Washington was appalled when he heard of this proposal, and wrote a carefully crafted letter to Congress emphasizing the overall shortage of supplies, lack of sufficient troops, and, in case some bright spark suggested it, the dangers of relying of militia. He stressed the strength of Quebec's fortifications and the Royal Navy's superiority over the French. In a more pointed letter to President of Congress Henry Laurens, which he asked be kept secret from Lafayette, he questioned how wise it was to encourage Gallic ambitions in Canada, mentioning that, during a conference with the marquis and his aides, Washington had "read in the countenances of some people ... more than the disinterested zeal of allies." He backed up these missives with a personal visit, which put paid to the concept. On the first day of the New Year, Congress dismissed the proposal.[114]

While these machinations were underway, a masterfully conceived document written by the French admiral Comte d'Estaing appeared on church doors in several lower Quebec parishes.

A DECLARATION ADDRESSED IN THE NAME OF THE KING OF FRANCE TO ALL THE ANCIENT FRENCH IN NORTH AMERICA

I, the undersigned authorized by His Majesty, and thence cloathed with the noblest of titles, with that which effaces all others; charged in the name of his Father of his Country, and the beneficent protector of his subjects, to offer a support to those who were born to enjoy the blessings of his government—

To all his Countrymen in North-America.

You were born French; you could never cease to be French. The late war, which was not declared but by the captivity of nearly all our seamen, and the principal advantages of which our common enemies entirely owed to the courage, the talents, and the numbers of the brave Americans, who are now fighting against them, has wrested from you, that which is most dear to all men, even the name of your country. To compel you to bear the arms of Parracides against it, must be the completion of misfortunes: With this you are now threatened: A new war may justly make you dread being obliged to submit to this most intolerable law of slavery. It has commenced like the last, by depredations upon the most valuable part of our trade. Too long already have a great number of unfortunate Frenchmen, been confined in American prisons. You hear their groans. The present war was declared by a message in March last from the king of Great Britain to both houses of Parliament; a most authentic act of the British sovereignty, announcing to all orders of the State, that to trade [with America] though without excluding others from the same right, was to offend; that frankly to avow such intention was to defy this sovereignty; that she would revenge it and defer this only to a more advantageous opportunity, when she might do it with more appearance of legality than in the last war:—For she declared that she had the right, the will, and the ability to revenge; and accordingly she demanded of parliament the supplies.

The calamities of a war thus proclaimed have been restrained and retarded as much as was possible, by a Monarch whose pacific and disinterested views now reclaim the marks of your former attachment, only for your own happiness: Constrained to repel force by force, and multiplied hostilities by reprisals, which he has at last authorized, if necessity should carry his arms, or those of his allies into a country always dear to him, you have not to fear either burnings or devastations: And if gratitude, if the view of a flag always revered by those who have followed it, should recall to the banners of France, or of the United States, the Indians, who loved us, and have been loaded with presents by him, whom they also call their *Father;* never, no never shall they employ against you their too cruel methods of war. These they must renounce, or they will cease to be our friends.

It is not by menaces that we shall endeavour to avoid combating with our countrymen, nor shall we weaken this declaration by invectives against a great and brave nation, which we know how to respect, and hope to vanquish.

As a French gentleman, I need not to mention to those among you who were born such as well as myself, that there is but one august house in the universe, under which the French can be happy, and serve with pleasure; since its head, and those who are most nearly allied to him by blood, have been at all times, through a long line of monarchs, and are at this day more than ever delighted with bearing that very title which Henry IV regarded as the first of his own. I shall not excite your regrets for those qualifications, those marks of distinction, those decorations, which, in our matter of thinking, are precious treasures; but from which, by our common misfortunes, the American French, who have known so well how to deserve them are now precluded. These, I am bold to hope and to promise, their zeal will very soon procure to be diffused among them. They will merit them when they *dare to become the friends of our allies.*

I shall not ask the military companions of the Marquis of Levi; those who shared his glory, who admired his talents and genius for war, who loved his cordiality and frankness, the principal characteristics of our nobility, whether there be other names in other nations, among which they would be better pleased to place their own.

Can the Canadians, who saw the brave Montcalm fall in their defence, can they become the enemies of his nephews? Can they fight against their former leaders, and arm themselves against their kinsmen? At the bare mention of their names the weapons would fall out of their hands.

I shall not observe to the ministers of the altars, that their evangelic efforts will require the special protection of Providence, to prevent faith being diminished by example, by worldly interest, and by sovereigns whom force has imposed upon them, and whose political indulgence will be lessened proportionably as those sovereigns shall have less to fear. I shall not observe, that it is necessary for religion that those who preach it should form a body in the state; and that in Canada no other body would be more considered, or have more power to do good than that of the priests, taking a part in the government; since their respective conduct has merited the confidence of the people.

I shall not represent to that people, nor to all my countrymen in general, that a vast monarchy, having the same religion, the same manners, the same language, where they find kinsmen, old friends, and brethren, must be an inexhaustible source of commerce and wealth, more easily acquired and better secured, by their union with powerful neighbours, than with strangers of another hemisphere, among whom everything is different, and who, jealous and despotic sovereigns, would sooner or later treat them as a conquered people, and doubtless much worse than their late countrymen the Americans, who made them victorious. I shall not urge to a whole people that to Join with the United States is to secure their own happiness; since a whole people, when they acquire the right of thinking and acting for themselves, must know their own interest: But I will declare, and I now formally order in the name of His Majesty, who has authorized and commanded me to do it, that all his former subjects in North America, who shall no more acknowledge the supremacy of Great Britain, may depend upon his protection and support.

Done on board his Majesty's ship, the Languedoc, in the harbour of Boston, the twenty eighth day of October, in the year one thousand seven hundred and seventy eight. ESTAING.[115]

Haldimand's biographer, Jean McIlwraith, postulates that d'Estaing exceeded his commission when he wrote this declaration and had it posted in Quebec, as it is now known that France had agreed not to pursue any personal advantage during the war; however, that fact was unknown to Haldimand, who could visualize his worst fears coming to pass. Over the coming years, the governor would be alert to every scrap of intelligence about the possibility of a Franco-American attack, and his concentration on this threat dominated his defensive and offensive strategies.[116]

Covert Vermont Negotiations

The British watched the conflict between New York and Vermont with a keen eye, as they could see the possibility of upsetting the rebellion by playing one against the other. They were fully aware of the commotion in Congress caused by Vermont's abortive Eastern Union, and of Ethan Allen's attempts to reconcile that body to his state's independence in the face of strong opposition by New York and New Hampshire. On December 24, William Eden, British undersecretary for the Northern Department, wrote to Sir Henry Clinton, now commander-in-chief America after Howe's recall, to suggest that Allen might be persuaded to withdraw support for the rebellion. "He may ... be easily tempted to throw off any dependence on the Tyranny of the Congress and made useful to Government by giving him and his adherents the property of all the Lands appropriated to the Rebels and making that Country a

General Sir Henry Clinton (1730–1795), British Commander-in-Chief America.

Separate Government dependent on the Crown and the Laws of Great Britain."[117]

This supposition led to the Secret Service in Canada conducting covert negotiations with members of the Vermont Council in hopes of bringing the state back into the British fold, which continued until 1791, long past the end of the War for American Independence.[118]

CHAPTER TWO

MOHAWK REGION

"Victims to the Rage of their savage Neighbours"

THE SCRAMBLE

For the British, a most alarming result of the failure of St. Leger's expedition was the danger that the Six Nations Confederacy would abandon the Royal cause. At a minimum, such a break would seal the fate of the Mohawk Valley and northern Pennsylvania, as the Crown did not have sufficient strength to wage war in those regions without their support. Although unlikely, the possibility of the Six Nations taking a neutral stance under the persuasive influence of the rebels' Indian commissioners could not be discounted, nor could the possibility of the confederacy siding with the rebellion, either of which would threaten British control of the Great Lakes, if not all of Quebec.

Even before St. Leger's retreating troops arrived at Oswego, Six Nations Indian Department agents took action to maintain the wobbling alliance. Two primary figures led these endeavours — Major John Butler,[1] a deputy agent of the Six Nations Department, and Lieutenant-Colonel Daniel Claus, who had nominally commanded the expedition's Native contingents as Indian superintendent of the Western Expedition. Claus had formerly been deputy superintendent of northern Indians, with responsibility for the Seven Nations of Canada under Sir William Johnson, but had been bumped from that role by Governor Carleton's creation of a Quebec Indian Department. When Claus went to Britain to pursue the restoration of his position, John Butler was sent to Fort Niagara to manage Native affairs and was elevated to the role of deputy agent to give weight to his position. For some opaque reason, this enraged Claus.

Although it was through Butler's unstinting efforts that the majority of the confederacy and its affiliates had come on side with the British, Claus arrived back from England with a commission to command St. Leger's Natives, causing a rather shocked Butler to take a back seat. Yet it was Butler, not Claus, who went into action alongside the Native warriors in the bloody battle of Oriskany, which, it might be argued, was Claus's responsibility.

In simplistic terms, Butler's strength lay with the Senecas and Cayugas and Claus's with the Mohawks, although both men were well-known to all six nations of the confederacy, and each could play a leading role. How obvious their poor relationship with each other was to the Natives has become is a matter of conjecture; however, it is unlikely that those astute observers of human nature were entirely unaware.

If St. Leger had not been fully cognizant of the possible consequences of his failure, the two agents soon made him fully aware of what was at stake. From his Native allies' perspective, the campaign had been disastrous. As Joseph Brant had earlier warned would occur, they had been under the control of white officers except during the actual fighting, and their hard-won victory over the Tryon Militia was squandered when they were not allowed to advance into the valley below and finish the job. Of particular note was the fact that it was primarily Natives who fought at Oriskany. Further, the British Regulars, who had safely remained behind at Fort Stanwix (a.k.a. Schuyler), had allowed a rebel sortie to pillage the Native encampments without mounting an effective counterattack.

Claus met with the Mohawks before the expedition left Stanwix. Brant proposed "to pass the Mohawk Villages[,] secure their Women and Children and collect what Indians he could in his way to join Gen. Burgoyne by way of Saraghtoga." Claus provided him with some funds, presumably to be shared with his fellow Mohawk headmen.[2] One hundred and fifty of Brant's Native volunteers, whom he had personally raised since 1776, left for settlements along the Chemung River and the east branch of the Susquehanna. Senior department ranger James Secord and some fifty rangers, who had been released to winter at their homes and return to Niagara in the spring with cattle, travelled with them, as did many of Brant's white volunteers who went to Oquago.[3]

At Oswego, Claus arranged for the handful of Niagara traders located there to supply clothing to the Natives who had lost their packs at Stanwix, and St. Leger sent to Montreal for a shipment of Indian trade goods to prove continued good faith. Butler promised to conduct a major council in the near future when he returned from Montreal with the king's merchandise. A second purpose of his trip was to accompany three confederacy headmen to visit Governor Carleton to discuss the Six Nations' future role.

These were, at least, his obvious motives, but his shock at having been supplanted by Claus had been severe, and he needed to cement his personal position with the governor and put forward his concept for expanding his personal contribution to the war effort by raising a battalion of rangers to fight alongside the Native allies.

Claus remained with St. Leger and immediately took action to retain the Natives' favour by assigning several well-regarded persons to winter at their villages. Two Indian Department officers, Captain John Johnston and his nephew Lieutenant William Johnston, were encouraged to return to William's usual residence near the Seneca town of Canadesaga. Lieutenants John Docksteder and George McGinnis were posted to Cayuga Castle and were joined by John's brother Frederick. Most significant, Claus persuaded the sexagenarian Sarah Kast McGinnis, an adopted Iroquois, to join her son George. In her youth, she had lived as an Native woman, acquired their language, and was loved and highly regarded by the Cayugas and Senecas.

Claus recognized the need to offset the anticipated storm of rebel diplomacy and brought the headmen together. He urged them to "be revenged upon the rebels for the loss of their chiefs at Fort Stanwix and for some of their peoples being put in irons and confined at Albany." Their response was plain and direct — supply our needs, unleash us, and we will follow our own path of war.[4] Claus later reported their words and thoughts to the deputy American Secretary: "[O]ur Hatchet is dull, on account of being restrained these two years from acting agst the rebells, and our expedition to Fort Stanwix not sufficiently equipt, that they intend taking up the Hatchet their forefathers gave them, wch was burried in a deep pit, but very sharp, and would force its way wherever pointed, without controul; at the same time they declare that they only mean to restore peace to the country, and make the king's children to repent and return to their duty."[5]

The confederacy's chiefs sent wampum belts to the western Indians to advise them of their plans and to recommend they "follow their example." Before Claus left Oswego, their couriers returned from the nations "living on the Ohio and Misisipy," who rather exaggeratedly stated they were "all in the King's interest ... [and] will act with more vigor and spirit."

In response to St. Leger's instructions to collect warriors to reinforce Burgoyne on the Hudson River, Claus was able to recruit forty-odd men, primarily Canajoharies from Brant's volunteers, although most of his Natives had already returned to their villages. The Mississaugas in particular had blotted their copybook by the blatant looting of their European allies during the retreat, and they probably returned to their villages until the scandal subsided.

Warnings arrived in Carleton's Quebec City office from Lieutenant-Colonel Bolton, the commandant of Fort Niagara. He had been visited by a Seneca headman who reported that the rebel Indian commissioner General Philip Schuyler was industriously spreading accounts of British reverses among the Indians. Schuyler had invited the Six Nations to a council at German Flatts to restore their former chain of friendship, saying he did not blame them for what had happened, and had warned long ago that John Butler would lead them to ruin. Further, five hundred rebel troops were repairing the damage to Fort Stanwix and, as soon as St. Leger left Oswego, Schuyler would take post there with a considerable force.[6]

Butler's Beating Order

John Butler and the three Six Nations chiefs arrived in Quebec City about September 14 and met with Carleton. The headmen told the governor of the confederacy's concerns that St. Leger's retreat left their country wide open to rebel incursions. This situation could be readily offset by the British taking permanent post at Oswego, which would demonstrate their commitment to protect their allies. This was an old request, which Bolton's report made all the more compelling.

A report from Fort Niagara's commissary, Edward Pollard, had arrived for Butler, and he privately shared this with the governor. Pollard confirmed that the Senecas were uneasy because the troops had left Oswego, leaving their country open to the rebels. Some were upset with Butler and wanted to know when he would return.

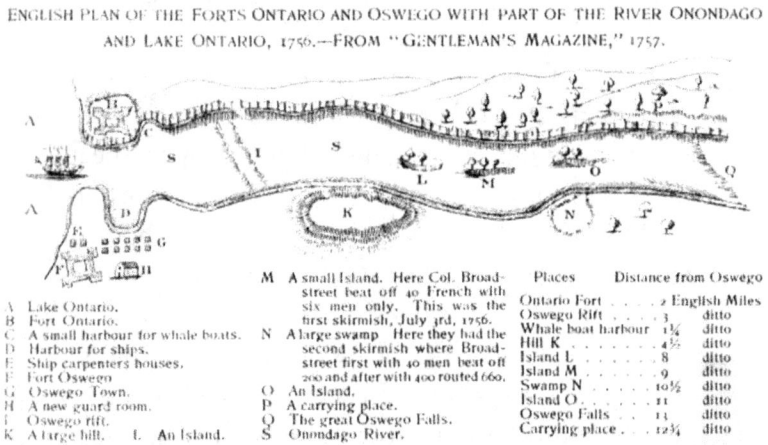

Oswego's fortifications midway through the Seven Years' War.

They had heard of Burgoyne's defeat and that Howe was in trouble. Pollard wryly warned Butler to return speedily, "[if] Government thinks the savage interest worth their notice."[7]

Pollard's letter added fuel to the headmen's request for a fort at Oswego. Although Carleton recognized that the army in Canada was too small and overcommitted to be taking on such a venture, he promised the envoys that Oswego would be occupied in the spring of 1778. Perhaps he thought his replacement would have arrived by then, which would allow him to turn his back on the issue, but it might have been better if he had kept to his earlier decision to avoid such issues altogether, as this pledge would later haunt Quebec's administration.

When Butler had the opportunity to address his own affairs, he opened the discussion by repeating some of the choicer comments Claus had made about Carleton's management of Native affairs at the time of the invasion, which angered the governor and made him receptive to the agent's request to raise a corps of rangers. As this corps would be positioned to operate with the Natives, there would be little conflict with Butler's primary responsibility as a deputy-agent for the Six Nations.

> To John Butler Esqr appointed Major Commandant of a Corps of Rangers to serve with the Indians.
>
> By virtue of the power and authority in me vested by the King, I do hereby authorize and empower you, or such officers as you shall direct, by the beat of the Drum, or otherwise, forthwith to raise, on the Frontiers of this Province, as many able bodied men, of His Majesty's loyal subjects, as will form one Company of Rangers, to serve with the Indians, as occasion shall require: which Company shall consist of a Captain, a first Lieutenant, Second Lieutenant, three Serjeants, three Corporals and fifty private men; and when you shall have compleated one Company

as aforesaid, you are further empowered to raise and form another in like manner, and of like numbers as the first, and so on, untill you shall have compleated a number of companies of rangers as aforesaid, not exceeding in the whole eight companies; observing that the first be compleated, armed and fit for service, and have passed muster, before such person as shall be appointed for that purpose, by some one of the Commanding Officers of His Majesty's Troops, nearest to where the said companies so raised, shall be at the time, before another be begun to be raised. And of which eight Companies, or such part thereof as you shall be able to raise, you shall be Major Commandant, two of the Companies aforesaid (to be composed of people speaking the Indian language and acquainted with their Customs and Manner of making War) for their encouragement shall be paid at the rate of four shillings New York Currency by the day,[8] non Commissioned Officers in proportion from the day of their inlisting, and the other said companies (to be composed of people well acquainted with the Woods) in consideration of the fateague they are liable to undergo, shall be paid at the rate of two shillings New York Currency by the day; Non Commissioned Officers in proportion, the whole to cloath and arm themselves at their own expense. You and the Officers so raised, to be paid as is customary to the Officers of like rank, in his Majesty's service, and you are carefully to obey and follow such orders and directions; as you shall from time to time receive from me, or the Commander in Chief for the time being, or any other of your superior Officers, according to the rules and discipline of War, in pursuance of the trust hereby reposed in you.

Given under my hand and Seal at Quebec this 15th day of September one thousand seven hundred and seventy seven and in the Seventeenth year of the Reign, Guy Carleton.[9]

By taking this unilateral action, Carleton ignored Claus in his role as Indian superintendent of the Western Expedition and trod firmly into Guy Johnson's bailiwick as the Six Nations' superintendent. He instructed Butler to march as soon as possible with the Rangers already enlisted and a large body of Iroquois and their allied nations to join Burgoyne. He was to send an express advising the general of his strength and expected time of arrival.[10]

Of note, Butler's monumental expenses incurred since the fall of 1775 were approved with little scrutiny and paid in Halifax currency, fully one-third more than the value of York. In contrast, Claus would go through hell trying to get his much more moderate expenses approved, with Carleton sloughing him off as being outside the governor's authority.[11]

Women's Assistance

Mary Brant had taken her family to Cayuga Castle after being forced out of Canajoharie by the Oriska Oneidas and their rebel friends. As a Mohawk matron and the widow of Sir William Johnson, she had immense influence across the confederacy. Claus observed, "one word from her is more taken Notice of by the five Nations than a thousand from any white Man without Exception." She was thoroughly wed to the British connection and acutely conscious of any unrest among the Iroquois. Claus maintained that shortly after Burgoyne's defeat she had found the Iroquois "in general very fickle & unstable." Even Old Smoke (The-Smoke-has-Disappeared, Sayenqueraghta), the Confederacy's War Chief, was wavering, and when she attended a council held at Canadesaga, she addressed him publicly, reminding him of his former close friendship with

Sir William, to whom "he so often declared & promised to live and die a firm Friend & Ally to the King of England and his Friends." Her persuasions were said to have restored Old Smoke's morale and that of the other attendees, and "they promised her faithfully to stick up strictly to the Engagements to her late worthy Friend and for his & her sake espouse the Kings Cause vigorously and speadily avenge her Wrongs & Injuries."[12]

At Cayuga Castle, Sarah McGinnis took firm action on the king's behalf when an Onondaga courier arrived with Schuyler's belts. The headmen consulted her, and as a woman of consequence, she acted decisively, "seized upon and cancelled the Belts, telling them that such bad news came from an evil spirit, and must endanger their peace & union as long as it was in their sight, and therefore must be buried under ground which she would undertake to do." Schuyler's wampum went no further; his diplomacy had been effectively stymied.

Rebel Natives

Butler reported to Carleton that on his return voyage, he had stopped at Deer Island and discovered that the necessary provisions and presents for raising a new body of Native warriors had been forwarded to Fort Niagara. Before sailing there, he heard from some Senecas that the Onondagas had joined the Oneidas and Tuscaroras in the rebel interest and taken up the hatchet from commissioners Philip Schuyler and Volckert Douw to fight against Burgoyne. This was in part true — a substantial body of Oneidas and Tuscaroras had taken up the rebel hatchet at Schuyler's Albany council, but only a handful of Onondagas, which scarcely represented a tribal commitment.[13] The prisoners taken by these volunteers were traded for the three Iroquois warriors captured at German Flatts with the Indian Department officers — Butler's son Walter, Peter Ten Broeck, and William Ryer Bowen — who, Butler's informants advised, continued to be held in irons and "cruelly treated."

When at Niagara, Butler acted on advice from some Seneca and Cayuga friends and sent a message instructing the disaffected Indians to deliver up the rebels' war axe at an upcoming council. Before this council began, he had such strong assurances from the Senecas of the confederacy's continued friendship that he wrote to Sir William Howe, General Henry Clinton, and Colonel Guy Johnson. His message to Clinton is most revealing, as Butler states that he and Joseph Brant were "ready to await your orders," indicating his willingness to work with the Mohawk despite Claus's contention that the two men were constantly at odds and in competition. Butler added, "Nor could I perceive that the ill success of General Burgoyne warped the majority of them from His Majesty's interest in the smallest degree."

His message to the disaffected prompted the attendance of "all the Onondagas and Tuscarora chiefs with the greatest part of their young men." They delivered up the rebels' axe with a belt acknowledging their fault and a promise to follow no other advice except from the British in the future. As the historian Barbara Graymont points out, these promises were fantasy, as the bulk of the Onondagas stayed neutral until 1779, and the Tuscaroras continued to supply manpower to the rebels throughout the war.

Butler reported to Carleton that "the whole of the Six Nations, except the Oneidas, are determined to act heartily and with vigour this winter.... Their operations, I believe, will be principally directed against Pennsylvania and Virginia." Craftily, he buried in his report's final paragraphs some disagreeable news. "In obedience to Your Excellency's orders, I would have endeavoured to join General Burgoyne's Army with a body of Indians, but it was not in my power, having neither provisions or clothes necessary for them but what was at this place. But before I could collect the body necessary for such an attempt, we received the unfortunate account of the fate of that army." Considering Burgoyne's defeat, this was indeed fortunate, but surely Carleton asked himself what had happened to the Indian trade goods he had sent to Niagara.[14]

The same day, Butler wrote to Captain Francis LeMaistre, Carleton's deputy adjutant general, that he had expected that a number of blank commissions would be forwarded to Niagara to be completed as he saw fit, but LeMaistre advised that this supposition was incorrect. Consequently, Butler pointed out that the majority of his recruits were still on the frontiers of New York and Pennsylvania, and to send men on the dangerous task of collecting them without being able to promise them rank consistent with the number of men they brought in would be difficult. He requested guidance on how to proceed, and asked for clarification of his own commission, as he understood he was to be ranked as a major in the army, but was now unsure.

He reported sending John Depew of Wyoming, a senior ranger in the Indian Department, to the Pennsylvania frontier to bring in the rangers St. Leger had released to go home after the Stanwix siege had been raised. He enclosed a roll of his son Walter's company along with a list of men recommended as officers for two new companies, and again recommended his second son, Thomas, to command one.[15]

Tory Hunting

After the Oriskany tragedy that shattered the Tryon County militia, vengeful Tory-hunting went on apace in the Mohawk Valley. Shortly after the battle, a number of prominent Tories' wives were taken up and lodged under guard in the Johnstown house-cum-tavern owned by the Six Nations Indian Department captain Gilbert Tice, including Mrs. Tice herself. The committee of safety noted that numbers of Tories were hiding in the woods, where they were supplied by their families, and that the women of these men were behaving very rudely and actively spiriting up resistance to the rebel cause. They lamented the death or capture in the battle of a senator, two assemblymen, their militia brigadier, two colonels, a major, a major of brigade, five committee members, and many captains and junior officers. Michael Ittig, one of their captains, had even "forgotten his duty" and taken the enemy's protection.

The committee investigated "the great revolution" at Dorlach, which had resulted in Jacob Miller's militia company joining St. Leger at Stanwix. It was reported that Dorlach's "chief of the Tories" did his utmost to seduce others and "tied a hand kerchief to a stick and cried out a Hurray for King George." William Newberry of Fort Hunter admitted to seducing others at Dorlach to march to Stanwix, and Adam Young was found guilty of supplying Miller's men with provisions during their march. When a fellow who had refused to do duty in the militia had been taken "in full arms and accutrements," he snapped his musket at the guard.

And there were individuals who purloined the goods and livestock of Tory families whose husbands and sons were hiding in the woods or were away in loyal Provincial regiments. A man who had returned from serving with the enemy was sent to join Gansevoort's Third New York in place of another man. Another fellow was fined £10 for damning some officers and committeemen, and harbouring a Tory. Former Tryon Militia colonel Henry Frey, an avowed loyalist whose brother John had been captured while serving as the Tryon militia's brigade-major, had another brother, Barent, who had run off to serve under John Butler. Henry refused to sign an association supporting the rebellion, and was considered such a threat to the Whig cause that he was exiled from the county for the duration of the war.

George Herkimer had been appointed the colonel of the battalion of Tryon County Minute Men on September 19, 1775, and was a county committee member until he resigned in October 1775, perhaps resigning then as colonel as well. A month later, he was discharged as a captain of the 4th Tryon County militia regiment for striking a man "contrary to the Law of Arms," presumably one of his soldiers. George was the brother of the deceased militia brigadier Nicholas Herkimer, and of Johan Jost, who had run off to join the Six Nations Indian Department. When he attempted to take over Nicholas's estate, he was warned off by committee chairman Peter S. Deygart, presumably because he was of dubious loyalty to the rebel cause.[16]

Southern Tryon's commissioners of sequestration impressed a number of men as guards to protect them as they went about their nasty duties of looting the properties of the disaffected. Archibald Thompson and Thomas McMicking, who had been in arms with John McDonell and Adam Crysler in the loyalist uprising in Schoharie in August 1777, and a third Scotsman were forced into this guarding role. How they might have performed if an armed confrontation had occurred is an open question. The virulent Captain Alexander Harper commanded this detachment and submitted a payroll for January 1778 for "Guarding the Commission of Sequestration Whilst they were Collecting and Selling the Personal Property of Persons Absconded to the Enemy."[17]

Only two months later there was a measure of ironic humour when the rebellious settlers in southern Tryon, the very area that the commissioners of sequestration had combed through while confiscating Tory properties, petitioned the state legislature for protection from predatory Tories and Native bands. The worm had turned.[18]

Oquaga Wavers

Butler's report of firm Native support for the Crown's cause was all very well, as it was made from the safety of the stone-walled fortress at Niagara with its impressive "French Castle," its redcoats and Rangers, its harbour for the king's vessels that controlled Lake Ontario, and its warehouses of Indian trade goods — but on the eastern margins of Indian Territory, the atmosphere was not nearly so comforting.

The sachems from the villages around Oquaga recognized their vulnerability to reprisal, as many of their warriors had eagerly responded to Brant's persuasion and taken a major role in scouring the communities across the Stanwix treaty line for provisions — and, more damning, taken a key role in the Oriskany ambush. The headmen sent an envoy to an Ulster County militia colonel, asking that the state forgive their young men and promising they would recall them. Their towns would not take offence for any of their warriors killed at Stanwix, and hoped to be recognized as neutral. This was typical Native diplomacy, entirely outside European tradition, and to white eyes nothing more than duplicitous.

The Ulster colonel forwarded the information to Governor Clinton, requesting instructions. The state council's members were insulted and resolved that the residents of the Oquaga towns should be considered enemies, whereas the Oneidas were allies of the state, and any attacks upon them would be seen as attacks upon Yorkers. That many Oneidas resided at Oquaga was either unknown, or ignored. The colonel was to advise the sachems:

> [I]f their young Men are fond of Fighting and choose to be in War ... they can come & join us who are their Brethern born, in the same Country against our common Enemies and we will pay them as we do our own young Men who go out & fight for us. The Indian may see what Reliance is to be put on the Promises of Butler and his Friends by the shameful Manner they have fled from Fort Stanwix leaving their Cannon Tents ammunition & even their Provisions behind them, tho' they boasted they would take that Fort & proceed to Albany in a Short Time & that our People dare not fight them.[19]

More Rebel Native Diplomacy

On January 1, Schuyler met with the Mohawk neutralist sachem Abraham Tyorhansere, who admitted that many Fort Hunters had been inimical to the United States, but not those remaining in the village, who asked for a document to guarantee their safety. Schuyler replied that the resentment of the people who threatened their community appeared just, as many of those people's relations and friends had been "inhumanly butchered by the Indians of your Castle," and it was believed "you might with proper Exertions have prevented the Mischiefs derived from their Defection." He could not give them the document they sought, and advised Abraham to go home, assuring him that the threats would not be executed.[20]

The Northern Department's Indian Affairs commissioners met at Albany on January 9. Present were Generals Philip Schuyler and Oliver Wolcott, and Timothy Edwards and Volckert P. Douw. Congressman James Duane presented four resolutions prepared by Congress. After due consideration of these instructions, the commissioners responded to Congress that they would invite the Six Nations to a council at Johnstown on February 15, observing that the good fortune enjoyed by "american arms" had not had "that effect on the Indians in general and the Senecas and Cayugas in particular which we expected ... the latter have hitherto continued to threaten revenge for the loss and disgrace they sustained in the engagement with the late Genl. Herkemeyer [Herkimer]."

Congress had suggested that the Six Nations be persuaded to undertake an enterprise against Fort Niagara, but the commissioners were convinced that such a polite approach would not yield positive results. "We are humbly of opinion that we should ... in

James Duane (1733–1797), New York state representative in the Continental Congress.

the most peremptory Terms *command* them to bury the hatchet they have taken against us to evince their contrition for past misconduct and [convince us of] the sincerity of their future views by joining our Arms and immediately committing hostilities on the Enemy."[21]

Schuyler's council planned for mid-February would be after Butler's was finished at Niagara. An invitation was sent to James Dean at Kanowalohale, who forwarded it with two emissaries, an Oneida and Tuscarora. Upon their return, they advised that the Onondagas paid little attention to the invitation, and the Cayugas none at all. They had left the belt with Old Smoke at the Seneca town of Canadesaga, who said he would respond after conferring with the Genesee Castle chiefs, but he left little doubt as to the answer, emphasizing that "the wounds of his warriors killed at Fort Stanwix were still bleeding."

The belt was ultimately returned to Dean with a message of rejection by all the Cayugas and Senecas. "[T]hey had no ears to hear any messages … neither would they nor any of their people attend their calls, adding that the blood of their people was still reeking which he (Schuyler) was the occasion of spilling." Dean apologized for not being able to report the particulars of Butler's recent council; however, he understood "that very large presents were made the Savages besides ample Reparation for all the Losses in goods &c. which they sustained near Fort Schuyler [Stanwix]." Further, their former "Onondaga Friends had delivered up our Hatchet and declared against us." A large party of Onondagas was expected at Kanowalohale in a few days, and it was first thought they would proceed to Johnstown for the council, but Dean had been told that they and the Cayugas would take their lead from the Senecas, whom he reported had recently "committed several Depredations upon the Frontiers of Virginia," where they lost a principal warrior.[22]

Brant on the Move

Troubling rumours persisted that the rebels from the Wyoming Valley in northern Pennsylvania were planning to attack Indian Territory. In late January, Brant decided to leave Niagara and winter at Cayo-Kwen in preparation for returning to the towns of Unadilla and Oquaga on the east branch of the Susquehanna River, from where he could gather accurate intelligence. This move complied with plans he had discussed with Daniel Claus the previous autumn.

John Butler was concerned, as he feared Brant would prompt rebel reaction before Old Smoke had gathered his forces for the campaign. Brant took some twenty Mohawks with him, and sent a message to Claus in the hands of the Fort Hunter warrior John Oteronyente, claiming that "all the five nations are in good spirrits and more united now than they ever has been yet since the troubles began except the Oneidas and a few others." He sent agreeable

John Hill Oteronyente, a Fort Hunter Castle Principal Warrior (detail from Benjamin West's portrait of Colonel Guy Johnson, ca. 1776).

news from westward, but chose not to write of any plans for the coming campaign for fear his letter would go astray. In any event, Oteronyente would tell all the news. Brant asked Claus to have two of the finest silver gorgets crafted with the king's arms and sent to him at his first opportunity. His closing comment revealed the strong personal relationships between their two families. "My sister and family joins me to give our Best compliments to Mrs. Claus and remain your sincere friend & servant." He sent a similar message to Guy Johnson in the hands of the Oquaga Mohawk chief, John Tayojaronsere.[23]

Patrols from Quebec

Governor Carleton instructed Sir John Johnson to organize a system of patrols into the upper Hudson, Mohawk, and Connecticut River valleys. The operatives were primarily drawn from Johnson's regiment. Sometimes they were augmented by Natives, but more frequently, the two bodies functioned separately. Major Campbell of the Quebec Indian Department assisted Johnson in organizing the Seven Nations' participation. The first patrol set out on February 3 and the programme continued until April 17.[24]

More Rebel Diplomacy

On January 24, General Schuyler sent a letter to Colonel John Greaton, the Continental officer commanding at Albany, enclosing a copy of a speech from the Oneidas and Tuscaroras. They requested a detachment of troops to be quartered at Kanowalohale to erect a stockade fort for the protection of the village. This was by no means their first request, as the Oneida sachem Thomas Spencer had made an appeal to Schuyler to defend the Oneida communities soon after St. Leger's retreat, particularly in view of the Mohawks' destruction of their Oriska village. Schuyler noted that, if this assistance were granted, the warriors would be less concerned about the security of their families and more inclined to join in the fighting.

The request must have been uncomfortable for the Oneidas, as it was an admission that they were incapable of providing their own security. They were aware that their skills lay in a war of movement and stealth, not in the sedentary task of defence, yet to invite an alien culture into their community required a difficult decision.

On the 26th, Schuyler wrote to Henry Laurens, the president of Congress, about four disparate topics. First, he asked for additional members to be appointed to the Indian Commission, as two of the current members, Edwards and Wolcott, were often absent, which caused delays in addressing pressing business. He mentioned the Oneida request for a fort and garrison, as they feared the Senecas would fall upon their village in its defenceless state. Although this matter was not strictly his responsibility, Schuyler, as New York's senior Continental officer, implored Laurens to supply seven or eight larger guns for the defence of Fort Stanwix, with an appropriate body of artillerists. Finally, he wrote about a Frenchman whom he had encouraged to travel to Quebec the previous winter to persuade the Canadiens of France's friendship. The fellow had allegedly induced five hundred Canadiens to desert the British service, and he asked Congress to reward the man.[25] Had this mysterious fellow actually been the cause of Burgoyne's shortfall of Canadien support?

On February 8, Schuyler again wrote to Laurens repeating much of James Dean's report from Fort Schuyler (Stanwix). In his flowery way, he described the state of the Senecas and Cayugas. "These haughty Nations cannot brook the Disgrace which they sustained from the Militia of Tryon County under the late brave and worthy General Herkimer ... and from the Garrison of Fort Schuyler under the Command of the gallant Colonel Ganesvoort [sic]. Their Resentment has undoubtedly been highly irritated by the insidious arts and Bribes of our Enemies, who at a Treaty held at Niagara ... have had an opportunity to give an Edge to their Animosity." Schuyler was claiming that the Tryon militia brigade's bloody defeat in some way disgraced the Senecas and Cayugas. Certainly, their casualties in the battle infuriated them, but it may have been Willett's unopposed looting of their empty camps that most bruised their pride.

Schuyler reported the defection of the Onondagas, and, by referring to rumours uncovered by one of Dean's couriers, predicted expeditions against New York's western frontiers, Virginia, and Pennsylvania by the Ottawas, Ojibways, Wyandots, Mingoes, and other tribes in concert with British troops. He urged Congress to provide the commissioners with answers to his previous dispatch, emphasizing that it was their

> opinion that vigorous preperations aught to be made not only to defend the Frontiers, but to chastise those Nations by carrying the war if possible into their country. Till they feel the power and the just Resentment of the united States there can be no Safety for the defenceless inhabitants. The Militia who lost their Leaders and many of their brave men taken at the German Flatts [Oriskany], suffered the additional misfortunes of being deprived of their Crops. If they should again be called upon [to serve] in planting or Harvest Time their Families must be deprived of all Subsistance. Indeed they are very sore from what they have already suffered and want Time to repair their past Calamities. Little therefore can be expected from their Exertions willing as they are to give their aid. The Oneidas and Tuscaroras are still very friendly, but far from being capable of an active part, are under well grounded apprehensions of falling victims to the Rage of their savage Neighbours.... [I]t is become indispensibly necessary to erect some Fortress and station a small Garrison in their Country for the Security of their women and children.... The Garrison of Fort Schuyler, which consists only of one Regiment may be able to defend that Fortress but cannot repel

the Incursions and Ravages of the Enemy and if it should so happen that Tryon County & the western District of Albany County should be deserted, to say Nothing of the Distress of Individuals the Difficulty of supplying our Armies with Flour would be insurmountable. The Treaty will be held about the middle of the month. We cannot defer it long, and should be relieved from the utmost anxiety by the Instructions from the honorable Congress.[26]

Butler's Rangers Captured

Butler reported to LeMaistre that a detachment of two hundred rebels had taken prisoner three Native warriors and thirty of his men, who had been sent home by St. Leger to collect cattle for

Postmortem portrait of Major John Butler (1728–1796), Deputy Agent, Six Nations Indian Department, and officer commanding, Butler's Rangers.

the Niagara garrison. Those who escaped dispersed, and several returned to their homes.

The Senecas and Cayugas were seriously alarmed by repeated rumours of coming attacks on their villages by the "masterful Connecticut settlers in Wyoming, who had already set the State Government of Pennsylvania at complete defiance." These concerns set the primary objective for the coming campaign. Butler reported that Joseph Brant, Aaron Hill, and about twenty-eight other Mohawks would go to the frontier villages if an alarm were raised, and that he would march with all the Rangers he had at Niagara, and with as many Mississaugas as he could collect. Perhaps he sensed that Carleton had made a hollow promise, as he closed with the reminder that the Six Nations were urging the British to occupy Oswego.[27]

Oswego or Deer Island

Colonel Bolton reported to the governor on the last day of the month that it would be necessary to send a strong detachment as early as possible in the spring to either Deer Island or Oswego with a large quantity of provisions for the upper posts. He and Butler believed that, unless a considerable force took post at Deer Island, the rebels would cut off their supplies from Lachine, which he thought would be no difficult matter to accomplish, and would be of the greatest consequence for Niagara, as the Natives would send their women and children to the fort in the face of an attack. On one occasion, twenty-seven hundred Natives had congregated at Niagara, and all the beef received from Detroit was consumed in six or seven days. To illustrate his vulnerability, Bolton enclosed a return of provisions currently in store for the garrison. Until provisions arrived from Lachine, he would order a small supply again from Detroit to guard against accidents, but he worried that Detroit would be unable to comply due to the number of Natives assembled there that winter. Bolton had bought up all the spare cattle from the Indian bands, and paid the soldiers 1 shilling NY per pound for all the pork they saved.

He believed he had used every possible method to prevent the garrison being distressed and to keep the Natives content.[28]

Butler wrote to Carleton on February 2, repeating that he had "the strongest assurance of the fidelity of the Senecas and Cayugas, who are the leading people of the Six Nations." Despite his several disagreements with Brant, and the conflict that Claus continuously encouraged, Butler showed himself magnanimous in his representation of the young Mohawk. "Mr. Brant, who is ... very deserving of the character of an active and intelligent man and very willing to do everything in his power for the public good, having represented that he had been employed for two years past without any allowance and out of hopes of receiving any reward for his past services from Col Guy Johnson, had desired me to lay his situation before Your Excellency, praying that you will allow him some certain pay for his future support.[29]

After the prime hunting season was past and the snow had crusted over to allow for easy snowshoeing, the Seneca and Cayuga war captains began a series of diversionary raids against Pennsylvania's backcountry, conforming to Old Smoke's strategy. Spies were stationed all along the common borders of New York, Pennsylvania, and Indian Territory to watch for rebel forces assembling.[30]

Tryon County's Problems

More than Tory-hunting occupied the Tryon County committee. In two disparate measures, the members organized the public distribution of salt, so necessary for food preservation, and passed a resolution that no black person was allowed to travel at night without a lantern, and without a permit from his master or some other appropriate person. No one was allowed to sell spirits to black people.

The German Flatts subcommittee complained to the county chairman that Colonel Bellinger, commander of the German Flatts regiment, was unwilling to garrison Fort Dayton, which left the military stores housed there unguarded. Bellinger opined that Fort Stanwix was overcrowded, and troops from there could be spared for Dayton.

The subject of George Herkimer came up again. On March 4, an Oriska Oneida named Hendrick testified that Herkimer avowed he was as good for the king as his brother Han Jost, and that he pretended to be well-affected to the rebellion to avoid being taken up. Herkimer had asked Hendrick to conduct him to Oquaga, from where he would make his way to Niagara. Two European residents acted as witnesses for this accusation. The same day, the county committee chairman, Peter S. Deygart, lodged a complaint against George Herkimer for uttering threats and insults against his person.[31]

A Ridiculous Rumour

The Marquis de Lafayette had been sent north by Congress to command an expedition against Canada. While in Johnstown at the Indian council, he heard rumours that Governor Carleton's nephew, Major Christopher Carleton, had been spying for some time in the Mohawk Valley. The major was thought to have entered the country through Oswego, and the marquis wrote to Colonel Gansevoort at Fort Stanwix to send out parties to apprehend him. The astounding sum of fifty guineas, hard money, plus any funds that Carleton had on his person, was offered as a reward to bring him in alive.[32] Although Christopher Carleton was a very capable officer, it seems most unlikely that he would have been flitting about the country when there were so many Provincials and Natives to take on the task at far less risk to the British service.

A Major Council at Johnstown

Three United States Indian commissioners were in attendance — Schuyler, Douw and Edwards — as were New York congressman

James Duane, Major-Generals Lafayette and Conway, Brigadier Ten Broeck, Albany's mayor Barclay, and many New York and Massachusetts military officers and officials. Seven hundred and thirty-two Natives attended, including women and children. None were Senecas; only a handful were Cayugas.

On March 9, a speech and belt were delivered by Schuyler and interpreted by James Dean. The commission delivered a severe message, demanding the Natives' strict neutrality and threatening punishments for future transgressions.[33] As was customary, the council then closed for the day to allow the Native headmen in attendance to develop their reply.

The next day, the Onondaga chief Tenhoghskweaghta rose to answer. He noted that the substance of the commissioners' message was directed at the Mohawks, Onondagas, Cayugas, and Senecas, and, with no Senecas in attendance, it was difficult to answer. He suggested that the commission's belt be taken to the Onondaga central council fire and deliberated upon there, in accordance with the directions of the sachems of those nations.

The chief noted that giving an answer would be fraught with many difficulties, as even his own nation was divided in sentiment, similar to the whites over their own quarrel. As to the Senecas, they had long since forsaken the central council fire, and had spurned several invitations. He assured the commissioners and officers that messengers would be dispatched to the Senecas as soon as he returned to Onondaga Castle and begged their patience awaiting an answer. He continued, "Brothers — We cannot but express our great satisfaction at the wisdom of your speech. That you say there is yet Room for us to make atonement which [gives] us Hope of peace. We find that the Congress are slow to anger."

A second belt addressed to the "Friends of the Six Nations" was spoken to by the same chief. This message agreed that some peoples were "unwise to throw off their affection and turn Enemies to their native land," but "Times are altered with us Indians. Formerly the Warriors were governed by the wisdom of their uncles the Sachems but now they take their own way & dispose of themselves without consulting their uncles the Sachems — while we wish for peace and they are for war." Addressing the commissioners' advice that many Indian nations to the southward had allied with the United States, he expressed concern that the tokens of this alliance with the Creeks had been hidden in a box, rather than given to him to take to Onondaga. "We want to relate this good news to our Confederacy[,] but without these Tokens we shall not be credited."

Then, the Oneida's senior sachem, the Grasshopper, spoke on behalf of his people and the Tuscaroras. He agreed with Tenhoghskweaghta — "Formerly, the Sachems were instantly obeyed by the Warriors, but now the latter have thrown off all Regard to their council."

The commissioners responded, stating that any Natives present who were inimical to the United States and would wish to give Butler an account of this council should come to the interpreter, James Dean, and he would repeat what had been delivered the day before. This would address Butler's accusation that the details of earlier councils had been deliberately misrepresented. Such individuals would be given supplies for their journey to Niagara. Instructions were given that the belts from earlier councils that had been brought to Johnstown be taken back to Onondaga. A final request was that news of the militia prisoners taken in the battle of Oriskany be delivered to the commission.[34]

Schuyler Recommends Action

Schuyler reported the council's details to Congressional President Henry Laurens. It was expected from their "inimical Disposition and revengeful Resolutions" that the Mohawks, Cayugas, Senecas, and the majority of the Onondagas would soon begin hostilities. Consequently, it would "be prudent early to take measures to carry the war into their Country as it would not require a greater Body of Troops to destroy their Towns than what would be necessary to protect the Frontier Inhabitants who already labour under the

Henry Laurens (1724–1792), President of Congress.

greatest apprehensions that they will soon experience the Ravages and Cruelty of these Barbarians."

A "trusty Indian" had advised Schuyler that the British would occupy Oswego. If this were true, there would be little hope for Indian neutrality. Schuyler concluded that the British were pursuing the French strategy of surrounding the rebel frontiers with a line of forts from which to supply the Natives and act as a safe haven to which they could retire. Such a situation would oblige the United States to maintain a large body of troops on the interior frontier, and Schuyler again recommended that Congress take early and vigorous measures to counteract this likelihood. The most effective means would be to occupy Oswego and reduce Niagara. Assuming troops and salt provisions could be assembled, he thought all other arrangements, such as boats, could be made by the end of May. He acknowledged that the enemy's Lake Ontario fleet might prove troublesome, but pointed out that the French navy had failed to prevent Bradstreet from reducing Fort Frontenac in 1758.

The allied Indians had requested that a trade be opened at Fort Stanwix. They had made note of the great advantage the British enjoyed over the United States in the matter of the Indian trade. Schuyler advised that the Oneidas' and Tuscaroras' request for the building of a picket fort at Kanowalohale had been passed on to Lafayette to act upon.[35]

General Washington Wants Warriors

In the Continental Army's miserable, frigid camp at Valley Forge, Pennsylvania, General Washington made a proposal to a congressional committee that was meeting there. He pointed out that with relative impunity, Howe's army was rapaciously foraging the countryside around Philadelphia for provisions, and suggested the employment of allied Native warriors to discourage them. Two or three hundred Indians combined "with some of our woodsmen would probably strike no small terror into the British and foreign troops, particularly the new comers." After some deliberation, the committee approved the concept and enthusiastically suggested that four hundred Natives be recruited.[36]

French Officers Sent to Kanowalohale

Circumspectly, Schuyler pared back Washington's request to two hundred warriors, and passed on the task of collecting them to Lafayette, who assigned the building of the fort and the recruitment to three French engineering officers. Lieutenant-Colonel Jean Baptiste Gouvion was to design and supervise the construction. The Oneidas had already prepared the timber; Lieutenant-Colonel Willett was to supply the tools, and the Tryon militia, the additional labour. Captain Louis de Tousard was to recruit warriors, and the third officer would be the courier between Kanowalohale and Stanwix. The marquis forwarded Washington's request and an encouraging speech from Schuyler to Marinus Willett, the acting commandant of Fort Schuyler, and requested he inform the Oneidas.[37]

COMMITTEES OF SAFETY DISSOLVED

From the time of their creation in mid-1774, New York's committees of safety had slowly but surely assumed control of all political and judicial affairs. As so many committee members were themselves judges, the committees often usurped the role of the highest courts of law, even after the new state constitution of 1777 provided for county judges, and frequently penalized or imprisoned disaffected persons without jury trials. In Tryon County, allied Oneidas were at times encouraged to pillage Tory holdings, and the properties of the Mohawks who remained at peace in the county were plundered by the rebel Oneidas with impunity. Indian commissioner Schuyler wrote to the Tryon Committee on March 11, warning them to stop such abuses, but his appeal received scant attention. Ultimately, excesses committed statewide prompted the legislature to abolish all committees of safety, and the governor to appoint a conspiracy commission.

Yet, even after all the other state committees had dissolved, the Tryon committee refused to submit. "They feared that [the] Commissioners of Conspiracy, as government appointees, would be men of wealth, of influence, and therefore moderates." The final blow was struck when the committee ordered armed men to break into the county jail and release Melchart Van Deusen, a committeeman from Canajoharie district, who had been legally confined for want of bail "upon Civil Process as the suit of Abraham Gerritsen." Then, the committee proceeded against Gerritsen, ordering him to pay costs.

When the state legislature learned of the case, it sent a strongly worded document, dated May 17, pointing out that these irregular proceedings went against decisions made by a constitutionally qualified magistrate, and the legislature's decision that all actions against persons suspected of disaffection were to be undertaken by the Commission for Detecting and Defeating Conspiracies.

> [T]he Intention of the Legislature is that no Committees should act after the Qualification of the Civil Officers and that in these Officers together with Commissioners all the power should be exercised — In this County as well as all the Lower Counties the Committees have Ceased and we doubt not but on the Receipt of this you will dissolve yourselves, for you will observe that as your Proceedings are illegal that the Persons whom you prosecute have a right to bring actions against you severally for Damages, which you may Rely will be the Case provided that outrages Committed in Consequence of Your Proceedings are not settled in a friendly manner. We therefore advise that your Conduct for the future may be to heal that Breach which you have so evidently made.[38]

With its activities condemned by the state, the committee had no choice but to dissolve.[39]

Schenectady Aggravated

On March 20, fifty-five deeply aggravated Schenectady citizens, including several prominent militia officers, petitioned Governor Clinton with complaints. First, a building that had been purpose-built as a barrack had been converted into a hospital, and the troops were instead billeted with the residents, but made no payment for the firewood they consumed. Second, the hospital's commissary and several officers serving under him were believed disaffected. Third, great partiality was being shown to Albany residents over Schenectady's. When the militia was called out, Schenectady sent three men to every one sent by Albany. This last complaint agreed entirely with General Stark's observation about the unreliability of Albany City's militia.[40]

Anxiety at Cherry Valley

In March, Colonel Samuel Campbell and Lieutenant-Colonel Samuel Clyde, both of the 1st Tryon militia regiment (1TCM), which was nominally headquartered at Cherry Valley, rode to Johnstown to plead with Lafayette for a proper fort to be built there and garrisoned by Continentals. As a temporary solution, the general organized a rotation scheme whereby militia would garrison the crude works around Colonel Campbell's home. Lafayette wrote to Washington to explain the community's needs, and forwarded their request for a Regular garrison, but it was some time before approval was given for a fort, and even longer before Continentals were sent.[41]

More Tory-Hunting

It was well-known in Tryon County that Brant had been supplied by several willing donors the previous year, and a search was undertaken to identify and remove them before the new campaign season began. On March 28, George Knouts deposed to Justice Peter S. Deygert that he had been taken prisoner by Brant the previous summer at "old Mr. Tunnicliff's." Knouts saw Brant give Tunnicliff a note for £36 for three oxen. A servant lad told Knouts that Tunnicliff had given Brant 5 cwt of cheese and ten or twelve cows. Further, Tunnicliff's son was there, and had worn a piece of yellow lace in his hat, the same identifying token that Brant's men wore.[42]

Guy Johnson in Exile

Colonel Guy Johnson, the Six Nations superintendent, reported to Lord Germain from New York City on March 12. He was in virtual exile, far from the scenes of action; however, he had been ordered to attach himself to Sir William Howe and take his instructions, and so in New York City he remained. Howe showed no interest in Johnson or his responsibilities, and the superintendent floundered in anonymity. Having received a copy of Bolton and Butler's message to "General Clinton or Officer commanding Hudson's River or Sir William Howe," with its assurances of Brant's and Butler's readiness for service, Johnson forwarded these same offers to the American Secretary, clearly hoping for official orders to employ the Natives in the petit-guerre, which would keep them out of the clutches of rebel emissaries.[43]

The Loyal Natives' Strategy

Daniel Claus reported that Brant and Old Smoke came together in the late winter to plan the coming campaign. Although Brant's reputation had undoubtedly been enhanced within the confederacy when he demonstrated his ability to raise and maintain a strong party the previous year, it is difficult to assess how much credit for the Mohawks' performance in the Oriskany battle should be given him versus other prominent war captains such as Deserontyon and the Hill brothers, who had surely been forward in the action. So, the question arises: Was Brant, a junior war captain, really the only Mohawk to develop plans with Old Smoke, one of the confederacy's principal war chiefs? Did that wise and competent elder Seneca exclude the confederacy's second principal war chief, Cornplanter, from the deliberations? What of the Cayugas? Yes, in the confederacy's hierarchy, the Cayugas were junior to the Mohawks and Senecas, but were they simply sideliners in the planning? More likely, Claus's report was simply another instance of him embellishing the reputation of his favourite at the expense of others.[44]

Whatever the case, an agreement was reached that the Senecas and Cayugas would concentrate on the New York/Pennsylvania border and rid themselves of the threat from the defiant Wyoming Valley settlements, and that the Mohawks would operate in the Mohawk region and bring off the rest of their people, who remained in their home communities, known as castles. With regard to rescuing fellow Mohawks, it seems that Brant would concentrate on his home town of Canajoharie, and the Fort Hunters on their own town, where it was thought that many families captured during the retreat from Burgoyne's defeat were being kept under the malevolent eye of the rebels. This division of responsibility made geographic sense, as Brant's headquarters on the edge of Indian Territory was closer to Canajoharie, and the Fort Hunters in their refuge at Lachine were within striking distance of their town.

It is noteworthy that there was no plan to attack the Oneida and Tuscarora villages, despite great concerns in those quarters. Nonetheless, considerable effort must have been made to avoid their hunters and patrols when crossing through their territories.

Ironically, the Allegheny Senecas, who had been so forward in promoting peace from 1774 to 1776, began the first dance, following Old Smoke's instructions by unleashing unrestricted partisan warfare against Pennsylvania's frontier settlements. One of their primary war captains, Kayashuta, a former peace diplomat, became a fierce enemy of the rebels.

Attacks on Fairfield and Salisbury

Considering that the focus of so many reports was on the intentions and activities of the Six Nations, it is surprising that the first party to maraud in the Mohawk Valley was one of Sir John Johnson's patrols led by Ensign William Redford Crawford of the Royal Yorkers. Crawford was a Johnstown saddler who, it seems, spoke the Mohawk and Mississauga dialects, as he spent much of the war seconded to the Indian Department at the Lake of Two Mountains Mohawk community of Kanehsatake and, in 1783, was responsible for negotiating the Cataraqui and Bay of Quinte land concessions with the Mississaugas. With him on this venture was Royal Yorker corporal Jacob Countryman, a farmer from Canajoharie District; Severinus Casselman of the Palatine District, who earlier had been a captain in the 4th Tryon County Militia; and the three Bowens — likely Luke, William Jr., and West — the last a Tribes Hill resident who at times served as a Mohawk interpreter. Whether these rankers were temporarily seconded to the Quebec Indian Department or were simply volunteers from the battalion is unknown. One source claims there were more Tories than Natives participating in the marauding, but no other European names have surfaced. It has been claimed that the Tories were dressed as Natives, which may have been for practical reasons, although the implication is that it was for purposes of disguise. The party was fifty strong; the Native element was composed of Mississaugas and probably Kanehsatakes, although unfortunately none of the war captains or principal warriors was identified.

There was snow on the ground, so the party travelled on snowshoes. They were so early in the season that surprise was complete. Their first target was the small settlement of Fairfield, eight miles north of the town of Herkimer and three miles east of West Canada Creek, which they struck in mid-March. Claims were made that the community was divided in politics, but that was true for almost every hamlet in the Mohawk Valley, so why this was considered significant is a mystery.

Across the Mohawk Valley, families had been moving to less-exposed locales, as was the case with Cobus Mabee's family. Two Native acquaintances of the family approached their home, intending to capture the father; however, he was already at his new place in Canajoharie with his wife and two young children. Two older children had been left behind, and Mabee's son was cutting up potatoes to feed their cattle when the Natives found him. He shouted a warning to his sister, who hid in some cornstalks, but was himself mortally wounded and scalped. Ten Fairfield men were captured; one fellow was too old to travel and too bald to scalp, so he was left behind untouched. After setting alight some farms that probably belonged to Whigs, the raiders crossed the Jerseyfield road and took a father and two sons captive, burned their buildings, and slaughtered their livestock for provisions.

At the Salisbury settlement, they took a father, his two sons, and another man. The father was permitted to return home because of his age. No one was killed, although the farms were thoroughly plundered. After stopping to craft snowshoes for the captives, the party retired by the old Jerseyfield road. Historian Nelson Greene observes, "This raid was one of the earliest of the war and was not marked by the bloody ferocity which characterized the later ones."[45]

Dangerous Looting

In response to complaints from Mohawk Valley Natives, the rebels' Indian commission opened an investigation. It was obvious to the commissioners that the looting of Native properties would simply encourage, if not guarantee, retaliation, and that some sort of justice was required. On April 20 and 21, in his role as a Palatine District justice, Colonel Jacob Klock, the acting brigadier of Tryon's militia, took depositions from witnesses regarding the looting of the Mohawks' Canajoharie Castle, specifically the home of Mary Brant. It was deposed that a great many citizens had been seen stealing ironwork, furniture, cookware, livestock, harnesses, mirrors, lanterns, window glass, vegetables, and corn. While it was well-known that the Oriska Oneidas had taken part in the plundering and destruction, they could be excused, as their own village had been destroyed by Mohawks; however, several witnesses implicated former committee chairman Peter S. Deygart, and his wife and son, as ringleaders, and testified that his daughter had been seen parading about in Mary Brant's gowns. A witness said that the Oneidas told him that they had been goaded into the looting by Deygart. It was noted that similar thefts and destruction had occurred at the Fort Hunter Mohawk village. No evidence has been found of Deygart being reprimanded or punished, despite the fact that many had given evidence against him. It is likely that local opinion prevented any penalties.[46]

Walter Butler Escapes

After persistent petitioning by Walter Butler and several of his acquaintances about the Albany jail's unhealthy conditions, Walter, Peter Ten Broeck, and William Ryer Bowen had been moved to Richard Cartwright Sr.'s house, where men from Alden's Massachusetts regiment were posted as guards. When Cartwright contrived an opportunity for their escape, Ten Broeck demurred, but Butler and Bowen made the break. One source says Butler got his guard drunk; another says a guard was killed during the escape. Whatever the case, the pair set out on April 21 to cross the Mohawk Valley on horseback to Indian Territory.[47]

Kanowalohale

Lafayette's three French officers arrived at Kanowalohale in early April with "black belts and yellow guineas" to encourage recruiting. Although the Oneidas were dismayed about the number of warriors Washington wanted to enlist, the community was open to his call because of the promised fort and detachment of Continentals. Colonel Gouvin set to work designing and laying out the installation, and Captain de Tousard began to recruit. Gouvin's efforts were soon stalled when the Tryon militia declined to supply any labour, in part because of the need to plant crops, and in part in fear of raids on their farms, and Stanwix refused to supply troops because of the garrison's weakness.

Despite these reverses, a request for assistance directly from Washington, the United States' "great warrior," appealed to Oneida pride, and they began to gather volunteers. This process was assisted when word came from Onondaga that the Senecas and Cayugas were going to attend the grand council, which offered hope for reconciliation. Lafayette cynically commented that they had been motivated by their "love of the French blood mix'd with the love of some French louis d'or."

Forty-seven warriors, primarily Oneidas, with a few Tuscaroras and an Oneida woman, Polly Cooper, followed Tousard to join Washington at Valley Forge. Many were Oriskany veterans; prominent were the Oriska war captain, Han Yerry Tewahangarahken, and his brother Han Jost Thahoswagwat; the sachem Thomas Spencer; Henry Cornelius; Jacob Reed; Blatcop Tonyentagoyon; and Reverend Kirkland's Native assistant, Deacon Thomas. As was customary, the village's principal sachem, the Grasshopper Ojistalale, addressed them: "Keep in mind that warriors sustain an important character. They can do much good or Commit Great Enormities." Acts of abuse or plunder against innocent, helpless persons would be "beneath the Character of a Warrior." A final piece of advice was to shun alcohol. The band departed Kanowalohale on April 25 for the 250-mile trek southwards.[48]

The contingent arrived at the Valley Forge cantonment on May 15. A Continental soldier gloated, "This will make the tories fear for their scalps." Washington exhibited his great qualities of leadership, and went out of his way to be welcoming. Over time, every warrior had an opportunity to meet the "Great Chief Warrior," and he gained their admiration. At the same time, he gave repeated orders not to supply them with alcohol "on any pretence whatever."

Another Continental described the Natives as "stout-looking fellows and remarkably neat for that race of mortals." They were armed with firelocks, tomahawks, and, like the Stockbridges, who were also serving with the Continentals, the traditional bow and arrow, which each warrior had mastered in his youth. For close-range exchanges, the bow was without peer. It was virtually silent, left no betraying signature, and was quick to reload. The troops were amazed at the Natives' skill in the bow's use, and were entertained by them firing at marks.

Polly Cooper, the Oneida woman, gained considerable fame in the camp by showing the soldiers how to prepare nourishing soups using corn brought from Indian Territory and mixing it with locally procured fruits and nuts. Her generosity was rewarded by Martha Washington's gift of a shawl.

Action at Barren Hill

After a few days' rest, the Natives and ten Frenchmen, including Captain de Tousard, were assigned to Captain Allen McLane's Independent Partisan Corps, which was part of a sizeable force commanded by Major-General Lafayette, consisting of five fieldpieces, the New Hampshire Continental Brigade, and six hundred Pennsylvania militia. Washington's protégé was to conduct a reconnaissance-in-force to determine whether the British, as rumoured, were about to evacuate Philadelphia, and simultaneously to harass their foraging parties. Lafayette marched his force out of camp on May 18 and took a position in the small village of Barren Hill, posting McLane's Partisans and the Natives south of the village on the Philadelphia Road.

The war party's only action occurred on May 20. The Indians were scouting down the road ahead of McLane's Partisans when they heard cavalry hoof beats. Quickly setting an ambush among the trees lining the roadsides, they sprang the trap with a fusillade of arrows, musketry, and war halloos, which threw the British horsemen back on their main body to regroup. The Natives collected some discarded cloaks, then swiftly retired, running from tree to tree. Having regained their composure, the dragoons came pelting after them, followed by light troops at the trot. The Natives and Frenchmen turned, fired, and ran on again, loading on the move. McLane's Partisans had pulled out, leaving no one to back the French and Natives, so their retreat became a race for Matson's ford on the Schuylkill River, where Lafayette's force was recrossing.

Tousard wrote to Henry Laurens, "I have had the occasion to acquaint the british light horse with the hollow [halloo] of the

Indians, and their hability in firing.... [They] fired pretty smart though running away, and I have seen myself five or six [Dragoons] killed." Thrown by his horse, Tousard said he owed his "liberty, perhaps more, to two Indians, and two Frenchmen who stood constantly by me" while he regained his feet.

Two Oneidas were captured; they were stripped of their weapons and marched into Philadelphia, where a Hessian observer described them as "handsome and well-built people, who had a rather deep yellow skin." According to a plaque marking the fighting, the Natives had six men killed, an uncomfortably high percentage of those engaged. Disastrously for Kanowalohale, the accomplished young sachem Thomas Spencer was among them. He had been the rebels' firm friend. In June 1777, he had led four Oneidas into Canada to gain intelligence, and was at Akwesasne, where he heard Daniel Claus give details of the upcoming St. Leger expedition. Back in Tryon, he urged the committee to be strong and defend Fort Stanwix, and, true to his word, he had fought beside the militia at Oriskany. He had been selected a Bear Clan sachem in early 1777, and displayed common sense as a political leader and impressive courage as a warrior — virtues not always found together in a sachem. Indeed, he was a great loss.[49]

Despite this sacrifice on behalf of the rebellion, the fort and stockade promised them for Kanowalohale were not built until 1779, and a Continental garrison never appeared.

Rebels' New Fort

As the war progressed, military installations in Tryon County were refurbished and new ones built. A blockhouse known as Fort Plank was erected east of Forts Herkimer and Dayton on the river's south side, and in April, the 5th and 6th companies of the 1TCM were called out to expand the structure into a full fortification, with palisades and two gun positions. On May 1, the 4th company rotated the duty, and near the end of the month, Colonel Samuel Campbell ordered out the entire regiment and sent Coapman's 5th company to Cherry Valley to garrison the fort for a few days.[50]

Brant at Oquaga

The snow was gone by late April when Brant set out for Oquaga, presumably with the twenty-man party that wintered with him at Cayo-Kwen. Over the weeks, he assembled some 350 men; two-thirds were Native, most of whom had followed him to Stanwix in 1777. Some thirty or so were Canajoharies, with Mahicans, a few Oquaga Oneidas, and the Schoharie Mohawks with some Senecas and Onondagas, who were likely Brant's clan relatives, plus some from the affiliated nations, the Delawares, Nanticokes, and Connoys. He had recalled his sixty-odd European volunteers who had wintered at home or in the Indian villages, and another thirty to forty new loyalists joined. By May 15, 1Lieutenant Barent Frey of Captain William Caldwell's Company joined him with sixteen Butler's Rangers. Brant and Frey were friends from the happier days in the Mohawk Valley, and made good working partners.[51]

Brant's first task was to collect provisions for Butler and Old Smoke. His men scoured southern Tryon for corn, grains, and livestock, and gathered these supplies at Unadilla. He was also expected to recruit loyalists to serve in Butler's Rangers or his own party.

Rumours were afloat at Kanowalohale that Brant intended to attack Cherry Valley. Two Oneidas travelled there to alert the village to Brant's plans, and advised them to move away. A Cherry Valley committeeman wrote to Governor Clinton with the alarming news that Brant would arrive four weeks after March 28, and claimed there were 1,500 Indians and Tories at Unadilla, only forty miles from Cherry Valley.[52]

John Butler Deploys

Butler, Captain John Powell, a handful of Indian Department rangers, and some seventy Butler's Rangers left Niagara on May 2 and travelled to Canadesaga to meet with Old Smoke. The major's pack train carried a large store of arms and ammunition to supply the Natives and Depew's recruits. Butler was concerned about the possibility of deserters compromising the campaign, and gave orders to hunt down and kill without mercy any from the Rangers.

While at Canadesaga, the major was overjoyed to receive his son Walter and William Bowen with several loyalists they had collected during their hazardous trip through the valley. He gave Walter his commission as senior captain of Rangers, but he was too weak to go on active duty, and travelled on to Fort Niagara with Bowen, arriving May 17.[53]

A Failure of British Strategy

Craftily, Old Smoke asked Butler how many British troops would co-operate with the Six Nations. The war chief was not interested in having direct support from the Regulars, as he intended to conduct his campaign in the Native fashion; however, he wanted to put the agent on the griddle to make a point. Butler was forced to admit that it would only be his Rangers and Indian Department officers who would participate. Old Smoke inquired into what Governor Carleton had to say about plans, and Butler had to admit another uncomfortable fact — the governor had not been heard from.

On May 4, a letter from Carleton caught up with the major, but disappointingly, it gave no guidance: "The Conduct of the War having been on all sides taken out of my hands the beginning of last campaign, I cannot pretend to give Major Butler any instructions relative to the movements of the Indians or give any directions about the offensive measures they have in view." Lieutenant-Colonel Bolton was of more help when he agreed that Butler must support the Iroquois if they began operations before Carleton's successor should arrive and send new instructions.[54]

Butler marched to Unadilla just outside Indian Territory at the junction of the river of that name with the Susquehanna, and set up temporary headquarters. Unadilla was an ideal base; all of its white inhabitants were loyalist, and, with two grist mills, bread would be available, as long as grain could be collected. Food was a genuine concern; the Rangers had met hardship on their travel through Indian Territory, and Richard McGinnis recalled, "we many a time had very hungry times. I was under the necessity of giving a hard dollar for four small Indian cakes, and sometimes could not get it at all."[55]

British Occupy Deer Island

In response to the loyal Natives' request that a depot and fortress be built closer to Indian Territory, Carleton directed Bolton to establish a post on Deer Island, the location of St. Leger's staging area the year before. The island lay near the confluence of Lake Ontario and the St. Lawrence River. As noted earlier, the Six Nations preferred Oswego, but the governor thought it impossible to support an installation there, considering the present state of the army in Canada. Bolton instructed Captain Potts of the 8th Regiment's Light Company at Oswegatchie to dispatch a subaltern and twenty men to the island, and sent forty others from Niagara to support him. On the first day of his command, the island's commandant dropped dead, and Bolton replaced him with Captain John Mompesson, formerly Detroit's commandant. His primary duties were to care for the public and commercial goods arriving from Montreal, see to their proper storage, and, when appropriate, see to their reloading on sailing vessels or bateaux for movement up the lake.

The small, bulbous extension off the south-west corner of the island was chosen for the location of warehouses and docking facilities. Two deep bays were on either side of this extension, and provided safe harbours for shipping. Once the building commenced, merchants' agents and Natives flocked to the scene. Off-duty soldiers were hired to build the commercial storehouses. Mompesson soon recognized that the new post required some protection, and persuaded the Mississaugas to mount screening patrols on the mainland.[56]

Brant Forages

Brant began foraging for provisions soon after arriving at Oquaga. He visited the tiny Butternuts settlement just across the treaty line with six warriors and a couple of "Green Coat soldiers," and ordered the nine families there to go with him if they were friends of the king, or they could remain behind; either way, he was taking their cattle. Four families immediately followed him to Unadilla; the remaining five and two single men followed later.[57]

Barnabus Kelly, who lived at Butternuts, recalled Brant arriving with forty loyalists and two Natives, perhaps on a different occasion. They bought seventeen-odd cattle, 7 cwt of cheese, and forty or more skipples of flour. Brant gave notes of payment in the names of John Butler and a Captain Servos, who was said to be Sir John Johnson's uncle. Persafor Carr, who lived close by at Major Edmeston's, sent word that he had forty skipples of corn for them. Ranger John Young read aloud a proclamation from Major Butler asking all friends of the government to join Butler with their cattle and families.

At the Delaware River settlements, the Natives got about seventy head of cattle and some horses. Some seventy local inhabitants joined them at Oquaga.[58]

Brant's First Raid

Brant chose to take action, which was a pre-emptive decision, considering the strategy he had supposedly developed with Old Smoke. His party of three hundred Natives and whites arrived outside Cherry Valley on May 25 and hid on a height called Lady Hill.

From this vantage point, Brant saw a militia company drilling at Campbell's house, which had been surrounded by a log-and-earth embankment. He concluded that the garrison had been alerted, and decided not to attack. Ironically, the "soldiers" were young boys at play with wooden muskets.

Brant and five warriors outposted the road to see whether any couriers could be taken with useful intelligence. As it happened, 2Lieutenant Mathias Wormwood of Hess's Company, 2TCM, had been sent to Cherry Valley to advise that Colonel Klock would reinforce the garrison the next day. He was riding to the village with his friend Peter Sits, the company's ensign. The two riders were challenged to halt, but spurred their horses to escape and were fired upon. Wormwood fell mortally wounded, and Sits was taken prisoner. This proved a sad event for Brant, as the lieutenant had been a friend before the war. Legend has it that the Mohawk knelt to inquire whether his wounds were mortal. When Wormwood replied yes, he was dispatched and scalped, although not by Brant himself.[59]

Joseph Brant Thayendanegea (1743–1807), Canajoharie/ Oquaga Mohawk War Captain.

Cobleskill

Having left Cherry Valley before troops investigated the gunfire, Brant set course for the small, straggling community of Cobleskill on an eponymous creek that flowed into the Schoharie Kill. Twenty families were spread along some three miles of its fertile flats. Although the residents had not built any fortifications, they had formed a company of the 15th Albany County militia regiment [15ACM], commanded by two local men — Captain Christian Brown and Lieutenant Jacob Borst.[60]

The settlement's first inkling of trouble was the sighting of several Natives apparently wandering about aimlessly. Brown alerted his company, and sent a runner to Middleburgh for assistance. Captain William Patrick of Alden's Massachusetts Continentals was in garrison there, and set out with thirty men. They arrived at Brown's home on May 26, where they stayed for three days before moving to Lawrence Lawyer's farm.

Patrick and Brown posted scouts, but nothing untoward occurred until May 29, when Lieutenant Borst, his brother Joseph, and one of the Freemeyers were several miles up the creek. Freemeyer was fishing a few hundred yards from the Borsts, when suddenly, two Schoharie Indians, Chief Hanyery and Ones-Yap, burst from cover and confronted the brothers with a loud, intimidating shout. No doubt the Borsts were very much on their guard as the men approached, although the warriors offered a pleasant enough salutation. After these friendly words, the Natives chastised the brothers "for being in the woods, to shoot Indians who did them no harm." Joseph replied that they meant no hurt to those who were friendly. Hanyery sidled up and playfully gripped Joseph's firelock, threw open the pan, jerked the priming out, and exclaimed in Mohawk that it was good this was done.

Joseph released his gun and grasped Hanyery's, twisting the flint out of the jaws and making a similar comment in Mohawk. The chief let go his firelock and grappled with Joseph, who forced him to his knees. While they wrestled, Ones-Yap told the lieutenant that he should surrender, but Jacob stepped back and fired a ball into his challenger, causing Hanyery to break loose from Joseph and run for cover. The lieutenant took up his brother's firelock and fired at the chief's back without realizing the pan was empty, which allowed Hanyery to escape.[61]

The Schoharie Mohawks had suffered a great many losses to disease in the recent past, and likely had no more that fifteen warriors at this time. During the Tory uprising the year before, they had lost one of their warriors, so the death of Ones-Yap was significant and would have to be avenged.

On the morning of May 30, a reconnaissance patrol from Schoharie under Captain Miller arrived at Lawyer's. After the officers exchanged intelligence, several of Miller's men volunteered to remain with Captain Patrick. When Miller left, Patrick marched his reinforced company to committeeman George Warner's place, the southernmost farm in the settlement. Warner's son and another fellow had returned from alerting the inhabitants of Cherry Valley the same day that Ones-Yap had been killed. Freemeyer recalled that just before Patrick's men arrived, several Indians were seen running back and forth across some fields. The militiamen were sure this was a ruse to lure them into an ambush. The officers conferred, and decided to send out three men as scouts; however, they were only a short distance into the woods when they were fired upon. Freemeyer recollected that all the troops set off in haste to rescue the scouts and pursue the enemy.

Jeptha Simms's account is different in several details. He wrote that Patrick's troops had been at Warner's for a short time before some fifteen to twenty Indians were spotted. The whole force set out in pursuit, but not before Captain Brown voiced his fears of an ambush. Patrick ridiculed that idea, implying that Brown was cowardly, which goaded the militia officer into agreeing to march. Simms wryly observed the similarity to what Nicholas Herkimer had endured the year before at Oriskany.

Freemeyer — who, it should be remembered, was a participant in these events — recalled that, after meeting the scouts, the two companies had chased the Indians for about a mile when they came across "a small knoll of some two or three hundred yards in length and about four feet in height," behind which the warriors lay hidden.

> [O]n the side the Indians lay, the surface of the earth near the knoll seemed ... to be somewhat lower than on the opposite side. Behind the knoll the Indians had driven stakes into the ground, fastened a stick across the top, on which they had put pieces of blankets and stuck a hat or cap thereon in order to deceive.... An excellent device, too, as ... many[,] in their zeal to destroy the enemy, and not being able to distinguish well for the smoke occasioned by the firing, were deceived and fired at the supposed bodies of the Indians, while the real Indians were lying or stooped below their imaginary men and firing upon [the rebel] party.

Reports suggest that it was at this point the militiamen hung back. Once Captain Patrick thought he had the measure of the enemy, he ordered his men to fix bayonets and charge. Freemeyer claimed the captain and a lieutenant were immediately shot down, and the charge melted. The number of Indians was so clearly superior to the rebels that Brown ordered a retreat, which turned into a scramble to get away.

Simms mentions nothing about the attempted bayonet charge, but states that Patrick was struck in the thigh after several of his men were felled. Two fellows attempted to carry him off the field, but the trio were surrounded by warriors and killed. Simms claims that Patrick's Lieutenant Maynard was spared when he gave a Masonic distress sign to Brant.[62]

Meanwhile, the others clambered for safety. One of the Fester brothers was run down and mangled by the Natives' dogs before being killed. Three Continentals and two militiamen took shelter in George Warner's house. When they engaged the pursuing Indians, the warriors stopped to deal with them, allowing the rest to continue their flight toward Schoharie. Having no success with musketry, the raiders set the house afire. The three militiamen, including a second Fester brother, perished inside the building, and the two Continentals attempted to escape. One was shot and killed, the other taken prisoner and tortured to death. A party that returned after the Indians had left discovered that this fellow's body had been cut open, and his intestines attached to a tree. Legend says a roll of Continental currency was thrust into one of his hands, presumably signifying Native derision about the worthlessness of the paper currency and the rebel cause. Claims were made that the Natives fired some fifty to ninety balls through one of the house's windows, but, as the building was destroyed by fire, one has to puzzle how this count could have been made.

When family members heard the brisk firing, they cleared off into the woods to hide, or headed cross-country for safety in Schoharie. Some families huddled in the woods for two or three days.

Freemeyer recalled that the Whigs had twenty-one men killed, including officers, and nine wounded. Five men were captured, and ended up in lower Quebec. A comment that more than half of the Continentals and militiamen were casualties appears accurate. Except for George Warner's older house, all of the settlement was destroyed — some twenty barns, stables, and houses. Horses that evaded capture were shot dead.

Postwar claims were made that the Natives lost as many men as the rebels or more, but how could this be so? Were any of the warriors who cleverly lured Patrick into the ambush killed or dangerously wounded? Were any who hid behind the knoll in ambush killed? Were any of the pursuers killed by those who were fleeing? Perhaps the warriors who confronted the five men in Warner's house took casualties before firing the building; however, the supposition that some historians have made that the war party's losses matched or exceeded those of the defending force is fantasy. In part, evidence for this contention was provided by man of mixed Native and black descent who had been with the raiders. He returned after the war and ingratiated himself with a highly suspect claim that twenty-five dead warriors and Tories were buried in a mud hole on a local farm. He also said that seven of the wounded enemy died on their way to Canada. The details of his claim are highly dubious, as Brant's force did not retire to Canada. More reliable is Mary Brant's report that a Cayuga chief was wounded and a Schoharie warrior killed — surely Ones-Yap.

James Belknap, one of Patrick's men, had a harrowing experience. After taking a ball in his right hip, he was carried to safety by militiaman Lawrence Lawyer. They found a hollow log inside which Belknap was able to hide, then Lawyer continued his flight to Schoharie. The next day, Belknap emerged from hiding, stiff and cold, and perched on a nearby fence, likely pondering what to do next, when he spotted a pair of Indians approaching, carrying bundles of plunder. He allowed himself to fall backward into thorn bushes. The two Natives came near and halted to share a bottle. When their two dogs put their paws on the fence and growled, the warriors paid no attention, and soon set off. Once the dogs and Natives were gone, Belknap extracted himself from the bushes, no doubt nursing many scratches to add to the discomfort of his wound. He cast his eyes over the ruins of several buildings, then spotted George Warner's old house still standing. Carefully making his way to the building, he went inside and found food on the table. After eating, he lay on a bed and fell asleep. Later that day, two men from Schoharie found him and helped him to Middleburgh, where his wound was dressed.[63]

As noted previously, the day after the fight, Stark reported to Gates that he had requested the assistance of Albany County's militia brigadier, and Ten Broeck had promised to help after church was over, but could not "do any business before, for fear of frightening the town into fits." Stark already nurtured a poor opinion of militia, and the brigadier's reply only served to stoke his fire. The following day, he reported that a detachment of Alden's Continentals and Schoharie militia had sortied to confront the raiders, but most of the militia "poltroons" stood by while the Continentals did their duty.

On June 2, Stark replied to Gates's order that Alden's regiment be sent down to reinforce the army at Fishkill. He wrote, "No news could give the troops here more pleasure than to hear of their being removed, as they have lost all confidence in the militia since the affair at Cobuskill." No doubt Brown had objected to Patrick's decision to pursue the Natives, but there is no evidence that he or his men "stood by" and watched the disaster, or deserved such damning criticism.[64]

Brigadier Ten Broeck had come to Schoharie, and reported on June 2 that he had sent Lieutenant-Colonel Yates with 150 Schenectady militiamen to Cobleskill, where they and a Schoharie detachment collected and buried the dead. A pit was dug near George Warner's burned house, and the charred corpses of the three soldiers who had been taken from the cellar, including one who had fallen into a tub of soap and was recognized by his tobacco box, were buried there. They were laid in the pit with the mutilated remains of those lying nearby. Freemeyer's brother Jacob was one of latter group, and his butchered body was identified by his knee buckles. Farther afield, other pits were dug, into which Patrick and other soldiers were placed.

On the grand scale of the war, the Cobleskill raid was nothing but a pin prick, but its real significance is that it heralded the harrowing existence that would be endured by the Mohawk region's inhabitants over the next four years.

Larger Raid from Quebec

Just as the hubbub over Cobleskill faded, Tryon County was attacked again from the north. This raid's primary purpose was to recover the Mohawk families that had been captured during their retreat from Burgoyne's army.

Captain John Ross, who had been seriously wounded in the 1777 battle at Hubbardton while commanding the 34th Regiment's Grenadiers, had recuperated in Montreal. As his company had surrendered at Saratoga, he was unemployed when he returned to duty. Probably at the insistence of Governor Carleton, who believed that Regular officers should lead all detachments that included Natives, Ross was chosen nominally to command the new raid. Although Carleton's distaste for Indian raids was pronounced, the avowed purpose of recovering Mohawk families would have met with his approval.

Simms reports that a handful of Tryon County loyalists formed the European element, and named the Bowen brothers of the Royal Yorkers (who had been with Ensign Crawford on a previous raid); a fellow named Loucks, of whom there were three in the regiment; and men named Lintz and Sweeny, who do not appear on regimental rolls at this time.[65] Perhaps the loyalists hoped to collect family members and valuables abandoned when they came to Canada, or were seeking revenge on the more notorious rebels, as they carried lists of their names.

John Ross (1744–1809), Captain, 34th Regiment, by David Martin.

In addition to commanding his Royal Yorkers, Sir John Johnson was responsible for the Secret Service and the mounting of forays into the valley. He had a great many scores to settle, as did his brother-in-law, Daniel Claus, and their guiding hands can be seen in the selection of the secondary targets to be struck, perhaps without the governor's knowledge or input.[66]

Two primary individuals who most likely motivated and directed the raiders were Fort Hunter's senior war captain, John Deserontyon, and his coadjutor, Isaac Hill Onoghsokete. The force assembled at Akwesasne, where the war captains recruited a number of warriors to assist in their efforts, and increased the Native contingent to about one hundred men.

On June 2, the force arrived at Sir William Johnson's Fish House on the southern bank of the Sacandaga River, some eighteen miles north-east of Johnstown. They made camp, then divided into several small parties to pursue various goals. Over the next few days, the raiders roamed at will through Sir John's vast estates and, according to rebel reports, passed through several small communities entirely unopposed.

On the first day, some men who were working on the roads four miles from the Sacandaga River were captured and taken to the Fish House. A lame fellow named Hendrick Warmwood was released, and when he arrived among friends, claimed that his Native captors had been two hundred strong and were less than a third of the raiding party. He was so shaken by the experience, he warned that a thousand militiamen could not stand against them.[67]

At the Shew farm near the Fish House, the father of the family, Godfrey Shew, was visited by a friend and neighbour, militia serjeant Solomon Woodworth; Woodworth had discovered that the house of another neighbour, Robert Martin, was suspiciously abandoned, and had come to make inquiries. As it was late, Woodworth stayed the night, and the family made preparations against an attack by placing a large pile of stones at the top of the staircase, where son Jacob was stationed to repel intruders. After a fitful night, Godfrey and his son John set out with Woodworth to find out what had happened to Robert Martin. On their way, they came across a fine buck deer, and John shot the animal, thus announcing their presence to a party of a dozen warriors, who swept them up and added them to a number of other prisoners.

The war party headed for the Shew farm. Jacob Shew had been posted to keep a lookout upriver, and after a boring two-hour vigil, he spotted a canoe coming down from Summer House Point. He ran home to warn his mother and brother Stephen, blundered into the party of Natives, and became their sixteenth captive.

An ironic exchange occurred at Shew's house. Godfrey had always warmly welcomed visits by local Mohawks, and knew several among the party, including two of the Hill brothers, Aaron Kanonraron and David Karaghgunty, both of whom had always professed lasting friendship. Back in his own home, Godfrey boldly took on the role of host, and looked after the wants of his old friends. Observing their reserved and emotionless expressions, he reminded them of their former pledges. Unmoved, David grunted in Mohawk that he did not understand. Clearly, the war had changed their perspectives.

The homes of the other captives had been thoroughly plundered, and Shew's place received the same treatment. After Catrina Shew and her youngest children were sent outside, the house was set afire. The war party was about to depart when the loyalist William Bowen, who had also benefited from Shew's hospitality in earlier days, saw that Shew's barn was still standing, quickly took up a fire-brand, and set it alight.

Despite the man's covering of paint, Godfrey Shew recognized a loyalist named Loucks, and chided him that he need not hide his true character. Chastised, Loucks washed himself and did not paint again during the raid. The Shews' large supply of maple sugar had been discovered, and the raiders lopped off chunks with their tomahawks and gorged themselves, but gave none to the captives.

Catrina Shew and her youngsters set out on the eighteen-mile trip to Johnstown. At Summer House Point, she was assisted in crossing Kennyetto Creek by an elderly Irish Tory named Kennedy, and she spent the night in Mayfield at the home of Warren Howell, where she was kindly treated. Howell was a Tryon militia lieutenant who later went to Canada to join Sir John's second battalion, in which his brother John was serjeant-major.[68]

That same day, 3rd Tryon's colonel, Frederick Visscher, his Exempts' captain, Jelles Fonda, and four other rebels reported from Caughnawaga that they had been at Fort Johnstown earlier in the day when Fonda's servant brought word that halfway between the Sacandaga River and Johnstown he had seen about a hundred painted warriors in the woods. He recognized some Tories who were with them, and saw they had taken several prisoners. Visscher and Fonda were in the midst of taking the fellow's sworn statement when two expresses arrived to report that Natives were destroying everything above the town. The officers hurried home and collected their families, then went to take refuge in the Caughnawaga church. There were only seven armed men with them for defence, as all of 3TCM had gone to the relief of Cobleskill, Cherry Valley, and German Flatts. Visscher pled for assistance, as he worried they would "fall an Easy Prey to the Enemy and we are also much afraid Some of our Neighbours will act against us."[69]

Two days later, Visscher and his lieutenant-colonel, Volkert Veeder, wrote to Albany County's brigadier from the Caughnawaga church, advising that the enemy's force of three to four hundred men was encamped at Mayfield. A Tory had told an old friend that the raiders would strike another blow before they departed, and the sachem, Hans Crine, the Fort Hunter Mohawk neutralist, said there had been no danger along the river earlier, but from now on, everyone must take good care, as the raiders would not withdraw without committing more mischief. Three small 3TCM companies had returned from Vroman's Creek, but could not be kept together. No assistance was appearing from anywhere, and they went home to defend their families. Just as Visscher was concluding his letter, word arrived that the enemy was making bark canoes to take their prisoners to Canada.[70]

The Mohawks had been able to collect their Fort Hunter kin, and brought off everyone there — some twenty to thirty families — except a few neutralist diehards who had refused to leave the year

Left: *Caughnawaga Church.*

Below: *Historic plaque at the site of Sir William's Fish House (New York State).*

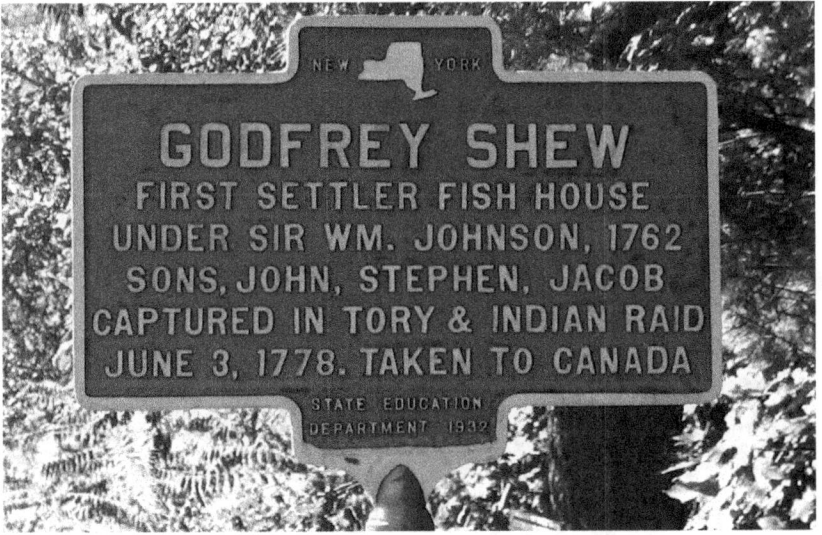

before. Six Royal Yorker recruits had been collected, and while few rebels were killed, seventeen noted offenders had been captured, three in arms. Relative to later excursions, only a few properties were burned, but immense alarm and despondency had resulted.

As the raiding party had grown substantially, two large elm trees were felled and their bark used to build two additional canoes. Four horses had been taken during the raid, and some of the raiders set off overland with them. On the first night, Woodworth so convincingly feigned illness that he was allowed to go down to the river bank to vomit, and he slipped away to freedom.[71]

That same day, Jelles Fonda wrote to Ten Broeck bemoaning the fact that Albany County was unable to assist the Mohawk District. Captain John Little's Tory father-in-law had threatened that all the people at Caughnawaga and roundabouts were to be taken and their houses burned. Mrs. Kelly from Sacandaga reported that her husband, who tended the gristmill there, had been shot dead at her side and the mill burned. Fonda reported that the Tories carried written lists of people they were targeting. He had sent to Colonel Klock for assistance, and was awaiting his response.[72]

Klock wrote to Ten Broeck from Caughnawaga on June 6. He had information that the raiders had been on the north side of the Mohawk, opposite Nicholas Herkimer's lovely home, where they were attacking Tilleborough near Stone Arabia and were destroying that place. He postulated, "It is impossible for us to defend the County, for whenever we march from one place to defend another, the places we leave are attacked." He asked Ten Broeck for "the assistance we owe each other," and asked that he inform General Stark about what was happening.[73]

After the raiders' return to Quebec, Sir John Johnson was unenthusiastic about the results and wrote to Claus, "I am happy to find the Mohawks have accomplished their errand … but wish with you, and am much surprised[,] that they did not bring off some persons of more consequence and strike a blow of more weight, as they certainly had it in their power. I think they were wrong in burning my mills, &c.; the breaking up of the settlement can injure no one, but me."[74]

A postscript to this raid occurred when Godfrey Shew, four of his sons, and some five other Mohawk District prisoners were being held prisoners on a ship in the St. Lawrence River. They sent a petition to Sir John, who knew them as his tenants, stating they wished to be exchanged for British and loyalist prisoners being held in the United States. Johnson refused their request, and came aboard the vessel to propose that they enlist in the Royal Yorkers. A few days later, Johnson's recruiting serjeant, Nicholas Hillyard, a Johnstown tailor well-known to the prisoners, came aboard to swear them in, but all declined.[75]

Merely Predatory

New York Congressman James Duane was in Albany when he wrote an urgent letter to Governor Clinton on June 6. "[T]wo parties of the Enemy have enterd the Country for the sole purpose of ravaging and murthering the defenceless Inhabitants. They consist of the Indians under Brandt's Influence and our own Tories. If they had any fixed object in View, they would not be formidable but in an Enterpize merely predatory & conducted with every make of the most execrable Barbarity, they inspire Terror & can commit infinite Mischief." He also made an astute observation, to which far too little attention was paid: "The garrison of Fort Schuyler [Stanwix] … might as well be in the moon for the Enemy take Care to leave it at a sufficient Distance."[76]

A day later, Mayor Barclay of Albany wrote to thank Governor Clinton for his efforts to obtain a body of troops to protect the northern and western frontiers. Referring to the raid led by Captain John Ross, he noted, "The Ravages by them already committed near Sacondago … in addition to that of Cobus Kill, has so struck the Militia of Tryon County that few of them can be Collected together, the principal part of them being employed to secure their Families from the Barbarity which is to be apprehended from a wanton, Cruel and Savage Enemy." He reported that some five hundred raiders had landed at Gilliland's Creek and divided into two elements. One contained those at Sacandaga; the second would strike farther westward. Before requesting Clinton to visit Albany to inspire the people, he commented that the dilatory and uncertain turnout of the militia was caused by worries about the disaffected among them.⁷⁷

Anxiety in Tryon County

Lieutenant-Colonel Clyde, 1TCM, wrote a heart-wrenching report on June 5 to Brigadier Stark from Cherry Valley.

> The inhabitants of Bowmans Creek have left their inhabitations; Springfield likewise; and the people of Newtown Martin have come into our settlement, and joined with us to make a stand against the enemy. They have brought their cattle with them, and families, so that in all we may reckon, on a moderate computation, there is 600 or 700 head of cattle, and they all feeding within the circumference of about ¾ of a mile, which must inevitably fall into the hands of the enemy, if some immediate help is not sent us ... and our wives and children [will be] massacred by a savage enemy. We have made the utmost efforts to stand the enemy and protect our lives and liberty; but cannot stand it much longer, without very timely assistance; and if we should be obliged to give up this settlement, consider what a quantity of provision is here for the enemy; which would enable them to harass the other settlements continually, as they would have no provisions to look for.... Brant lies but about 20 miles from us upon Charlotte River, and as one party comes in, the other goes out, to the destruction of the smaller settlements. The militia that are with us are quite out of patience; and we are afraid they will leave us; and were we to be attacked in the place where we have made a stand — sorry we

are to think so, but more to say it — there are not over 30 men that would stand their ground.[78]

Judging from what happened a few weeks later, some of the Springfield inhabitants must have tired of the cramped quarters at Cherry Valley and returned to their homes.

Old Smoke's Ploy

Old Smoke saw the possibility of creating a useful diversion by responding to the Onondaga summons to a confederacy council to hear the messages from the rebels' Johnstown council. Big Tree Kaoundowana was the leader of an outspoken peace faction among the lower Senecas, centred on his village of Kanaghsaws at the foot of Conesus Lake. The chief and his followers wanted to visit the rebel commissioners to arrange the exchange of a rebel officer for their chief Atskeorax, who had been captured in Pennsylvania. This visit could be beneficial, as the rebels would be gratified to receive Seneca emissaries, and would be distracted from Old Smoke's movements through Indian Territory in preparation for mounting his major expedition. Butler supplied a rebel militia officer for the exchange, Lieutenant John Jenkins from Wyoming, and added his own voice to Old Smoke's cautions to Big Tree not to proceed beyond Kanowalohale, in case of entrapment, which could lead to a hostage situation.

On the day before Brant struck at Cobleskill, General Schuyler wrote to President Laurens in Congress, "The Conduct of the Savages is mysterious and embarrassing. The twenty Senecas mentioned in Mr. Deane's last letter as coming down with a prisoner is expected in a few Days. I purpose detaining them here until the prisoner I wrote for some Time ago arrives from the Southward." He theorized that while these emissaries were at Albany, there would be no further hostilities committed, and suggested Congress forward troops before the Natives went home. "I think one thousand men with half the garrison of Fort Schuyler[,] such militia as may be procured in Tryon County and some of the Oneidas and Tuscaroras would be quite sufficient to burn the Cayuga Town and some of the Seneca Villages. Unless these people are made to feel our power they will, I fear, continue hostile as long as the Enemy keeps possession of Canada, and afford them such ample supplies as they have hitherto done." He inquired about the Seneca chief Atskeorax: Was he alive, and if so, when might he arrive at Albany?[79]

Big Tree proceeded to Onondaga and found that the Oneidas and Tuscaroras were deeply disappointed, as the promised delegations of Cayuga and Seneca headmen had not appeared. Miffed, they declined to intercede with the rebels' commission on behalf of the neutralists. When the disgusted Oneidas and Tuscaroras left for Kanowalohale, Big Tree's party followed, and on May 24, they set out for Albany and arrived on June 6. Lieutenant Jenkins was delivered up to the commissioners as a sign of good faith, and the neutralists asked when they could expect Atskeorax in exchange. Unknown to the commissioners, the chief was already dead; he had been captured at the head of a raiding party in the Delaware's West Branch valley and murdered by a militiaman while asleep in a guardhouse.[80]

On June 16, a letter was sent from York Town, Pennsylvania informing Schuyler of Atskeorax's death and suggesting the fact be concealed.[81] Accordingly, Schuyler arranged for Big Tree's Senecas to visit Washington's army, and afterwards the Congress in Pennsylvania. While most of his party was permitted to return home, Big Tree and two companions remained with Schuyler as de facto hostages, just as Old Smoke and Butler had predicted.

Tory Captain Tice

Governor Carleton was annoyed by the Six Nations Indian Department rangers who were idling in Montreal. Their senior officer was Captain Gilbert Tice, and in mid-March the governor ordered him to take his men to Niagara. Tice was a thorough-going Johnson man, and had no desire to return to John Butler's sphere, so he delayed his departure while assembling supplies, preparing boats, and petitioning the governor to pay his men's salaries. Tice left Montreal at the end of May with some one hundred men, including nine officers, eighteen rangers, and forty-five warriors, mostly Canajoharie Mohawks. His first stop was Akwesasne, where he used a Six Nations wampum belt to invite the village's Iroquois to join him in operations against the rebels. By appealing to the community's pro-British element, he persuaded over twenty-five keen warriors to join him, which later hampered the efforts of Major Campbell in an already politically divided atmosphere.[82]

Walter Butler in Quebec City

Debilitated by his prison experiences, Walter Butler travelled to lower Quebec, where the medical facilities were better. On June 4, he delivered his father's report to the governor concerning the plans for the upcoming campaign, with several requests and recommendations, and answers to some outstanding inquiries.

The major advised that his Rangers would accompany the allied Natives to Unadilla on the Susquehanna River in Indian Territory, where they would be near the frontiers of New York, Pennsylvania, and New Jersey. This location would facilitate the collection of supplies. As he had no instructions to the contrary, Butler held to Guy Johnson's broadly phrased strategy that the Six Nations and their affiliates would join Clinton's main army at some time somewhere in New York province. Being located in Unadilla facilitated this possibility; meanwhile, he would "break up the back settlements of Pennsylvania ..., Jersey and other parts of ... New York in order ... to distress the enemy...." He again reiterated the Six Nations' intentions to support the king's arms in America.

Regarding the governor's questions about Indian Department expenses, he advised that the charges incurred after he joined St. Leger were solely on Colonel Claus's account, not on his. As to Tice, Butler was ignorant of how much funding he had drawn, or about which men the funds applied to, other than £100 that Tice had given to the Natives at Niagara when he arrived from New York City in 1776. Tice claimed that he was commissioned a captain in the army and his pay of 10s/day had been received from General Howe, and that he did not belong to Butler's "part of the Department," nor did he expect any pay from Butler. For this reason, Tice and his men were not on Butler's departmental returns.

The entry of France into the war had caused unrest, particularly among the Native bands that had previously enjoyed good relations with that country. No doubt Butler's spies had brought word of the three French officers at Kanowalohale. To address this issue, the major recommended the incorporation of a Canadien company in the Rangers. He also requested a small brass fieldpiece, and approval for an adjutant and quartermaster. His regiment's recruits were "nearly destitute of clothing and necessaries," and his beating order provided no bounty for joining. Further, the requirement that the men pay for their arms caused them great debt, and subjected Butler to many losses when they were killed or died of natural causes. And each officer's expense of buying a horse to carry his necessaries on campaign made a bat and forage allowance a necessity.

An important repeat request was for official commissions for the Indian Department's officers. Without these, they would be treated no better than "public murderers and highwaymen"[83] should they be taken by the enemy.

Bolton's Report

Colonel Bolton, whose fort was the headquarters for the Six Nations' Indian Department, was uneasy over his unavoidable relationship with the Natives now that Major Butler and most of the department's officers were in Indian Territory. He reported on June 5 that "Parties of savages with scalps and prisoners are daily coming in, some with and some without [Butler's] orders to be clothed, notwithstanding they have in general received presents more than once since I have been here, which must soon amount to a very considerable sum."[84]

Congress Warns of Major Indian War

Congress's Board of War concluded from the reports of widespread hostilities on the frontiers that a major Indian war was brewing. The members believed that defensive actions would be an inadequate response, and recommended an expedition of 3,000 men against Detroit to punish the Ohio and Lakes' Nations, and a similar attack to punish the Senecas and Cayugas and drive off the British if they had occupied Oswego. The effort against Detroit was authorized by Congress on June 11, and Major-General Horatio Gates was nominated to command with a remarkably large fund of $932,743.[85]

Governor Clinton was closer to the New York frontier's agonies than the Board of War, and made practical suggestions to address the problem. On June 11 he wrote to Continental brigadier Stark and militia brigadier Ten Broeck, advising that Alden's regiment would remain in the north "for the Security of the Western Frontiers." He believed Unadilla was the rendezvous for the raiders, and opined that an expedition against that place would be "the only effectual Means for giving Security to the inhabitants." He had asked Ten Broeck to advise Stark on the propriety of such an action, and for Colonel Klock to furnish militia for this service.[86]

Yet neither Clinton nor Stark appreciated the grievous situation in Tryon and bordering Albany County. Both lay entirely open to incursions from Indian Territory and Canada. Tryon was particularly affected, as much of the harvest had been left in the fields after the Oriskany disaster the previous year. The settlements dare not miss another one, which meant the farmers had to tend their fields, not march in the militia in pursuit of raiders. In addition, the militia had taken a hammering at Oriskany, which, coupled with the flight of many surviving families, meant the brigade's numbers were substantially reduced.

Ten Broeck's orders of June 12 announced that a proportion of Albany County's brigade would be embodied to counter the enemy's depredations in Tryon. A quarter part of eight regiments would be called into service for one month, and formed into a single regiment with field officers. Officers and NCOs would be supplied by each regiment in proportion to its contributions. The men would assemble completely armed and provisioned for the march to Albany, and arrive no later than June 23. They would be relieved in one month by an equal number of men, should the service require it, and the officers commanding regiments would form detachments for such a relief.[87]

Stark wrote to Klock on June 14, reminding him that Governor Clinton had ordered him to form two companies of rangers, and noting that Clinton was surprised it had taken so long for the order to be complied with. He chastised, "Your exertions in this affair will do you honor, and your neglect will be your disgrace and your country's ruin. You can not expect people of this State and neighbouring States to leave their families and farms to relieve you if you do nothing for yourselves. If you expect relief, you must first exert yourselves."

Two days later, Stark took a whack at the Tryon Committee.

> I received yours of the 14th, wherein you complain that you are in bad circumstances. I am of the same opinion with you; but you may blame yourselves for it in a great measure. The governor ordered the officers of your county to raise two companies of rangers for the defence of your frontiers, and exempted you from making up your proportion of the continental troops. Had that order been complied with, you might have been safe; but it was

neglected, and you suffer.... [Other officers] say that they are obliged to raise their proportion for the army, while you were exempted, and now you want them to guard your frontier.[88]

On the 15th, the vocal citizens of Schenectady warned the governor, "the people are flying and crowding into this town in great numbers, and by the best information the enemy are really round about there, and are determined to destroy, and burn up that whole county, and unless soon relieved, we undoubtedly believe they will effect it, and the loss that will arise there to the unhappy individuals of that part of the country will be nothing in comparison to the loss of the United States, as it is one of our principal wheat countrys."[89]

Meanwhile, General Gates was in an entirely different world. Although he was responsible for all military activities along the Hudson River and in the north, his concentration was on the threat

Major-General Horatio Gates (1727–1806), Commander, Northern Department (Hudson Highlands).

of a major British thrust from New York City. He had stripped almost all of the Continentals from Albany and Tryon County, but at the last moment had been persuaded to leave Alden's regiment in the north. One gets the impression that Gates would have preferred to ignore everything north of Fishkill, as he was so easily persuaded that very little was threatened up there. On June 17, he advised Stark that his interview with Big Tree's Seneca party had persuaded him that "Stark would not have many real alarms in his district." This opinion played very well into Old Smoke's strategy of allowing Big Tree to conduct his mission. Presumably, Gates thought the incursions at Cobleskill, Fort Hunter, and Tilleborough were of little account, which indeed they were, compared to a threat from New York City.[90]

Oneida Concerns

James Dean, Fort Stanwix's resident Indian agent, reported to Schuyler on June 15 that the Onondagas' attempts to convene a general council were not going well. A Cayuga chief, who was leading a war party with Brant, had sent a runner to his people, saying he was surrounded by "white people and in danger of being cut off, unless they afford him speedy relief." Dean thought this appeal would result in a strong reinforcement of Brant's party. The Oneidas predicted that "a vigorous war" would commence between the United States and the Six Nations once the commissioners' belt was returned, and they asked to move their people "down among our Inhabitants," or that a body of troops be marched west of their towns as a protective screen.[91]

War Party in Schoharie

On June 18, Colonel Vrooman reported that a war party had taken William Bouck, a young woman, and four black people as prisoners from Bouck's farm two miles north of the Upper Fort. The Natives had been seen at Henrick Mattice's on Breakabeen Creek on the morning of the 15th. As Mattice was a suspected Tory, the party may have sheltered there. Lieutenants Harper and Vrooman and forty militiamen went in pursuit, came upon the party, and retook the prisoners, but the Native men jumped down a precipitous rock face and escaped, leaving all their kit behind except their arms. The warriors had told a local Tory, who likely took pleasure in spreading the alarm, that a larger party would come in four weeks to burn out the Schoharie.[92]

Tory Hunting in Albany County

A report from the conspiracy commissioners of June 20 was sent to Albany's representatives in the senate and assembly at Poughkeepsie. A party of rangers had been sent to Pasink west of Cooyeman's to apprehend "One Garnet" and seven other Tories, who had hidden in the woods there for over a year.

Thomas Garnett was a Tory recruiter who had worked with James Hewetson in 1777 to raise men for Sir John Johnson's brigade. Hewetson had ultimately been caught and hanged, but Garnett escaped and was sentenced to death in absentia. He gathered his recruits together and made contact with the leaders of the loyalist August uprising in the Schoharie, but for some unknown reason, failed to join them. His efforts to join Burgoyne's army also failed, as did an attempt to board the British shipping at Esopus, when his party was repulsed by fifty rebel militiamen.

The rebel rangers missed capturing Garnett's party, but found a fourteen-year-old lad who said that an express from New York had arrived for Garnett about ten days earlier, carrying dispatches for westward. The lad advised that another courier was expected in a day or two with instructions for Garnett. He thought the greatest part of the people in the neighbourhood were disaffected, and had engaged under Garnett. The commissioners reported that there were so many places harbouring notorious offenders that they simply did not have enough men to address the issue. Calling out the militia was not an answer, as many of them were disaffected and would send warnings. In fact, despite the greatest secrecy surrounding the rangers' party, the commissioners were convinced some villain had leaked their purpose, allowing Garnett to escape. Permission to raise another fifteen rangers was requested.[93]

Manpower and the Unadilla Expedition

Ten Broeck reported to Clinton that he and Stark agreed that an expedition against the Natives was sensible, but questioned what forces could be raised. As only one hundred Berkshire militiamen had arrived at Albany, Stark seemed intent on keeping Alden's Continentals in the city. Ten Broeck had ordered out one quarter of his brigade's nine regiments, and expected them to assemble at Albany by June 23. They would be sent to relieve the Tryon militia and those men of his brigade who were already in service at Schoharie and in Tryon.[94]

Seven days later, Ten Broeck advised Clinton that Tryon's field officers were unanimously in favour of a Unadilla expedition, and thought that a one-thousand-man force would be required for success, of which the county would supply four hundred. As to the Albany brigade's contribution of nearly six hundred men, only two hundred had marched, so Ten Broeck had met with his field officers to urge them to furnish their quotas, but very few had responded to their summons.[95]

On June 24, the Albany brigade's co-operating field officers established the duty rotation for command of their composite regiment in Tryon. This tour would be commanded by Colonel Peter R. Livingston, Lieutenant-Colonel Jacob Ford, and Major Jacob Van Schaick; however, on July 1, Ten Broeck had second thoughts about this decision, perhaps because the tour would include the ambitious expedition against Unadilla. In confidence, he advised Governor George Clinton that he thought Livingston was "very Improper" to command any troops for this expedition, and asked that a Continental officer be assigned to the project. If the fellow were of lower rank than Livingston, then the colonel would be ordered away, and the brigade would be extricated from this embarrassing situation. He recommended Lieutenant-Colonel Marinus Willett of the Third New York.

The governor replied the very next day, which indicated there were excellent communications between Albany and Poughkeepsie. He chastised Ten Broeck for appointing an officer in whom he lacked confidence to such an important command, noting that some other duty could have easily been found for him. Clinton approved of Willett, and had ordered him to Poughkeepsie. Before the expedition proceeded, Clinton recommended the Indian commissioners be consulted to avoid any bad consequences. In a postscript, he asked that he be informed of the date the expedition set out, as it might be useful to mount a diversion.[96]

By July 1, Stark had accepted the governor's recommendation, and wrote to Gates about an attack on Unadilla. In a show of his disdain for his Tory opponents, Stark made ridiculous predictions about the outcome. "Unadilla is about sixty miles from Cherry Valley. It is concluded that the expedition can be made in a month. Should the party meet with success, they will secure all our western frontiers, and give such a check to the tories in these parts that they will never dare to lift up their heads again."[97]

Old Smoke's Expedition Assembles at Tioga

By June 24, Old Smoke and Butler had assembled their men at the small Iroquoian village of Tioga Point, where the Chemung River entered the Susquehanna on the Stanwix treaty line. North of Tioga, on the flatlands, was a Seneca community of seventy log houses called Queen Esther's town, where Esther Montour held sway. She was a granddaughter of the Madame Montour who, years before, had ruled the Seneca castle of French Catherine's Town, at the head of Seneca Lake.[98]

The war chief and agent strove to build up supplies and recruits, and sent out scouts to gather intelligence. They had five hundred-odd warriors, primarily Senecas, Cayugas, Delawares, and perhaps some Shawnees. Native and white recruits dribbled in constantly, but the flow of foodstuffs was inadequate. Ranger Richard McGinnis recalled meeting some loyalist families passing through on their way to Niagara, and trading a woman "an excellent white shirt for four quarts of rye meal and glad to get it."[99] Raiding continued throughout the border country, but by the end of June, the last of the marauding war parties had joined Old Smoke.

Old Smoke summoned Brant to Tioga. Although the conduct of the campaign had supposedly been agreed to in earlier discussions, the war chief's expectation was that Brant would bring his men to join in the attack on the Wyoming Valley; however, the Mohawk had no such intention. His focus was on the Mohawk Valley, as he had declared earlier, and he arrived with only a few of his lieutenants. At the same time, Barent Frey and his Rangers rejoined their regiment.

During a week-long war council, the rivalries that haunted the Six Nations' war effort upset the plans and expectations of all the leaders. Brant was determined to maintain his autonomy, as he considered himself Guy Johnson's personal representative. As such, he declined to take orders from John Butler, and as a member of the Eastern Door of the Longhouse, his objectives did not dovetail with the Seneca keepers of the Western Door. Butler was careful with Brant, considering him a contrary but rather special subordinate, whereas Old Smoke and the other chiefs saw him as no more than "a junior, though promising, captain."[100]

Old Smoke was concerned that his force was inadequate for the assault on Wyoming, and thought he needed Brant, his men, and his inventory of provisions, but it was not to be. During the discussions, Butler was cautious in his approach, agreeing to support the two factions in sequence — first Old Smoke, then Brant. When the Mohawk left, none of the principal leaders was happy with what had transpired. On June 27, the members of Old Smoke's force boarded their rafts and canoes and set off for Wyoming.

Chapter Three

THE WYOMING AND WYALUSING CAMPAIGNS

"Stand firm and the day is ours!"

Background

Some historical background information about northern Pennsylvania's Wyoming Valley is essential to understanding why the region was targeted by the Six Nations in 1778. In 1662, King Charles II granted a strip of land in present-day northern Pennsylvania to the colony of Connecticut, and nineteen years later, he granted a much larger region, which included the first strip, to William Penn. This confusion bred a conflict similar to the turmoil between New Hampshire and New York in "the Grants," but with a major difference. The Grants story lacked the complications of strong indigenous interests.

The Iroquois Confederacy claimed Native title to the Wyoming valley, and because the dispossession of Native peoples was occurring all over colonial America, the confederacy recognized that European incursions were soon to follow these Royal grants, and directed its vassal tribes to settle there as buffers. The Shawnees established a village in 1701 and, over time, Munsees, Nanticokes, and Mohegans settled in and about the valley.

By the early 1750's, Connecticut's population had expanded threefold, and much of the colony's soil had become fatigued. Two land companies were formed to establish settlements in the Wyoming Valley. These enterprises received the co-operation of the Iroquois Confederacy, which casually abandoned the rights of their affiliated tribes. Some claim that the land was purchased from the resident Munsees by getting their delegates drunk before completing the transaction, but whatever the case, the underlying agreement was that the resident Natives would vacate the valley. Those affected were outraged, not only over the companies' methods, but at their reputed mentors, the haughty Iroquois, who had so cavalierly brokered the sales to their own advantage.

Virginia Colonel George Washington precipitated a world war in May 1754 when he killed a French officer who was on a peaceful diplomatic mission. Events tumbled together and the war gained momentum. The next year, the British sent a two-thousand-man army of Regulars and American Provincials to capture Fort Duquesne (Fort Pitt.) Their column blundered into a classic Native ambush set by 640 western and Canada Indians, supported by 450 Canadiens and some French Regulars. Only 350 British troops emerged unscathed.

Many tribes, including the Delawares and Munsees, took up the hatchet against the English colonists and, by the time the campaigning season ended, hundreds of farmsteads along the Susquehanna and Delaware River valleys had been destroyed and their occupants driven off. Historian Robert Grumet wrote of the settlers' retaliations, "The inclination toward vigilantism ... metastasized into a mindless viciousness that would soon grow into something much more murderously malignant." Grumet lists retaliatory atrocities committed by Europeans, often without distinction between the guilty and the innocent, as being an Indian was guilt enough. Scalp bounties were authorized, settlers fortified houses, provinces built forts on the frontiers, raiding parties were mounted.

Many Natives soon recognized that the war was going against the French, and that the British would prevail. Some decided a change of alliance was necessary, or at the very least, saw a need to play one power against the other in the time-honoured tradition. Delaware and Shawnee headmen from the Wyoming area attended a 1756 council conducted by William Johnson, Britain's agent of northern Indians, and, with the persuasion of the Six Nations, accepted an alliance against the French, but other Susquehanna region vassal tribes remained at war with the colonists until 1758, when a general peace was brokered at Easton, Pennsylvania.[1]

In April 1763, the Delaware chief Teedyuscung, who had been prominent in developing the Easton treaty, was burned alive in his house. Although the perpetrators were unknown, the chief's son, Captain Bull, struck a Connecticut settlement at Mill Creek in the Wyoming Valley in October and killed some twenty settlers, captured several others, and drove off the rest. For the next few years, the valley's only Europeans were fur traders.

In 1768, it was the turn of Pennsylvania settlers. They built a blockhouse at Mill Creek and began to survey and parcel the land. Early the next year, Connecticut men returned to the valley and built Forty Fort — named in honour of their first forty settlers. They were followed in May by a two-hundred-man party led by John Durkee, which built its own fort across the river, christening it Fort Durkee. Next month, a body of armed Pennsylvanians, dubbed Pennamites, ordered the Yankees out of the Wyoming Valley. By September, the Connecticut men were gone, but back they came in 1770, and took Fort Durkee from the Pennamites. John Durkee laid out a townsite for Wilkes-Barre, named after two sympathizers in the British Parliament. The Pennamites upped the ante and built Forts Wyoming and Ogden in an attempt to slow or stop Yankee encroachment into the region.[2] They were dissatisfied with Pennsylvania's government, as the legislation that had been passed to uphold their land grants had no effect on the settlers on the Yankee side of the river.

In January 1770, Connecticut settlers under Zebulon Butler's leadership recruited a group of thirty-nine Scots-Irish vigilantes from Lancaster County, known as the Paxton Boys, to assist in defending their claims. Led by Lazarus Stewart, the Boys had been formed in 1763 to retaliate against the Natives who had attacked settlers during the Seven Years' War and Pontiac Uprising. The Boys perpetrated several bloody, indiscriminate massacres, and in consequence, were at odds with Pennsylvania's government — so serving with Yankees posed no problem. The Boys were promised lands in Hanover Township, on the Yankee side of the river, if they would help take the Pennamites' forts and territory. A month later, the Paxton Boys, assisted by ten Yankees, retook Fort Durkee. In March, one of Stewart's men was the first to be killed in the conflict during an unsuccessful Pennamite attempt to recapture the fort; however, the Pennsylvanians were successful in September. Yet the fort changed hands again in a surprise attack led by Stewart in December.

In January 1771, Captain Ogden's Pennamites built a new installation closer to the Yankees than previously, and named it Fort Wyoming. Simultaneously, they laid siege to Fort Durkee, but their demand for surrender was met by gunfire, which killed Ogden's brother. Stewart and his men feared being charged with murder, and, outnumbered by the besiegers, snuck away in the night and crossed country to Connecticut. Captains Zebulon Butler and Stewart returned to the valley in July. Possession of the various forts see-sawed back and forth, with settlers of both persuasions being run off; however, during the next four years, the Yankees succeeded in expanding their settlements, building additional forts and gristmills, and surveying five townships — Wilkes-Barre, Kings Town, Pittston, Hanover, and Plymouth. The Pennamites complained bitterly to the Continental Congress, but simply received the fatuous advice to settle the issue of ownership.[3]

In June 1774, a Wilkes-Barre town meeting voted that Westmoreland's residents organize themselves into companies to defend the country in the same manner as Connecticut. Prompted by the armed confrontation at Concord, Massachusetts, Connecticut's General Assembly proclaimed in May 1775 "that the town of Westmoreland shall be one entire regiment distinguished and called by the name of the 24th Regiment, and have the same powers and privileges and advantages as other regiments of this colony by law have." Zebulon Butler was appointed colonel, Nathan Denison, lieutenant-colonel, and William Judd, major. By October, ten companies had been organized and officers appointed.[4]

In August 1775, seven hundred Pennsylvania militia, under Colonel William Plunkett, marched into the Wyoming Valley, and in September pushed back the outnumbered Yankees from the Susquehanna's west bank. Connecticut raised four hundred men under the command of Zeb Butler, now a colonel, but it was Captain Stewart, with only twenty men, who confronted the Pennsylvanians at Rampart Rocks on Christmas Eve, causing them to retire to their camp on the east side. On Christmas day, Stewart's company caught the Pennsylvanians re-crossing the river to Wilkes-Barre, and broke up their attack. They regrouped and attacked the Yankee positions at Rampart Rocks, but were forced to withdraw. What was known as the First Yankee-Pennamite War was over.

Yet there was little time for the Yankees to savour their victory, as the war in the east had expanded, and on March 6, 1776, sixty-six Westmoreland men organized a military company and offered their services to the Continental Congress to "engage in the common cause as soldiers in defense of liberty."

In August, the Continental Congress approved the raising of two Independent Continental Companies specifically for the defence of Westmoreland County, naming Robert Durkee and Samuel Ransom as captains. Colonel Zebulon Butler acted as their commissary and paymaster. The companies received two hundred pounds of powder, and a proportionate amount of lead. In mid-September, Congress sent four thousand dollars to Colonel Butler for the independent companies, and Major Judd mustered them. Each company was composed of a captain, three subalterns, four serjeants, four corporals, a fifer and drummer, and seventy-six privates. Both were recruited to full strength by September 17, when Judd completed the muster. The men provided their own arms, accoutrements and clothing.[5] In December, orders came from Washington's headquarters in Bucks County for the two independent companies to join the army at Morristown, New Jersey, where they joined Connecticut's 6th brigade and participated in the battle of Millstone River in January 1777.

Early that month, Congress received word "that certain tribes of Indians living in the back parts of the country, near the waters of the Susquehanna ... under the protection of the Six Nations" were on their way to Easton, Pennsylvania, to hold a treaty council. Congress appointed a commission to meet with the emissaries in the hopes of detaching the Six Nations from their British allies — or, at a minimum, having them commit to neutrality. When the Natives passed through Wilkes-Barre, their party numbered seventy men and some one hundred women and children, including Big Tree of the Senecas, and Cayuga, Munsee, Conoy, and Nanticoke headmen. While all very promising, the treaty went nowhere, as the delegates scarcely represented the Six Nations, which surely the commission recognized.[6]

While they continued on duty with the Continental Army, Wyoming's two independent companies were looked upon as a battalion, with Durkee commanding. They participated in the battle of Bound Brook in April, at Brandywine in September, and Germantown in October, then went into winter camp with the army at Valley Forge.

A Native Delegation

On September 21, a deputation of three Native chiefs arrived at Wilkes-Barre. They were William Nanticoke of the Nanticoke-Conoy tribe, Indian Joseph of the Onondagas, and Navondigwanok, or Captain Johnson, of the Senecas. They brought a message from the Onondaga Council, which had been approved by the Chenango chiefs. "Brothers, we are unwilling to have Forts built up the River, but wish you would be content to build forts here among the lower settlers. A Fort at Wyalusing will block up our new made, wide and smooth road, and again make us strangers to one another."[7]

Colonel Zebulon Butler replied with many traditional sentiments, and concluded with this disingenuous claim, "Brothers, we hope you are not surprised at our building forts. It is not for fear of you and the Six Nations, our brothers, but for fear of Johnson and

Butler from Niagara. That fort we think of building at Wyalusing is for your defense as well as ours; for if Butler and Johnson do come down the River we think they will likely fall upon you — in which case you can flee to Wyalusing and be safe with our people, your brothers. Therefore we hope your minds will be easy on the account, as we design your good as well as our own."[8]

After this exchange of mutual friendship and reassurances, the participants retired to enjoy some drinks, and, while inebriated, one of the envoys revealed that their intention had been to lull the settlers while preparations were being made for an attack. In understandable disregard for the sanctity of Indian messengers, the delegates were taken hostage and their wives sent home to advise their communities of their predicament. Once the hostages were seized, the pro-rebel settlers up the river, as far north as Wyalusing, withdrew to the relative safety of the Wyoming settlements."[9]

Tory Recruits Captured

A number of settlers, many of them migrants from New York, had located in the Up-the-River district some eighty miles north-west of the lower Westmoreland settlements. They were suspected of supporting the Crown, and, in January, a committee from Wilkes-Barre was sent to advise them that the Westmoreland folks were not about to attack, as long as they conformed to Connecticut laws and the resolutions of the Continental Congress.[10] Despite those assurances, in October, Lieutenant Asa Stevens and nine men were sent upriver, and returned with five suspect Tories. In late November, Lieutenant John Jenkins was scouting at Wyalusing when local Tories turned him over to the neighbouring Native people, who took him to Fort Niagara. When word of Jenkins's capture and rumours that the loyalists were banding together with intentions to stir up the Tioga Natives reached Colonel Denison, he marched several hundred of the 24th Connecticut militia some eighty miles into the Wyalusing area on January 3 and dispersed the conspirators; he took some thirty prisoners, and spoke to the Native people at Tioga, believing he had calmed them. Eighteen captives were sent to Connecticut, where they were "treated as prisoners of war, having been taken in arms against the United States."[11]

Many of the prisoners had been rangers in the Six Nations Indian Department under John Butler in 1777. When the Stanwix siege was lifted, St. Leger gave the Up-the-River district men permission to return to their homes to bring their families to Niagara, and, at the same time, drive in as many beeves as possible for the garrison. Denison's arrival caught the men in the act of preparing to come away. Senior Ranger James Secord was their leader. There appears to have been little sense in the choice of who was released and who was jailed. Secord and Michael Showers, both of whom had been at Stanwix, were released, but Philip Buck, Adam and John Young, and Jacob Bowman and sixteen-year-old Adam Bowman were sent to Connecticut. All but Adam Young had been at Stanwix.

Jacob Bowman and his wife Elizabeth were Mohawk Valley-born. Jacob had been granted land on the upper Susquehanna as a Seven Years' War veteran, and left his father's settlement on Bowman's Creek, Canajoharie, to begin anew. Historian Hazel Mathews reports:

> At the time of Jacob's arrest his house was pillaged, his grain destroyed, his cattle driven away, and his wife and children left without provisions and with only one blanket between them. Soon after her husband and eldest son were marched away Elizabeth gave birth to her seventh child, and to keep the family from freezing, barefoot eleven-year-old Peter cut and drew wood on a hand sleigh. They might have perished had not friendly Indians brought them provisions, and shoes and a blanket coat for Peter. In the spring Elizabeth Bowman took her children to the Mohawk Valley where they planted corn and potatoes.[12]

In late March, Senior Ranger John Depew, the recruiter from the Up-the-River district, brought the news to Fort Niagara of James Secord's party having been taken. He claimed to have engaged almost one hundred area men for Butler's Rangers,[13] raising the question of where such a large number of recruits came from. Historian Stephen Young offers an analysis: "Those joining the Loyalist regiments were ... either former Yankee collaborators in the Pennamite-Yankee War or newcomers who settled upriver after that conflict was over, including several large families of recent German or Dutch origin. This latter element, the newcomers, held little, if any, sympathy with either Connecticut's or Pennsylvania's claims of jurisdiction in this region."[14] Colonel Zebulon Butler prepared a list of sixty-one "Tories who joined the Indians." Of the names on his list, only three were Yankees. It is claimed that most were transient labourers, or hunters and trappers, although Young's study shows them to be farmers. Six on his list were of one family, the Wintermoots, who originally had come from Minisink, New York; four were Secords, three were Pawlings, and three were Larraways.[15] Why pay so much attention to a gang of Tory renegades? Simply because they were so prominent in the July attack on the valley.

Defence of Westmoreland

On January 1, 1778, Colonel Zeb Butler was given command of the 3rd Connecticut Continental Regiment. In March, the Continental Congress ordered the raising of another independent company in "the town of Westmoreland County ... for the defense of the said town and settlements on the frontier in the neighbourhood thereof against the Indians and enemies of these states...."[16] Captain Detrick Hewitt was given command. On April 11, Congress approved the sending of 175 firelocks, 200 cwt of powder, and 800 cwt of lead for the county's militia in the care of Nathan Denison, who had just been promoted to full colonel in place of Butler, with George Dorrance as his lieutenant-colonel.

About February 13, three men were taken prisoners by Tories and Indians near Wyalusing. One, an old man, was released, but the other two were taken to Niagara, from where they were released as not having been in arms, and sent to Montreal.[17] Throughout the winter, the Wyoming settlers had frequent indications that the Indians had "some mischievous design against them," whereas the Senecas and Cayugas became more and more convinced that the Wyoming settlers posed a dangerous threat to their southern border.[18]

Through April and May, the Westmoreland Independent Companies guarded Hessian prisoners at Lancaster; then, on June 1, Colonel Butler, who was home in the valley on furlough from his Continental regiment, rode to York to request the return of the companies to Wyoming because of fears of an attack. When word of his request was received at Lancaster, Captains Durkee and Ransom resigned their commissions and set off immediately for the valley with twenty-five of their men. The two companies, which had been reduced by sickness and military service, were then combined, and command given to Captain Simon Spaulding, formerly a lieutenant of Durkee's company. After some delay, Spaulding's company marched for Wyoming.[19]

Raids in Western Pennsylvania

By April 1, raiders had brought in seventy scalps to Niagara. Early in the month, three large Cayuga and Seneca war parties, totaling almost three hundred warriors, set out simultaneously for the Pennsylvania backcountry settlements north of the Forbes Road, between the Susquehanna and the Allegheny Rivers. The largest party, of 125 Senecas, went to the settlements along the headwaters of Kiskiminetas Creek in Westmoreland County, which upper Seneca and Lakes' Nations parties had ravaged several months before. Their intention was to bring away any of their relatives and friends who were in villages and camps within reach of the Wyoming settlements, sew panic among the inhabitants, and drive them into the interior.[20]

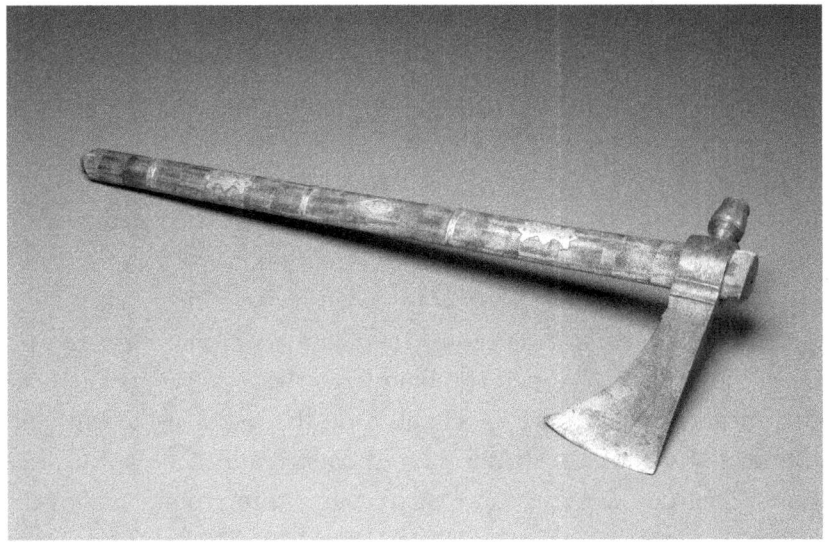

Seneca pipe-tomahawk, ca. 1800.

A message was received by the Seneca headmen from Colonel Nathan Denison and Judge Jenkins of the Wyoming Valley, inviting them to visit the settlement. The Senecas were most mindful of the three peace delegates held somewhere in Westmoreland, and turned to Major John Butler, requesting his assistance with a body of troops so they could visit Wyoming in such force that obtaining the release of the hostages would be assured. The message served as a catalyst for the disasters visited on the valley in the summer.[21]

LIEUTENANT JENKINS RETURNS

On June 2, Lieutenant John Jenkins arrived home after his experience of being taken to Albany by the Seneca chief Big Tree. Jenkins reported that the chief for whom he was to be exchanged had died of smallpox, and that Big Tree refused to accept any other trade, and was going to take him to Seneca Castle to be disposed of by the grand council. After Big Tree's party left Albany, Jenkins escaped with the assistance of a friendly young chief. As his account was at considerable variance with the rebel commissioners' version, it is difficult to judge its veracity.

Whatever the case, Jenkins said that Up-the-River Tories at Niagara had been insolent and abusive to him. They threatened to return to Wyoming in the spring, drive the settlers away, and take possession of the country for themselves.[22] This was hardly news, but certainly did nothing to calm the situation.

On June 5, a party of Natives and six Tories struck near Tunkhannock, some twenty-five miles upriver from Wilkes-Barre. They captured several men and plundered the local Whigs. News of the incident came to the lower valley on the night of the 6th, and the next day the inhabitants worked to strengthen their fortifications. That day, another alarm arrived, this time from a settlement called Shawnee.[23]

Loyalsock Creek

Although the focus of this chapter is on the Wyoming Valley, not all the raiding along the Susquehanna occurred in Westmoreland County, and there were attacks and tragedies on the lower river during May and June. An ambush on June 10 precipitated major consternation when a party of six men, three women, and eight children came to Loyalsock Creek to make a crossing in their wagon. A local man, who had heard firing that afternoon, warned them not to proceed, but they continued on and fell into a Native ambush. At the first fire, one fellow was shot in the temple; then some twenty Indians, yelling war cries, sprang from concealment. The five remaining men of the travelling party took to trees and opened fire, which permitted a boy and girl to escape. The Indians came on fast, and the men fled in the wagon, but before it was out of sight, they saw the warriors tomahawking the women and the other children. The two escaped children ran down the road to Lycoming Creek, where they told of the attack, but their story was too garbled to be understood correctly. A messenger brought word

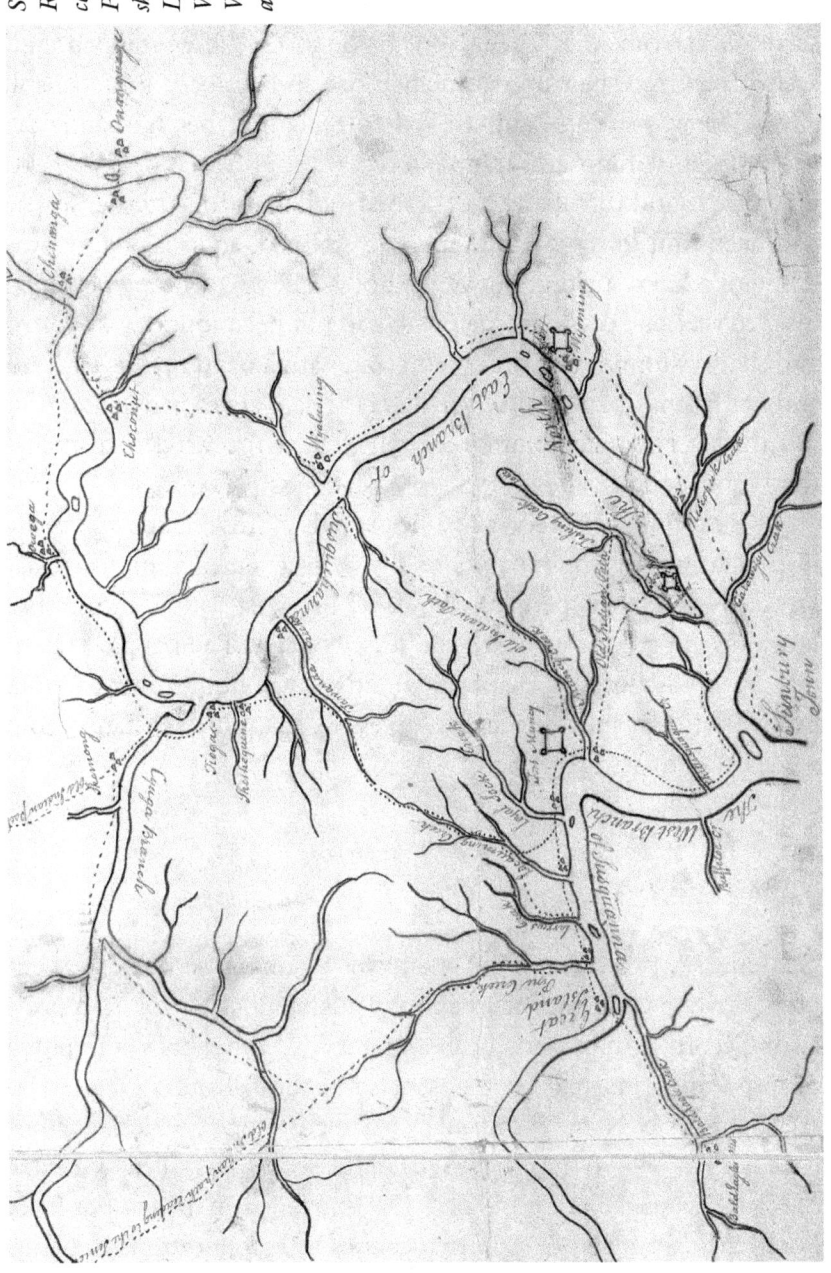

Susquehanna River in central Pennsylvania showing Loyalsock, Wyoming, Wyalusing, and Tioga.

of the incident to Fort Muncy, farther upriver, and an armed party rushed to the scene, where they found two dead men; darkness had fallen by that time, and they went downstream to Lycoming Creek to wait for first light. Next morning, they discovered a revolting scene: one woman had been shot through the body, stabbed, and scalped; another had been tomahawked and scalped, but was still alive. She was sitting, and seemed to recognize her husband; she leaned against him, and then expired without a word. A boy and girl were found tomahawked, stabbed, and scalped. Another fellow had been shot in the back, then axed, stabbed, and scalped; he was left with a knife sticking out of his body. The boy who had escaped insisted that one of the women who had not been found was nearby, and she was found near the creek, lying with a hand under her head and her brains oozing onto her fingers. The Natives had lain in wait in a thicket of tangled plum trees, which gave the attack its name — the Plumtree Massacre.

A local colonel noted, "A panic prevails in this county. It is really distressing to see the inhabitants flying away and leaving their all, especially the Jersey people, who came here last winter and spring. Not one stays, but sets off to the Jerseys again. The people in general are so discouraged that I am afraid we will not be able to make proper stands against the enemy, unless we get more assistance from some other quarter."[24]

Tunkhannock

On June 12, two scouts from the lower Wyoming settlements went up the river a couple of miles above Tunkhannock to John Secord's farm. Secord had formerly been a member of the rebel's committee of inspection, and had been absent since the fall of 1777. He was serving as a Six Nations Indian Department ranger, which may not have been known to the rebels. One of the scouts was killed by a party of Natives, and the other escaped. On June 17, a six-man scout from Fort Jenkins went upriver in two canoes to reconnoitre the enemy.

Six miles below Tunkhannock, the leading canoe's crew landed on the western shore, climbed the bank, and was surprised by a party of warriors and Tories. They scrambled to their canoe, shouting a warning to the second canoe, and paddled hard to get behind an island, away from the gunfire pouring down on them. One fellow was killed; another had his paddle shattered in his hands, and the third, Joel Phelps, was wounded. One of the Tories was a Butler's Ranger private, Elijah Phelps, the brother of Joel and the brother-in-law of the dead canoeist. The second canoe escaped unscathed. On the 26th, Captain Hewitt led a scouting party up the river, and returned four days later with news that a large enemy party was above.

The morning before Hewitt arrived with the warning, a twelve-man party had left Fort Jenkins and ridden upriver about six miles to tend their fields. Remarkably, only two men, the brothers Benjamin and Stukley Harding, took firelocks. The party divided into smaller groups; one worked a cornfield, another tended fields on an island, and a third worked onshore close to a tannery. Near evening, two known Tories, Michael Showers and Jacob Anguish, both Butler's Rangers who happened to be without uniforms, appeared at the Hardings' cornfield and offered to replace the guards. Another Harding brother, militia captain Stephen Harding, suspected treachery and went to get their horses, and the Tories left. When Stephen returned, he discovered that his brothers had quit work and followed the Tories into a ravine. He heard them being fired upon, and when he investigated, saw they returned fire, then clubbed their firelocks to fight the Indians until felled by spears and hacked with tomahawks.

The second party was captured near the tannery. Those on the island attempted to escape by canoe, but were fired on by Natives lying in ambush. A few got away. Stephen Harding made his way back to Fort Jenkins with news of the attacks. Word of the incident was immediately communicated down the valley, and caused great alarm and consternation.

Colonel Zebulon Butler was still at home on leave from the 3rd Connecticut Continental regiment, and at the inhabitants'

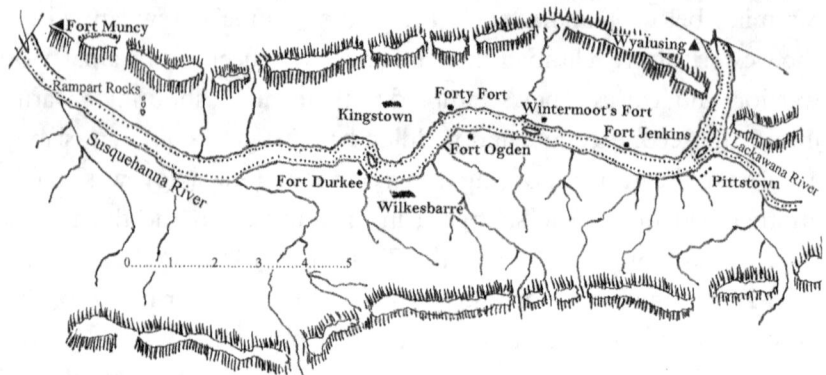

Wyoming Valley settlements and forts.

request, assumed command of local defence. On July 1, Colonel Butler, along with Colonel Nathan Denison and Lieutenant-Colonel George Dorrance of the 24th militia regiment, marched with all the forces in and about Forty Fort to the scenes of the attack. The Harding brothers' scalped and mutilated corpses were found, with many spear wounds through their bodies. Two Natives were lurking nearby. One was shot where he sat; the other fled into the river and was killed there. The brothers' bodies were taken to Fort Jenkins and buried in its graveyard.

The Massive Raid

On June 29, Old Smoke's expedition arrived about five miles above Wyoming. The main body was composed of 464 Natives, primarily Senecas, and 110 Butler's Rangers. That same day, two Native men and a woman, who may not have been part of the raid, were killed and scalped by a rebel scouting party.[25] A day later, the raiders arrived in the valley and encamped on a high point of ground overlooking the whole area. In addition to his co-war chief, Cornplanter, Old Smoke was supported by several senior confederacy captains and sachems — Sagwarithra, a Tuscarora; Gahkoondenoiya, an Onondaga; Fish

Blacksnake Thaonawyuthe (Chainbreaker), a Seneca Warrior of Kendaia, d.1859.

Carrier, a Cayuga, and a number of notable Senecas — Sequidonquee (Little Beard) and his principal warrior, Hiakatoo; Jeskaka (Little Billy); Honeyewus (Farmer's Brother); Dahgonwasha (Twenty Canoes); Donnegeosha (Jack Berry); Gahgeote (Half Town); Blacksnake; and Cornplanter's brother, Ganiodaio (Handsome Lake.)

John Butler reported that, when the bodies of the woman and two men were discovered, the Natives were infuriated, and a party was immediately dispatched, which soon returned with scalps and eight captives. A pair of loyalists came into the camp and informed Major Butler that the local defence force numbered about eight-hundred effectives.[26] The Natives were upset by the intelligence brought by their scouts that the settlers had fled to the safety of their many forts. They immediately wanted to plunder and burn the farms and run off the cattle, but Butler persuaded them to hold together until he could take action against the forts.

The Westmoreland militia was marching upriver to retrieve the Hardings' bodies on July 1, when Old Smoke's expedition arrived at a point opposite Wintermoot Fort and encamped. The next day, Major Butler sent Lieutenant John Turney to summons the fort, and the garrison immediately accepted the following terms.

> This doth hereby Certify that Lieut. Elisha Scovell his Surrendered his Garrison with all his people to Government and to remain as Neuteral during this present Contest with Great Britain and America, on Consideration of which Colonel John Butler Superintendent of the Six Nations of Indians their allies &c., with Kayingwarto the Chief of the Sanake Nations and the other Chief Warriors of the Six Nations do promise that they Shall live in the Quiet Possession of their Places with their Families and Shall be daily protected from Insult as far as lies in their Power and provided they Should be taken it is our Desire that they may forthwith be Released.[27]

The speed and ease of this capitulation led the rebels to conclude that the garrison was comprised primarily of Tories, which may have been true, as six Wintermoots — a well-known Tory family — served in Butler's Rangers during the war. Yet, in common with the other members of the garrison, that family was relieved of its livestock.[28] Butler set up his headquarters in the fort. That evening, Rangers captain William Caldwell led a detachment to Fort Jenkins, which surrendered on similar terms to those of Wintermoot after skirmishing had killed six men of the seventeen-man garrison, although the condition of not bearing arms in the future was not accepted.

During this day of threat and terror, the farmers and their families gathered at Forty Fort, about four miles below Wintermoot, and at Forts Durkee, Wilkes-Barre, and Ogden farther below.[29] A list of the troop distributions places the 1st, 2nd, and 3rd militia companies and Hewitt's at Forty Fort, the regimental headquarters. The 7th company had been consumed at Forts Wintermoot and Jenkins. The

An impression of Forty Fort. Unknown artist.

4th company was at Pittstown Fort across the Susquehanna, the 5th and 6th companies were at Wilkes-Barre Fort, and the 8th was in the Lackawana settlement.[30] The senior officers sent expresses to militia companies downriver, hoping to get some assistance, although they held little expectation of much help from Pennsylvanians.

On the morning of July 3, a flag arrived at Forty Fort carried by Daniel Ingersoll, who had been captured at Wintermoot Fort. He was accompanied by a loyalist and an Indian. This last delivered a message to Colonel Denison from the headmen, saying the Natives had come at his invitation and would speak with him, either as friends or foes. The loyalist delivered Major Butler's demands for the unconditional surrender of the post with the public stores, and the surrender of Hewitt's Independent company. The major promised to grant good terms, but also threatened that, should they refuse, he would move on the fort at once in full force. Denison boldly replied that "he was determined to fight, & that he would have all our Scalps before Night."

Denison then sent an express to Colonel Zeb Butler at Wilkes-Barre, requesting him to come immediately. Butler ordered the two Wilkes-Barre and the Hanover companies to march to Forty

Fort, and they arrived by one o'clock. As well, orders were sent to the other parts of the valley to send reinforcements.[31]

Cornplanter and ten of his Senecas climbed a hill overlooking Forty Fort to count the accumulating militiamen and Hewitt's company. Their assessment provided the expedition with an accurate appreciation of their opposition. In contrast, no scouts had been able to view the Crown Force, and the rebels had little information.[32]

As soon as Colonel Zeb Butler arrived at Forty Fort, a council of officers was held. They agreed not to capitulate, and to hold the fort at all costs. They also decided to delay negotiations for as long as possible to allow more reinforcements to arrive, and sent a flag to Major Butler requesting a conference to discuss his demands. Simultaneously, scouts were sent out in hopes of learning the enemy's strength, location, and movements.

The rebels' flag had gone about halfway to where it was thought the enemy was camped when it was fired upon by Natives and Tories, and turned back. The rebel officers discussed the situation and decided to send a second flag, but this was also fired upon and forced to return. Then, some of their scouts returned to report that they had not got near enough to the enemy's camp, but thought they were still near Wintermoot Fort. They had seen Natives on the move in every direction, many collecting the horses and cattle that roamed the woods. Other scouts came in and advised that the enemy were moving toward Forty Fort, and their strength was not greater than that of the Whigs. With so many Natives prowling around the abandoned settlements, that observation could have been correct.

A welcome reinforcement arrived in the form of Captains Durkee and Ransom, with two lieutenants and some men from the Independent Companies, but they could offer no idea of when Captain Spaulding might arrive with the combined company. Their detachment fell in as supernumeraries.

To prevent further destruction of the settlements, the officers' council decided to attack and beat back the enemy. Lieutenant Jenkins was left in command of the fort, with a handful of senior men as a garrison, and great numbers of women and children. A column was formed of Hewitt's and the 24th regiment's militia companies, over a hundred men and lads who were not enrolled in the militia, and some stragglers from the outlying settlements. They marched from the fort with a Continental flag flying, a fife shrilling "St. Patrick's Day in the Morning," and drums beating. After about a mile, the column stopped on a hill around which Abraham's Creek formed an elbow. The hill rose twenty feet, and the creek protected their front and right. A branch of the stream and a marsh protected their left, leaving the rear open, should a retreat prove necessary.[33]

Some Natives who were collecting livestock had spotted the rebels on the march at about 2:00 p.m., and reported to Old Smoke and John Butler. The Natives were in high spirits over this news. Now they could meet the enemy on their own terms in the woods.[34] Ranger captain William Caldwell, who was setting fire to Fort Jenkins, was recalled to join the main body.[35]

The Yankees sent out another flag from their position at Abraham's Creek, but it was no more successful. An adventurous scout returned after having skillfully reconnoitred the enemy. His mate had been killed, and he was slightly wounded. His observations were that the enemy was in turmoil, and perhaps preparing to leave the valley, which caused much confusion. Had Major Butler's morning threat been nothing but bluster? Surely if he meant to attack, he would have done so by now. Some officers opined that the invaders' strength had been overestimated by the timid. Perhaps the Ranger leader made the threat simply to avoid pursuit. The discussion grew heated, which was of no help in making an informed decision. Other scouts arrived with reports that the enemy was devastating all the upper settlements, and probably intended to cross the river to Pittstown and take the fort there and plunder and burn. This speculation added fuel to the arguments. The hotheads in favour of advancing had grown tired of flags, and demanded the column march. They were convinced the invaders' force was too small to withstand the column, otherwise they would have followed through with their threat. More circumspect officers believed their current defensive position would protect the lower valley until reinforcements arrived. At this point, a lieutenant arrived with the welcome news that Spaulding's company would arrive on Sunday, which added weight to the cautious approach, but held no sway with the impetuous, who pointed out that their arrival would be too late. Were they to stand by and allow the enemy a free hand, like cowardly poltroons? Were they to creep back to the fort and await deliverance? It was pointed out that there were not enough provisions to withstand a long siege.

Similar to the morning argument between Nicholas Herkimer and his Tryon Militia officers before Oriskany, the arguments became personal. The former leader of the Paxton Boys, Lazarus Stewart, who at this juncture was serving as a private in the Hanover company, charged Colonel Butler with cowardice, and threatened to report him to headquarters. Colonel Denison put Stewart under arrest, but the Hanover company flew into an uproar, which led to their captain resigning. The men immediately elected Stewart in his place, and threatened to revolt if an immediate advance were not ordered.

Up to this point, Denison had been quiet, except for his intervention with Stewart. He now voiced the need for careful, well-considered action; however, too many men had become inflamed by the disagreements, and their opinion prevailed. Colonel Butler discharged the newly elected Captain Stewart from arrest, and the order to march was given.

The column proceeded to a second hill, where a halt was ordered. Scouts came in to report that the enemy looked to be leaving the valley and had set fire to Wintermoot Fort, which rising smoke confirmed. The men were eager to pursue the enemy, and the column marched toward the burning fort, halted, and formed a battle line that extended for some fifteen hundred feet. Captains Durkee and Ransom and their two lieutenants were detailed to mark off the ground and form the line as the column deployed left and each company took its position. Colonel Butler took command of the right wing, assisted by his adjutant and a major. Colonel Denison, assisted by Lieutenant-Colonel Dorrance, commanded the left wing.

Battle Joined

Between four and five o'clock, the Crown force saw that the rebels were about a mile from their position. To give the impression they were retiring, Major Butler ordered the burning of Forts Wintermoot and Jenkins. Although Butler enthusiasts suggest the major set the structure of the ambush, it is more likely that Old Smoke and his war captains were the primary designers. Graymont reports that they chose an open wood, placing all the Rangers on the left flank, and the main body of the Native fighters on the right, beside a swamp. All lay flat and were dead quiet, while a number of Native "teasers" were sent to lure the rebels forward.

Butler's historian Ernest Cruikshank describes the dispositions somewhat differently, noting that John Butler posted his Rangers in a "fine open wood" that extended from an impenetrable marsh to the river. The Natives were located on the Rangers' right flank, and formed into six distinct parties. Fire was to be held until a signal was given by Old Smoke. Cruikshank makes the colourful claim that Butler laid aside his cocked hat, wrapped a cravat over his head, took up a rifle, and placed himself in the Rangers' centre.

The centennial commemorative account of the battle made this rather contradictory report of the topography: "Yellow and pitch-pine trees, with scrub-oaks about breast high, were everywhere

Detail of an alleged Butler's Rangers' musket. John Butler purchased his regiment's firelocks and only rarely drew from government stores. This item was collected in Niagara-on-the-Lake, Ontario, from a Ranger descendant (confidential source).

over the plain. There were very few trees of any size. The Indians were accustomed to burn the plain over every year, to make pasture for deer and other game, and thus destroyed the growth of trees of large size."

The rebels advanced in a single-rank battle line[36] for almost a mile, until they were about two hundred yards from Wintermoot's burning stockade, with their right flank on a hill and the left about 130 yards from the swamp. A halt was ordered, and scouts were sent out to reconnoitre. As the scouts advanced, individual Indians would pop up, fire, and run off, some in one direction, some in another.

The rebel officers began to worry that there might be more of an enemy force than they had thought, and called a halt in order to make inspirational addresses to their troops and instruct them to "Stand firm the first shock, and the Indians will give way. Everything depends on standing firm the first shock."[37]

The rebel line was then counted off into odds and evens. The odds were to advance ten steps and halt, then the evens would advance past them another ten paces and halt. The Wyoming Commemorative account says that every time a rank halted, the men fired a volley. Graymont claims that the rebels advanced in these alternating bounds without firing until two hundred yards from where they thought the enemy was hiding, then gave a volley. Whatever the case, there was no response from the Crown force, other than individual warriors rising, firing, and scampering off. The line advanced, and second and third volleys were delivered, until the rebels were about one hundred yards from the hidden, silent foe.

Graymont records that Old Smoke then gave his warriors the order to fire, and their discharge was immediately followed by that of the Rangers. Cruikshank reports that Old Smoke gave a shrill whoop, which was repeated by his six parties and the Rangers. Another account recalls the events differently, stating that the first enemies to appear in numbers were the Rangers — a squad arising, firing, and retreating, to which one of the officers shouted, "See! the British retreat! Stand firm and the day is ours!" The rebel line advanced again, and another squad of Rangers rose, fired, and fell back. Another shout: "The British retreat! The day is ours!"

If Graymont's account is accurate, the Crown forces' first fire was so close and so accurate that the rebels suffered greatly. The main body of warriors immediately began to manoeuvre around the rebels' left flank, forcing them to fall back.

Once again, the various accounts are at odds. Cruikshank reports "a deliberate and deadly volley," but the commemorative version makes no reference to the Crown forces' opening volleys; it simply confirms that the Natives manoeuvred around the rebels' flank.

> Our men had now arrived at a point just opposite Wintermoot Fort, on their right, and on the edge, in front of the only cleared space on the plain, which was an open field of three or four acres. They continued their advance slowly and cautiously, when they soon found the British in full force in front, standing up to the work, though apparently yielding ground. The firing now became general along the lines on both sides. Our people felt they were gaining ground and driving the enemy before them.
>
> Too much attention had been devoted to the movements of the British in front, to properly observe and understand the movements and dangers of the other portions of the field. The British lay behind a log fence which ran along the upper side of this cleared field down to the foot of the hill at a marshy spot, and were largely concealed and protected by it. The Indians, lying behind the marsh, on the other side of the field, which ran diagonally across the front of our line, and concealed behind its dense shrubbery, had not manifested their force on the field, and their location was not really known. When the settlers had advanced fully into this cleared field, and were, as they supposed, driving the enemy before

them, the Indians broke from their covert and fell upon their left, yelling like demons, pouring in their fire and pressing to close quarters with the spear and tomahawk.

Their [Natives'] numbers were sufficient not only to outflank the left, but to turn it and gain the rear. Col. Denison, on discovering this movement, at once gave orders for the left to fall back, and form an oblique line to the position of the right, and thus bring the left into a position to face the enemy.

The order was not fully understood, or was imperfectly communicated, and hence the movement was confused. In the midst of the noise and confusion, the word oblique was understood by some to be retreat, and the line was not formed, but the left began moving in on the right in a broken, confused mass.

The officers, meantime, made every possible effort to have their orders understood, and to restore order and bring the men to face the enemy and stand their ground, but in vain. Col. Dorrance fell, severely wounded, while riding along the line gallantly laboring in this vain attempt. The mistake was a fatal one and could not be retrieved.

Observing that their left was collapsing in panic, the rest of the rebels thought a general retreat had begun, and the action soon turned into a rout. Cruikshank says that the warriors darted ahead to cut off the rebels, and "drove them in confusion towards the river. After that they offered but little resistance, and a merciless pursuit began. Many tried to swim the river, and were shot or drowned in the act." Some of the fleet of foot made it back to Forty Fort; others managed the swim to the other side. The action had taken thirty minutes, from the opening volley to the panicked retreat.

The Battle's Outcome

The commemorative account claims the Crown force greatly outnumbered the Yankees, "three to one"; by 20 percent was more like it, however, and it was also likely that the enemy was much more professional than they.[38] To be sure, the Natives were trained warriors from childhood, but most of the Rangers were no better trained or adept than their foe. That the Rangers were better led is true; that they were more disciplined and patient is also true. The commemorative account also includes many lurid, patently ridiculous tales of prisoners being horrendously tortured, and stories of patricide and fratricide on the part of the Rangers.

The fact is that the Natives finished the battle on their terms, and killed all who were, or had been, in arms. John Butler reported that 227 scalps were taken and only five prisoners, and commented that the Natives were so infuriated over their losses at Oriskany that he could scarcely persuade them to take even those few. His later account said that 376 rebels had been killed, and his Indian Department lieutenant, Adam Crysler, claimed 460.[39]

Two participating rebel officers provided body counts. Colonel Zeb Butler reported about two hundred; Colonel Nathan Denison was more precise: 268 privates, one colonel, two majors, seven captains, thirteen lieutenants, eleven ensigns — total, 302. As Zeb Butler was not at Forty Fort the next day and Denison was, he was likely better informed, and in view of the staggering defeat, perhaps Zeb Butler had a motive for playing down the losses.[40]

The disproportionate casualties during this action are astoundingly similar to those of Oriskany. According to Butler, one Native man was killed, and two Rangers and eight Natives wounded. The Seneca warrior Blacksnake recalled years later that six Natives were killed, including two war chiefs, and Cornplanter's biographer reports five Senecas, two Cayugas, and one Onondaga killed.[41] Whichever is correct, the comparison to the rebels' losses is staggering.

More Forts Surrender

The next morning, the three stockades at Pittstown near the Lackawana River surrendered on the same terms accepted at Fort Jenkins. Mills, homes, and barns were already burning, and the Natives had rounded up an immense drove of beeves.

Colonel Denison arrived in Major Butler's camp the next day with a clergyman to negotiate the sparing of the rest of the Westmoreland settlement. At this time, he reported the defenders' battle losses as noted above, and advised that only sixty of the four hundred-plus men who had marched out to battle had escaped. Fourteen of those were Continentals, most likely of Hewitt's Independent Company, which had been posted on the right flank of the rebel line, and therefore away from the Natives' turning manoeuvre. It soon became apparent to the major that Colonel Zeb Butler and the other Continental Army survivors had fled the valley, having earlier been threatened with captivity.[42]

Interpretation of John Butler in a period-correct uniform.

Major Butler offered Denison the same conditions that he had proposed before the battle.

Westmoreland, July 4th, 1778.

Capitulation made and completed between Major John Butler on behalf of His Majesty King George the Third and Colonel Nathaniel Denniston of the United States of America.

Article 1st. That the inhabitants of the settlement lay down their arms and their garrisons be demolished.

Article 2nd. That the inhabitants are to occupy their farms peaceably and the lives of the inhabitants preserved entire and unharmed.

Article 3rd. That the Continentals be delivered up.

Article 4th. That Major Butler will use his utmost influence that the private property of the inhabitants shall be preserved to them.

Article 5th. That the prisoners in Forty Fort be delivered up and that Samuel Finch in Major Butler's possession be delivered up.

Article 6th. That the properties taken from the people called "Tories" up the river be made good, and they to remain in peaceable possession of their farms, and unmolested in a free trade in and throughout this state as far as is in my power.

Article 7th. That the inhabitants that Colonel Denniston now capitulates for, together with himself, do not take up arms during the present conflict.

Signed: Nathan Denniston
John Butler
Witness: Zarah Beech, Samuel Gustin, John Johnson, William Caldwell[43]

As John Butler recalled in his services' memorial, "I ordered all their Forts to the number of twelve to be destroyed, but Forty Fort in which the greatest Part of their Women & Children were, was saved & not in the smallest degree molested or plundered." For everyone's safety, he insisted that all alcoholic spirits be destroyed before any Natives entered the fort, and that the fort's stores be displayed as booty. One of the prisoners recalled Butler's efforts to prevent the Natives from excessive plundering, "and even from taunting the inhabitants with their defeat."[44]

Yet all was not sweetness and light — one of the more likely tales associated with the battle was the grim death of Lieutenant-Colonel George Dorrance. As an officer in a fine uniform, sword, and accoutrements, he was one of the few taken prisoner, presumably for the ransom that might be expected. The day after the battle, his two captors were leading him to Forty Fort when he collapsed from exhaustion and stress. The Wyoming commemorative theorized that the two Indians killed him in their eagerness to get downriver, with its promise of more rich booty. One took Dorrance's scalp and sword; the other stripped off his coat and donned his cocked hat, which sported a feather. When the latter entered Forty Fort, he searched out the colonel's widow, and delighted in parading himself in front of her in her husband's finery.[45]

On the morning of June 4, John Gardner, who had been captured the day before the battle when the Hardings were killed, was displayed to his wife and five children. He was tied to a log, and near him lay a heavy pack of plunder that he was expected to carry north. After a goodbye, his captors slipped a rope around his neck, lifted the pack onto his back, and his family never saw him again. A story filtered back that when he reached his captors' village, he collapsed in exhaustion, and was given to the women, who tortured him to death.[46]

Despite the surrender terms and Major Butler's good intentions, he was unable to control the Natives. Colonel Denison later reported, "Nevertheless, the enemy, being powerful, proceeded, plundered, burned and destroyed almost everything that was valuable; murdered several of the remaining inhabitants, and compelled most of the remainder to leave their settlements, nearly destitute of clothing, provisions and the necessaries of life." A final enumeration listed the burning of one thousand dwellings and all the valley's mills, and the driving off of a thousand head of cattle, sheep, and hogs. Major Butler contentedly reported, "But what gives me the sincerest satisfaction is that I can with great truth assure you that in the destruction of this settlement not a single person has been hurt of the Inhabitants, but such as were in arms, to those indeed the Indians gave no quarter."[47]

Before withdrawing, Butler sent a party eastward to destroy the settlements along the Lackawaxen branch of the Delaware River.[48] No mention of the fate of the three Native delegates who had been earlier imprisoned in Wilkes-Barre has been found.

The Great Runaway

When the destruction of the Wyoming settlements was complete, the raiders marched away, driving their vast collection of livestock; however, most northern Pennsylvanians were unaware of their withdrawal. The Westmoreland disaster reverberated downstream, as hundreds of inhabitants fled the Wyoming Valley in widespread panic over the news of the invasion. A great many had crossed the river at Forty Fort the night after the battle and plunged into the woods, making their way to the mountains. Many more fled the night of the 4th.

Historian Frederick Godcharles wrote that "as the news passed down the North Branch of the Susquehanna and spread over the hills and valleys leading to the West Branch Valley it caused a general stampede, a wild, precipitate flight of the settlers from the upper region which has ever since been known as the 'Great Runaway.'" Two days after the battle, the news had reached across the entire North Branch Valley and as far up the West Branch Valley as Fort Antes.[49]

Some of the escapees came across Captain Simon Spaulding's company on June 5, and Lieutenant Jenkins fell in with them the next morning on their march toward the valley. When the company reached the mountains overlooking the Wyoming settlements, parties were sent out to help people who were still hiding in the woods, exhausted from fear and hunger. Spaulding's men continued this work for two or three days.[50]

When the news reached Colonel Samuel Hunter, the lieutenant of Northumberland County, who was commanding at Fort Augusta in Sunbury, he wrote to Colonel William Hepburn at Fort Muncy ordering all settlers to evacuate the region and fly to Fort Augusta, as there was insufficient militia to defend them. Hepburn complied, and sent messengers to the Muncy Creek farms and to Fort Antes on the Susquehanna's West Branch.[51]

Robert Covenhoven, who had carried Hepburn's instructions to Fort Antes, wrote of his experiences: "I took my family safely to Sunbury and came back in a keel-boat to secure my furniture. Just as I rounded a point above Deerstown I met the whole convoy from all the forts above. Such a sight I never saw in all my life. Boats, canoes, hogtroughs, rafts hastily made of dry sticks, every sort of floating article had been put in requisition, and was crowded with women, children and plunder...."

Hannah Miller of Muncy recalled, "Those in the rear could see the sky reddened at night by the lurid glare caused by burning houses and barns. The scene was one of appalling grandeur, and the impression made on the minds of those who witnessed it especially the young was so vivid and deep that it never was effaced, but like some hideous spectre of evil, was always before them to haunt their memories!"

Whenever an obstruction occurred at any shoal or ripple, the women would leap out into the water and put their shoulders to the boat or raft, and launch it again into deep water. The men of the settlement came down in single file, on each side of the river, to guard the women and children. The whole convoy arrived safely at Sunbury, leaving the entire range of farms along the West Branch to the ravages of the Natives.

Future senator William Maclay wrote from Paxtang on July 12:

> I left Sunbury and almost my whole property on Wednesday last. I will not trouble you with a recital of the inconveniences I suffered while I brought my family by water to this place. I never in my life saw such scenes of distress. The river and roads leading down it were covered with men, women, and children flying for their lives. In short, Northumberland County is broken up. Colonel Hunter only remained, using his utmost endeavors to rally some of the inhabitants, and to make a stand, however short, against the enemy. I left him with very few, I can not speak with certainty as to numbers, but am confident when I left him he had not one hundred men on whom he could depend.

Maclay felt that something charitable should be done for "the many miserable objects that crowd the banks of this river, especially those who fled from Wyoming." As a Pennsylvanian, he admitted that they were a people whom he "did not love very warmly at one time," but now he most sincerely pitied their distress.

Frederick Godcharles noted, "Several persons are known to have been killed by the Indians during the 'Great Runaway,' but it remains a most remarkable fact that almost the entire population moved from the settlements and for several days were in the open along the river and yet but few were killed." Perhaps not so surprising at all, for the Six Nations had withdrawn northwards, and so it was local Natives prowling the area — and they had their hands full plundering and burning abandoned farms.

The Expedition Returns to Tioga

Major Butler had scarcely arrived at Tioga when he was struck down with a violent attack of fever, ague, and rheumatism in the head. He was forced to retire to Fort Niagara, but before he left, he made the necessary arrangements. Captain William Caldwell, who was the corps's senior officer in the absence of the two Butlers, was to command field operations, and join Brant at Oquaga. Butler instructed Caldwell, "I would have you give orders to each party you may send out to burn and destroy everything they possibly can, and I imagine our Brothers can never be more service to Government than at the present juncture. If we can prevent the enemy from getting in their grain, their Grand Army (who are already much distressed) must disperse and their country, of course, become an easy prey to the King, their Father."[52]

Rebel Retaliation

Whatever criticisms might be made about Westmoreland and Northumberland settlers, it cannot be said that they lacked resiliency, or that Pennsylvania failed to respond to the disaster.

Colonel Daniel Brodhead's 8th Pennsylvania Continental Line was marching by stages to reinforce Fort Pitt when it received orders to divert northwards to Fort Augusta in Sunbury to restore some order to the settlements. From there, Brodhead continued on to Muncy, arriving on July 24.[53] Colonel Thomas Hartley, with his Additional Pennsylvania Regiment, was ordered to the Susquehanna, and arrived at Fort Augusta on August 1. Over one thousand militia had been ordered to reinforce Hartley, but only a fraction joined him. A week later, Hartley relieved Colonel Brodhead at Fort Muncy, which allowed the 8th PA to march south and resume their original mission.

Pennsylvanian Thomas Hartley was born in 1748. He had studied law, and practiced in York before the war. In 1774, he was elected vice-president of York County's committee of observation,[54] and he represented the county as a deputy at the Provincial Conference that year and at the Provincial Convention in 1775. His military career began in December 1774 as a militia first lieutenant; a year later, he was a lieutenant-colonel. In January 1776, Hartley was elected a Continental lieutenant-colonel, and served with distinction during

Colonel Thomas Hartley, commander of the Wyalusing Expedition.

the invasion of Canada. That December, Congress authorized the raising of sixteen battalions of additional infantry, and command of one was given to Hartley. His battalion served conspicuously during the battles of Brandywine, Germantown, and Paoli, with Hartley acting as a brigadier of Wayne's division.[55]

Hartley assigned his captain, Andrew Walker, to improve the Muncy fort and guard the returning settlers while they worked their crops.[56] On August 4, Colonel Zebulon Butler returned to Wilkes-Barre and set up Camp Westmoreland. Over the ensuing weeks, the fort there would be rebuilt and christened Fort Wyoming. On the 5th, he advised Hartley,

> I arrived at this place yesterday with about sixty Continental troops and about forty militiamen. We discovered two small parties of Indians yesterday, and fired at them, and discovered two other parties

this day. What numbers there is about is uncertain. If your honor should think it consistent to have some part if the troops under your command advance as far up the river as this place, or as far as you should think proper, I think it will be a means of keeping the savages from murdering and robbing the inhabitants if these frontiers.[57]

Hartley had some two hundred men to protect the frontiers. Obviously, this was an impossible task, and he decided the solution was to mount an offensive that would stop Native raiding by forcing them to secure their own villages. He wrote to the State Council on September 1.

> Since my last [letter] to the Council I have been out with several Detachments up the West Branch — tho' we are not certain we killed a single Indian; it would have been in our Power several Times since I came up here had we had some Horse. The Barbarians have frequently appeared in open ground & do fairly out run the most of white men. From my little observation I am dearly convinced of the utility of Horse, for however sagacious the Indians are, they cannot always chuse their own ground. The Horsemen should be armed with a sword, two Pistols & a short Rifle; the latter would be necessary to intimidate the Enemy, & the Soldier might occasionally act on Foot. I have wrote to the Board of War to send an officer & 12 Horse here; I hope they will comply.
>
> Captain Walker has been so industrious at Muncy as to have compleated all the Earth and Fas[c]ine Works, & nearly all the Stockade. I never saw as much work done by so few men in so short a time.
>
> We have a four Pounder mounted there; if we had four Swivels to place in the Bastions the Place

would be very secure with a small Garrison. It is to be remarked that since this Work has been begun, no Person has been killed within our Line of Posts.

I most earnestly wish that you would send up twelve Swivels for the County; in Case the withdrawing of the Militia they will be essentially necessary.

I am inducing the People to put in some Fall Crops. Several are returning to their Habitations, but with great Diffidence.

Yesterday morning three German militia, without arms and without Permission, went out of the Fort at Muncey to dig some Potatoes within sight of the Garrison; they were immediately attacked by one white man and some Indians. The Enemy discharged all their Pieces at once — one militia man fell and was scalped, one ran off; The other one was seised, and had a Tussel with a stout Indian, but was rescued by the Troops. One Cottner was killed, & one Capt. Martel was wounded on the 23d of August near Muncy.

Several Indians and Tories have appeared about Wyoming. One Family has been killed 15 miles on this side of it, & two near the Garrison. My Detachment from Northampton County is arrived there by this Time, but I am told their Cloaths are all torn by the woods; they are in the utmost want of Hunting Shirts and woolen overhalls or Leggins. I hope 200 of each will be sent up immediately. No medicine has yet arrived — the militia are very sickly.[58]

Hartley received approval for his expedition in early September, and simultaneously, Colonel William Butler's 4th Pennsylvania Continental Regiment was ordered from its base at Schoharie to form a junction with him at Tioga.

Hartley wrote to Zebulon Butler on September 10, illustrating that the Yankees and Pennamites had at last found common cause, if only temporarily.

> Upon a full consideration concerning the Indian country, and a view of the circumstances of our affairs, I have come to these determinations. That it is absolutely necessary that the troops at Wyoming, those on the west branch, and in this department, should effect a junction before they proceed against Chemung, where, I understand, a great part of the plunder taken from our unhappy brethren at Wyoming, and a body of Indians and Tories, are collected. I mean that this town should be approached by the Lycoming path to the mouth of the Towanda, and that the troops should sweep the country down river to Wyoming. This will give relief to our frontiers, and intimidate our enemies....
>
> I am informed many of your people have the highest inclination to go against some of the Indian towns, they may revenge the murders of fathers, brothers and friends, besides serving their country. You will detain Captain Kenney with a Sergeant and ten men of my regiment, a subaltern and twenty of Spalding's and Howe's men, of those who are the least able to march of which Captain Kenney is to take charge, under your immediate direction, in your garrison. That Captain Bush, with the residue of my regiment and the other troops at Wyoming, do march from thence on Monday next by the route of Freeland's Mills to Muncy Fort, near Wallis. They are to bring all the pack-horses, saddles, &c. with them. It is expected they will arrive at Fort Muncy the third night if their march, or the fourth day.

> It will be impossible to tell the troops or people where they are to march to. You must induce the militia to go — say they are marching against some Indian town. After they are marched, the garrison are to be informed that the men are gone to the West Branch to support the people there, who have been attacked by the Indians. The route to Muncy will justify the last; the Tories will be deceived. You will act in the best manner you can during the absence of the troops. I shall not, perhaps, go to Chemung (this is between you and I), and you shall be supported with all the troops in this quarter in case of emergency. A garrison will be continued near Nescopeck. You may communicate this letter to Captains Bush and Kenney; and also to Colonel Dennison and Mr. Stewart — under the strictest injunction of secrecy. Mr. Howe and Murray have had some intimations, but I dare say they will keep them secret. The inhabitants who go on this expedition will be back time enough to put in some Fall grain.[59]

British Indian Department Dispositions

On September 18, Lieutenant-Colonel Bolton sent Haldimand a "return of the disposition of the Rangers now employed on the frontiers of the Indian country."

> Captain Caldwell of the Rangers, Captain Powell of the Indian Department and Mr Joseph Brant: at the Aughquaga [Oquaga] employed in scouting from thence to the Delaware River as low as the Minisink to Schoharie as well to annoy the enemy as to gain intelligence.

Mr Pawling — also detached from Aughquaga with 30 Rangers and a number of Indians to Wyalusing upon the Susquehanna with directions to scout as low as Wyoming and watch the motions of the rebels said to be re-assembling there.

Mr John Young — detached from Aughquaga with 30 Rangers and Indians constantly towards the German Flatts and Cherry Valley.

Captain [John] Johnston — from the Seneca Country keeps constant parties of Indians out from thence to the West Branch of the Susquehanna and to the Juniata.

Mr Adams of the Indian Department — at Carleton Island (under the command of Captain Aubrey) employed in scouting from thence towards Fort Stanwix.

The Chiefs of the Upper Senecas have an attentive eye to Fort Pitt and the country around about it.

The body of the Rangers under the command of Captain Butler at Aughquaga and that neighbourhood are ready when joined by the Indians for an incursion into the enemy's frontiers or to assist in defending the Indian country in case of any attempts of the rebels.[60]

Hartley's Expedition

After he returned from his expedition, Colonel Hartley sent a useful explanation of the events to Congress:

> With a Frontier from Wioming to Allegany, we were sensible the few regular Troops we had could not defend the necessary Posts. We thought (if it were

practicable), it would be best to draw the Principal part of our Force together, as the Inhabitants would be in no great danger during our absence [and] make a stroke at some of the nearest Indian towns, especially as we learnt a handsome detachment had been sent into the Enemy's Country, by the way of Cherry Valley [William Butler's 4PA.] We were in hopes we should drive the Savages to a greater distance.[61]

Hartley offered a somewhat different explanation of affairs to Pennsylvania's Executive Council: "Anxious for the welfare & safety of these Frontiers, I wished if possible to drive the Savages to a greater distance; By acting on the Defensive only, this could not be effected. The times of the Militia were soon expired, we are now without any of them. I rec'd a letter from Mr Bryan, V. P., by which I understood Col. Morgan & [William] Butler were acting against the Indians on the waters of the Sasquehana, this with our former Inclinations induced us to push an Expedition to Tioga & its neighbourhood."[62]

Originally, he had planned on four hundred rank-and-file of his own regiment, plus seventeen mounted men under Captain Henry Carberry,[63] but when it was time to march, "we came to count and array our Force for the Expedition, [and] they amounted only to about 200 Rank & File.[64] We thought the number small, but as we presumed the Enemy had no notice of our Designs, we hoped at least to make a good Diversion if no more, whilst the Inhabitants were saving their grain on the Frontier." His report continued,

> In our Rout we met with great Rains & prodigious Swamps, Mountains, Defiles & Rocks impeded our march, we had to open and clear the way as we passed.... We waded or swam the River Lycoming upwards of 20 Times.
>
> On the morning of the 26th our Advance Party of 19 met with an equal Number of Indians on the Path, approaching each other, our People had the

first Fire, a very important Indian Chief was killed and scalped, the rest fled.

The *Royal Gazette*, the New York City Tory newspaper, wrote an account of this incident on November 7:

> [W]e are enabled by an authentic account from the back country to give our readers a true detail of the boasted advantage obtained by the rebel Colonel Heartly in his latest expedition to that country. On the 26th or 27th September a Seneca chief with twelve warriors, being on a scouting party near Tioga, was discovered by a party of Heartley's men who had the first fire, when the chief was killed. The warriors returned the fire and say they saw several of the enemy fall. They then retreated to young Mr Butler's party, who supposing the enemy very strong, retreated to Chemung, leaving about fifty cattle which fell into the enemy's hands....[65]

Word of Hartley's expedition had arrived in Indian Territory while it was still in its planning stages. The Senecas immediately raised an opposing force, as Chief Big Tree discovered when he returned home from his adventures with General Washington and Congress. During a stop at Kanowalohale, Big Tree had promised the Oneidas that "he would exert his utmost influence to dispose his tribe to peace and friendship with the United States," but when he saw that all the men at Canadesaga and Genesee were under arms to repel an invading rebel force, he and his followers also took up arms. The Senecas were to march on September 8, the Cayugas the next day, and all were to rendezvous at Tioga.[66]

Hartley advanced a few miles, and discovered a camp where some seventy warriors had been the night before. He reckoned they fled when hearing of his coming.

No Time was lost, we advanced towards Sheshecunnunck [Sheshequin], in the Neighborhood of which place we took 15 Prisoners from them, we learnt that a Man had deserted from Capt. Spalding's Company at Wioming, after the Troops had marched from thence, & had given the enemy Notice of our intended Expedition against them.

We moved with the greatest Dispatch towards Tioga, advancing our Horse, and some Foot in Front, who did their duty very well; a number of the Enemy fled before us with Precipitation, it was near dark when we came to that town, our Troops were much fatigued; it was impossible to proceed further that Night.

We took another Prisoner, upon the whole Information, we were clear the Savages had Intelligence of us some days [before] — That the Indians had been towards the German Flats — had taken 8 scalps and brought off 70 oxen intended for the garrison of Fort Stanwix — That on their Return they were to have attacked Wioming and the settlements on the West Branch again — That Colo. Morgan [i.e. William Butler from Schoharie] or no other Person had attempted to penetrate into the Enemy's Country, as we had been given to understand, and that the Collected force at Chemung would be upwards of 500, & that they were building a fort there.

We also were told that young Butler had been at Tioga a few Hours before we came — that he had 300 Men with him, the most of them Tories, dressed in green — that they were returned towards Chemung, 12 Miles off, & that they determined to give us Battle in some of the Defiles near it.

It was soon resolved we should proceed no further, but if possible, make our way good to Wioming.

> We burnt Tioga, Queen Esther's Palace or Town, & all the settlements on this side; several Canoes were taken and some Plunder, Part of which was destroyed.[67]

As to the significance of Queen Esther's village, The Royal Gazette was quite scathing: "[They] burnt what Mr Heartley calls Queen Ester's Palace or Town, which consisted of only three indifferent cabins covered with bark, inhabited by that ancient squaw and two other very feeble Indian women." What nonsense; the town had at least seventy log houses.

Colonel Hartley's report to Congress continued:

> Mr. Carbery with the Horse only, was close on Butler, he was in Possession of the Town of Shawnee, 3 Miles up the Cayuga Branch, but as we did not advance, he returned.
>
> The Consternation of the Enemy was great, we pushed our good Fortune as far as we dare, nay, it is probable the good countenance we put on saved us from destruction, as we were advanced so far into the Enemy's Country & no return but what we could make with the sword. We came to Sheshecunnunk that night.
>
> Had we had 500 Regular Troops, and 150 Light Troops, with one or two Pieces of artillery, we probably might have destroyed Chemung, which is now the recepticle of all villainous Indians & Tories from the different Tribes and States. From this they make their Excursions against the Frontiers of N. York and Pennsylvania, Jersey & Wioming, & commit those horrid Murders and Devastations we have heard of. Niagra and Chemung are the assilums of those Tories who cannot get to New York [City.]
>
> On the Morning of the 28th, we crossed the River and Marched towards Wyalusing, where we

arrived that night at eleven o'Clock; our men much worn down — our Whiskey and Flour was gone.

On the Morning of the 29th we were obliged to stay 'till eleven o'clock to kill and cooke Beef. This necessary stop gave the Enemy Leasure to approach.

Seventy of our Men, from real or pretended Lameness, went into the Canoes, others rode on the empty Pack Horses, we had not more than 120 Rank & File to fall in the Line of March.

Lt. Sweeny, a valuable officer, had the Rear Guard, consisting of 30 Men, besides five active Runners under Mr. Camplen. The advanced guard was to consist of an officer & 15. There were a few Flankers, but from the Difficulty of the ground & Fatigue, they were seldom of use.

The rest of our Little army was formed into three Divisions, those of my Regmt composed the first, Capt Spalding's the 2d, Capt Murrow's the 3d. The Light Horse was equally divided between front and rear. The Pack Horses and the Cattle we had collected, were to follow the advance guard.

In this order we moved from Wyalusing at twelve o'clock, a slight attack was made on our Front from a Hill, half an Hour afterwards a warmer one was made on the same quarter, after ordering the 2d and 3d Divisions to out Flank the Enemy, we soon drove them, but this, as I expected, was only amusement, we lost as Little time as possible with them.

At two o'clock a very heavy attack was made on our Rear, which obliged the most of the Rear guard to give way, whilst several Indians appeared on our Left Flank. By the weight of the Firing we were soon convinced we had to oppose a Large Body.

Capt Stoddard commanded in Front, I was in the Centre; I observed some high ground which overlooked the Enemy, orders were immediately given for the first & 3d Division to take Possession of it, whilst Capt Spalding was dispatched to support the Rear Guard. We gained the Heights almost unnoticed by the Barbarians, Capt Stoddert sent a small Party towards the Enemy's Rear; at this critical moment Capts Boone & Brady, & Lt King, with a few Brave Fellows, landed from the Canoes, joined Mr. Sweeny, and renewed the action there. The War Whoop was given by our People below and communicated round, we advanced on the Enemy on all sides, with great shouting & Noise, the Indians after a brave resistance of some minutes, conceived themselves nearly surrounded, fled with the utmost Haste, by the only passes that remained, & left ten dead on the ground.

Our Troops wished to do their duty, but they were much overcome with Fatigue, otherwise (as the Indians immagined themselves surrounded), we should [have] drove the Enemy into the River.

From every account these were a select body of warriors, sent after us, consisting of near 200 Men. Their Confidence and Impetuosity probably gave the victory to us.

After they had drove our Rear some Distance their Chief was heard to say, in the Indian Language, that which is interpreted thus: my Brave Warriors ... drive them, be bold and strong, the day is ours, upon this they advanced very quick without sufficiently regarding their Rear....

We had 4 killed and 10 wounded. The Enemy must have had at least treble the number killed & wounded.

They received such a Beating as prevented them from giving us any further trouble during our March to Wioming, which is more than 50 Miles from the place of action.

The officers of my Regiment behaved well to a Man. All the party will acknowledge the greatest merit and Bravery of Capt Stoddert, I cannot say enough in his favor, he deserves the Esteem of his Country.

Mr. Carbery with his Horse, was very active, and rendered important services, 'till his Horses were fatigued.

Nearly all the other officers acquitted themselves with Reputation.

Capt Spalding exerted himself as much as possible.

Capt Murrow, from his knowledge of Indian affairs, and their Mode of fighting, was serviceable. His Men were Marksmen and were useful.

The men of my Regt were armed with Muskets & Bayonets, they were no great marksmen, and were awkward at wood Fighting. The Bullet, and three Swan shot in each Piece, made up, in some measure, for the want of skill.[68]

The Pennsylvania Historical & Museum Commission describes the action:

> Almost immediately, the advance guard came under attack, but soon brushed the enemy aside. Another attack occurred thirty minutes later, and this also was beaten off. Then, at about 2:00 p.m., a major assault was launched against the rear guard. Undetected, Hartley led part of the main body inland to some high ground, from which he could encircle the Indians. Then the men in the canoes landed and struck from the opposite direction. The enemy, almost completely surrounded and taken by surprise, soon broke and fled, leaving ten dead from

a force Hartley estimated at almost two hundred. The Americans lost four killed and ten wounded.[69]

The lieutenant of Northumberland County, Colonel Samuel Hunter, added details of the expedition in his October 7 report from Fort Augusta in Sunbury to Vice-President Bryan, (a vice-president being Pennsylvania's version of governor):

> The 5th Ins't Col. Thomas Hartley returned from an Expedition he carried on against some of the small Indian Towns on the North Branch of Susquehanna, where he was informed there was a party of Indians and Tories assembled, but they being appraised of Col. Hartley's march by a party of Wariors he met coming to the West Branch, whome our People fired uppon and shot their Captain dead, uppon which the Indians fled imeadiately and alarmed the Towns Col. Hartly was bound for, so that they had time to put their familys and chief part of their Effects out of the way before he arrived there, and when he came to Tiaogo, [Tioga] where he took some Tories Prisoners, they informed him that there was a Town called Shamung [Chemung] about ten or twelve miles from there, where there was a Body of Indians, Tories & Regulars in Garrison, as good as six or seven hundred; Col. Hartley after consulting his Officers thought it most Expedient to return back without attempting Shamung, and so after destroying Tiaoga & Shesiken [Sheshequin] and bringing off fifty or sixty Head of Horned Cattle and some Horses they got there, beside several other articles our People brought with them in Cannoes.
> In the mean time the Indians was collecting a party to intercept Col. Hartly on his march to Wyoming, which they accomplished, and fired on our

People in front in this side of Wyaloosing, where the Indians had way-lay'd our People among a parsel of Rocks as they were marching through a piece of narrows along the River side, but Col Hartley's People returning the fire briskly made the Enemy give way, and marched but a little ways furder when they were fired on again in the rear, and after a brisk fireing on Boath sides for some time the Enemy retreated.

It must be acknowledged our People beheaved with Courage and Conduct in bringing off their wounded, all their Cattle and pack Horses; suppose the Enemy followed all the way to Wyoming and scalped four of Col. James Murray's men after they arrived there; as for a more minute account of this Expedition, I refer you to Col. Hartley's own Letters to the Board of Warr & Executive Council. But in the whole it was well conducted considering the number of men that went with Col. Hartley, not above two hundred and fifty, which shows that Officers and men beheaved with spirit in bringing with them five Indian scalps besides several more of the Enemy kill'd. Col. Hartley's loss was seven killed and eight wounded including those that was killed at Wyoming.

As for the Inhabitants of this County they seem very much afraid at present, hearing of such a large Body of the Enemy being so nigh as Shamung, and all the militia that was here from Lancaster County & Berks gone, as their times was Expired, and none here but part of Col. Hartley's Regiment, sixty men of Col. James Murray's Company of six month's men, and about one hundred of our own militia, which is doing duty in several parts of this County, which is no way adiquit to the security of the same, as I am certain the one half of this County is left vacant, and not more than one third of the Inhabitants that lived formerly here, is putting in any fall crop this year, so that Distress & Misery must ensue. If no Continental Troops is ordered up here this fall, nor no militia from other Countys bordering of us, I am afraid a number of those that has brought their familys back will leave the County again.

This Company of Col. James Murray's that was raised for six months, at present consisting of sixty men, has been in service no better than three months, and has not received any of their pay during that time, complains very hard, and I am certain they deserve their pay as well as any other Company I know in the Continental service. Agreeable to the orders I received from Council, each man that found himself in a good Rifle & Accoutrements was to be allowed Eighty Dollars, this is the footing this Company is rais'd uppon, and all little enough, for they wear a vast quantity of Shoes and Shirts as they are constantly on scouting partys, and is just now come in after being with Col. Hartley on this last Expedition, and beheaved Well which he can assert—there is [like]wise a number of the militia of this County that has not rec'd pay as the Paymaster has not got money enough to pay them off.[70]

Hartley concluded his report to Congress as follows:

Tho' we were happy enough to succeed in this Action, yet I am convinced that a number of Lighter Troops, under good officers, are necessary for this Service.
 On the 3d the Savages kill'd & scalped 3 men, who had imprudently left the Garrison at Wioming to go in search of Potatoes.

> From our observations, we imagine that the same Party who had fought us, after taking Care of their Dead & Wounded, had came on towards Wyoming, and are now in that Neighbourhood.
>
> I left half of my detachment there with five of my own officers, should they attempt to invest the place when their number is increased, I make no doubt but they will be disappointed.
>
> Our Garrisons have plenty of Beef & Salt, tho' Flour is scarce at Wioming.
>
> I arrived here with the remainder of the detachment on the 5th, we have performed a Circuit of near 300 miles in about two weeks. We brought off near 50 Head of Cattle, 28 Canoes, besides many other articles.
>
> I would respectfully propose that the Congress would be pleased to send a Connecticut Regiment to Garrison Wyoming as soon as possible, it is but 120 miles from Fish Kills. I have done all I can for the good of the whole. I have given all the Support in my Power to that Post, but if Troops are not immediately sent, these Settlements will be destroyed in Detail. In a week or less a Regiment could march from Fish Kill to Wyoming.

Again, his report to the State Executive Council contained slightly different information:

> Considering our numbers we pushed our good Fortune as far as we dare, we gave a present relief to the Frontiers & turned back the Barbarians from Deluging our Country with the Blood of Helpless Mothers & Infants.
>
> They are a strange enemy, they shun Danger when among us, but near their own Country they

fight brave, a number of circumstances happily concurred to give us the victory over them on the 29th Sepr....

It is too late for an Expedition against Chemung this Fall, we must only secure our posts for the Winter & early in the Spring, a Body must march against their Towns on this River, there are more Indians within 150 Miles of this, than within the like distance from Fort Pitt, where so many men are collected....

We are here on a Dangerous service, which gives us few opportunity's of gaining Laurels; we have a Vigilant & Dangerous Enemy, but it gives us pleasure to think we serve our Country & protect the helpless & innocent.

Hartley's Threat

When Hartley was at still at Tioga he had sent an accusatory, threatening message to the Native chiefs at Chemung:

> I am very sorry to find that so many inhuman murders have been committed by the young men of your country upon helpless mothers and infants. We have marked their tracks and lurking Places. This custom of killing women and children is contrary to the rights and laws of Nations. I cannot imagine these depredations have received the sanction of the Chiefs; I would therefore recommend that you would prohibit the like for the future, and prevent that barbarous practice of burning and killing prisoners.
>
> This is the more necessary as I can inform you that the success of the American arms has been such as to give the King of England no hopes of conquering us and has left them few Possessions in

America besides Canada, which must inevitably fall in another campaign. By continuing these measures, the prospect of peace and amity will be destroyed; your country as a natural consequence will be desolated by Fire and Sword, and unsupported by Britain you will fall prey to the united force of these States.

Several people have fled from the States and taken sanctuary with you — the only chance they have will be to surrender themselves to the mercy of their country. I warn you in time, you need not afterwards plead ignorance; we have with my Party done but small injury to the Indian possessions.

Those Warriors who meet us must be convinced they have not Women and Children to deal with. I shall conclude with wishing that your good understanding [of your actions] may be removed. Your conduct has been reprobated by the Ministry and Parliament of England.[71]

Barbara Graymont comments, "Although the Indians had not molested noncombatants at Wyoming, there had been a number of instances of small war parties having done so on the Pennsylvania frontier — sometimes wiping out whole families. Hartley had not been specific enough in his accusations. Already fanciful tales of Indian barbarities at Wyoming had come back to the Senecas, and were deeply resented."[72]

Native Reaction to Hartley's Expedition

Delaware scouts had shadowed Hartley's expedition from the moment it left Muncy, and runners carried word to the Senecas. Upon hearing of the threat, the Senecas quickly assembled four hundred warriors, leaving only their women and children to defend their villages.[73]

Colonel Bolton wrote from Niagara on October 12, noting that Walter Butler was with Old Smoke collecting a force against fourteen hundred rebels advancing from Wyoming into the Indian country as far as Tioga. He opined that "should the Indians be defeated I should not be surprised if they compelled the Six Nations in a short time to observe a neutrality." He advised,

> I have ordered all the Rangers here to march with the utmost expedition to Captain Butler's assistance and have also sent as many volunteers from the King's Regiment as I could possibly spare considering the weak state of the garrison under my command. This I thought absolutely necessary as Sungerachta and the Chiefs have earnestly requested a reinforcement and I believe Your Excellency will agree with me that whenever the Six Nations are forced into a neutrality these posts must be in danger notwithstanding everything a handful of men can do to defend them. Last year, when we had an army in Philadelphia and another in New York, I am convinced the enemy would have sent a strong body of troops here if it had not been for the determined resolution of the Indians to oppose them, of which I acquainted Sir Guy Carleton.[74]

Old Smoke, Cornplanter, Blacksnake, and other headmen decided to attack the invaders, and set off in pursuit with their warriors and Delaware allies. Their attack took place near the farm of Ranger recruiting officer John Depew, and the results are noted in Hartley's report (above). Graymont attributes their losses to a lack of caution and to overconfidence.[75]

Although some sources make much of Hartley's attack on the Six Nations, Sheshequin and Tioga were Delaware villages, and Queen Esther's Town mixed Delaware and Seneca. Hartley would have preferred to strike the Seneca town of Chemung, but was warned off. Nonetheless, his expedition, and the coming destruction of the mixed towns of Unadilla and Oquaga, would signal to the Six Nations that their homelands were indeed threatened. Thomas Hartley had proven himself an effective leader.

Also, the fact that Colonel Denison had acted for Hartley as a scout, despite having given his solemn pledge not to take arms again during the war, infuriated the Iroquois, who had once again given in to a European convention — the act of paroling enemies — that had turned against them.

Delayed Burial

An order was issued on October 21 at Camp Westmoreland in Wilkes-Barre for a lieutenant, two serjeants, two corporals, and twenty-five privates to parade the next morning as a guard for the party that was setting out to bury the dead killed in the July 3 battle near Wintermoot Fort. Accordingly, Lieutenant John Jenkins and his party fell-in on the morning of the 22nd. The burial party had two carts, as well as several shovels and two-tined wooden forks. Due to dry weather, the corpses were desiccated and shriveled, and very few could be identified. Two men easily lifted a body with their forks and loaded it into a cart. By the time the party had gone about halfway between Forty Fort and Wintermoot, the carts were full, and a large hole was dug, into which the remains were dumped. The party moved on to collect more, returning repeatedly to the large common grave. Even after this sad and trying work, only ninety-six bodies had been found — sixty of them from the battleground, the rest from the line of flight.[76]

CHAPTER FOUR

NEW YORK'S MIDWESTERN FRONTIER

Hostile Designs of the Indians and Tories

VULNERABLE SETTLEMENTS

A handful of thriving settlements lay west of the Catskill Mountains, along the Delaware River's East Branch in lower Tryon County, and to the south along the Delaware's main course. Along the river's tributaries, in Pennsylvania and in New York's Ulster and Orange Counties, there were many other established farming communities. All of these were targets for Joseph Brant's volunteers as sources of recruits and supplies.

This region was also home to earlier occupants, the Esopus and Minisink Indians, Delaware sub-tribes whose members spoke the Munsee dialect. Although they had lived peaceably with the settlers for decades, they were co-opted into the early conflict by Colonel Guy Johnson, the Six Nations Indian Department superintendent, who drew them to a major council at Oswego in October 1775, during which he failed to gain wholehearted support from the Six Nations, but managed to recruit 220 Iroquois and affiliated warriors to escort him to lower Quebec. When he arrived at Montreal, he and his deputy, Lieutenant-Colonel Daniel Claus, and Six Nations

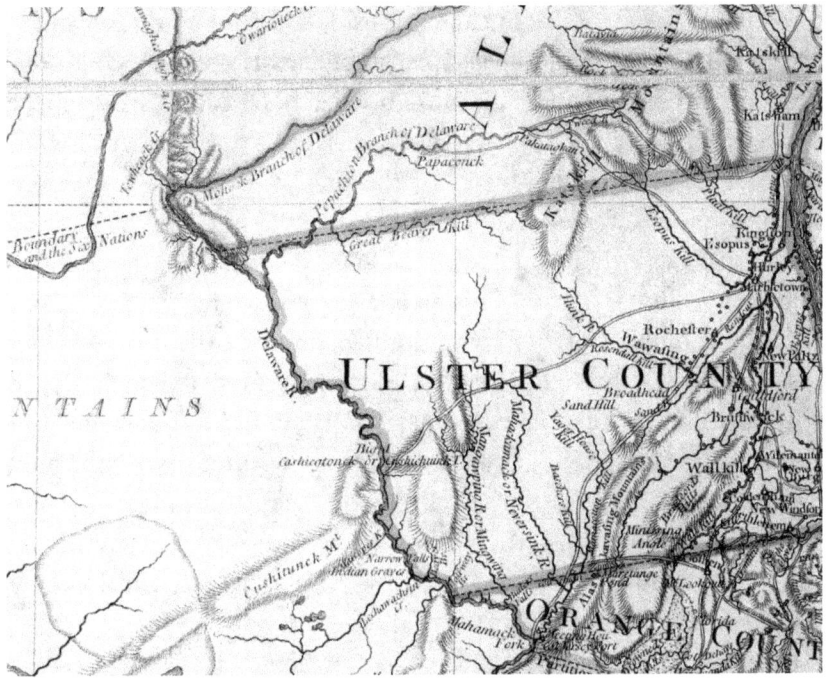

Southwestern Albany, Ulster, and Orange Counties.

volunteers were able to rouse a majority of the Canada Indians for the defence of Canada. Of course, news of these developments rapidly spread among the Esopus and Minisink Indians, and influenced their future behaviour as Six Nations affiliates.[1]

For loyalists who did not want to risk infiltrating New York City, and who wanted a more regulated method of opposing the rebellion than operating with Brant, there were two choices — Sir John Johnson's Royal Yorkers, or Butler's Rangers. Butler's recruiting was more wide-ranging than Johnson's, with parties roving as far as New Jersey and Pennsylvania with considerable success.[2]

In September 1776, the East Branch white settlement of Pepacton was repeatedly visited by friendly Natives urging the people to move away, and a few heeded this advice and went east to Kingston. Pressure continued to mount when Joseph Brant set his headquarters at Oquaga, and began roving the settlements for supplies and volunteers. Inevitably, political tensions developed among folk in the Delaware River communities. A Pepacton farmer complained in May 1777 that two of his neighbours, who were later under arms for the king, were "spreading lies and false intelligence to the great discouragement of the good subjects of the State." By August, relations had become so strained that the local Natives announced they would abandon Cookoze and move to Oquaga, as they feared the indiscriminate hostility of the Minisink and Esopus whites.

The campaign of 1777 was noteworthy for several expeditions and battles. In the middle states, Howe captured Philadelphia. In the north, St. Leger failed to take Fort Stanwix. Burgoyne lost his superb army at Saratoga, and Clinton captured two important Hudson Valley forts, burned Kingston, and threatened Esopus. Throughout the year, settlements west of the Catskills were in turmoil over divided loyalties, stirred by Tory recruiters and foraging parties from Indian Territory.

April saw the first raid of 1778, when Natives struck near Cochecton (Cushetunk) on the lower Delaware.[3] In May, Minisink's residents sent a deposition to Governor Clinton concerning threats emanating from Oquaga, and enclosed a letter written by Charles Smith, a Butler's Rangers' captain.

> Capt Charles Smith to Gentelmen offesers
> and Cummanders at the Meaneasinks
>
> These Cumes to Inform you That the Volanteers and Indens Doth Not Intend to hurt aney of the frunteers if tha keep thare Selves Still, and Minds thare Buysness, and Don't Hurt the [friends] to government; for we are Informed that that Inhabatance is Moving a way for feer of Us, and I am Cum Down My Self to this place to Dezier the Inhabtance, that that Need Not be a frade of aney Hurt, if they Stay at Home, But By thare Moving and Caring of fauls [false] News, in Rages the pason [enrages

the passion] of the Indens, But thare is one thing that I Dezier of you as a frind, that is to Move your gards Back, for that In Rages the Indens, and Will Be the ocassion of the Indens fauling on that place and Distring all Before them; and if you Do that, the Inhabatence May Live in Safatry; and if Not they Must Take What follows. I am one of the British offesers that am Sent to Look into these Maters, and a frend to all Human Nater, But your proceedince is Working your own Ruen [ruin], Which you Will find Before Long, if you Dont Take My Councel; and for Rob[b]ing and plundering of the Whigs it is Beneeth the Sparit of a British Offeser or Solder, altho you Have Made it your Buysness to Rob and plunder the frinds to Goverment yet the Davel has Not so Much Power Over Us as yet, and I hope Neaver Shall; But We Meen that Law Shall Take place in a Short Time and Make the gilty Siffer a Cording to thar Dezarts; and I Beag that you Wold Not Troubel the frinds to Goverment as Long as tha Lay Still; this is the advoice of a frind; for feer of Wors following So No More from yours.[4]

On July 5, Governor Clinton received the shocking news that Wyoming had fallen into "the Possesion of our most Inveterate Enemy." Coupled with the Cochecton raid, the Wyoming raid caused many Minisink families to move away. They complained, "Many of the Militia who are now placed as guards to the Frontiers, have neither Guns nor Ammunition & have it not in their power to purchase, because neither Guns or Lead are to be had; & a Few are not able to buy."

The governor had ordered out a frontier guard to gather intelligence, but the men remained at home, and the result had been the Cochecton incursion, which timely warnings might have prevented. Clinton now ordered Lieutenant-Colonel Jacob Newkirk,

2nd Ulster County Militia [2UCM], to strengthen the guards, but he could not think of what else might be done without weakening the critical Hudson River defences. He made it clear that he expected the militia officers to have their men "held in the most Perfect Readiness to march at a Moment's warning."[5]

On July 6, Brigadier Abraham Ten Broeck of the Albany County militia received an alarming report from a coach and chair maker from Acra in the southern county that armed Tories were constantly on the move past his house on the road from Catskill, on their way to Paghkatakean (Pakatakan). He told tales of suspected Tories, including a fellow named Smith, who, he reported, ranked as a major and an Indian superintendent. Smith had shown him a paper signed by John Butler, claiming to have fifteen thousand Natives and government men ready to join Admiral Howe's fleet at Catskill, and another paper that instructed "the friends to Government" to join him immediately or they would "share the same fate as the Rebels." These "friends" were to assemble at Pepacton and would receive four shillings per diem from the time they left their homes.

Smith claimed he had led the Cobleskill raid, and had twenty-two Natives at the lower end of Batavia in southern Schoharie, and "five hundred Indians & Government men back of the Mountains." He said there was a party back of Cherry Valley, another back of Schoharie, and the main body with Butler. As the chair maker lived in an exposed situation, he had disguised his allegiance so he could converse with the country's enemies, but on hearing the above intelligence, he thought it his duty to make his deposition.[6] Surely this Smith was the notorious captain whose threats and claims were so imaginatively exaggerated that they put everyone on edge.

Lackawack Raid

On July 10, Judge Levi Pawling took a sworn statement from Harmanus Dumond of Pakatakan. Two days before, Dumond and a number of men had gone downriver to Pepacton, where they

An interpretation of warriors lurking near a farm.

discovered a forty-man party — half Native, half Tory — under arms and set on destroying Lackawack and Rochester. Most of the Tories were local men like the Middagh brothers, John and Stephen, and John Snow, a Continental army deserter. Dumond was allowed to go on his way, and immediately reported to Colonel John Cantine, 3UCM, but before a detachment could be sent to interrupt the raiders, they struck at Lackawack and ran off the livestock. On their return march to Pepacton, about twenty Native and Tory raiders came across Robert Jones, who had escaped from Oquaga, which number suggests half of the raiding party had gone elsewhere. The raiders had seized two men from the tavern near the small Lackawack fort — the mistress's son, Jacob Ousterhout, and George Anderson, whose prize mare became booty. The pair was entrusted to three warriors and two women, to be taken to Niagara to collect the bounty.

Jones had somehow got free, and when rebel Lieutenant-Colonel Wisner of the 4th Orange County Militia [4OCM] interviewed him, he reported, "although we have some reason to suppose Jones to be a rascal and have confined him, yet his information we have good reason to believe in sundry particulars...." Indeed, Jones provided accurate and detailed intelligence about Brant's activities. He explained how he was persuaded to join Brant at Oquaga, and his intimate knowledge of the Mohawk war captain and his headquarters must have prevented the Lackawack raiders from suspecting him. He was with Brant when the captain was ordered to Tioga to meet with Old Smoke. Upon returning to Oquaga, Brant organized a party to raid Lackawack, but after a single day's march, they were recalled by news of an attack on Unadilla. Brant dispatched "all the white men he Could" from Oquaga, and two days later followed with "all the Indians at that place." That day, five Natives arrived at Oquaga and said that a large body of Senecas was on the march to Unadilla, and Captain Jacob left the next day with a collection of warriors. Strangely, Jones was left alone, and he took the opportunity to escape, and, on his way home, fell in with the Lackawack raiders. He told Wisner that Butler would not raid Minisink, but would go from Wyoming to join Brant on an expedition against Cherry Valley.[7]

Also on July 10, Wisner, with lieutenant-colonels Tusten, 3OCM, and Newkirk, 2UCM, reported to Governor Clinton that, because of "the unbounded disaffection and plotting lately discovered," they had taken their regiments to Minisink and "found things in the greatest confusion." Some men, with hundreds of women and children, were flocking from Wyoming, where "the most horrid scenes of savage barbarity" had occurred. The officers were unable to prevent them from continuing eastwards, although why they would have wanted to stop them was unstated, unless it were to prevent further panic.

Captain Abraham Cuddeback, 2UCM, had scouted Cochecton, and reported that some 250 Natives and Tories had assembled there to raid Peenpack and Minisink. The raiders planned to divide into small parties at the Mongaup River and strike simultaneously at several settlements, but hearing that a large body of militia was at Minisink, went no further. Instead, they attacked Lackawack again, killed some people, and took prisoners and livestock. Then, they set off across country for Oquaga, leaving scouts behind to forward intelligence. When the raiders were gone, the colonels dismissed their regiments, but recommended other drafts of militia be sent westward, assuming sufficient Continentals had arrived to garrison the Hudson River posts.

The very next day, Clinton reacted to reports from Ulster County colonel John Cantine and Judge Levi Pawling regarding a letter allegedly written by an Onondaga Indian and sent to the inhabitants of Kingston about "the Hostile Designs of the Indians & Tories on our Western Frontiers," which added credibility to Harmanus Dumond's earlier report. Clinton had also received a letter from Colonel Gansevoort at Fort Stanwix about a body of Regulars and Natives from Canada assembling at Oswegatchie in preparation to attack his post. Clinton reasoned that if the enemy planned to attack Stanwix, they would maintain small bodies of irregulars to harass the inhabitants and tie up the militia, preventing a reinforcement from being sent to Gansevoort's aid. He bemoaned that "this is the most critical & unfavourable Period to have the Peace of our Frontiers disturbed," as Washington's army had still not arrived on the Hudson, and he dared not withdraw the militia from the Highland's posts. As well, the harvest was imminent, and a large proportion of the militia would be unavailable for long lengths of time, so he was relying on the detachments of the 2UCM and 3OCM that were out towards Minisink and Peenpack. He urged Cantine to keep in touch with them, and to post more guards along the frontier.[8]

Major John Butler

Before Major John Butler left the Lackawanna River on July 8, he sent a party of raiders to Lackawack to destroy the settlement, collect provisions, and take prisoners. Excited rebels reported two hundred raiders; however, Butler had sent only two dozen warriors and Rangers under the command of the Munsee, Captain Mounsh. The force travelled the Lackawanna River north-eastward, then burned its way down the Lackawaxen valley to near Minisink, where Butler's recruiter, Captain Smith, had been causing considerable unrest. Mounsh's party killed several men, captured some others, and retired to the Munsees' old village of Cookoze, then on to Oquaga with a number of cattle, hogs, and sheep.

Major Butler arrived at Tioga on July 10. Despite the fact that couriers had been sent to New York City to obtain orders from the commander-in-chief for the conduct of the balance of the campaign, no instructions had arrived, and although a very large supply of livestock had been run off from Wyoming — Richard McGinnis recalled 900 cattle — lack of provisions continued as a serious problem. His Rangers were plagued by sickness, and, as already noted, the major was so incapacitated with rheumatism that he could not stay in the field; meanwhile, the Senecas, Cayugas, and Delawares wanted to return to their villages to display their trophies and tell of their exploits. Although Butler had committed to assisting Brant after his return, he found that the Senecas had little interest in co-operating with the junior Mohawk captain.

On July 12, the major wrote a series of instructions for Captain Caldwell. Butler had great confidence in William Caldwell; he had performed well in 1777 and during the Wyoming expedition, essentially commanding the Rangers with the major's oversight. The captain had earlier experience of Indian warfare, albeit from the opposite perspective, as he had participated in Lord Dunmore's War against the Ohio Indians before going to Niagara and joining Butler.

> You will, on receipt of this, proceed with all convenient speed to Ochquage, taking under your command all the officers and Rangers. On your arrival there, you will call a meeting of the Indians of that and the neighbouring villages and acquaint

them that I have sent you to join them either in the defence of their settlements or in any other offensive measures you and they may think practicable. And that I expect that they will use their utmost to supply you and party with provisions during your stay there.

I would have you send an officer and a few men with every party that goes out to annoy the country, which I strongly recommend to them, as by that means they may supply themselves and your party with provisions and prevent the enemy from getting in their grain....

You will without loss of time transmit to me every intelligence you may be able to collect on the designs and movements of the enemy, and if possible get intelligence of our army on the Hudson's River.

I would recommend to you to keep a good understanding between the Rangers and our Brothers, the Indians; and to consult with them on all occasions. Mr Joseph Brant will no doubt give you every assistance in his power.

All the Rangers that you meet with you are immediately to put themselves under your command so that you may have the greater number to assist our Brothers; taking down their names and the time they joined any of my officers on service there. You will enlist as many able bodied as can be well recommended for their loyalty into my Corps of Rangers.

You will acquaint my Brothers, the Ochquagas, that I shall remain at Canadesego until I shall be able to get a party ready to attack some parts of the rebel frontiers about the time their harvest is ripe. I have parties out on the Delaware, one of which I expect hourly; several others to the southward. The Five Nations are determined to give them no rest.

Your own judgement and good sense must direct you in many things, which no doubt will arise, but at present cannot be foreseen. My best respects to Mr Brant, the Chiefs and Warriors.[9]

After Butler's departure, the Rangers were still at Tioga when Jacob Hutsinger and Peter Simmons, who had families nearby, asked permission to visit them. Caldwell refused, but the men took advantage of being posted on guard and sneaked away, after destroying the arms of their fellow guards. The captain sent a party in pursuit, commanded by Lieutenant John Turney. When the pair was re-taken on August 18, Turney obeyed Major Butler's orders and had them shot. Their scalps were taken, brought to Oquaga, and hung up in Caldwell's tent. Richard McGinnis thought "this was not well done, as they might have made prisoners of them"; however, Butler's directives about deserters had been most explicit.[10]

A Butler's Rangers sword-belt plate collected in Niagara-on-the-Lake, Ontario, from a Ranger descendant (confidential source).

Their "bodies were left in top of the ground as not entitled to a burial. Queen Ester superintended the digging of a grave for the bodies and they were buried after the manner of the Indians."[11]

A Principal Granary

On July 12, General John Morin Scott, a New York Senator and the Secretary of State, reported to Governor Clinton from Hurley, immediately south of Kingston. He wrote, "The Situation of this Country is truly deplorable.... The Country breaking up and the Harvest probably abandoned." He thought his family and government records were unsafe, and was about to move away. He could not believe that such a valuable country was being left without defence, as it was a principal granary to the army. Nor could he believe that some two hundred miscreants were able to break up the whole extent of the country — surely three hundred troops could be found. He suggested sending Colonel Graham's Levies, which had been raised for protection of the frontiers, to the region. The disaster of Wyoming increased the danger. He had been told that three hundred of the enemy were on the way to Shamokin, and that another two hundred were going toward Hurley.[12]

The same day as Scott appealed to the governor, thirty-three men and women who had remained on their farms at Napenack (Napanoch) near Wawarsing petitioned as "Faithfull Subjects of the United States" for a stronger guard along their frontier, complaining that from the Lurenkill to Wawarsing there were only thirty-four militiamen, scarcely enough for protection, and keeping even them under arms threatened the harvest.[13]

On July 19, Brigadier Ten Broeck forwarded a letter to the governor from Vrooman at Schoharie warning of a large party of raiders coming up the Delaware's West Branch. They were rumoured to have made "a wide Road," perhaps to convey field pieces. Vrooman asked for reinforcements, but the harvest had just begun, and Ten Broeck had difficulty turning out a body of militia, so he pled for Continentals.[14]

All was relatively quiet in the upper Delaware area until July 30, when John Snow, the deserter from the 2nd New York Continental Line, was captured at Packatackan (Pakatakan) by Lieutenant Frederick Westbrook, 4UCM. Snow was suspected of having participated in the Lackawack raid, and also of being an armourer for Major Butler. When taken, he had a mare belonging to the Widow Cole, the tavern mistress at Lackawack, which was evidence of his guilt. Colonel Cantine warned that Snow was "a Daring Villian and Will Stick at Nothing to make his Escape." Snow said that Butler was at Oquaga and would attack Schoharie or Fort Stanwix, and had sent the Esopus Indian Ben Shanks to Pepacton and Pakataken to get all the Tories to join him.[15]

When John Burch came home to Pepacton from Albany, he heard that Major Butler and the allied Indians were in need of provisions. He sent a message that he would bring a supply of his own cattle and what he could collect from his neighbours, and Butler sent Lieutenant MacQuin [George McGinnis, 6NID] and two Native chiefs to assist. In early August, Burch took 136 cattle to Oquaga, along with forty local men he had persuaded to join Butler's Rangers. Recruit Joel Austin recalled the number as 110 cattle, twenty-nine of Burch's own and the balance his neighbours', and the number of men in the party between fifty and sixty. Whatever the actual numbers, this was a significant effort.[16]

Colonel Cantine reported the dispositions of some four hundred Ulster and Orange county militiamen stationed at Peenpack, Minisink, Lurenkill, Great and Little Shandaken, and at Hunk, where he had his headquarters. His report included the incredible tale of George Anderson and Jacob Ousterhout, who had been captured at Lackawack and led away by the Mohawk warrior who had commanded the raid. They were about twenty miles from Niagara when Ousterhout collapsed. Anderson overheard a plan to kill the invalid the next day and take his scalp, so he told Jacob in hopes of spiriting him up, but the fellow was done in. As was customary,

Anderson was laid between two young warriors that night, while the war captain and women lay on the other side of the fire. Anderson had managed to hide an axe, and, in the depth of the night, he took it up and killed the two youngsters, and stepped around the fire towards the captain, who started awake, but too late. The women escaped during the fracas. Exhausted or not, Ousterhout and Anderson made it to Hunk after nineteen days of trekking.[17]

Pepacton

On August 12, Colonel Cantine, who was acting as Ulster County's militia brigadier, sent a detachment from 2UCM under Captains Henry Van Keuren and Leonard D. Nicoll to Pepacton. Their orders read, in part:

> You will proceed to Papaconck and Down the River Delaware as far as where the Middaghs live; you will apprehend; all those upon said River who have taken an active part against the United States of America, especially those who have committed hostilities against the Western frontiers, and treat them as Enemies (tho with humanity), not distressing the Women and Children by taking their apperel or means of subsistance; you will be exceeding Careful not to hurt our friends (if any there be) and make

An example of an Eastern Woodlands' knife.

diligent inquiry who are our friends and who our enemies; you will act against John Middagh, Stephen Middagh, Hendrick Bush, Junr., and Nathan Parks, and all others who have lately committed hostilities at Lagewack, or any other parts of the frontiers, as open enemies; our friends you will give all the assistance you can in bringing them of with their effects, if they chuse to come.... George Barnhart you will apprehend and bring down and all others by whom goods [were] robbed from the inhabitants, our friends, being found.[18]

On August 14, Lieutenant-Colonel Newkirk reported to Colonel Cantine about a patrol that had inadvertently turned into a joint operation. The former had sent Mr. Tylar and thirty-seven Ulster militiamen to Cochecton. En route they fell in with a company of Continentals from Fort Penn, supported by Jersey and Pennsylvania militia on the same mission; in all, they totalled 230 men. Tylar was posted in the van of the combined force. He stopped a fellow who said there was no enemy near, but after another two miles, spotted a war party approaching. He had his men hide to allow the Natives to pass, on the supposition that the warriors would confront the main body and recoil onto an ambush he set behind them; however, the Natives' rearguard tripped his trap and opened fire. Some of Tylar's men retreated upslope and discovered a Native party above them, and diverted downhill to the river. Meanwhile, the rest of Tylar's men, who had remained in ambush, opened fire on their pursuers and dropped some. Two prisoners were taken, who said that the first party of thirty Natives and five whites was destined for Minisink, and that a second party was on its way, numbering one hundred, and Captain Butler would follow with his army. Tylar and a Pennsylvania captain advanced a mile farther, killed an Indian, and returned with his plunder. In total, the Whigs had taken three whites prisoner, killed one Native, and wounded four.[19]

By August 19, Cantine reported to Governor Clinton that Van Keuren and Nicoll had returned from Pepacton, bringing three well-affected families to safety. They took five Tory prisoners, thirteen horses (including George Anderson's mare, which had been stolen at Lackawack), and some cows. They heard that Major Butler's people were in great need of grain, and had asked the Pepacton farmers to thresh theirs and send it along. The day before their patrol arrived, John Burch, the Middagh brothers, and Henry Bush had gone off with grain to Oquaga. The patrol destroyed Burch's remaining crop.

The fate of George Anderson's mare became an issue. He had asked Van Keuren and Nicoll to look for the animal, but having found it, they put it up for sale. Anderson appealed to Governor Clinton, who ordered the two captains to return the horse to its owner;[20] however, the pair ignored his instruction, sold the mare, and pocketed the proceeds. Cantine observed that the officers had plunder in view, more than the good of their country. Indeed, the practice of plundering had become prevalent among the troops guarding the frontiers. Rarely were the troops of either side in uniform, so identifying friend from foe was very difficult, as a coming tale will reveal.

On the 19th, Cantine advised Clinton that there were only a few friends left at Pakatakan willing to provide information. The governor answered that it would be best to remove the grain and all kinds of provisions from both East Branch settlements, and, if that were not possible, to destroy it rather than have it fall into the enemy's hands. Cantine wrote back that it was impossible to remove the grain at Pepacton, and only with great difficulty from Pakatakan, as the rough road would not allow the use of teams.[21]

Shortly after daybreak on August 20, a war party of twenty Natives and a Tory named McDonald struck the Brookses' home at Peenpack, taking eleven prisoners and wounding a man who attempted to escape through a window. The house was thoroughly plundered and set afire, and the prisoners were strictly examined about the strength of the frontier guards and their ammunition supply. After threatening to destroy the whole settlement, the raiders stripped and released several prisoners. The wounded man's wife was able to return to the house and douse the flames, then made her way to the nearest guard post to give the alarm. A party was sent in pursuit, and came across the murdered and scalped corpse of the wounded man. The war party had taken a girl of about fifteen, two younger boys, and two little girls, five and three.[22]

Pakatakan

Cantine heard from Great Shandaken that the remaining few friends to the United States at Pakatakan had fled, leaving most of their effects behind. A girl of eighteen recalled that the women sat up all night, repairing clothes and stockings for the children by the light of "blazing wheat stacks" that were being torched to prevent the Tories and Natives from having them. Now the refugees asked for an escort to guard them while they went back to recover their goods. Cantine supplied a detachment with additional orders to seize any Tories they came across.[23]

So, on the morning of August 26, the refugees and their guard marched up the East Branch valley to Pakatakan, where they collected a few others who chose to leave. When the refugees had assembled all their goods, they left with the guard, but Harmanus Dumond and his neighbor John Burrows remained behind to gather up some last few items before departing.

The guard's convoy of women and children had just arrived at Great Shandaken when Peter Hendricks came rushing in with the news that two hundred Tories had raided Pakatakan, shot Harmanus Dumond "through the Belly," and taken away what cattle was left and the chattels of those residents who had not left.

This latest irruption was not quite as Hendricks reported.[24] As it transpired, a 200-man detachment from Schoharie had arrived in Pakatakan and passed themselves off as Tories in order to lure the inhabitants into revealing their support for the Crown and gain intelligence of loyalist activities. In the process, Harmanus Dumond was gut-shot and, as he lay dying, his personal effects were looted.

A distressed Colonel Cantine later reported, "Dumon was & has Been the Chief man we Depended on for Intelligence from that Quarter." Further, the Schoharie party plundered all the clothing of two staunch Whig families.[25] This little tragedy starkly illustrates the hazards of frontier life in a civil war.

Two Continental units had been posted to Schoharie on August 1 — Colonel William Butler's 4th Pennsylvania, and the residue of Daniel Morgan's disbanded rifle battalion under Captain-Commandant Thomas Posey. As soon as he arrived, Butler took action against the Tory threat, which included killing Butler's Rangers' captain, Charles Smith. Over the next several weeks, Butler's Continentals conducted operations that yielded a considerable amount of plunder, including a quantity of livestock, which Butler viewed as the troops' property to be disposed of as they saw fit, as they had suffered great fatigue "in bringing off those cattle out of the Jaws of a Savage Enemy." Brigadier Stark agreed, but New York authorities did not, and Albany County's committee of sequestration was moved to report, "We cannot find that they have taken any cattle or horses immediately out of the hands of the enemy,"[26] implying looting rather than the recovery of Tory plunder.

On August 24, Colonel William Butler ordered Captain Posey and a local militia captain, Alexander Harper, to scout Pakatakan. Butler set the scene by characterizing the settlement as "chiefly inhabited by tories and people who had actually been in arms against the country." Harper was an interesting choice, as he and his brothers were hot-headed, virulent rebels who often preferred action to reason. Two days later, the mixed force of riflemen and militia arrived in the Pakatakan area, where, in Posey's words, they behaved "as being in an enemies Country." They found Simeon Van Waggenen's place occupied solely by women. Harper aggressively questioned Simeon's wife, Catherine. He recollected, "I asked the Woman of the House if she was as Great a Tory as she Us'd to be. She Answer'd she was not a Tory, and if I Did not believe her, I might Enquire of Hermanus Demong who was a Tory"; by this, she probably meant that Dumond could sort Tories from Whigs, but her unclear answer may have led to the sad consequences that followed. Posey asked the women what had become of all the people, and was told that they had been taken down to the settlement. The two men called Catherine Van Waggenen a damned liar.

When a wagon was heard coming along the road, Catherine was asked who drove it. She replied that is was Dumond and Barrow. She recalled that the Schoharie men stopped the wagon and unharnessed the horses, putting Dumond and Barrow on one, then led them away.

In a subsequent investigation, Posey recalled things somewhat differently. He testified that after finishing with the women, his men marched on a half mile and came across two men, one driving a wagon, the other on horseback and with a gun slung across his back. Posey asked the driver where he was going, and was told he was moving his goods "into the Settlement," and that an Esopus scout had taken all the livestock and most of the inhabitants. He then asked if there had been a scouting party from Unadilla lately, or whether Butler or Brant frequently sent scouts. Dumond advised that they had sent parties at different times. Posey asked whether Dumond had assisted the enemy, and was told that "he had Assisted His King in whatever he was able to do, he had given them Beef, Cattle and such Assistance as he cou'd from time to time." Posey then ordered Harper to set three of his men to guard Dumond and Barrow.

Harper recalled events differently still. He testified that their detachment found Dumond with his loaded wagon, followed by Barrow, who was mounted and leading a packhorse. "I came up and Ask'd him his Name. He replied Demong." Then, according to sworn evidence, Harper continued his questioning.

> Harper: "Are you as Good a Man for the King as you Used to be?"
> Dumond: "Yes."
> Harper: "What did you ever do for the King, and how many Cattle Did you give to Brant's party?"

> Dumond: "I gave four Cattle and Supply'd them with all the Provision that lay in my power."
>
> Harper: "Will you supply them with any more?"
>
> Dumond: "I would but the Rebels have Carried them all to Esopus with my family."
>
> Harper: "I think you Look like a Rebel and I believe you are one."
>
> Dumond: "No, by God! I am no Rebel."

Harper asked Barrow how many cattle he had given Brant. Being told "one," he replied, "I believe you are a Churlish fellow for not giving more." Barrow replied that "it was all he had, excepting one Milks Cow."

And what did Catherine Van Waggenen recall in her deposition to Judge Levi Pawling on September 15?

> [A] party of Men who told her they came from Schogary, came to her house and Enquired where all the Men was. She told them they were all gone down to Marbletown by order of Coll. Contine, who had sent a guard for them, and she Expected another guard and then they were all to goe down to Esopus. They answered She Iyed, the Men was all gone to the Indians. She told them they were not, but was gone down with the guard that was come to fetch them. The[y] Insisted that she was a Dam'd Lyar, After a little time a waggon was heard. They askt her who that was with the waggon. She told them it was Hermanus Demun and John Barrow, who was come up in order to fetch some of their goods, that Dumun had moved down with his family the week before. By this time the waggon was at the house. Dumun was stop'd and the Horses taken out of the waggon. Duman and Barrow were put on one of the Horses, and so went away with them.

Not long after she heard two guns fired. About two hours after Dumon came to her house, and told her he was Shot, and that he believ'd he was a dead Man. Duman told her further that the[y] had threatened to carry him to [John] Butler, and that he told them he would Rather die than be carried to Butler; after which he attempted to Make his Escape from them and was Shott in Making the atempt. Some time after two of the sd. party came to the House and seem'd very Sorry that Demon was Shot. After this[,] Deponent though[t] the whole party was gone, there came two of the party and threatened to tomhawk Demon as he lay on his Death Bed, took his Shoes, Buckles and hat away with them. This Deponent further saith that the party took three horses ... the property of her husband, with many other things belonging to her, and further saith that Duman Died some time after.

Captain Posey deposed:

I Pursued with all possible expedition down the Delaware, thinking as those men had demonstrated themselves Enemies to the country by the confession they had made, that they only intended imposing on me with regard to moving into Esopus that perhaps it might be a party of the Enemy which had been there. When I got near the lower end of the Settlement (which was about six miles) I was told the Guard which had the Prisoners in charge had come up without them; upon which I ordered them to be Brought to me & ask'd them where the Prisoners were; they told me they (the Guard) had taken the Horses out of the Waggon, mounted the two Prisoners on a Horse and each of them (the

Guard) riding on the other Horse follow'd me; that after riding some distance the two Prisoners rode off to try to make their escape, upon which they (the Guard) immediately pursued & finding they (the Prisoners) were likely to get off thro' the Woods one of the Guard fired upon them & miss'd: they (the Prisoners) then dismounted one of them making his escape thro' the woods the other kept the road. After pursuing near a mile the one who continued the road was fired upon & Shot, who proved to be Demon; they (the Guard) left him in a House & made their way as Quiet as possible to the Party.

After my excursions down the Delaware in which I Gathered what Stock I possibly cou'd, which amounted to few, being chiefly drove off by the other party, I returned to the House that I had conversed with Women before mentioned in which I found Demon the person who was shot by the Guard. I ask'd him his reason for Running from the Guard; his excuse was that he thought we were some of Brandt's or Butler's men. I asked him how he cou'd think so when I upon meeting him, ask'd him if any of Butler's or Brandt's parties had been in the Neighborhood lately, upon which you reply'd there had & that you had Assisted Brandt & Butler in Beef. I ask'd him if he cou'd deny what he had said to me, upon meeting me first. He said no that he acknowledged he said what I had asserted & said he really had assisted the King. After which I left him & march'd on towards Schohary.[27]

Understandably, the uproar over this affair reverberated for some time, with Posey contending that "there is a number of People throughout the Frontier settlements, which Can Prove Dumond's Carrector to be Exceeding Bad." Although considerable doubt persisted about the behaviour of Posey's detachment, the furor subsided in early October when Governor Clinton wrote to Colonel William Butler, saying that he at no time intended to charge any of his officers with misconduct, but it appeared Harper made "Use of some Deception which might have betrayed a better Man than Dumond into Imprudent Expressions in his Situation."[28]

Meanwhile, Cantine sent a party of thirteen men to destroy any grain left at Pepacton. They returned on September 4 with Thomas Cumming, John Burch's overseer. They had confronted Henry Bush across a river, but he jumped behind a tree and saved himself from seven balls that lodged in the trunk. They also thought they had wounded Burch himself. They returned with a great many sheep, hogs, and cattle, and with deer leather, and had destroyed all the grain for twenty miles down the river, but not the Indian corn, which would have to be addressed later.[29]

Clinton was already angered over Colonel William Butler's troops' indiscriminate plundering of goods and livestock in southern Tryon, so when he wrote to Cantine on September 6, he vented about Ulster and Orange militiamen behaving similarly. "[I]t is contrary to every Idea of Justice & good Policy & [that it] will be productive of much Misschief is certain." Cantine was to prevent such abuses in the future, and to have the past rectified as far as was in his power.

Enclosed with this dispatch was a copy of a letter from two Esopus war captains, Ben Shanks and John Rinepee, which had been sent to Judge Levi Pawling:[30] "Your Old Friends the Esopus Indians had allwase ment to Screen Your part of the Country as much as possible in the Present Unhapy Contest as they had no Particular spite at you [but if] your Rangers Come out any more to hurt the Women & Children they will Revenge it Dredfuly on your Women & Children & will spare none tho they never ment to hurt them."

They further threatened that should the rebels kill any captives, they would burn alive all that they took.[31] Perhaps the Schoharie detachment had been as indiscriminate with the Native people who fell into their path as they had been about plundering the white inhabitants, regardless of their claimed political convictions.

Pepacton's loyalists had built a crude fort down the Delaware's East Branch, on its western shore, sometime in mid-July. This became known as the Tory House, and served as a rendezvous for parties that lifted livestock from the Whigs to send to Oquaga. John Middagh, Henry Bush, and Nathan Park made this place their headquarters, and by September they had become such a nuisance that Governor Clinton offered a cash reward for their capture.

At daybreak of September 5, a war party of Natives and Tories, led by the Esopus War captain Ben Shanks, burned three barns at Lackawack, killed and scalped two men, and took two other men prisoner. Captain William Telford, 2UCM, ordered a pursuit that was led by John Graham of the Hanover precinct's Company of Exempts, who acted as their lieutenant. After advancing some seventeen miles, Graham decided they had got ahead of the raiders. As it was late afternoon, the detachment decided to camp in a place Cantine criticized as "disadvantageous," fit for neither defence nor retreat.

After a half hour, they heard the enemy approaching. An Indian appeared about thirty yards in the van, and he immediately spotted the detachment, as it was so poorly concealed. The Native sank onto his haunches to make himself a smaller target, and one of Graham's men shot at him. The Indians rushed upon the detachment, and received their fire without taking casualties. The Whigs turned to flee, but their only choice was to climb a steep hill. Cantine reasoned that few would have survived if the Natives had pressed. Three men were killed and scalped, Graham amongst them.[32]

When Cantine heard of how few men had been dispatched with Graham, and that they had taken no provisions, he organized a second detachment of fifty-two fit men with five days' supplies. They set off the next morning under Captain Samuel Clark, the commander of an Ulster Independent Company. They had orders to pursue the Natives as far as the Middaghs' Tory House. When they were near, Clark was to send out a reconnaissance party to assess the enemy's strength. At five o'clock in the afternoon of September 8 or 9, Clark's militiamen attacked some thirty-five Natives at Downs Brook, near the Tory House, which was perhaps their camp. The fighting continued until darkness fell. At daybreak, the militiamen discovered the Indians had slipped away, leaving behind four dead warriors. Clark's party suffered two or three killed.[33]

This small action appears to have precipitated an evacuation of the Esopus Natives and their Pepacton Tory allies, as nothing specific is heard of them for the balance of the year. They may have withdrawn to Oquaga, although they were not caught there when Colonel William Butler destroyed that settlement a month later, so it is more likely that they joined the large collection of Natives and Rangers that had assembled at Tioga. Despite their absence, anxiety remained high in and about Ulster County.

When Colonel Cantine corresponded with the governor on September 18, he spoke of the poor response he received from several Ulster and Orange County regiments to his request for detachments. Clinton replied on the 21st, and mentioned a petition from Marbletown asking for a guard. He sought Cantine's recommendations about the number of militiamen necessary to mount an attack on Oquaga, and again offered a reward for the capture of Nathan Parks and the Middaghs.[34]

Sixty-nine-year-old Robert McGinnis arrived at Great Shandaken, and testified that he, his two sons, and four other men had been taken prisoner at the Unadilla River by some Oneidas on the 19th. Due to his age, Robert was released, and returned home. The next day, Joseph Brant arrived at his farm with about two hundred Indians and Tories on their way to Oquaga from German Flatts. Robert saw that the war party had a "very Large Number of Cattle," and some said that they would attack behind Esopus, near Rochester, next. In confirmation, a Cochecton man arrived at Peenpack on September 22 with news that Brant had gone to German Flatts with 450 men, and that Ulster County was his next target. Both informants concurred that Major John Butler had left for Niagara.

There had been considerable discussion back and forth about mounting an expedition against Oquaga. Cantine ruminated that six or seven hundred chosen men would be required. Judge Pawling believed that militiamen could not be relied upon, because they were called out by class, not individually selected; this was another way of saying that Continentals were necessary. Almost as an afterthought, he wrote that Brant had six or seven hundred chosen men.[35]

In reply to Colonel Cantine's complaints about the lack of response from some Orange and Ulster County regiments, Colonel Moses Phillips, 4OCM, explained to the governor that the county's frontier was open for a fifteen-mile gap, which was a common route for Native war parties, and, despite sending a request to Cantine for a detachment, it was local inhabitants who continued to form the guard. Clinton reacted firmly, hammering several nails into Phillips's arguments, reminding him that he had failed to attend a meeting of the two counties' field officers, during which it was determined what number of men would be necessary as guards and where they should be posted. He told Phillips that his refusal to turn out men when requested was totally unacceptable.[36]

Peenpack

On October 7, the day before Colonel William Butler's Schoharie expedition arrived at Oquaga, Brant's force of eighty whites and some Natives had left for Cookoze on the Delaware River. From Cookoze, the war captain launched an attack on the Minisink settlements on October 13. At about eleven o'clock in the morning, his men struck Peenpack, a pretty settlement on the Neversink River that had three forts. They took one blockhouse by storm, but the other two would not yield. A number of women and children were sheltered with nine men in the blockhouse called Fort Gumaer. The commander, Captain Abraham Cuddeback, 2UCM, had the women dress as men to thicken up the appearance of his tiny garrison. In any event, the Natives paid no heed to the blockhouse, and set fire to the settlement's houses and barns. Some shots were fired at a second blockhouse, known as Fort DeWitt. During the raid, six rebels were killed, and six taken prisoner. Philip Swartout Sr., a local committee of safety member, was one of those killed, perhaps by

Anthony Westbrook, one of Brant's most faithful volunteers, who could have been seeking revenge for the confiscation of his property earlier in the year.

The raid had proven quite futile, as it was found that recent rainstorms had swollen the rivers so high that cattle could not be driven across. A report from Easton, Pennsylvania alarmingly numbered Brant's force at 700, and said that Tories were flocking to join him.

Lieutenant-Colonel Newkirk, 2UCM, whose area of responsibility had suffered the attack, warned that all the posts along the frontier to Marbletown could be hit the next morning. In reaction, Colonel Johannes Hardenburgh, 4UCM, ordered seven companies of Lieutenant-Colonel Joseph Hasbrouck's 4OCM to march to Mamakating. Hardenburgh went there the next day to co-operate with Cantine, but found the enemy had withdrawn and dismissed part of the men, leaving the balance to wait for Cantine's return from his pursuit of the raiders. Having suffered yet another attack, Peenpack's inhabitants applied to the governor for the protection of a company of rangers.[37]

Governor Clinton was still unaware of the successful expedition against Unadilla and Oquaga when he wrote to General Washington on October 15. Like many other officials, he had high expectations of the benefits of destroying Oquaga, which were almost immediately proven unrealistic. "I am perswaded unless it can be destroyed & the Enemy thereby oblidged to retire farther Back into the Country that no Force however formidable will be able to protect us ag't their practices. Besides[,] the Enemy by occupying that Post, will soon acquire a very considerable accession in strength & Numbers." Although he was now aware of Colonel Butler's success, in a second letter he made several suggestions regarding how and from where an expedition should be conducted, likely to illustrate that he and his officers had spent considerable time discussing the issue.[38]

Despite William Butler's successful foray into Indian Territory, and the several forecasts regarding the great effect the destruction of Oquaga would have upon the Natives and Tories, major steps were being taken to protect Orange and Ulster counties in reaction to reports from Colonel Hartley, and from James Dean at the Oneida town of Kanowalohale. With the large collection of warriors and Rangers at Chemung, Governor Clinton had reason to expect "some Capital Stroke ag't our Frontier." The 2NY was on the march from Peekskill to Rochester, and the governor thought that all of his brother James's New York brigade would follow, except the 1NY, which was on the march to Fort Stanwix. The governor called out "into actual Service ... a greater Proportion of the Militia" from Orange and Ulster counties. He believed Minisink was in particular danger, and directed Cantine to give that area his particular attention.[39]

As a result of an examination of two Continental soldiers who had become separated from Colonel William Butler's expedition, three companies were dispatched from Schoharie to march to Cookoze and then on to Minisink. Clearly, reinforcements were being rushed from many points.[40]

On October 27, an alarm was raised by militia major Adrian Wynkoop, who had come from Rochester with intelligence about a large body of the enemy under Brant, who was at Cochecton waiting for a reinforcement of Senecas. Clinton requested that Colonel Van Cortlandt march the 2NY to Rochester, where the inhabitants would supply them with stockings and shoes.[41]

In the midst of all this anxiety and rushed preparation, the governor received information from officials in Kingston that detachments of Colonel Johannes Snyder's 1UCM were inadequately supplied with cartridges, despite having made the proper applications; this was particularly so with those men assigned to Shandaken, who had threatened to abandon their posts if the enemy appeared. Clinton issued an immediate order to supply Snyder's troops, and, after a quick investigation, discovered that certain officers had shown "scandalous Neglect," and advised they would be brought to "a most severe account."[42]

On November 13, Brigadier Ten Broeck reported to the governor about a sizeable British expedition of Regulars, Natives, and Tories on Lake Champlain that had destroyed farms and mills on the lake and the lower Otter Creek settlements in Vermont. A second tragic event was a devastating attack by Natives, Tories, and some Regulars on Cherry Valley, despite inclement campaigning weather.[43]

Colonel Van Cortlandt, 2NY, reported to the governor from Rochester on November 15 that he had visited Minisink with Colonel Cantine. He wrote of various troop postings, including the assignment of Pulaski's newly raised legion of lancers, dragoons, and light infantry, which he thought would allow for the militia's dismissal. He commented, "I am not apprehensive of the Enemy attempting any thing further this Season." In this he was correct, for the 1778 campaign had ended in Orange and Ulster Counties.

Future Actions

After the many disasters that had befallen New York, Pennsylvania, and now Vermont, Governor Clinton wrote to John Jay, one of New York's members of the Continental Congress, who was shortly to become president. Clinton gave his opinion on future actions, a foretaste of the Sullivan-Clinton expedition of 1779. "It is of the utmost Importance that some more effectual Measures than have hitherto been pursued be adopted for the Defence of the Frontiers & I am perswaded this can only be effected by Offensive Opperations, thereby carrying the War into the Enemy's Country."[44]

The Natives' Last Message of 1778

The final threat of the campaign was sent to Cantine when four chiefs from Indian Territory's lower region wrote a strongly worded warning to him, dated December 13.

> It is the Desire of the Seneca Cheifs and other Indians that you will Not in the Least trouble or moliest those People on the Delaware above Econack

[Equinunk?]. The Reason of this your Rables came to Oughquago when we Indians where gone from our place, and you Burned our Houses, which makes us and our Brothers the Seneca Indians angrey, so that we Destoryed men, women, and Children at Chervalle [Cherry Valley]. It is, therefore, the Desier of us Indians that those people Living about Shackaken are our Brothers [Esopus Indians]; we, therefore, Desire that you will Let our brothers live in peace, least you be worst delt with, then your Nighbrous the Ceryvalle People was. You may think it's a Hard winter will hinder us from Coming to you. I have Big Shouse [snowshoes] and can come in a few day to your place.... I will set my face again you, for if you hurt my people I shall fell the Strock for the Six Nations.[45]

Chapter Five

Back in the Mohawk Region

"A shocking sight ... of savage and brutal barbarity"

Incipient Mutiny

Sir John Johnson wrote to his favourite brother-in-law, Daniel Claus, from Quebec on July 2, reporting the confidential details of a conversation he had had with General Haldimand in the presence of Governor Carleton. Johnson had informed Haldimand that his regiment had hopes of being sent to New York City, and when that failed to happen, great uneasiness developed throughout the ranks. As an alternative, they wished "to be employed on the frontiers of the Province, where they cou'd be of most service, and cou'd hear from their distressed families, and send them some relief." The new governor asked Johnson whether he was acquainted with Deer Island and Lake Ontario, and Sir John answered that he had been on that route the previous year. Haldimand said that Oswego "was too distant to be supported from this Country, especially in the Winter, that he therefore thought Cataraughqua wou'd answer the end intended by the Indians." Johnson offered the opinion that Cataraqui would serve only those Natives on that side of the lake, but Haldimand held the opinion that "it would answer us better than any other Post and desired I wou'd consider of it."

Haldimand thought that Claus was best-acquainted with the Six Nations, so he would send him to their country to manage that department. Johnson agreed that his brother-in-law was "the fittest person and one the Indians approved of most." Carleton was mum during the conversation about the Natives' business, "whatever his thoughts might have been."

Sir John hoped that he and Claus could be posted together, or at least near to each other. If Claus could think of a plan that would achieve that, Haldimand requested that he send it soon. Johnson confessed to Claus that he could "scarcely think of taking my family to" Cataraqui, and added a postscript, "Remember me to Joseph [Brant] who I am told is arrived at Montreal; the General speaks highly of him."[1]

Later in the month, the unrest within the Royal Yorkers bubbled over into an organized protest bordering on mutiny. The rankers in five companies signed a protest over not being posted to New York City. In two of the companies, the men signed the document in a circle, which prevented anyone from being singled out as a ringleader. Colonel Watson Powell, who commanded Montreal district, was informed on July 22 by a Captain McDonell that his detachment had refused, to a man, to be sent to Oswegatchie. Sensibly, Powell spoke to the men, and discovered their objection was being separated from the rest of the battalion. In some manner he assuaged their concerns, and they returned to their duty. Nothing more came of this dangerous incident.[2]

Native Disgust

While the attack on Wyoming had been a marked success — similar to the mauling of the Tryon militia at Oriskany — both campaigns had a disturbing feature in common. After Oriskany, St. Leger had refused to allow the Natives and loyalists to reinforce their victory by penetrating the dispirited Mohawk Valley and subduing resistance there. At

Wyoming, John Butler had persuaded the Native leadership to allow clemency for the survivors in return for them giving their paroles not to serve again. Yet within weeks, the rebels began reoccupying and refortifying the valley, and officers whose parole had been accepted were back in service. The Iroquois were thoroughly disgusted.[3]

When Major Butler arrived at Canadesaga with the Senecas, he had with him several Ranger invalids, and a few loyalist families. He was immediately confronted by a serious problem. Despite Carleton's promises of the previous year, the British army had not taken post at Oswego while the Natives were absent in Pennsylvania; the rebels had taken advantage of this, and burned the handful of small buildings remaining there, as well as a quantity of ammunition and other public stores. The Senecas were deeply angered; quite clearly, the occupation of Deer Island was not an acceptable substitute. They had carried the war to the rebels and fulfilled their engagements, but the British had not, and their country continued to be unprotected. Before continuing on to Niagara, Butler assigned Indian Department captain John Johnston to stay in the village and attempt to mollify the Senecas, and encourage them to keep parties on the frontiers.[4]

Johnson Clan

On July 16, before word of Butler's major success in the Wyoming Valley had been received in lower Quebec, Sir John Johnson wrote to Daniel Claus, fully revealing the internecine conflict that existed among the loyalist leadership.

> The General [Haldimand] frequently expresses great apprehension of the rebels gaining over the Indians, to prevent which he often wishes you would go and reside in the midst of them, without interfering with Butler, as he does not wish to counteract anything General Carleton has done, especially while he is on the spot, being upon a very friendly footing with him.

I have given him a very plain and honest account of Butler and his son, not concealing a single circumstance of his whole conduct that has come to my knowledge, and I think I can plainly discover that a change in his opinion of this great man's merit and services will soon take place, if not already the case.

He asked me yesterday what he would be about all this time, that he thought he would have struck a blow ere now. I told him I thought I might venture to assure him that was not his intention, and that I believed he would remain where he was, or thereabouts, till he could join the army from York with safety, or till it would be too late to do anything.

He told me the other day that young Butler was a pretty genteel man. I took the opportunity to give my opinion of him very freely, since which he has asked what he was doing here. I told him he was waiting his orders and perhaps to accomplish something more for himself and his father. He only shrugged up his shoulders. From all I can judge, I think you may carry out any point in reason, but I think it best to be entirely silent upon the subject until Sir Guy's departure which will be next week, I believe.[5]

Of course, Johnson's opinion that Butler did not intend to "strike a blow" before joining the army from New York City was quite true, but that decision had been taken out of his hands by the Iroquois and Delawares, and the result had been a great victory.

Daniel Claus responded four days later, addressing Haldimand's suggestion that he take a post in Indian Territory. While Claus's observations had much truth, his introverted sentiments did him no credit.

I am much obliged to you for the contents of yours by last post, and thereby perceive (as I had expected) that Mr Butler's Patron, before leaving Canada, has endeavoured to influence his successor as much as in his power in favour of his Minion; but I apprehend the latter will prove no great credit to his recommendations, and perhaps ere long make him regret of his having countenanced him at all.

As to my residing empty handed or properly fixed and established in the Six Nation's country would appear mean and despicable in the eyes of the Indians and do more hurt than good, besides acknowledging Butler my superior in every respect. As long as we are able to maintain the command of the lakes and Upper Posts there is no fear of losing the interests of the 6 Nations and surrounding Indians, and Joseph and Mary Brant will out do fifty Butlers in managing and keeping them firm with proper directions from a Governor or Superintendent under the influence of the Commanding Officer at Niagara, and a vast deal of money and provisions thereby saved to the Crown for all the needless sums have hitherto expended by Butler upon the Indians, have rather injured the King's interest by giving the Indians a precedent of asking and expecting presents without doing any service for them which will make any Superintendent hereafter odious to them unless he follows Mr Butler's steps in this respect.[6]

This ridiculous posturing by the Johnson clan served no real purpose other than to vent their spleens. Butler was making a great reputation for himself and his Rangers among other loyalists. William Knox, Germain's undersecretary, heard the following from a member of New York City's Royal council: "Butler, you'l hear, is going on very rapidly on the frontiers; he strickes more terror and occasions more distress to the rebels than all your other military operations put together; if that man had a few thousand men with him th[at] is now here adoing nothing, he wou'd give a mortel blow to the Rebellion in a very short time."[7]

Brant Offended

Brant wrote to his friend Persafor Carr regarding news he had received that a fellow named Smith, who lived near Carr, had corn to spare. Smith had already sent five skipples, but Brant needed all that could be spared. He asked Carr to send one or two of his men, especially a fellow named Elias. He also needed all the firearms that

Captain Joseph Brant wearing one of his silver officer's gorgets. Painted by Gilbert Stuart, 1786.

Carr could spare. He mentioned having heard that the Cherry Valley people were very bold, and that they had called his men wild geese. Indeed, Captain Robert McKean of Cherry Valley had left a written challenge on an Indian trail saying that he would turn Brant into a goose, which the Mohawk viewed as a great insult.[8]

Continentals on the March

By July 11, the rebels' Unadilla expedition was stalled. Ten Broeck was unsure whether Willett was going to command, and a date for setting out had not been chosen. The relief detachments from his brigade had not arrived to replace the first tour in the Schoharie and Mohawk Valleys, and there was widespread dissatisfaction at men being called up for service at harvest time. How the relief would be accomplished was of great concern.[9] A partial answer came on July 18, when Washington ordered Colonel William Butler, his 4th Pennsylvania Continental regiment, and part of Morgan's Rifle corps to march to Wawarsing in Ulster County. From there, they could be called to Albany or westward, as exigencies would dictate.[10]

Springfield and Andrewstown Attacked

Brant's volunteers struck the Lake Otsego settlements on July 18. This was a raid to obtain provisions, not to kill rebels, although the farms were razed to the ground to remove them from production. The raiders were at Springfield about 11 in the morning, rounded up the inhabitants, herded the women and children into one house, led off the livestock, loaded provisions onto horses, and burned the rest of the buildings, wagons, farm implements, and haycocks in the fields.

When five gun discharges were heard at Cherry Valley, the garrison commander, Lieutenant-Colonel Jacob Ford, 9ACM, ordered out two patrols to discover the cause. Seventeen more discharges were counted, and Ford had an alarm gun fired. A report came in that Springfield was in flames. As Ford had so few troops, he decided to send no more men out, and arranged those he did have "in the best manner possible" for defence.

Brant's war party moved on to Andrewstown, where they came across four men and three women who had earlier abandoned their farms. They had returned to harvest hay, and made preparations to stay a few days. The men were at work just after breakfast when a party of Natives and several Tories suddenly appeared. A seventeen-year-old, who had sworn never to be taken alive, was near his house, rushed inside, and was taking a musket down from its pegs when he was shot through a window. His father was blocked at the door and ordered to catch a horse in a nearby field, with a promise that he would be spared if he were successful; as he climbed a fence, however, he was gunned down. Three men who were working at a distance from these events managed to escape to Fort Herkimer. The women, who had been baking bread, were told by the party to surrender some of their clothing, but thereafter were ignored and told to make their way to Fort Herkimer.[11]

Having rounded up about two hundred horses and cattle, Brant's party left with fourteen male prisoners, although they soon released two old men. In the evening, Ford sent out a thirty-man scout that returned that night and reported that Springfield was in ashes. Ford had sent an express to Colonel Jacob Klock, and expected reinforcements to arrive on the 19th. His report continued,

> I am informed that there is a small Company of Rangers on their way to us. I have about 80 men fit for Duty here besides some of the inhabitants. I have not time to make a proper return of the Garrison at this time. The People here are in the greatest Distress. There is Piquets made round the meeting house and all the women and Children and there Houshold Effects are Crouded into that place, for protection, and they are so thick, it seems to me that they must

> Die there. And there are so few men here that it is not in our power to protect them, Except they are together and the inhabitants have determined that they must Carry away there Families Directly, Except there Can be men sent them, for they are every moment Exposed; and for my part I must fully agree with them for the Distressed Circumstances here I can not give you an Idea of[.] The Post is all open to the Enemy and nothing to hinder their Coming; and so few men here is only a Bait for them; and I think if this post is Evacuated that the Mohawk River will not stay so, that I Conceive the Supporting of this post is of great Consequence to the Northern inhabitants; at least there should be four or five hundred men here and a Good Commandant to be Steady here, and a Number of Continental Troops with the Militia.... The Enemy that have done this mischief have taken another Route where they was not Expected by the inhabitants that was acquainted with the Country. It must be that they Came round back of the Lake were they have had a great way to travel, and where we have had no Scouts....

Brant's war party travelled down the Susquehanna to Tunnicliff's place, and left there the next day.[12] Tunnicliff and Persafor Carr had come to America on the same vessel, and had settled in the newly opened settlement area that had resulted from the Treaty of Fort Stanwix in 1768. Both men chose to assist Brant as soon as he set his headquarters at Oquago in 1776.[13]

When Colonel Klock made his report, he noted:

> As soon as the News came, I ordered imediately the Militia to march to stop the progress of the Enemy. The same Instant I received a Letter from Coll. Peter Bellinger of the German Flats, that the Enemy

was burning Houses within four Miles of the Flats praying for Assistance. I did order up five companies of the Palatine and Cona Johary Battalion; The rest I marched straight to Andrewtown; ordering Coll. Bellinger to join me in order to intercept if possible the Enemy. But on my March thiter I learnt that the Enemy was gone; and nothing was left.... I got information, that still a strong party of the Enemy was left to do mishief. As soon as the Flats Militia was on the March in the woods, the Enemy fell out at the Flats took two prisoners and killed one Man. Several People, who have been prisoners and did Escape, affirm, that Brandt was the Comander, and that his party consists of about five hundred. So much is certain, that his Number encreaseth dayly; many very lately did run off moved by Disaffection; others join him moved by fear, and severall are forced to tacke up Arms against us, or to swear Allegiance to the King of Britain. We are informed and Brandt boasted openly, that he will be joined at Unatelly [Unadilla,] by Buttler, and that within eight Days he will return and lay the whole County waste.

Committeeman John Franks and several others from German Flatts went in pursuit, first stopping to bury the dead at Andrewstown, then, guided by a half-dozen friendly Natives, followed Brant's party as far as Young's settlement at the Little Lakes. They may have discovered that the war party was too far in advance, or decided that discretion was the better part of valour, as they stopped to plunder and burn the farms of two known Tories — that of the settlement's founder, Adam Young, who may have been with Brant's party, and of his neighbour.[14]

Klock said that reports of the dreadful sights of Springfield and Andrewstown put the inhabitants into the greatest consternation. As they saw no prospect of speedy assistance, they could speak "of nothing but flying off" — and harvest time was at hand. It was with the greatest difficulty that men could be persuaded to serve for more than a few days. Then came the colonel's emotional appeal to Governor Clinton: "Your Excellency, the comon father of the good People of this State, upon whose fatherly Exertions the People of this County relieth, and which keepeth the many poor, the numerous widows and the fatherless still in hopes, will, we fervently pray, grant us such speedy relief, as your Ex'llcy in your wisdom shall see meet; & In case it should be an impossibility; to afford us any Assistance with Batteaus, to bring off wifes and Childern, that they might not be a prey to a cruel Enemy."[15]

Just two days before Klock composed his report, General Schuyler sent an equally distressing letter to the governor. He had heard from the Oriska Oneidas about the destruction of "Anderson's purchase [Andrewstown] and Springfield," and that the enemy's next target would be German Flatts. After that, they would attack Canajoharie and its adjacent villages. Schuyler emoted, "It is much to be Lamented that the finest Grain County In this State is on the point of being Entirely ruined for want of a body of Continental troops. If any are to be sent, the Greatest dispatch should be used and then, perhaps, they may still come in time to save part of the Settlements and numerous fine crops of wheat."[16]

Colonel Vrooman, at Schoharie, wrote to Brigadier Ten Broeck about warnings he had received from a Frenchman, who had heard from an Oquaga Indian of a likely attack on the valley. Supposedly, the enemy was cutting a wide road through the woods, perhaps to bring fieldpieces, and he pled for assistance. Ten Broeck wrote to Clinton, enclosing a copy of Vrooman's letter. He was having great difficulty in getting the militia to turn out, as they were just beginning to bring in their harvest, and he yearned for a body of Continental troops.[17]

Undoubtedly, Clinton felt bombarded, as even before Klock's appeal reached his desk, he replied to Schuyler, "I have long feared that this woud be the Fate of our Frontier Settlements." He had advised General Gates of his concerns, and had attempted to turn out a respectable force of militia, "and had my Orders for that Purpose been executed, I flatter myself that the present as well as the former Depredations committed by the Tories & Savages might have been prevented." He did have some good news to impart. As soon as the Grand Army arrived at the Hudson River, Gates issued an order for a detachment of Continentals under Lieutenant-Colonel William Butler to march to Wawarsing in Ulster County, where he was to halt, awaiting further orders. When Clinton sent Gates an express with the news of the attacks on the Otsego Lake communities and the threat to German Flatts, the general issued an order for William Butler to continue on to the Schoharie Valley. Heartening though this news was, Clinton recognized that this assistance would scarcely be adequate, and added that "Genl. Gates is in no ways Apprehensive of Danger to the Northward or Westward of Albany," and the general put his faith in the arrival of large bodies of Massachusetts militia to resolve the issue. The governor confessed, "Indeed, Sir, we have no hope left but in the Exertions of the Militia" of Albany and Tryon Counties.[18]

A decision was made on July 20 about the quota of men from each regiment in the Albany brigade that would be sent to Schoharie and Cherry Valley. Colonel Knickerbacker, 14ACM, was to command the 415 men ordered for Schoharie; another 373 were for Cherry Valley. All of this was rather academic, as Ten Broeck had ordered the Schenectady regiment to Schoharie when he received Klock's and Ford's reports. He had eighty of his brigade already posted there, over and above Vrooman's regiment, and one-quarter of the Half Moon regiment was en route to Cherry Valley. Colonel Livingston had been posted at Johnstown with fifty men, and when he tried to get them to march to Cherry Valley, they had refused, claiming it was too close to the time of their relief. Then they deserted and left for home. Ten Broeck had had no success in assembling a relief for the first tour already in Tryon County. Exclusive of the Schenectady regiment, he had ordered 698 to turn out, but only 220 responded.

None of the expected Massachusetts militiamen from Hampshire County had arrived in Albany, and the Berkshire militia had returned

Cherry Valley and environs. The proximity to Fort Herkimer, Canajoharie, Cobleskill, and Schoharie is obvious. Detail from John Montresor, Paris, 1777.

home, except for thirty men. Bedel's New Hampshire regiment had only fifty men in the city. He was in a desperate situation.[19]

Five principal men from the German Flatts district wrote to Governor Clinton on July 22, complaining that, after the destruction of Springfield and Andrewstown, their communities were continually threatened by scalping parties, and that Brant had told the two old men he released that, once he joined Butler, German Flatts would be attacked in about eight days. The principal men had written to General Stark for assistance, and hoped the governor would support their plea, adding they had not had time to get in their harvest. "Last

Year, at the time of the siege of Ft Schuyler [Stanwix], we could get no assistance till too late, by which means we lost most part of our harvest, and the remainder was almost spoil'd.... [W]ithout the desired Reinforcement, we are under apprehensions, that this Harvest, will prove a great deal worse."[20]

The long-awaited arrival of Continental troops at Cherry Valley occurred on July 24, when elements of Colonel Ichabod Alden's 7th Massachusetts regiment arrived. Captain Benjamin Warren wrote in his diary, "About four o'clock arrived at the garrison, which was a meeting-house picketted in, with a large number of distressed inhabitants crowded in, men, women, and children: drew some rum before the men and placed them in their several quarters. The inhabitants received us with the greatest tokens of joy and respect, and it was like a general jail delivery. They began to take the fresh air and move into the nearest houses from their six weeks' confinement in that place."[21]

Local militia lieutenant-colonel Samuel Clyde had a rather different memory of these events. He wrote, "Col. Alden arrived with the continental troops, who immediately ordered us out of the garrison which we had made ourselves. He would not allow us the liberty to keep one chest in it, saying that he would protect us. Few of us having wagons to hide our effects away, were obliged to carry them back to our houses again." Clyde's comments suggest that much of the thrill of seeing the Massachusetts men subsided rather quickly.[22]

The 4th Pennsylvania and the residue of the 2nd Rifle corps arrived in Albany on July 27. Stark reported to Washington that they had great need of clothing, and would be unfit for scouting without a new issue. Nonetheless, he would send them immediately to the frontiers to "protect the affrighted inhabitants, whose fears are but too well grounded."[23]

Colonel William Butler, who commanded the 4PA and the combined detachment, was the brother of Richard, who had been second-in-command of Morgan's Rifles, so a warm relationship obtained between the two units. The Butler brothers had been in the fur trade in the Ohio country before the war, and had a working knowledge of many Native peoples. Washington told Stark that he had great confidence in Butler to command frontier troops, and in his personal capabilities as a woodsman. He was an enterprising officer, well-acquainted with the Native mode of warfare.

Morgan's 2nd Rifle corps had been disbanded, and the two companies sent north were the remnants. Captain Thomas Posey was the commandant, and his company commanders were Captains James Parr and Gabriel Long. Parr's company was predominantly composed of Pennsylvanians, and Long's, of Virginians.

A strength return taken the next day showed the 4PA at 131 all ranks, with 128 fit and present for duty. Long's company returned fifty-four, and Parr's, fifty-five, for a total of 109. Strangely, the riflemen were reported to need more shirts, shoes, and overalls than the total strength of their corps. They were also woefully short of blankets, knapsacks, and canteens. Apparently, the 4PA was in similar straits. Most of the riflemen had repairs made to their rifles at Albany, and were ready to march by July 30. About sixty riflemen set off that day, with a brass fieldpiece and an iron three-pdr, although without any shot. This vanguard arrived in Schoharie the next day, and Colonel Butler followed with the rest of the force over the next few days. As Butler thought the Middle Fort was the most likely target for an attack, he set up his headquarters there, and had the two guns mounted. Major Jost Becker of the local militia reported that one of his scouts had recently been at Harpersfield, and had been driven off by the enemy, who were constantly skulking about.

The great advantage of Continentals over militiamen was their total focus on military duties. They had no distractions, like nearby farms and families. Whether they were content with their lot in the service or not, all of their efforts could be concentrated on being soldiers. Washington's instruction to Colonel Butler was to take immediate offensive against the Indians and Tories, but when Stark posted Colonel Alden's regiment to Cherry Valley, a question of seniority of command arose, which — fortunately for the rebel cause — never became an issue.[24]

British Fortify Deer (Carleton) Island

By July 28, three companies of the 47th Regiment under Captain Aubrey, two companies of the Royal Yorkers, and twenty-eight artificers were at Deer Island, building a fort and shipyard there. The yard was being relocated from Oswegatchie, so that it would be closer to Lake Ontario. As noted above, Governor Haldimand had originally selected Cataraqui, the former site of a French fort and yard; when the detachment boated upriver, however, it stopped at Deer Island, and naval Lieutenant John Schank surveyed the possibilities there. He was persuaded that the island was a better location, and sent a message to Haldimand with an explanation of the island's benefits. The governor returned his approval.

Presumably, the Regulars would garrison the site and form construction parties to saw planks and make shingles and mortar, and the Provincials would cut and draw timber, clear the landward side, and patrol the island and mainland with the Natives. Two extremely competent junior officers had leading roles. Engineering lieutenant William Twiss would execute the plans for the fortification, and Schank would design the docking installations for the Provincial Marine.[25]

The fort was located on a sixty-foot-high bluff, overlooking both harbours and the storehouses below. To the north and north-east, works were built, with three gun bastions dominating the island's interior, and gun positions were constructed atop the bluff to protect the harbour. The fort was at such an elevation that enemy bombardment by small naval ordnance would be ineffective. At some point during the construction, the island was renamed Carleton Island, and the fort, Fort Haldimand.

Governor Carleton Departs

On July 30, Guy Carleton sailed from Quebec City, leaving Haldimand free to determine future strategy. In contrast to his predecessor, the new governor pursued an aggressive style of defence that, if it had been applied in 1775, might very well have saved Canada from invasion. Home and frontier defences were to be improved, and all of the governor's resources, in particular his Native allies, would be employed to harass the rebels constantly, create military and political havoc, and establish a wide band of no-man's-land, preventing the rebels from readily mounting a new invasion. Haldimand recognized the importance of the western fur trade to the health of lower Quebec, and realized it could not be protected without the assistance of his western Native allies, to whom he would give serious attention.[26]

Haldimand wrote to Lieutenant-Colonel Bolton on July 31, advising that he was sending the trained engineer Captain Robert Mathews, of the 8th King's Regiment, to Niagara. Mathews would be under Captain Twiss's supervision while erecting additional log houses to accommodate the reinforcements to be sent in the autumn.

Captain Walter Butler was about to return to his regiment, and would take with him Robert Guthrie, a former surgeon's mate at the hospital, and Lieutenant John McDonell (Aberchalder) of the 84th Royal Highland Emigrants, who had requested to join the Rangers. Haldimand noted that McDonell was "well spoken of for his gallantry and activity."[27]

Charles Smith

The Butler's Rangers' recruiter, Captain Charles Smith, wrote to Captain Butler from Harpersfield on July 27, reporting that he had been diligent in his recruiting, but with the harvest at hand, many men had declined to leave their homes before getting their grain cut. Now that this had been accomplished, he expected many to come with him. Some were concerned the rebels would destroy their properties before the British army occupied the area, and Smith had given them the greatest encouragement. Others had heard that the loyalists who had gone off were suffering from want of provisions, and that the Native people took away much of what was collected, but Smith denied this. Smith had been on his way to join Walter, but fell in with Archibald Thompson, one of Brant's volunteers, who had said something that prompted Smith to turn back to collect his men. He would bring men from northern Catskill communities like Beaver Dam and Hellebergh. He confessed that he was "obliged to say more than the truth to encourage them to come out." Schoharie-area loyalists expected Butler to come to their aid, and were making preparations to assist him, although few men were to be had there, as they were generally struck with terror, and were hoping the British shipping would come up the Hudson again.

Smith wrote of the northern army giving the rebels a "sad stroke," which likely referred to John Ross's raid. Smith would join Butler soon, and be painted like a Native when he marched in front of his men, as would some of his recruits. He asked that "his brethren" be given notice of this. Smith wrote a second note to Brant. He mentioned that he had met Thompson, and, as a result, had "made bold to write to the friends of Government in your name," and hoped that Brant would not be offended by this. The magic of Brant's name! Smith gave the message to a Native runner named The Beaver, with a little tobacco for the war captain.[28]

A Tory Murdered

On August 9, a report was sent to Governor Clinton from Albany that a party of riflemen had captured Archibald Thompson "back of Schoharie," and killed "a certain Servos, a noted and zealous defender of the King's bad cause." Colonel Butler's report added some details. He said that when he had arrived in the Schoharie Valley, he had immediately dispatched a subaltern with a scout on a reconnaissance. This comment makes the patrol sound almost random, but that was not the case, as the scouts travelled directly the twenty-five miles to the holdings of the "noted villain" Christopher Servos, who was a supplier for the Tories and the Natives, and demanded his surrender. Servos offered resistance by raising an axe, while his wife Clara pled with the riflemen to spare him. Timothy Murphy, who became an anathema to local Tories, made a ribald jest to the woman, and shot Servos dead. The man could easily have been disarmed and made prisoner, but he was a notorious Tory, and better off dead and out of the way. A search of the premises uncovered Captain Smith's letters to Butler and Brant.

Before the scout returned from Servos's, intelligence was received from General Stark about Captain Smith marching his recruits through the valley. A detachment of Pennsylvania Continentals and Captain Long's riflemen was sent to intercept. They cautiously marched up the Schoharie Kill, and, about fifteen miles above the Upper Fort, they spotted Smith's party on the other side of the creek. Smith was in full Native dress, and Long took a careful bead and shot him through the head. Of Smith's twenty-four recruits, all but one managed to escape. Only one of Long's men was wounded in the fracas. Long collected Smith's scalp, and sent it to Stark as a trophy.

Colonel Butler noted that Smith's letters said that he would bring his recruits to Servos's on the coming Sunday. Further intelligence revealed that another body of the enemy was going to rendezvous there, and divide into two parties — one to attack Cherry Valley, the other to attack Schoharie. The colonel dispatched Major Church, with 120 men, to a canoe landing about five miles downriver from Servos's to lay an ambush to prevent them landing; however, the enemy, likely having heard of Servos's killing, chose not to come. Church's detachment brought back fifty-two horned cattle and forty-nine horses, so their efforts were not unrewarded. Colonel Butler sold the livestock and held on to the funds, awaiting a decision on whether the money should be distributed among his troops, or turned over to the committee of sequestration.

The colonel was unhappy. Since his arrival, these two incidents had been his only offensive actions; however, that would soon change, as his goal was to attack Unadilla and Oquaga. Meanwhile, he could be content that the arrival of his Regular troops had prompted numbers of disaffected people to beg for protection, and take the oath of fidelity to the United States.[29]

The Tunnicliffs

On August 10, Cherry Valley received another warning that Brant intended to mount an attack on the settlement. It was known that the Tunnicliff family was one of Brant's major suppliers, and to disrupt the Mohawk leader, Colonel Alden dispatched Captain William Ballard, with sixty men, to arrest John Tunnicliff and his son William. The troops found a great deal of livestock collected near the main trail, apparently for Brant's men to pick up. Ballard continued on some fifteen miles to Butternut Creek, where several Tory families were located, and his party returned with seventy-three head of cattle, forty sheep, fourteen horses, and fourteen Tories, including the Tunnicliffs, but whether anything had been learned about Brant's intentions is unknown. The next day, Ballard took the prisoners to Albany.

General Stark gave instructions to Colonel Alden to "Divide the Plunder as ... will do most Justice to the Party" rather than turning it over to the commissioners of forfeiture and sequestration. A later inquiry by Albany's conspiracy commission bemoaned "the Spirit of plundering" so prevalent among the Continentals, particularly Alden's regiment at Cherry Valley. "We cannot learn," they informed the governor, whether the livestock's owners had "acted such a Part as to forfeit their Property.... We have had persons sent down by [Alden's] under pretence of being guilty of Treason, but suspect in fact that the motive proceeded only from having a better opportunity to appropriate their Effects...." When Alden heard that the Tunnicliffs, and some others taken up at the same time, might be released, he wrote to Stark, "you may inform the Commitee that if they send them Back, I will again take them Prisoners," so the commissioners kept the Tory suspects in close confinement.[30]

An officer of Alden's named Wheelock led a scout of six men to Tunnicliff's on August 16, where they had a brush with a Native band and killed a warrior. Three days later, word arrived that Brant's party was to be at Tunnicliff's, and Major Stacey marched 150 men around the foot of Lake Otsego, and, after covering seventeen miles, lodged in some houses. On the 21st, Stacey's detachment marched through low and swampy ground, crossed a couple of creeks, and at noon was atop a mountain overlooking Tunnicliff's house. No enemy could be seen, so Stacey split the force, and had the two elements rush down to surround the house. They found some women and a boy inside, along with a sumptuous meal, obviously prepared for expected guests. A shot rang out in the nearby woods, and some figures were seen to run off, but the women refused to supply any information. When the boy was threatened, he admitted that Natives had been there that morning.

After devouring the meal, Stacey's force set out along the foot of Schuyler's Lake, and marched about nine miles to (Jacob?) Schuyler's house. There was no sign of the enemy, and the detachment spent the night there. A party was dispatched to Unadilla, presumably during the night, as they were able to take three prisoners out of their beds without being discovered, and brought them to the major. Under examination, the captives revealed that Brant's party of four to five hundred men planned to draw ammunition the next day, and then march for Cherry Valley or German Flatts. Another prisoner claimed Brant had two thousand Natives and Tories, and yet another told the same story about a coming expedition, but gave the enemy's number as between four and six hundred. According to him, one hundred were at Unadilla, the rest at Oquaga.[31]

Clinton's Worries

The issue of what was to be done with the plunder taken from the Tories came to the fore. Governor Clinton wrote to Colonel Butler on September 8. He displayed sympathy for the thoughts of rewarding the troops who had collected the goods, but worried about the danger of tempting the men to commit acts against the well-affected, and added a comment that betrayed his poor opinion of General Stark: "I am more than ever convinced, that offensive Operations ag't the Savages & Tories is absolutely necessary, & could, therefore, have wished that the plan by you proposed to Genl. Starke had been carried into execution, especially as (if I know the man) it must have been much better than any he can devise."[32]

A Daring Scout

An extremely daring scout was conducted by John McKenna, one of Captain Parr's Pennsylvania riflemen. He left Schoharie's Middle Fort on August 17, and arrived at Unadilla two days later, where he met up with several former acquaintances who had joined the Tories, and consequently had no difficulty mixing with the crowds. In casual conversation, he heard that there were between four and five hundred whites in the area, and maybe five to six hundred Natives. Walter Butler was said to be at the Chemung with 1,100 Natives. Brant was at Oquaga, but it was said he would not make an attack until the British sallied from New York City. McKenna quietly slipped away from Unadilla on August 24, and arrived in Schoharie to give his sworn testimony on the 29th.[33]

Dumond Killed

While McKenna was on his adventure, Colonel Butler sent 150 men to tour the headwaters of the Delaware and Susquehanna Rivers. As seen in the previous chapter, on August 26, Captain Posey's scout captured two men, and turned them over to the militia. When the pair attempted to escape, one fellow, Harmanus Dumond, was mortally wounded at Pakatakan. There was consternation when it was discovered that the dead man was a Whig spy, who had thought that Posey's riflemen were Tories. Further investigation suggested Dumond had also been assisting the Tories. Whether true or not, Posey and the militiamen were off the hook.[34]

Stanwix's Garrison

Colonel Gansevoort, the commandant of Fort Stanwix, added to General Washington's woes on August 13 with accounts of desertions from his garrison. Since March 26, he had lost three serjeants, two corporals, and twenty privates from his regiment, and a bombardier, gunner, and matross from the artillery. Prior to that date, several men had been tried by general court martial for desertion, but had not been punished, because the sentences had not been approved by General Stark. Sometime in June, a spy from British General Clinton had been discovered attempting to woo Irishmen in the regiment to desert. The man confessed, and was tried by court martial, but again his sentence had not been approved in Albany, and he still lay in irons in the fort's jail.

Gansevoort's officers had detected a growing sense of unrest among the men, and had heard expressions of unwillingness to stay another winter. There was no question that Stanwix was a bleak, isolated, frozen posting. The Third New York had been there since the spring of 1776, and had undergone a harrowing siege, so the men were within their rights to expect some relief; however, the officers knew that likely would not occur before winter, and something had to be done to re-establish firm discipline.

An unfortunate opportunity arose when five men deserted on August 10. Tuscarora warriors were sent in pursuit, and overtook the fugitives fifty miles from the fort, on their way to Canada. An October 15 court martial sentenced them to death, and the fort's officers recommended an immediate execution to set an example. This situation was exacerbated when a 3NY party, which had driven cattle from German Flatts, came back to the fort missing six more deserters, who were immediately pursued without success.

The colonel had word from his Native allies that the Tories had secretly recruited seventy men in the garrison to rise up when the Crown's forces made an appearance, which pushed Gansevoort into accepting his officers' recommendations. The men were sentenced to be shot at the head of their regiment on October 16, yet on that same day, six more deserted, and two more went five days after the execution.[35]

Doubting the Oneidas

In early September, a soldier was killed and scalped outside Stanwix's gate. Some of the garrison charged the Oneidas with complicity in the killing, and this accusation was taken very hard by the headmen, who sent a party of sachems and chiefs to meet with the fort's temporary commander, Major Robert Cochran. The headmen denied any knowledge of the killing, and voiced their irritation at being suspected. Previous commanders had treated them with respect, but now they were being neglected. Cochran assured them of his goodwill, and together they drank toasts to mutual friendship, but the event remained irksome to the Oneidas.[36]

Tory Recruiting

On August 27, two Royal Yorker recruiting officers, Thomas Garnett and Roeleff Van De Car, set out from their hiding place in the Catskills. Garnett had had only seven men when he earlier escaped from the rebel rangers, but over time he had collected thirty-nine recruits, and raided several rebel farms, where he collected provisions and took a black slave. The loyalists set off across country, heading for Indian Territory for a rendezvous at Oquaga.[37]

Captain William Caldwell and two hundred Rangers were with Joseph Brant at Oquaga when Captain Gilbert Tice and his party of Indian Department rangers and Canajoharie and Akwesasne warriors arrived near the end of August. His 125 men were a very welcome addition, as Brant knew Tice well, and thoroughly trusted him. Then, on September 1, a pleasant surprise: Garnett and Van De Car arrived with their thirty-nine men, and put themselves under Tice's command.[38]

Scouting Stanwix

Captain Aubrey, 47th Regiment, the commandant of Carleton Island, forwarded a return to headquarters of eight prisoners who had been sent down from Niagara, and reported sending Lieutenant Jacob Adams of the Six Nations Indian Department to Fort Stanwix with a Native party — likely Mississaugas or Oswegatchies — which had brought in two prisoners taken near the fort. The Natives kept one of the prisoners to show their people, as a display of their competence. Adams had heard that the rebels had 540 men at the fort, and were strongly fortifying. Further, they had asked for five thousand men, to mount an attack on Major Butler.[39]

German Flatts Attacked

Caldwell set out from Oquaga with Brant's volunteers, Tice's and Garnett's combined parties, and his own companies of Butler's Rangers. The force totalled over four hundred men. Along the way, they captured a five-man Oneida scouting party. Brant's Natives made it very clear that they did not trust the prisoners to accompany the war party, and he left several guards to watch them so they could not raise a warning.[40]

German Flatts had expected a raid all summer. The area was a ripe, plum target, with barns bulging from an excellent harvest. A patrol of nine men had been sent on a reconnaissance down the Unadilla River, and was surprised by Brant's vanguard at the Edmeston settlement. In the ensuing skirmish, only one of the scouts, John Adam Helmer, had been able to escape. Circumspectly, he bravely held back, and lay behind a tree to watch the main party pass. Having counted about two hundred men, he concluded this was about half of the whole. When he set out at a run to warn the Flatts, he was spotted by several warriors, who set up a pursuit. A noted athlete, Helmer outran them, and made it to the settlement on the night of September 16 to give warning. His clothes were "torn to tatters, his eyes bloodshot, his hands, face, and limbs lacerated, and bleeding for the effects [of] the brambles and bushes through which he had forced his headlong flight."[41]

Caldwell's force arrived at the Flatts an hour after Helmer. Heavy rain was falling, and the raiders sheltered in a gully near Rudolph Shoemaker's tavern, where Walter Butler's party had been taken the year before. They had no idea that the settlement had been warned, and that virtually every man, woman, and child had taken refuge in one of the two forts — Fort Herkimer on the Mohawk River's south bank, Fort Dayton on the north. When Caldwell's force divided the next morning and went on a rampage of plundering and destruction, they met no opposition. Sixty-three houses, fifty-seven barns, and five mills were burned, and 235 horses, 229 cattle, 269 sheep, and ninety-three New England oxen being held for the troops at Fort Stanwix were led away. A resident who had failed to evacuate was shot, and another fellow died inside his burning home. Although no attempt was made against either fort, the inhabitants suffered scenes of devastation on every hand. The attack was a major disaster.[42]

A militia force of three to four hundred German Flatts' men pursued the retreating raiders — one suspects not all that eagerly — as they turned back after discovering and burying their dead scouts at Edmeston's settlement. Some Oneida scouts who were with the militia fell upon the farm of Persafor Carr, one of Brant's primary suppliers, killed his servants, and took the family prisoner.

When word of the attack on the Flatts reached Cherry Valley, a force of 180 men under Major William Whiting, 17ACM, was dispatched to pursue the raiders, but when they arrived at the Butternuts, they gave up and turned back.[43]

Governor Clinton reacted to the news of this raid by severely criticizing Brigadier Ten Broeck for not supplying sufficient men from his brigade for the defence of the frontiers. He noted that Tryon County's militia was quick to react after the fact, but were, of course, too late. Once again, Clinton gave voice to his displeasure with General Stark: "It does not appear to me that he pays the least Attention to the safety of the Frontiers." He asked where Alden's regiment was stationed and how it was employed during the German Flatts' disaster, so that he could inform General Washington.

On September 24, the governor wrote to Washington, informing him that he had ordered the commanders of the Albany and Tryon militia brigades to keep one-fourth of their commands posted on the frontiers, and, although these instructions had not been fully complied with, a substantial force had been constantly on that service. For a variety of reasons, including the lack of Continental troops, the measure had been ineffective, and Clinton was concerned that many valuable settlements would be lost, and Fort Stanwix put at risk. The governor again expressed his dissatisfaction with Stark, noting that Clinton had only received two letters from him concerning his command, and neither was of any consequence. Clinton believed Stark was paying a greater share of his attentions to Vermont, helping — in Clinton's words — "the disaffected Subjects of this State on the Grants, in establishing their usurped Government." As it happened, Stark's orientation would persist until 1781, when he would be personally disappointed by Vermont's lack of response in his hour of need.[44]

ONEIDAS ATTACK BUTTERNUTS

Somehow, the five Oneidas taken by Brant's force escaped from their guards, and made their way directly to Kanowalohale. As noted, their elders had earlier been stung by the attitude of Fort Stanwix's garrison, and they saw a possibility here of making a stroke in favour of their allies. A war party of Oneidas and Tuscaroras was assembled, and attacked one of the Unadilla villages and the nearby Butternuts. Whatever guards had been posted were run off, and the rebel warriors burned houses and barns, took livestock and ten prisoners, and released a prominent local Whig, whom Brant had captured nine weeks before. It was later claimed, "Our Warriors were Particular that no hurt should be Done to Women & Children. We Left four old men Behind who were no more able to go to War."

Richard McGinnis had strong memories of this attack. He had been given leave from the Rangers to come home to the Butternuts to recover from an intermittent fever. His family planned to go to Niagara when the raiders returned from German Flatts, and had buried most of their effects in preparation. When the rebel Natives struck, Richard's brother John was found in a field collecting horses, and they bound him strongly. His father was near the house, and he called to Richard to come out and identify these Natives; Richard told him they were rebels. A rebel Indian McGinnis knew, named Fowles, warned him to stay still, but he refused, and the warrior levelled his piece and shot him with buckshot through the ear.

Richard and his father managed to escape into the house and exchanged shots with the war party, until the warriors shouted they would kill John if the two men did not surrender. They complied, and came out of the house. It was likely at this point that Brant's prisoner, William Dygert of Fall Hill, who had been left in John's care, was released. Richard pled for his father to be left behind, as did the man himself, and the war party agreed. They took John and Richard away, but soon decided they had made a mistake, and returned to retake the father; however, the older man had wisely hidden in the woods, and could not be found. Richard recalled that "These villains then broke open the chest and took from thence my brother John's watch. Tygert [Dygert] got the watch and a watch belonging to my father; there was some silver money, buckskins and many other articles." He wrote:

> It is the greatest presumption to trust on the veracity of any savage whatsoever; for they will undoubtedly deceive you as they did us. And I have the greatest reason to believe that Brant knew that these savages were on their way, when he met them, to destroy our settlement, as he never sent us any word, which

he could easily have done to put us on our guard to have escaped to the woods. And therefore when he and his party returned from the destruction of ye German Flatts back again to our place, what the rebel Indians had not time to destroy, Brant and his party destroyed for us. Brant's Mohawks went in our house, ripped up the feather bed and took the Tick with them. Every hog they took. My father's horse and he was obliged to go to the Indians and beg for his horses with tears in his eyes and much pleading he got two of them back. I was informed Brant took the other, and all living creatures they took clean off. His Indian savages took my father's horses and Brant himself went with my father to get his horses from them. By much entreaties he got them. I was informed on my coming to Canada that Brant himself carried off my father's mare, the best of the three horses.... We was taken the 19th day of September. As soon as the savages had bound us they took us to a thick hemlock swamp on the Unadilla Creek where we were pinioned to small saplings sitting in about 4 inches of water. They now talked of killing us and we expected nothing else as they held the tomahawks over our heads, but thanks be to God, our lives were spared for we was not hurt in the least.[45]

A delegation of about one hundred Oneida and Tuscarora warriors went to Fort Stanwix to apprise Major Cochran of their deeds, and deliver six prisoners as proof. They told of burning Unadilla and the Butternuts, taking five men captive at each settlement, and releasing four old men "who were no more able to go to war." William Dygert was turned over to Cochran so he could be returned to his friends. The headmen claimed they had avenged the soldier who had been recently scalped,[46] and said to the major, "We hope you are now Convinced of our Friendship towards you & your

Great Cause." A seventh prisoner was given to some visitors from Kahnawake and taken to lower Quebec, and the eighth was adopted as a son by the Oneida sachem, the Grasshopper.[47]

Meanwhile, in the Schoharie Valley, a return of the current tour of Albany County militia was made on September 20, showing 225 men of all ranks, from eight different regiments and the local 15th Albany. Although Governor Clinton was critical of the Albany brigadier, this was a sizeable commitment.[48]

Anguish in Tryon County

Several principal men of Tryon County wrote despairingly to Governor Clinton from Canajoharie on September 28, noting that, because of the attacks on Springfield, Andrewstown, and German Flatts, at least 150 families were "reduced to Misery and Distress."

> Notwithstanding we have repeatedly wrote our Situation down and asked Relief, we have obtained none except Colo. Alden's Regiment…. Woeful Experience teaches us, that the Troops in Cherry Valley are by no means a Defence for any other Part of the Country….
>
> Strange as it may appear to your Excellency, it is no less true, that our Militia by Desertion to the Enemy and by Enlistments into our Service, are reduced to less than seven hundred Men. Indeed if these 700 would do their Duty and act like Men, we might perhaps give the Enemy a Check, so as to give Time to the Militia from below to come up, but, Sir, they are actuated by such an ungovernable Spirit that it is out of the Power of any Officer in this County to command them with any Credit to himself — for notwithstan'g the utmost Exertion the Officers have nothing but Blame in Return.

And blame is exactly what they received two weeks later, when the governor responded to Colonel Klock. He cited examples of other counties that were facing similar depredations, and yet were meeting their responsibilities. He chastised him regarding the failure to raise two ranging companies, and over the poor turnout of the county's militia regiments, criticisms heard before. He urged the county to take the offensive, and apply courts martial to offenders when appropriate.[49]

Continentals Counterattack

Colonel William Butler was eager to start his expedition against Unadilla, despite the fact that much of the clothing he had ordered months before had not yet arrived. Prior to September 21, Butler's intelligence noted that Brant had seven hundred men at Oquaga and Unadilla, and on about October 1, spies advised that Brant had left both places. That day, Butler sent Lieutenant William Stevens of Parr's rifle company with a dozen men, and a militia subaltern with sixteen militiamen, to patrol the roads and pathways leading into the valley and prevent intelligence leaks. The expedition was assembled on the 2nd — 161 officers and men of the 4th Pennsylvania; seventy-seven officers and men of the rifle corps; twenty-one officers and men of Lieutenant William Dietz's militia ranging company; and eight militiamen acting as guides and packhorse handlers, for a total of 267 men.[50] They carried provisions for six days on their backs, and another five on the packhorses. The force suffered from heavy rain and poor roads, but made it to the Delaware River's headwaters by October 3. They followed the course of the Delaware for two days before climbing over the mountains to arrive at the Susquehanna.

Lieutenants Stevens and Reuben Long were sent to take up some inhabitants who lived within four miles of Unadilla. Butler continued the march in the night in order to come near the settlement and make his attack in the morning. They had gone about seven miles when they came across the two lieutenants, with a prisoner who said that the enemy had left Unadilla some days before for Oquaga.[51]

On the 7th, Lieutenant Stevens was sent to Unadilla to capture a Tory to act as a guide for the expedition. As Stevens went to Unadilla and back without difficulty, the Tory he collected, John Glasford[52] by name, was obviously expected to reveal targets for destruction, not to act simply as a guide. Before the force arrived at Unadilla, it had to cross the Susquehanna on three occasions. When the advance party reached the opposite shore at the last crossing, a set of tracks was discovered. Worried that the force's presence had been discovered, the tracks were followed without success for eight miles.

At ten o'clock that night, the competent Lieutenant Stevens was sent to reconnoitre Oquaga. He returned on the 8th, and provided a good description of the settlement. There had been a heavy rain that morning, and the force's arms had to be dried and cleaned before movement. When the troops arrived at the Susquehanna shore opposite Oquaga, they faced a 250-yard, waist-deep ford. Butler arrayed his riflemen in the van, with orders to flank right and left if fired upon, and the musketmen would charge forward from behind with bayonets fixed; however, the crossing was made without opposition, and the town quickly occupied. Butler claimed in his report that the enemy had left the town that day in the greatest confusion; however, he had earlier reported they had left at least a day before that, and other evidence indicates there had been no rush or confusion about their departure.

As a ruse, many fires were lit, to make the force appear larger. The village had forty good houses of squared logs, shingled roofs, glass windows, and stone chimneys. The colonel noted that "it was the finest Indian Town I ever saw." Horses, cattle, dogs, poultry, furniture, vegetables, and two thousand bushels of corn were taken. Livestock that could not be driven off was butchered. It was also claimed that some Native children who had been hiding in the cornfields were killed, and that the troops may have raped female prisoners, an act considered utterly taboo in Native culture.

Major Church took a party across the river the next morning, and burned ten frame houses and a corn bin, cut down apple trees, and took some cattle. When a few packhorses strayed, some unarmed soldiers went to look for them, and one was shot in his side and skull, which blew away part of his brain. When the shots rang out, Butler marched his whole force toward the discharges, but nothing more occurred.[53]

While the main body of troops lay hidden in the woods, Butler sent Captain Parr to burn the lower Tuscarora village, about three miles off. When Parr returned, the force burned the main town and destroyed the crops. At three in the afternoon, the raiders set off, recrossing the river with the Grenadiers in advance, bayonets fixed. As the march continued, any stray buildings that were found were torched, including the small upper Tuscarora village of Cunahunta.[54] On October 10, an incessant downpour caused the creeks and rivers to rise, making crossings more difficult. In one instance, the horses had to swim, and trees were felled for the troops to cling to. In another, the troops crossed on horseback, and it took twenty trips to get everyone over, during which seven muskets were lost. Arriving at Unadilla, on the south side of the Susquehanna, all houses, a saw mill, and grist mill were burned, except for Glasford's, who would now have to persuade his fellow loyalists that he had been coerced, or they might take vengeance on him.

While the force rested on October 11 and cleaned their arms, a raft was fashioned to take Lieutenant Long and one of his men across the river to torch the buildings on that side — which raises the question about what part of Unadilla the Oneidas and Tuscaroras had destroyed earlier. Perhaps the settlement was so widespread that there was no shortage of targets.

One ford defied crossing, and the force diverted across high ground, became lost, and marched six miles in the dark before discovering their error. At this time, the man who had been wounded expired. The force trudged on, and ran out of provisions, with only an ear of corn for each man until they arrived at the Middle Fort on October 15. Butler ordered thirteen rounds to be fired by the forts' guns, no doubt in recognition of the thirteen rebelling colonies, and the troops fired a *feu de joie*.⁵⁵

In Butler's belated report to Governor Clinton, dated October 28, he made a prediction about his expedition that may have given him cause for regret later: "I am well convinced that it has sufficiently secured these Frontiers from any further disturbances from the Savages at least this Winter."⁵⁶ Native and Tory resiliency was always underestimated.

Much was made of this expedition. Considering it was the first serious counterattack in the Mohawk region against the loyal Natives and their Tory allies, and was a successful strike with only a single casualty, there is every reason to give Butler and his men kudos. It is, however, rather comic that so much attention was paid to the physical aspects that they had to overcome — constant heavy downpours, water crossing after water crossing, swollen water courses, inadequate provisions, threats of sudden combat, mountains to be climbed — which entirely ignored the fact that their enemies faced these same rigours over and over and over again.

A likely unforeseen result of Oquaga's destruction was the impact upon the rebels' faithful allies — the Oneidas and Tuscaroras. The area was home to substantial elements of both nations, and, whether pro-rebel or neutralists, they, like so many white settlers, had not been able to move to more friendly locations. Now they had lost their homes, clothing, furniture, farm implements, livestock, and harvests. Blood and clan relations were strong forces, so seventeen refugees went north to Kanowalohale, which was an already deeply stressed community, short of provisions and other supplies.

Late in the month, Good Peter Agorondajats, an Oneida sachem who had left Oquaga earlier in the war, led a delegation to Albany to plead with the Indian commissioners on behalf of the newly arrived refugees. He noted that they were true friends of the rebellion, who had not been able to remove themselves earlier because of their commitments. Among many other requests, he asked for documents identifying these people as being "under the protection of the united States," and these requests were granted.⁵⁷

Good Peter Agorondajats, an Oneida sachem.

STANWIX RELIEF

Fortunately, Colonel Gansevoort was going to get the relief his regiment was desperate to receive, but it would take some time to get organized. On October 17, the day after the deserters' executions, General Washington wrote to General James Clinton about the reassignment of the First New York, Continental Line. "I have determined to send Col. Van Schaick's Regiment to Fort Schuyler to relieve Col. Gansevoort. You will signify this to Col. Van Schaick that he may be preparing for it. So soon as the Cloathing, Expected in camp, arrives; he shall have an order for a competent supply and will then proceed." Vessels were to be provided to convey the regiment up the Hudson to Albany.[58]

Attack near Fort Herkimer

On October 23, at Fort Herkimer in German Flatts, a black woman and three young girls under ten were looking for cows behind the fort. While the woman continued with the task, the three girls climbed a hickory tree to collect nuts. Instead of cows, the woman saw six Natives approaching, and ran for the fort. As she passed the girls, she yelled, "Wilder Kummer!" which they chose to ignore, perhaps thinking they were safely hidden in the branches. If so, they were deceived, and when the warriors came up, their leader, Flat Kop, a well-known Tuscarora, ordered the youngsters to come down. The two Sharrar sisters, Margaret and Nancy, immediately complied, but their companion, Lucinda Bellinger, refused, and Flat Kop shot her. She fell on the other side of a fence, and her killer was about to climb over to collect her scalp, but saw a young fellow emerge from a barn and point what looked like a firelock his way. This was Lucinda's brother, Peter, and he carried a pitchfork, not a gun, but his gesture was effective in dissuading the warrior.

Meanwhile, the woman's shouts and the gunshot had alerted troops, who could be seen coming their way. Picking up the sisters, the Native party made off into the woods and got away. The girls' mother must have been in deep distress, as she had already lost her husband, Christian, the year before, in the battle of Oriskany.[59]

British Progress at Carleton Island

In mid-September, Governor Haldimand received reports from Engineering Lieutenant William Twiss. Two hundred bushels of lime had been produced in a newly-built kiln, and a like amount of charcoal prepared. A saw pit, a storehouse, a smithy, and a carpenter's shop had been erected and clad. A general hospital was well underway. Two hundred twenty-foot-long pine logs and ten thousand shingles had been fashioned for building barracks, the first of which, some 175 feet long, would be completed in mid-October.[60]

Johnson Hall Excursion

Lieutenant William Redford Crawford was again chosen for a mission in October. Combining with Lieutenant William Byrne and thirty-one Royal Yorker Light Bobs, Crawford and a party of Kanehsatake Mohawks went to Johnstown to recover Sir John's iron chest of family papers and parchment land patents that had been hastily buried in 1776, before he escaped over the Adirondacks. Johnson's considerable fortune was tied up in land, and these papers were his grants and tenant records.[61]

The little expedition set out from Sorel, but what route was followed in and out of New York is unknown. En route, Byrne went lame, and Crawford continued on with the detachment. Their arrival was unopposed; however, when the chest was unearthed and sprung open, it was found that the papers were a sodden, useless mass, as the lid had not been properly secured in the rush to leave. Byrne advised that the chest "was taken up from under the Earth at the place directed to them by the said Sir John Johnson namely in the garden in front of Johnson Hall." When opened, it was "found that a great deal of water had been lodged therein which on the sd Chest being taken up was let out and … the said Papers Parchments &c for a considerable time had laid under water and … the Parchments being entirely rotten and nothing but the Seals thereof remaining and intermixed with other papers in such a manner that the same were wholly obliterated and destroyed by the wet and quite illegible." Sir John reported to Governor Haldimand, "they brought off the Ruins of my Papers, none of which are legible; my loss … at the lowest computation [is] twenty thousand Pounds.… [T]he Indians and six Prisoners … are gone to Colonel Claus."[62]

Butler's Arrogance

When Walter Butler returned from Quebec City, he was eager to get into the field before the campaign season ended, and he joined Captain Caldwell on the Chemung River at Tioga, where a large collection of Seneca and allied warriors under Old Smoke and Gilbert Tice's and Thomas Garnett's parties were gathered. Garnett received a very nasty surprise when an arrogant young Butler indulged in an outburst.

> I was very Ill Treated by him, He said I had no business to carry Men Thro his Camp nor neither had any Other Corps upon the Continent any Right to Inlist Men upon the Frontiers but himself and Threatened to send me in Irons to Niagara But Thro delacacy he would Suffer me to pass, And ordered me to depart the Camp the next Morning by Nine OClock, and likewise put one of my Men under Guard that was wiling to go with me and Threatened to Hang him — He also took my Negro Slave and Sent him to Niagara and there detains him[.] I was obliged to depart the Camp within the limited Time with only Five Men, Altho the Greatest part of them was Inlisted and Sworn as early as the year 1777 for Sir John Johnson's Brigade, who fled to him for Safety.[63]

Young Butler was living a fantasy. His father's Rangers had no monopoly on recruits in northern New York. Sir John had been the major-general of militia in the northern section of the province before the war, so if anyone could claim an exclusive position, it was he. Walter's intemperate behaviour would have a major impact on the closing of the campaign, and added considerable weight to Claus's criticisms of his family.

Brant had meant to join with the Senecas and Butler at Oquaga, but that was impossible now. He travelled first to Cochecton, on the

Delaware River, along the Pennsylvania border, where he left twenty of his men, probably to visit their families. He had received word that the rendezvous had changed to Owego, just beyond Tioga, where he and the rest of his volunteers arrived on October 22, after a march of nine days from Peenpack.

Walter Butler had a collection of fifty Regulars of the 8th (King's) Regiment, about 150 Rangers, with Captains Caldwell and the newly-minted John McDonell, and Indian Department officers Captain John Johnston and Lieutenant Adam Crysler. His Native contingent numbered 321, of which fifty may have been attached to Brant. In the absence of Old Smoke, Cornplanter was the senior war chief.[64]

A lengthy council was held to discuss the next target, and Cherry Valley was chosen. The combined force was on its way by October 29. Brant wrote a letter that day to a friend at Niagara, advising that he and young Butler had been quarrelling over his white volunteers. For some inexplicable reason, Butler objected to the yellow lace the men wore in their hats as an identifier, which was a simple excuse to exercise his imagined right to recruit exclusively on the frontiers. The acrimony became so strong that Brant contemplated leaving the expedition, but the warriors persuaded him to stay, although ninety of his whites fled to the woods under the threat of being treated as rebels by the Rangers. Walter's arrogance had got the best of him again.[65]

General Hand's Report

Brigadier Edward Hand had been appointed to replace Stark as northern commander. A few days after his arrival in Albany, he sent a scathing report to General Washington concerning his predecessor.

> I think it my duty to Acquaint your Excy that I arived here on the 24th & Communicated my instructions to Genl Stark. I had reason to expect

that in compliance with your orders I should be made acquainted with many particulars necessary for my Gouvernment in this Command, but found myself much mistaken, Genl Stark left this place on Tuesday 27th without Communicating a Single Circumstance except what I could Collect from the Inclosed returns, which are the Best I am yet Able to make your Excelly.

I requested a return of the Troops in Garrison here, & the duty they did, but recd none from him, he Verbally inform'd me that the present Garrison Consisted of 9 or 10 Privates with two or three Non Commissiond Officers of Col. Aldens Regt as a Guard for himself, and two Compys of Massachusets Militia whose time of Service would expire on the last of this month, which however I found not to be the case.

The Act by which they were Raised entitles them to a very Generous Bounty from their own state exclusive of the Continental pay, but expresly says they are to Serve untill the 1st of Jany next, unless Sooner discharged.

With what propriety Genl Stark could discharge them Sooner, when, as he confesses in his letter to their Officers discharging them, (a Coppy of which I transmit yr Excy in his own words) that I could not possibly procure a man to Guard the Stores here, I hope for the Good of the Service he will be obliged to make Appear to your Excelly.

I believe it will not Appear Strange to your Excy that the Men pay very little regard to the Genls recommendation to stay a week longer[.] I Yesterday[,] to no Effect, made use of every Argument I could think of to induce them to continue a few days, and was Strongly Seconded by their own Officers. [T]odays

Orders, (an Extract of which I inclose) will with the Exertions of the Officers I hope have a better Effect. [I]f not my only dependence is on an Application made to the Commanding Officer of Militia of the State in this Quarter — as the Continental Troops are too far distant & cant be spared from the Frontiers untill the winter Sets in....

Provisions are now forwarding to Fort Schuyler, & the Commy has promised me to use his Utmost Efforts to supply every other ... as speedily as Possible.

As the Greater part of the Troops on the Frontier are Almost naked, and the Winter Approaching, I intend [to] Send an Officer from each Corps to head Quarters for a Supply of Cloating for them.[66]

Relief of Fort Stanwix on the Way

Colonel Goose Van Schaick had preceded his 1st New York Continentals to Albany, so that he could put his family's affairs in order before taking post at Fort Stanwix. The last day that the regiment did duty at the Continental Village or at Peekskill was November 4. Thereafter, they were on the move north to their assignment on the frontier.[67]

Another Small Raid

At daybreak of November 3, a party of eight to ten Natives and Tories came to Peter Hansen's at Tribes Hill, took him and his servant prisoner, and ordered his wife and children to empty all the effects from the house, which they set afire with the barn. The wife and children were set loose, and Hansen and the servant carried off to Canada. Colonel Visscher, 3rd Tryon, sent a party in fruitless pursuit.[68]

Cherry Valley Attacked

On November 4, Colonel Alden wrote a detailed letter to Washington, reporting his actions since his arrival in Cherry Valley. In view of the sentiments expressed by the village's residents to General Hand three days later, his closing comment was surprising: "Likewise there never has Been a good understanding & agreement with the Inhabitants of this part of this State & the Soldiery of the Massachusetts, therefore if it Could be thought for the Good of the Publick that My Regiment may be Releived & Join the Brigade it Belongeth to it will give Great satisfaction to the Officers & Soldiers."[69]

Colonel Gansevoort sent Alden a warning about a possible attack, which he had heard about from an Oneida who said an Onondaga had come to Kanowalohale from the Tioga branch of the Susquehanna River, where there had been a large meeting of the British Natives and Tories, during which it was decided to attack Cherry Valley. Young Butler was to head the Tories. Alden replied on November 8, noting his obligation to the colonel for the receipt of the information, although circumstantially he seems to have thought the advice was nothing more than another "Indian rumour."[70]

The townsfolk begged Alden to allow them to move their possessions into the fort and stay there overnight. Coincidentally, General Hand was at the settlement, on a tour of his command, when Gansevoort's warning was received. The general was presented with a letter signed by twenty residents, begging him to allow Alden's men to remain, "as they now are acquainted with our country and the roads and haunts of our enemy; so that by their means we may be secured from slaughter and devastation." Hand recommended that the inhabitants be allowed to store their goods in the fort, but once he was gone, the colonel would not permit it, saying he was worried his soldiers would be tempted to plunder. He assured the residents he would have good scouts patrolling, and would be able to give timely notice of an approaching enemy. Despite these assurances, his greatest error was to have himself and many of his officers continue to live in the warmth and dryness of various local homes, at a considerable distance from the fort.[71]

In fairness to the man, Cherry Valley had been warned by friendly Natives and county inhabitants of coming attacks for two years, and nothing had happened, other than Brant's killing of Wormwood. Further, the season was far advanced, and the weather predictably poor, as William Butler's expedition against Oquaga and Unadilla the month before had discovered.

On the 9th, Alden sent out three scouting parties. One of these, composed of a serjeant and eight men, went down the Susquehanna toward Butternuts — unwittingly, straight into the path of the advancing enemy.

Hand had returned to Albany by the time he wrote to Governor Clinton on November 10. He forwarded a copy of Gansevoort's warning, and noted that Cherry Valley and Schoharie were

> very Scantily supplied with Provision & Ammunition.... [A] Number of Parties are out from Schoharry, Cherry Valley & Connejohary to make discoveries, I waited on Colonel Klock who promised to Reinforce Col Alden with 200 Militia and to Collect a Body at Connejohary to Act Ocassionally[.] Genl Tinbrook has Ordered a Reinforcement to Schohary and Stores are now on their way from Scnectady and this place for Cherry Valley & Schoharry, the Enemys Rout must be with in 25 or 30 Miles of Schoharry so that Col. [William] Butler must undoubtedly get in their Rear, if he does not find himself Strong enough to attack them in Front, have Ordered Col Vanscaicks Reg to proceed as expeditiously as possible to Connejoharry from which [he can] Guard the supplies to Cherry Valley & the [deliveries] made before my Return which will be Tommorow warrant it shall detain them the more effectually to secure a warm Reception for the Enemy.

> Your Excellency will likewise receive inclosed the Coppy of a Letter received from Fort Edward respecting the appearance of an Enemy at or near Crown Point, their numbers are trifling and meant only as a Deversion if an Attack from Tioga intended — Measures are taken to prevent their being able to affect any thing of much Consequence, on the night of the 2d Inst two men were taken & an House & Barn Burnt near Johnstown, three of the perpetrators of this Villany are known[.][72]

Hand was clearly intent on taking action where Stark had been strangely remiss. That day, he ordered the storekeeper at Albany to forward immediately three hundred pounds of powder and six hundred of musket ball, with one thousand flints and an appropriate amount of cartridge paper, to Cherry Valley. A like amount was to be sent to Colonel Butler at Schoharie.[73]

Butler's Advance

Walter Butler's expedition had taken a common route up the west bank of the Susquehanna as far as the mouth of Schenevus Creek, which they forded, continuing along the east bank. The vanguard discovered tracks before dark. Following these, the Natives in the expedition came across a fire with nine men spread around, sound asleep. Perhaps these fellows had absorbed their colonel's nonchalant attitude about the threat. All nine were quickly seized — none escaped.

It was later claimed that the scout's serjeant was of the Tory persuasion, and an acquaintance of young Butler, probably to explain the fellow's willingness to yield so much detailed information under questioning. He provided the regimental strength of the 6MA, and the local militia — three hundred and 150, respectively — and the billeting arrangements for the senior Continental officers in a home some four hundred yards from the fort, and for many junior officers in nearby homes. It was also learned that the settlement had been warned of their approach two days previously.[74]

Butler convened a night council to discuss this intelligence. He theorized that, although the settlement had been warned of the attack, it was unaware of their party's proximity; he proposed to march directly to the settlement as soon as the moon rose, surround the houses, and capture the Continental officers. All participants concurred; however, a fall of alternating rain and snow throughout the night greatly discouraged the Natives, who refused to move before daylight, and the force lay in a frigid, fireless camp, wrapped in sodden blankets and capotes.

Historian Samuel Campbell claims that some of Butler's men, who were well-acquainted with Cherry Valley families, came to him in the night and requested permission to infiltrate the village and warn their friends, but he refused, reasoning that the families were so interconnected, word would soon spread to the Whigs.

As first light dawned, "[I]t was resolved that Captain McDonell, with two subalterns and fifty chosen Rangers, should march with the body of the Indians; and with one part surround the houses and cut off communication between the fort and inhabitants, while the other began the attack upon the fort which I was to support with the main body of Rangers."

With the tactical dispositions set, the raiders crept forward in a light rain and foggy mist, through several inches of snow and dripping branches. About a mile from the fort, the Native van halted to listen to the sounds of woodcutting. Perhaps while their captains decided on the course of action, two of their number, probably young warriors, slipped away and fired at a pair of men cutting wood, killing one and wounding the other, who made his escape.

This breaking of discipline electrified the warriors, and the various leaders set off at a run with their war parties. The Seneca war captain Little Beard Sequidonquee, who had most likely been part of the vanguard, led his party directly to the Wells house, where the Continentals' senior officers were reported to be billeted. Because they relied upon firearms more than did the Natives, the Rangers were not as quick off the mark, and delayed to check their guns' readiness after hours of rain and snowfall.

Brant did not hesitate. Since joining the Senecas at Owego, he recognized that his allies were deeply angry over recent events. Despite the rebels' decisive victory in the Wyoming Valley, many of their senior officers who had been paroled by John Butler had immediately returned to the service. Then, the Seneca discovered that the forts they had destroyed were already being rebuilt, and they heard that the rebels were insulting them by labelling the big battle a massacre, although they had only killed men in arms. Not long after they had withdrawn northwards, Hartley's Continentals and the paroled Colonel Denison had struck out of the Wyoming Valley into lower Indian Territory and burned several Native villages. Then, William Butler's Continentals had dared to enter Indian Territory, and destroyed Oquaga. It was obvious that the rebels had not learned their lesson; the Senecas and their allies brooded deeply over these incidents and harboured a raging thirst for revenge, which Brant knew all too well. He realized the Senecas would not know who were loyalists among the inhabitants, and he also thought that Walter Butler was too inexperienced to sense the danger.

When a wholesale advance began, Brant recognized the Wells family's peril. Robert Wells had been a close friend of Sir William Johnson and John Butler, and had accompanied Joseph and his wife and child down the Susquehanna in 1769. Brant knew all of the family, and considered them good friends. He set out to save them, taking what he believed would be a shortcut, but was slowed while crossing over soft, ploughed ground.

There are different versions of what happened next. Some sources claim that the wounded woodcutter arrived at the Wells house and warned the officers. Other sources state that a Mr. Hamlin was riding into the village and came across Natives running through the woods. They challenged him, and when he failed to reign in, they shot him in the arm. Despite his wound, he spurred his horse and galloped to the Wells house to give the alarm, and then went to the fort. All sources agree that Colonel Alden was not greatly excited, thinking the Natives were nothing but a handful of stragglers. Besides, it seems the officers were enjoying a mess breakfast at the time.[75] The colonel did alert his house guards, but did not immediately leave for the fort, a decision that sealed his fate.

Before Alden's guard could assemble, Little Beard's party struck the house. The Wellses were strangers to the Senecas; the fact that Continental officers were being billeted by them would have been enough to make them guilty of complicity with the rebellion, and they were struck down without mercy. Robert Wells, his mother, his wife, three sons, and three servants were gone in a twinkling. A daughter who ran to hide behind a woodpile was found and tomahawked. Rumours persisted that a white ranger who was with the party killed the father as he knelt in prayer. The guards were similarly dispatched or taken prisoner.

Lieutenant-Colonel Stacey attempted to escape, and was quickly captured; however, Alden broke free and ran for the fort. He was hotly pursued by a warrior who called on him to surrender. Alden repeatedly turned and snapped a pistol at him, but as frequently happened, it misfired. Growing impatient, the warrior unerringly threw his tomahawk, which struck the colonel's head and felled him. The warrior ran up and lifted the scalp. Alden was dead.

A warning gun had been fired at the fort, and Major Daniel Whiting, along with several soldiers and inhabitants, streamed there for safety. Massachusetts private Henry Scott reported that

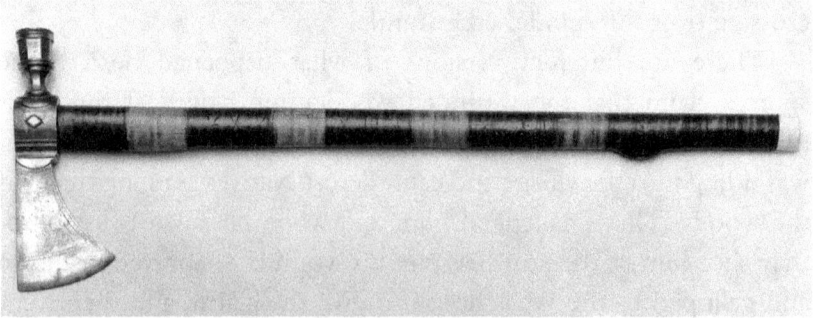

Pipe-tomahawk.

thirty-nine soldiers were washing their clothing in a stream, and rushed to get back.[76]

Brant arrived to find the Wells family's corpses littering the ground, and Senecas plundering the house. It was soon alight, and the regiment's colours perished in the flames. The war captain knew there was nothing to be said to his allies; the deed was done, and he feared it would be repeated throughout the village. He quickly explained his fears to his running mate, the Oquaga Mohawk chief Little Aaron, and urged him to visit several houses to save the inhabitants.

Little Aaron rushed to the home of Reverend Dunlop. He arrived too late to save Mrs. Dunlop, but was able to rescue the aged clergyman and his daughter, leading the pair outside, where he stood beside them in the rain while the house was plundered and set on fire.

A fellow named Mitchell saw Natives approaching his house, and ran to safety in the woods. When he returned, he found his wife and four children scalped, and his house plundered and burning. He managed to extinguish the fire, and found one of his daughters still alive. When he saw a second party about to arrive, he again hid, and saw William Newberry, a Butler's Ranger from the Mohawk Valley, tomahawk his daughter.

A party surrounded the house of militia colonel Samuel Campbell, and took prisoner his wife, her four children, and her parents. Like the others, her house was plundered and set afire. The colonel's son William was able to escape to the woods with a black servant, and they made their way to Fort Plank, where the father was stationed.[77]

Lieutenant-Colonel Clyde's wife gathered her eight children (one an infant) and an apprentice lad, and fled to the woods. They hid under a log, where they lay in the wet snow, praying and listening to the movements and yells of the Natives as they passed nearby. The butt of one native's gun struck the log and frightened everyone. The mother clapped her hand over the infant's mouth, and the lad muzzled the family dog.

Brant entered a house and found a woman calmly engaged in her chores. Surprised, he asked her why she had not taken flight when all of her neighbours were being killed around her. She replied, "We are [the] king's people." He said, "That plea will not avail you today." Coolly, she returned, "There is one Joseph Brant; if he is with the Indians he will save us." He explained that he was Brant, but he did not have the command; however, he would do what was in his power to save her. Seeing several Senecas advancing on the house, he told the woman to get in her bed and feign sickness. When the warriors entered, the Mohawk told them there was no one there, other than a sick woman and her children. The Senecas moved on. When they were out of sight, Brant went outside and gave a long, shrill call. Soon after, several Mohawks crossed an adjoining field at high speed. When they came up, Brant asked, "Where is your paint? Here, put my mark upon this woman and her children."

This was done, and is credited with saving the family. This tale is often expanded to Brant and his men marking doorjambs with his totem, like the Passover, and saving many others; however, none of the many histories consulted confirms it, although the historian Samuel Campbell reports that Brant's totem was put on many of the prisoners, which he would have heard from his grandmother.[78]

Young Hugh Johnston was inside the fort when he saw Natives advancing on the village, and rushed out to Mrs. Cannon's house, where his father, the regiment's chaplain, was lodging. He helped the minister, his wife, younger children, and a local lad escape and hide in the woods.

Another fortunate family was the Ogdens. When Mrs. Ogden heard the alarm, she grabbed a blanket and fled with her children into the woods. From there, she made her way north to the Mohawk River, where she was joined days later by her husband.[79]

Captain Benjamin Warren, 6MA, wrote of the attack from the garrison's viewpoint. "The enemy pushed vigorously for the Fort, but our Soldiers behaved with great spirit and alertness; defended the Fort, and repulsed them after three hours and a half smart engagement. Twelve of the regiment beside the Col. Killed, and two wounded."[80]

Many rebel historians state that the garrison took no action against the attackers because they were greatly outnumbered. Yet, if Alden's had about three hundred men, and the local militia 150, as stated by the captured scout serjeant, their total would have substantially outnumbered Butler's 150 Rangers and fifty British Regulars, who were concentrating their attention on the fort. With the Natives rampaging through the village, killing and capturing people, and pillaging and burning buildings, a well-organized sally might have disorganized the attackers, and allowed more inhabitants to escape. One account advises that Captain Ballard attempted an ineffectual sortie as the enemy was withdrawing, which the raiders tried to cut off, but reinforcements from the fort prevented it.[81] Likely, the shock of the surprise and the loss of two senior officers prevented more assertive action.

John Dain, the regiment's orderly serjeant, wrote in his journal:

> [T]his Morning About ten a Clock the Enemy Surrounded the Fort[,] the Number of them we Cannot tell[.] We think thare Was betweain Seven or Eight hundred of them Endion [Indian] and toreys[.] In the first phase thay Killed the Cheaf Col. and took the Left. [Lieutenant] Col. Prisoners And Likewise Left. Holden[,] Ensign Garrett and the Docters mate Prisoners With them — Samuel procter, Samuel Woodsum[,] Charls hudman and Joseph Smith that Went outt A Scoutt the Day before this was took Prisoners[.] With them likewise Was a Good many more belonging to sd Redgt[;] the Enemy Is Killed A Good maney of our men Which we have found all Readey beside Sevearl more missing all thay Killed Belonging to our Regt thay used in the Most Barbous Maner And Also all the Enhabbitance Men Women and Children thay Used in the same Manner.[82]

Butler's account makes for an interesting comparison.

> Although our design of surprising the fort was thus frustrated, we nevertheless made an attempt, firing upon it for the space of ten minutes at about 70 yards distance, which was briskly returned both by the musketry and cannons. When finding it inaccessible on this part, I moved with the Rangers to explore the other side, destroying in our way a block house which the rebels had abandoned on our approach. But perceiving the Indians dispersed over the settlement, killing and taking prisoners the inhabitants, plundering and destroying the buildings, &c, I found it absolutely necessary to move again with the whole of the Rangers and take possession of an eminence which commanded the fort on the side we first attacked.
>
> In order to prevent a sally while the Indians were scattered as aforesaid, we remained in this position till late in the evening, though it rained incessantly. We retired about a mile further and there passed the night.[83]

After the Indians and Tories had retired, the garrison persisted in keeping the gates shut, which meant that many inhabitants who had escaped the slaughter were left outside "where they lay all night in the rain with children who suffered most."[84]

That first evening, some seventy captives were marched in a body through the snow, past the burning, smouldering ruins of the Continental storehouse and their homes and outbuildings to a point about two miles south of the fort, where the raiders had camped for the night. Large fires were kindled around the camp's perimeter, and the prisoners were herded into the centre around another large fire, where they could be readily watched. They were given nothing to cover themselves except what they had with them. If they chose to lie down, it was upon frigid, wet ground. The exultant voices of the warriors, recounting their deeds and dividing the plunder, could have been heard in every quarter.

Legend has it that Lieutenant-Colonel Stacey had been stripped naked and tied to a stake to be tortured and killed, but Brant passed by and recognized the colonel's Masonic sign of distress, and saved his life. If true, this indicates that Stacey had prior knowledge of Brant's Masonic membership (perhaps he had heard of Lieutenant Maynard's good fortune), or perhaps the Mohawk was wearing the order's emblem on his clothing.[85]

At seven o'clock that evening, Colonel Frederick Visscher, 3TCM, wrote from Johnstown to General Hand in Albany with a report about the attack on Cherry Valley. A Lieutenant Debe had escaped from there after seeing the Wells house on fire and the enemy surrounding the fort. Captain Parker had been with him, and went to Schoharie to warn them there. Debe thought that all the regiment's field officers had been taken prisoner; as he rode off, he could hear the cracks of constant firing.[86]

The next morning, the raiding force divided into elements. Captain John McDonell, sixty Rangers, Brant, and fifty warriors were sent back to the village to complete the destruction. The weakest of the Rangers and Native parties herded and led off the livestock. Butler failed to persuade the Senecas to leave the women

Native-trade silver Masonic emblems.

and children behind, and they were divided into smaller parties for ease of control and led away. Butler and the balance of the Rangers held back to support McDonell, should the garrison attempt a sally. When McDonell and Brant completed the burning, they gathered another large drove of horses and cattle to add to those already taken. Butler noted that the garrison had remained cooped up inside the works as spectators, and offered no resistance against the continued destruction.[87]

Yet, Butler's account was not entirely accurate. Massachusetts's Lieutenant McKendry recorded that on the 12th, a party was "Sent out and fetchd in Col Alden and Buried him under Arms with firing three vollies over his Grave."[88] And at daylight, Mrs. Clyde asked their apprentice, James Simon, who had been hiding under the log with her and the children, to sneak his way to the fort and see if the American flag was still flying. If it were, he was to run to the fort and obtain her husband's assistance, should he still be alive. Simon was successful, and Mrs. Clyde was rescued by a sally party of fourteen volunteers, led by her husband. The day before, she had missed her eldest daughter in the rush to gain safety, and hoped the girl had found her way into the fort, but this was not the case. The little ten-year-old — afraid, drenched and freezing — had been hiding all night, and when she approached the fort at daylight and saw sentinels on the walls, wrapped in blankets, she turned to flee, thinking they were Natives. Fortunately, she was seen, and brought safely in to join her father, mother, and siblings.[89]

McKendry continued, "Brant came with 100 Indians 8 … o'clock A.M. to attack ye fort ye Second time but receiving two or three Shots from the Cannon gave Back [and] left ye Fort 3 'Clock P.M. [The garrison b]rought in a No of the Dead Bodies." Rangers' Captain McDonell sent Lieutenant John Turney forward with a flag, presumably to discuss surrender terms, but he was fired upon and withdrew.[90]

Captain Warren recalled that the Indians attacked on the second morning, and were driven off by the fort's guns. Of course, this may have been Brant's tactical ploy to forestall a sally. After that attempt, he noted that the Natives completed the destruction of the village.[91]

Once again, if there were some four hundred soldiers, Continental and militia, in the fort, what was to stop a large sally driving off McDonell and Brant, other than a disastrous state of morale?

News of the attack on Cherry Valley reached Colonel Van Schaick in Albany on the morning of November 12. Despite being on a much-deserved leave with his family, he immediately rejoined his regiment, and by noon, he had the 1NY marching towards the Mohawk Valley.[92]

On the second morning, Butler and Indian Department captain John Johnston ("to whose knowledge and address in managing I am much indebted") persuaded the Senecas to allow twelve loyalist captives, who had been hitherto sheltered by the "humane assistance" of Brant and Captain Jacobs of Oquaga, to return to the village.[93] How these purported loyalists were going to be received by the troops and survivors in the fort bears some thought. They had nothing to go back to, any more than their rebel neighbours did, although there might have been some common feeling among all the victims, as they had all suffered the same pain and anguish.

In fact, the raiders released all the women and children, except the families of Colonel Campbell and State Congressman John Moore,[94] whom Captain Butler retained in hopes of exchanging them for his mother and sisters. In a letter dated November 12, which he gave to the returning women, he advised General Schuyler of this intention. His claim to have done everything in his power to avoid the butchery was true of the night of the raid in the camp, and the days following; however, his rather haughty, moralistic tone gave him a reputation he was never able to shake.

> I am induced by humanity to permit the persons whose names I send herewith, to return, lest the inclemency of the season, and their naked and helpless situation, might prove fatal to them, and expect that you will release an equal number of our people in your hands, amongst whom I expect you will permit Mrs. Butler and family to come to Canada; but if

> you insist upon it, I do engage to send you, moreover, an equal number of prisoners of yours, taken either by the Rangers or Indians, and will leave it to you to name the persons. I have done every thing in my power to restrain the fury of the Indians from hurting women and children, or killing the prisoners who fell into our hands, and would have more effectually prevented them, but that they were much incensed by the late destruction of their village of Auguaga by your people. I shall always continue to act in that manner. I look upon it beneath the character of a soldier to wage war with women and children. I am sure you are conscious that Colonel [John] Butler or myself have no desire that your women or children should be hurt. But, be assured, that if you persevere in detaining my father's family with you, that we shall no longer take the same pains to restrain the Indians from prisoners, women and children, that we have heretofore done.[95]

Brant had captured a fellow named Vrooman, whom he knew from before the war. After they had gone a few miles down the trail, he decided to release the man quietly, and told him to go back down the trail a couple of miles and collect some birch bark. He was sure his real purpose was understood, yet several hours farther along, who should reappear but Vrooman with the unwanted bark. There was nothing for it but to take him along.[96]

An individual with the initials M.R., whose sister and niece had been taken by the enemy, arrived in Cherry Valley to help collect and bury the dead, and assist the survivors to get organized to leave. He wrote:

> I was never before spectator of such a scene of distress and horror. The first object that presented, was a woman lying with her four children, two on

each side of her, all scalped; the next was the wife of the Reverend Mister Dunlap [Dunlop], likewise scalped, stripped quite naked, and much of her flesh devoured by the Indian dogs. But it would be tedious to mention all the shocking spectacles that were to be seen.... Of the wretched surviving inhabitants, there are 182 who have neither house nor home, nor a morsel of bread; are almost naked, and a great part of them without a penny to purchase any of the necessaries of life: And in all this massacre, there were but three men of the place killed, all the rest being helpless women and children. A great part of the sufferers, both killed and prisoners, were people much suspected of tory principles, and greatly depended on protection from Brant and Butler, who conducted this bloody and inhuman business.[97]

There is disagreement about the day the Tryon County militia arrived. The historian William Campbell reports that two hundred came on the 12th and assisted in the burial of the dead,[98] and Captain Warren reported their arrival between nine and ten o'clock that morning; however, in contradiction, there was a letter written on the 12th at 10:00 p.m. by Colonel Klock from John Moore's place, which he said was about four miles from Cherry Valley. "I arrived here this Evening with upwards of three hundred Men with an intent to march to Cherry Valley to morrow at break of day."[99] Did Klock record an incorrect date? Did he mean November 11? According to several participants, apparently not.

Yet another mystery was raised by a pension deposition of Nathaniel Potter, 17ACM, who claimed that when word arrived of the attack on Cherry Valley, Klock's force marched to within two miles of the settlement and camped for the night. A lieutenant from Cherry Valley was said to have got a drummer, and beat up for volunteers to march immediately to the settlement's aid. Potter said four companies rallied to him, but Colonels Klock and Gordon ordered them to stop, and threatened to have the rest of the force fire on them if they did not obey. The militia arrived "when the sun was about 2 hours high and the Tories and Indians went away about sunrise."[100]

Lieutenant McKendry recorded in his journal, "[November] 13th — Col Clock arriv'd at fort Alden 12 O Clock A.M. after a long cowardly March of 12 miles with 400 men[. He l]eft ye fort in about one hour and march'd back for Mohawk River."[101]

William Feeter, 2TCM, was in Klock's force, and recalled arriving within a few miles of Cherry Valley and encamping at a small house for the night. When they arrived at the settlement the next day, the garrison was "Collecting the dead into the fort." Daybold Moyer, 2TCM, also served in Klock's force, and he recalled staying at Bowman's Creek on the first night and reaching Cherry Valley "the second day after it was burned," i.e., November 13.[102]

Lodowick Kring, 2TCM, arrived with Klock. The militia found many of the houses still burning, and helped to put the fires out and gather the dead for burial.[103] According to Private Thaddeus Scribner, the militia arrived two hours after the raiders departed, and assisted in burying the dead. He recalled that the troops from Fort Plank were hurried back when word of Brant's attack south of the fort was received.[104]

The historian Francis Halsey found it incredible that Klock had not arrived before the attack, noting that the distance was only twenty miles, and the road "old and well travelled." General Hand had ordered Klock to pursue the enemy "if he found it practicable"; however, once on the scene, he decided not to do so, because "the enemy had gone too far to be overtaken," and his men were short of provisions and ammunition.[105] Captain Warren was disgusted with their performance. "Though there were 300 men between this and the river most of them together before we were attacked, yet they came within four miles and laid there until they were assured the enemy was gone off."[106] The vituperative militia captain Alexander Harper was particularly critical in a letter to Governor Clinton dated December 2, stating that Klock had come to Cherry Valley and "warmed himself, turned about, marched back without affording the distressed inhabitants the least assistance or release, even to bury the dead, or to collect the small remains of their cattle or goods." In a second letter, Harper expanded his theme; Klock "did not stay above two or three hours, notwithstanding the enemy had not retired above six or seven miles from the settlement." Harper was similarly unforgiving of Colonel Frederick Visscher, 3TCM, who arrived soon after Klock and similarly withdrew, reputedly not even assisting in burying the dead.[107]

What none of the critics give credit to is the effect the Oriskany battle had on all of the Tryon leaders. With exaggerated rumours of the size of Cornplanter's force, and the Natives' well-deserved reputation as fighters, as well as the reputation the Tories had gained in their own right, is it really any wonder that the colonels did not want to blunder into another ambush?

In contrast, Warren was impressed by his fellow Continental's response. "Col. [William] Butler, though near forty miles off, marched and got near and would have been the first to our assistance, had we not sent him word they were gone off." Warren's final comments spoke of the disastrous state of Alden's Massachusetts men, who only the week before had been hoping to be relieved. "We are here in a schocking situation; scarcely an officer that has anything left but what they have on their backs."[108] William Butler's relief force had been seven miles from Cherry Valley when they received an express from Major Whiting advising that the raiders had left on the 12th, and "had march'd twenty Miles before Evening," which convinced the Pennsylvanian that overtaking them was out of the question.

Whiting wrote of the attack in a report to General Hand, dated November 13. Either naively, or disingenuously, he stated that the enemy "notwithstanding all our endeavours to the contrary, surprised us." He advised that one of the captured scouts had been compelled to guide them to the officers' quarters, which, disregarding the menace of painted Seneca warriors, must have given rise to the rumours of the serjeant having Tory leanings. The major provided a partial list of the officers captured, and mentioned the killing and capturing of the inhabitants and their livestock and the burning of their homes and buildings. From his next lines, it is clear that the major did not consider the brief visits by the Tryon militia to have contributed much. "Notwithstanding the earliest and repeated dispatches to the river have had no reinforcement from there." Alarmingly, he noted, "Had it not been for a barrel of powder and half a box of cartridges belonging to the town our ammunition would have failed us." He closed with a postscript: "We have a soldier with his leg broken that's necessary to be amputated. The surgeon has no instruments; request a case to be sent if possible."[109]

Brigadier Ten Broeck sent a brief report of the attack to the governor, and advised that, at the request of General Hand, he had ordered three regiments to march to Schoharie as reinforcements.[110]

A Tragedy

During the march that day, Mrs. Campbell's family experienced a tragedy. Both of her parents, the Cannons, were with her; her father had been wounded, but was managing to get along; however, her mother was unable to maintain the pace, and, before her eyes, a guard struck the elder woman dead. Mrs. Campbell was clutching her eighteen-month-old child in her arms, and must have hesitated at the gruesome sight, as the guard drove her forward by threatening with his bloody hatchet. A couple of days later, responsibility for Mrs. Campbell and her family fortunately fell to an older Native, who was far more conciliatory than her mother's killer.[111]

Captain Warren's Account

Captain Warren wrote about the second day after the initial attack: "Nov. 13 — In the afternoon and morning of the 13th we sent out parties after the enemy withdrew; brought in the dead; such a shocking sight my eyes never beheld before of savage and brutal barbarity; to see the husband mourning over his dead wife with four dead children lying by her side, mangled, scalpt, and some their heads, some their legs and arms cut off, some torn the flesh off their bones by their dogs — twelve of one family killed and four of them burnt in his house."[112]

General Consternation

Fifteen days later, Brigadier James Clinton wrote to his brother, the governor, with "a genuine account of the slain, and prisoners taken": thirty-one had been killed "and barbarously massacred;" thirty-three carried off; thirty-eight made prisoners and permitted to return."[113]

Rumours and alarums were now general up and down the river. Lieutenant-Colonel Clyde arrived at Fort Plank from Cherry Valley, and reported to Colonel Gordon that Fort Alden had been taken by storm that day at noon. Clyde had been with a burial party, and had collected the few effects that the Natives had missed or ignored, when he heard cannon fire from the fort. He ran toward it, and could "not see any one in the outside, but heard dreadful yells of Indians and cries of murder in the inside." Gordon sent an appeal to Colonel Goose Van Schaick in Albany to march his 1NY regiment up as quickly as possible, and have them "ready to assist us in case they should come toward the river this morning."

At eleven o'clock that night, Jelles Fonda wrote to Van Schaick from Johnstown. He had received word from Colonel Bellinger at German Flatts that Fort Plank was under attack. Bellinger had heard cannon fire, as did the express rider who had brought him this news. Fonda pled with Van Schaick to march his regiment immediately. Of course, the 1NY was already on the march.

The next day, General Hand wrote to Governor Clinton from Schenectady to advise that he had recommended that Colonel Klock use the three hundred militiamen he had collected to pursue the enemy if practicable; however, the lack of ammunition and provisions, and the fact that the enemy had gone too far to be overtaken, "induced the Colonel to lay aside all thoughts of a pursuit and disband his Regiment." On receipt of this advice, Hand had turned back from Caughnawaga and arrived at Schenectady in the evening, where he received word that Fort Alden had fallen. He reported that Van Schaick's 1NY regiment had arrived at Fort Johnson on the morning of the 15th, and would push forward with all dispatch to Fort Plank.[114] The number of express riders moving back and forth through the valley must surely have been legion.

More Killing

During the withdrawal, Cornplanter's war party killed a family named Buxton, who resided on Butternut Creek, and burned their farm.[115] Senecas also plundered a place known as Sleeper's Mills, but did not find a quantity of cash that Mrs. Sleeper had hidden among some rags. John Sleeper was away, and his wife and ten children were left unharmed, but destitute. When Brant came on the scene, he was distressed that the family had been attacked, as John Sleeper had been one of his willing suppliers. He offered some cash to Mrs. Sleeper, which she declined, as she thought it had been taken from other settlers — which, in Brant's case, was unlikely.[116]

Although Brant had joined in the withdrawal, he only went part way before deciding to remain in the valley, take a prisoner, and burn the home of the dead brigadier Nicholas Herkimer. He set off with four of his warriors, but for some reason did not attempt Herkimer's place, striking instead the Chyle settlement near Fort Plank, where the party burned four houses and barns and took three prisoners, and Brant uttered the threat that "he would still have the river."[117]

Raiders' Casualties

Warren reported that the Cherry Valley garrison's first supply of provisions since the original attack arrived on November 15. In the afternoon, a scout of a serjeant and eight men, sent out by Colonel Alden and presumed killed, returned safe.[118] Although the timing does not seem quite correct, it is possible that it was the arrival of these fellows that prompted the firing by the garrison and led to Clyde's exaggerated report of the fall of the fort, as he reported to Colonel Visscher that "[t]he reason of the Alarm was by a Scout of ours that went out last Sunday that we expected was taken, it got in safe, they appearing in their Blanketts, were taken for the Enemy, when the mistake was found out [it] caused the noise that we heard, and the small arms that was fired."[119] Fort Alden had a very nervous garrison!

Warren reported that when the released women and children arrived at the fort, they said that the raiders had a number of wounded. With some satisfaction, he theorized that the enemy had had more men killed than the defenders. He noted that there had been a "thick snowstorm" all day, and that by the day following, there was almost a knee-deep accumulation; however, his thoughts about the raiders' casualties were wishful thinking, as Lieutenant Hare brought word to Fort Niagara before the Rangers' return that the former had one man wounded, and the Indians two.[120] Captain Butler was more specific in his report: "We are happy in not having lost a man; our fifer-major, one private and three Indians only, wounded." He listed the Continentals killed as "the Colonel, 2 Captains, 2 Lieutenants, one Ensign and 20 Privates; the Prisoners a Lieutenant-Colonel, a Lieutenant, an Ensign, the Surgeons Mate & 10 Privates." One wonders if the fife-major was wounded when Captain McDonell's flag was spurned by the garrison.[121]

After all the inhabitants' corpses had been attended to in Cherry Valley, there was nothing to keep the survivors there, and they migrated to the Mohawk River, where they received assistance and temporary lodging. Whether any of the local militia stayed at the fort is unknown, but the 6MA were left in garrison amid the stark desolation until the following summer, when the post was abandoned.[122]

Walter Butler's Report

Captain Butler and his Rangers were at Unadilla on November 17 when he wrote a detailed report to his father. In addition to the information noted above, he added, "I have much to lament that notwithstanding my utmost precaution and endeavours to save the women and children, I could not prevent some of them falling unhappy victims to the fury of the savages. They have carried off many of the inhabitants prisoners and killed more. Among the latter is Coln. Cloyd, a very violent rebel." That last was wishful thinking, as Lieutenant-Colonel Clyde was very much alive. Butler reported the release of some women and children, and the good offices of Joseph Brant and Captain Jacobs. He also complimented the performance of Captain John McDonell, "whose activity and spirit on every occasion does him much honour and to whose conduct I am much indebted." In a postscript, he recognized the men of the 8th Regiment, who "were particularly alert in every point of duty." Was Walter displaying good leadership with these sensible acknowledgements, or perhaps courting allies to defend his role in the raid? He also reported news of several movements of British and rebel troops, including the planning at Albany of an expedition against Carleton Island. Several of the raid's prisoners predicted that "the rebels intend to invade Indian Country in the spring with an army of 3,000 men."[123]

Clinton's and Hand's Recommendations

By the 17th, the 1NY had arrived at Caughnawaga. After a short halt, Van Schaick ordered the resumption of the advance at midday, after turning over command to his lieutenant-colonel, which allowed him to resume his leave.[124]

This same day, Governor Clinton set the tone for the coming campaign of 1779 when he wrote to John Jay, a New York State representative in the Continental Congress. After advising Jay about the destruction of Cherry Valley, and the erroneous report of the loss of Fort Alden, he got to the meat of the matter:

> Fatal Experience has more than sufficiently taught us the Impracticability of defending our extensive Frontiers by the Militia of the County & the small Proportion of regular Troops imployed in that service against an Enemy acting upon a desultory Plan. There are so many Passes leading into the Different important Settlements to the Northward & westward which equally claim attention, that when the present Force is distributed for their Defence it becomes too weak to resist the united strength of the Enemy employed against any particular Point.... This is the 7th valuable settlement in the state which this season has been destroyed exclusive the Injuries & Distresses experienced by Individuals. The Public have lost by the Destruction of these settlements some of the principle Granaries in this State from whence alone the army might have drawn supplies sufficient, at least to have prevented their present want.
>
> It is of the utmost Importance that some more effectual Measures than have hitherto been pursued be adopted for the Defence of the Frontiers & I am perswaded this can only be effected by Offensive Opperations, thereby carrying the War into the Enemy's Country, For which Purpose a proper Force ought to be imployed. I might say raised for, unless the Enemy at N.Y. [City] leave us I can't think a Competent Force can be detached from the Main Army without leaving it too Weak. If the Enemy are suffered to continue their Depredations much longer the Consequence may be fatal, as this state will be disabled from furnishing any supplies to the army & hitherto they have depended upon it for Bread.[125]

Brigadier Hand wrote a detailed report to General Washington on November 18, advising that the reports of the fall of Fort Alden and the attack on Fort Plank were in error. He had taken action by approving a petition from the Mohawk District inhabitants for a blockhouse for fifty men, to be built at Sacandaga to cover the route that Ross and other raiders had employed earlier in the year. He recommended removing the 6MA from Cherry Valley, now that the settlement was destroyed, and offered some suggestions for alternate postings. Although he had not been in conference with Governor Clinton, he held similar thoughts about what was needed to defend the region. "I am firmly of Opinion that untill the Season & other Circumstances will admit of our Acting Offensively against the Savages, or Prosecutg some other Measures that May attract their Attention we will not be secure here, so extensive a Frontier, can never be defended against the Indian incursions of a Numerous Enemy, especially when they for the most part to be opposed by Militia harrased by Continual Alarms & dispersed over the whole Face of the Country."[126]

Relief for Stricken Families

The arrival of Colonel Campbell and Congressman Moore in Albany prompted Abraham Yates Jr., a prominent politician, to observe to the governor that New York State had no formal provision for granting relief to families that had suffered the complete loss of their properties and effects. He recommended that Congress empower an officer in every quarter of the country with the powers and means for this purpose, chargeable upon the Continent, i.e., the United States. A similar letter was sent by the governor's brother, Brigadier James Clinton, advising that he had authorized the commissary at Schenectady to issue each family a week's provisions.

The governor responded to Yates on December 3, comparing the Cherry Valley tragedy to that of German Flatts, and noting that the assistance rendered to the victims of the latter had been approved on the basis that the relief granted would continue as long as the inhabitants garrisoned and maintained Fort Dayton; however, a similar condition was not applicable in the former case. He requested that Albany County provide assistance to the Cherry Valley sufferers until the state legislature was able to address the issue.[127]

Cayugas Threaten the Oneidas

While the uproar over the Cherry Valley atrocities echoed throughout the Mohawk region and beyond, the Oneidas, who for many months had anticipated retaliatory attacks by their Iroquoian brothers, were threatened by the Cayugas. In mid-December, Peter Johnson, a Cayuga emissary, visited Kanowalohale to deliver a litany of accusations and suspicions, to wit: the Oneidas had broken the confederacy's three-hundred-year-old bond of concerted action; the losses of the British-allied tribes at Oriskany were attributed to them; they were providing intelligence to the rebels, and perhaps had assisted the rebels in destroying Unadilla and Oquaga. It was noted that the Oneidas "had Exposed themselves to the severe Resentment of the other tribes," and that the Cayugas could no longer protect them. If they would not take up the hatchet against the rebels, then they must remain neutral and move to the Susquehanna River, so they would "not be trodden under Foot by the Kings People who intend to pass by you in the Spring." A few days after this ultimatum was received, Good Peter Agorondajats visited Lieutenant-Colonel Van Dyck at Fort Stanwix to discuss the Cayugas' challenge. For the Oneidas to stay true to their commitment to the rebel cause, they needed protection and supplies. The fort that had been promised to them earlier in the year still had not been erected, nor had the promised troops arrived.[128]

to them until you shall at length convince them that such indiscriminate vengeance taken even upon the treacherous and cruel enemy they are engaged against is as useless and disreputable to themselves as it is contrary to the dispositions and maxims of their King in whose cause they are fighting.[132]

Brigadier James Clinton and Captain Butler Exchange Letters

Walter Butler's letter to General Philip Schuyler, which he had written at Cherry Valley on November 12, received an acerbic reply from Brigadier James Clinton of the New York Continental brigade. There is nothing conciliatory in Clinton's message, and the brigadier's disdain for the behaviour of the Natives and Tories is most obvious.

As young Butler's whereabouts were unknown, a Flag was sent with Colonel Campbell — as a most interested party — and two other officers. They were to attempt to search Butler out and deliver the message.

> Should the prisoners be in any of the Indian villages and in condition to be moved, you will be pleased to send them to the nearest of our settlements, or if you do not choose to do that, I will send proper persons to treat and receive them at any point you may appoint.
>
> I am not informed if Mrs Butler and her family and such others as will be given in exchange for those you have in captivity and those you have suffered to return as you mentioned in your letter, would choose to move in this inclement weather. If they do, they shall be sent; if not, they may remain until spring, and then they may either go to Oswego or Canada at their option.

Should the prisoners taken at Cherry Valley, or any others belonging to the State of New York, be at Niagara, it will be impossible for them to return until spring. And then I request that they may be sent to Oswego or Fort Schuyler [Stanwix], and that you will send notice of your determination, that provisions may be made accordingly.

Don't flatter yourself, Sir, that your father's family were detained on account of any consequence they were supposed to be of, or that it is determined they should be exchanged in consideration of the threat contained in your letter.

I should hope for the sake of human nature and the honour of civilized nations that the British officers had exerted themselves in restraining the barbarity of the savages; but it is difficult even for the most disinterested mind to believe it, as numerous instances of barbarities have been perpetuated when the savages were not present have occurred, or if they were, the British force was sufficient to have restrained them had there been a real desire so to do.

The enormous murders committed at Wyoming and Cherry Valley would clearly have justified a retaliation and that your mother has not fallen a sacrifice to the resentment of the survivors of those families who were barbarously massacred is owing to the humane principles of which the conduct of their enemies induces a belief that they were utter strangers to.[133]

The Oneidas could conceive of no method for the rebel officers to deliver the letter safely, so finally Colonel Campbell left it at Kanowalohale, from where it was taken to Niagara by an Oneida emissary. A long delay ensued before Walter made a carefully considered reply on February 18, perhaps coached by his father and

Lieutenant-Colonel Bolton. Only his final comment displayed a measure of pique.

> I could wish Mrs Butler and family, including Mrs Sheehan and son and Mrs Wall, were permitted to go to Canada in the spring, even should the exchange be fixed at Ontario [Oswego.]
>
> It's not our present business, Sir, to enter into an altercation or to reflect on the conduct of either the British or Continental Forces, or on that of each other; but since you have charged (on report, I must suppose) the British officers in general with inhumanity, and Colonel Butler and myself in particular, in justice to them and in vindication of his and my own honour and character, I am under the disagreeable necessity to declare the charge unjust and void of truth, and which can only tend to deceive the world, though a favourite cry of the Congress on every occasion, whether founded on truth or no.
>
> We deny any Cruelties to have been committed at Wyoming, either by whites or Indians. So far to the contrary, that not a man, woman or child was hurt after the capitulation, or a woman or child before it, or taken into captivity. Though should you call it inhumanity the killing of men in arms in the field, we in that case can plead guilty.
>
> The inhabitants killed at Cherry Valley does not lay at my door, my conscience acquits me.
>
> If any are guilty (as accessories), it's yourselves, at least the conduct of some of your officers. First Colonel Hartley of your Forces sent to the Indians the enclosed, being a copy of his letter, charging them with crimes they never committed and threatening them and their villages with fire and sword and no quarter. The burning of their villages then inhabited

only by a few families your [Native] friends, who imagined they might remain in peace and friendship with you, till assured a few hours before the arrival of your troops that they should not even receive quarter, took to the woods; and to complete the matter, Colonel Denniston and his people again appearing in arms with Colonel Hartley after a solemn engagement not to bear arms during the war.

And Colonel Denniston not performing his promise to release a number of soldiers belonging to Colonel Butler's Corps of Rangers then prisoners among you, were the reasons assigned by the Indians to me, after the destruction of Cherry Valley for their not acting in the same manner as at Wyoming. They added that being charged by the enemies with what they never had done and threatened by them, they had determined to convince you it was not fear that prevented them from committing the one, and that they did not want spirit to put your threats against them in force against yourselves.

The prisoners sent back by me, or any now in our or the Indians' hands, but must declare I did everything in my power to prevent the Indians killing the prisoners, or taking women and children captive or in any wise injuring them.

Colonel Stacey and several other officers of yours will acquit me and must further declare they have received every assistance before and since their arrival at this post that could be got to relieve their wants.

I must, however, beg leave, by the by, to observe that I experienced no humanity or even common justice during my imprisonment with you.[134]

Notes

Chapter One: Lake Champlain, Upper Hudson River, and Lower Quebec

1. **Whitcomb**: Mike Barbieri, "Living History" (hereafter Whitcomb), *Rutland Historical Society Quarterly* 8.4 (Fall 1978), 25–39; Robert K. Wright, Jr., *The Continental Army* (Washington: Army Lineage Series, Centre of Military History, United States Army, 1989), 200.
2. Gavin K. Watt, *Poisoned by Lies and Hypocrisy: America's First Attempt to Bring Liberty to Canada, 1775–1776* (Toronto: Dundurn Press, 2014), 86, 129–46, 152; http://en.wikipedia.org/wiki/Timothy_Bedel.
3. Caleb Star, trans. and ed., *Memoir and Official Correspondence of Gen. John Stark, with Notices of Several Other Officers of the Revolution…* (hereafter *Stark Correspondence*) (Concord, NH: G. Parker Lyon, 1860), 142; Max M. Mintz, *The Generals of Saratoga, John Burgoyne and Horatio Gates* (New Haven: Yale University Press, 1990), 228; Paul L. Stevens, "His Majesty's 'Savage' Allies: British Policy and the Northern Indians During the Revolutionary War: The Carleton Years, 1774–1778" (hereafter "Allies") (PhD diss., State University of New York at Buffalo, 1986), XXIII, 1530; Wright, 122fn. Wright cites letter from Hazen to Gates, October 26, 1977.
4. Journals of Congress, 1777–78, vol. 3, 10; E.P. Walton, ed., *Records of the Council of Safety and Governor and Council of the State of Vermont, to which are prefixed the Records of the General Conventions*

from July 1775 to December 1777 (hereafter *Vermont Minutes*) (Montpelier, VT: Steam Press of J. & J.M. Poland, 1873), I, 217n.

5. **Conway cabal**: http://en.wikipedia.org/wiki/Conway_Cabal.
6. Mintz, 229, 230; www.ushistory.org/valleyforge/served/lafayette.html.
7. Board of War to Lafayette, January 20, 1778, Library of Congress, Manuscript Division, George Washington Papers.
8. **Rebel occupation, 1775–76**: Gustave Lanctot, *Canada and the American Revolution, 1774–1783*, trans. Margaret M. Cameron (Toronto: George G. Harrap & Co. Ltd, 1967); Watt, *Poisoned*, 162.
9. Stevens, "Allies," XXI, 1437, 1438.
10. Stevens, "Allies," XXIII, 1532, 1536; Colin G. Calloway, *The American Revolution in Indian Country: Crisis and Diversity in Native American Communities* (Cambridge, U.K.: Cambridge University Press, 1995), 73.
11. *Vermont Minutes*, I, 227–29; Stevens, "Allies," XXIII, 1532.
12. Ebenezer Mack and Jules Cloquet, *The Life of Gilbert Motier de La Fayette, etc.*, (2013), 65–69, https://books.google.ca/books/The_Life_of_Gilbert_Motier_de_Lafayette.html?id=Zx) RAAAAYAAJ&redir_esc=y.
13. *Vermont Minutes*, I, 225.
14. Ibid., 226. For details of the men's services under Burgoyne and after, see Gavin K. Watt, *The British Campaign of 1777 — Volume 2: The Burgoyne Expedition — Burgoyne's Native and Loyalist Auxiliaries* (Milton, ON: Global Heritage Press, 2013).
15. **Warner**: Walter S. Fenton, "Seth Warner," *Proceedings of the Vermont Historical Society*, New Series, VIII.4 (1940), 346. Curiously, this promotion was not recognized in later documentation. Warner had been favoured with a 1775 appointment as colonel of the Green Mountain Regiment over the flamboyant Ethan Allen. However, Ethan's brother Ira harboured great resentment and, from his key role in postwar government, may have been instrumental in having Warner's promotion removed from historical documentation. Ibid., 335; *Vermont Minutes*, I, 74.
16. Barbieri, Whitcomb.
17. Michael Barbieri research; Abby Maria Hemenway, ed., *The Vermont Historical Gazetteer*, 3 vols. (Claremont, NH: Claremont Manufacturing Co, 1877), III, 1082–83.
18. Stevens, "Allies," XXIII, 1533; Carleton to Germain, June 19, 1778, in Historical Section of the General Staff, ed., "The War

of the American Revolution, The Province of Quebec under the Administration of Governor Frederic Haldimand, 1778–1784," in *A History of the Organization, Development and Services of the Military and Naval Forces of Canada From the Peace of Paris in 1763 to the Present Time with Illustrative Documents* (hereafter *HSGS*), vol. 2 (Canada: King's Printer, n.d.), II, 256, ex LAC, CO, Series Q, V.15, 256.

19. Stevens, "Allies," XXIII, 1532, 1533.
20. *Vermont Minutes*, March 6 and 8, 1778, I, 228. A "block-fort" was built by Ethan Allen in 1773 in New Haven, on the falls of Otter Creek, ibid., 228n.
21. Ida H. and Paul A. Washington, *Carleton's Raid* (hereafter Washingtons) (Canaan, NH: Phoenix Publishing, 1977), 25–27; *Vermont Minutes*, I, 227, 245–46; Paul L. Stevens, *Louis Lorimier in the American Revolution, 1777–1782: A Mémoire by an Ohio Indian Trader and British Partisan* (Naperville, IL: The Center for French Colonial Studies, Inc., 1997), 4, 5. **Philo**: Possibly Lieutenant Philo Hurlburt, QLR. Prior to the war, he had been a Green Mountain Boy who came away with Samuel Adams of Arlington in early 1777. For details of his service, see Watt, *Burgoyne's Auxiliaries*, 158n17. Another possibility is Philo Hard, perhaps of Arlington, who was chosen as 2Lieut in Brownson's Coy, Warner's Regt, but chose not to serve. He served Burgoyne as a conductor of wagons during the expedition. Details of his later service have not been found. See Watt, ibid., 72; Stevens, "Allies," XXIII, 1533, 1534. Stevens postulates the raid was led by a Royal Highland Emigrants' officer, with some men of his regiment and other loyalists, probably Queen's Loyal Rangers. He claims the RHE officer was killed, along with Chamilly de Lorimier and a warrior. He claims further that the party had eight wounded, five killed, and six captured. I have found nothing to substantiate these contentions, and believe that Captain Sawyer would have reported such a triumph and mentioned whether Tories had participated. I contend that Lorimier conceived and led the raid, acting upon Philo's intelligence, and employed his band of loyal Kahnawakes, likely with Campbell's specific permission. To further my theory, I consulted Kim Stacy, who has spent decades researching the two RHE battalions ("No One Harms Me with Impunity: The History, Organization, and Biographies of the 84th Regiment of Foot [Royal Highland Emigrants] and Young Royal Highlanders, During the Revolutionary War 1775–1784"

[manuscript in progress, 1994.]) Stacy searched his database and found no reference to the death of an RHE subaltern in 1778, nor to an RHE raiding party against Shelburne, Vermont.
22. Stevens, "*Allies*," XXIII, 1534, 1535.
23. Schuyler to Laurens, Albany, March 15, 1778, in Maryly B. Penrose, ed., *Indian Affairs Papers, American Revolution* (Franklin Park, NJ: Liberty Bell Associates, 1981), 120–21.
24. *Vermont Minutes*, I, 246.
25. Ibid., 247, 248.
26. Ibid., 248–50; http://en.wikipedia.org/wiki/Elisha_Payne. **Cumberland County**: "Cumberland county, the first established in the grants, was erected by the legislature of the Province of New York, July 3, 1766, and comprised about the district of territory now occupied by Windsor and Windham counties. It probably received its name from Prince William, the Duke of Cumberland.... At the first session of the legislature of Vermont, in 1778, the State was, on the 17th of March, divided into two counties, the division line being fixed February 11, 1779, the territory on the western side of the mountains being called Bennington county, and that on the eastern, Unity county, though the latter name was changed back to Cumberland on the 21st of the same month." *Gazetteer and Business Directory of Windsor County, Vt., for 1883–84*, vol.1, 21–25.
27. *Vermont Minutes*, I, 251.
28. Ibid., 252, 253.
29. Ibid., 253, 254. **Smith**: ibid., in Warner's 1775, see 6, 7. As major, 5th regiment, May 28 1778, see 260.
30. *Vermont Minutes*, I, 6, 256–59. **Brownson**: Gideon Brownson of Sunderland was the fifth captain in Warner's Regiment, appointed July 26, 1775. He was later a major in the Continental service, and then a militia general.
31. Gates to Conway, Fishkill, May 18, 1778, *Stark Correspondence*, 143.
32. Gates to Stark, Fishkill, May 18, 1778, and Commissioners to Stark, Albany, May 18, 1778, *Stark Correspondence*, 144.
33. Barclay to Stark, Albany, May 20 1778, and Stark to Gates, May 21, 1778, *Stark Correspondence*, 146, 147.
34. Stark to Gates, Albany, May 24, 1778, and Gates to Stark, HQ, May 30, 1778, *Stark Correspondence*, 151, 155.
35. Stark to Gates, Albany, May 31, 1778, *Stark Correspondence*, 156.
36. Stark to Gates, Albany, June 2, 1778, *Stark Correspondence*, 157, 158.
37. Stark to Gates, Albany, June 4, 1778, *Stark Correspondence*, 159, 160.

38. Gates to Stark, June 8, 1778, *Stark Correspondence*, 161.
39. Bolton to Carleton, Niagara, April 8, 1778, and Butler to Carleton, Niagara, April 10, 1778, Smy transcripts, HP, AddMss21756.
40. *Quebec Gazette*, June 4, 1778.
41. Council minutes, June 9, 1778, *Vermont Minutes*, I, 263, 264. **Redding**: Watt, *Burgoyne's Auxiliaries*, 187; Dr. H. C. Burleigh, *The Bones of David Redding* (printed by author, n.d.); John Spargo, *The Story of David Redding Who Was Hanged* (Bennington, VT: Bennington Historical Museum, 1945). Hanging of Tories and suspected Tories, or disaffected persons, was a common occurrence in the United States. In contrast, no rebels were hanged in Quebec during the revolution.
42. Council minutes, June 12, 1778, *Vermont Minutes*, I, 264fn; Chilton Williamson, *Vermont in Quandry: 1763–1825* (Montpelier, VT: Vermont Historical Society, 1949), 79.
43. *Vermont Minutes*, I, 265, 266.
44. Ibid., 267–69. **Fletcher**: biography of Samuel Fletcher taken from a "History of Eastern Vermont," found at www.rootsweb.ancestry.com/~vtwindha/hev/hevbio632.htm.
45. Gates to Stark, Peekskill, June 17, 1778, *Stark Correspondence*, 163, 164.
46. Allen to Stark, Bennington, June 18, 1778, and Stark to Allen, Albany June 20, 1778, *Stark Correspondence*, 164–65.
47. **Allen**: Vermont negotiations. See Gavin K. Watt, *A Dirty, Trifling Piece of Business, Volume I: The Revolutionary War as Waged from Canada in 1781* (Toronto: Dundurn Press, 2009), on the hanging, 361–64; and Vermont negotiations, *passim*.
48. Stark to Gates, Albany, June 29, 1778, and Stark to Gates, July 7, 1778, *Stark Correspondence*, 166, 179.
49. See http://davidlibraryar.blogspot.ca/2010/11/timothy-bedel-papers-and-andrew-park.html; www.nhhistory.org/finding_aids/finding_aids/Bedel_Timothy_Papers_1880.001.pdf; President Weare to NH's Congressional delegates, Exeter, August 19, 1778, *Vermont Minutes*, I, Appendix G, 413.
50. Stevens, "Allies," XXIII, 1536–39.
51. Stark to Hampshire County's brigadier, Albany, June 23, 1778, *Stark Correspondence*, 168.
52. Stark to Gates, Albany, June 26, 1778, *Stark Correspondence*, 170, 171.
53. *Quebec Gazette*, June 27, 1778; Haldimand to Germain, Quebec, July 25, 1778, HSGS, II, 47, 48, ex CO, Q15, 162–66.

54. Stark to Weare, Albany, June 28, 1778, *Stark Correspondence*, 172–73.
55. **Welch**: see "Roll of Warner's Additional Corps (Green Mountain Boys)," in James A. Roberts, *New York in the Revolution as Colony and State* (hereafter *New York in the Revolution*), 2 vols. (Albany: State of New York, 1904), 61, 62; "David S. Welch," in *The Revolution Remembered: Eyewitness Accounts of the War for Independence*, edited by John C. Dann (Chicago: The University of Chicago Press, 1980), 274–77.
56. Stark to Gates and Stark to Warner, Albany, July 9, 1778, *Stark Correspondence*, 176, 177.
57. Gates to Stark, White Plains, July 16, 1778, *Stark Correspondence*, 181; **d'Estaing**: b.1729; d.1794. Served in India during the Seven Years' War. Governor of Antilles, 1763–66. Vice admiral, 1767. "D'Estaing was an energetic commander, but his lack of naval experience caused him to be diffident before smaller British forces. His caution and hesitancy greatly disappointed the colonists during a crucial phase of the war." He commanded the National Guard at Versailles at the outbreak of the French Revolution and was guillotined in Paris during the Reign of Terror. See www.britannica.com/EBchecked/topic/193274/Charles-Hector-count-dEstaing; Washington to d'Estaing, July 14, 1778, Library of Congress, Manuscript Division, George Washington Papers.
58. Stark to Gates, Albany, July 15, 1778, *Stark Correspondence*, 177.
59. Williamson, 72, 73; *Public Papers of George Clinton, First Governor of New York, 1777–1795, 1801–1804* (hereafter *PPGC*), 6 vols. (New York and Albany: State of New York, 1902), III, 552.
60. "Narrative of John Peters, Lieutenant-Colonel of the Queen's Loyal Rangers in Canada, drawn by himself in a letter to a friend in London, Pimlico June 5, 1786," *The Daily Globe*, Toronto, July 16, 1877, found in the AO, H.H. Robertson Papers; Mary Beacock Fryer, *King's Men: The Soldier Founders of Ontario* (Toronto: Dundurn Press, 1980), 224.
61. Haldimand to Peters, Quebec City, July 25, 1778, LAC, HP, B62 (AddMss21722), 14, 15.
62. Flora J. Rhicard, "The Road That Never Was," in *Rovers, Rebels and Royalists*, Missisquoi Historical Society Reports 18 (1984): 80–89.
63. Haldimand to SJJ, Quebec, July, 16, 1778, *HSGS*, 47, ex LAC, HP, B80, 17; Haldimand to Peters, July 16, 1778, HP, B62 (AddMss21722), 17; "Joseph Langlois dit Traversy (1728–1806): Un agent secret au service des Américains," www.familleslanglois.com/

deja-parus/Joseph%20Langlois%20dit%20Traversy%20-%20Un%20 agent%20secret.pdf; Haldimand to Germain, Quebec, July 28, 1778, *HSGS*, 48, ex CO, Q15.
64. Bayley to Gates, Newbury, July 13, 1778, *New Hampshire State Papers*, vol. XVII, V.4, 240, www.rootsweb.com/~vermont/History HazenMilitaryRoad.html.
65. Peters to Haldimand, August 11, 1778, Washingtons, 10; Watt, "The Quebec Indian Department 1777–78," *Burgoyne's Auxiliaries*, 327–33.
66. Barbara Graymont, *The Iroquois in the American Revolution* (Syracuse: Syracuse University Press, 1972), 175, ex Claim of Daniel Claus, American Loyalists, XLIIII, 423, 424; Stevens, "Allies," XXII, 1455.
67. Stark to Washington, Albany, July 31, 1778, *Stark Correspondence*, 183.
68. Stark to Chittenden, Albany, July 29, 1778, *Stark Correspondence*, 183.
69. Clinton to Congress, Poughkeepsie, September 7, 1778, *PPGC*, III, 743.
70. Stark to Washington, September 15, 1778, *Stark Correspondence*, 189, 190.
71. Stark to British Commander at Crown Point and Stark to Chittenden, Albany, September 24, 1778, *Stark Correspondence*, 190, 191; Chris McHenry, compiler, *Rebel Prisoners at Quebec, 1778–1783: Being a List of American Prisoners Held by the British During the Revolutionary War* (Lawrenceburg, IN: printed by author, 1981).
72. Council minutes, September 30, 1778, *Vermont Minutes*, I, 274.
73. Haldimand to Germain, October 15, 1778, Washingtons, 10, 11.
74. **Carleton, Christopher**: b.1747, England; d.1787. Ens, 3rd, December 12, 1761. Ens, 31st, February 12, 1762. Lieut, 31st, July 29, 1763. Capt-Lieut, 31st, December 25, 1770. Capt, 31st, September 23, 1772. Maj, 29th, September 13, 1777. Bvt LCol, 29th, February 19, 1783. See John A. Houlding, "The King's Service: The Officers of the British Army, 1735–1792" (u.p., n.d.).
75. John Enys, *The American Journals of Lt John Enys* (hereafter *Enys*), edited by Elizabeth Cometti (Syracuse: Adirondack Museum and Syracuse University Press, 1976) 23; Washingtons, 16.
76. **Chambers:** On March 24, 1779, Haldimand requested Germain promote two naval officers — John Schank and William Chambers. Schank commanded on Lakes Ontario and Erie, and Chambers, Champlain. At the time, Chambers was acting locally as master and commander, with the rank of captain, which he had done for some two years, and Haldimand wished to have this officially confirmed.

This was done on April 8, 1780. James M. Hadden, *A Journal Kept in Canada and Upon Burgoyne's Campaign in 1776 and 1777*, edited by Horatio Rogers (Albany: Joel Munsell's Sons, 1884), Appendix 18, 542–44.

77. Haldimand to Chambers and Haldimand to MacBean, October 17, 1778, Washingtons, 17. **Royal and Mantelet**: George Smith, *An Universal Military Dictionary…* (Ottawa: Museum Restoration Service, 1969; first published in 1779 by J. Millan), 158, 227.
78. *Enys*, 23.
79. **Enys**: A prolific writer of detailed, insightful records of two tours of duty in North America. The second tour included a private visit with General Washington and his family in 1787 before Enys returned to England. Rather unusually for the time, Enys's entire career was in the 29th Regiment. Lieutenant, February 1778. Captain, 1783. Half-pay, 1783. That fall, he was restored and given orders to join the regiment in Canada. Served at Forts Haldimand, Frontenac, and Ontario. In Britain, he was promoted to major, March 1794, and lieutenant-colonel, September 1796. He retired in 1800. *Enys*, xvii–xxxiii.
80. Washingtons, 33, ex "Return of the Commissioned Non Commission'd Officers Drumrs & Private Going on the Expedition Under the Command of Maj Christopher Carleton"; **29th Rangers**: Major H. Everard, *History of Thos. Farrington's Regiment subsequently Designated The 29th (Worcestershire) Foot 1694 to 1891* (Worcester: Littleby & Company, The Worcester Press, 1891), Chapter V. Everard offers some details on the creation of Ranger companies in several British regiments in 1779, and notes that the 29th had such a company in 1778. Everard, who consulted Enys's journals in the preparation of the regimental history, states that Enys served in the Ranger Company, but does not say when, and Enys's published journal does not provide this information.
81. Powell to Haldimand, October 24, 1778, Washingtons, 18.
82. **Campbell**: Carleton's journal hints that this Campbell was a loyalist, living on Lake Champlain, who had risked collecting intelligence. Michael Barbieri, a New England historian, thinks he may have been William James Campbell, who was involved in intelligence affairs for Haldimand. More likely, he was George Campbell, who saw service under Burgoyne first in the King's Loyal Americans, then in Munro's bateaux company. At the end of the campaign, he appears to have returned home. A George Campbell served as a guide for

Major Carleton during his 1780 raid. By 1781, he was a serjeant in Breakenridge's Company, King's Rangers, and was on Secret Service work that year. By 1784, he was a serjeant in Pritchard's Company. See Watt, *Burgoyne's Auxiliaries*, 249; Gavin K. Watt, *The Burning of the Valleys: Daring Raids from Canada Against the New York Frontier in the Fall of 1780* (Toronto: Dundurn Press, 1997), 102; and Gavin K. Watt, *A Short Service History and Master Roll of James Rogers' 2nd Battalion, King's Rangers* (Milton, ON: Global Heritage Press, 2015).

83. Christopher Carleton, "Major Christopher Carleton's Journal, Isle aux Noix, November 14, 1778" (hereafter "Carleton's Journal"), transcribed in Washingtons, 85.
84. *Enys*, 25, 26.
85. **Johns**: Neither Carleton nor Enys provides Johns's given name. I have identified him circumstantially. Solomon Johns killed a man in the summer of 1777 in the Otter Creek Valley, and fled to join Burgoyne. Postwar, he petitioned that he was employed "upon several very hazardous & fatiguing Scouts." He was appointed a lieutenant in Rogers's King's Rangers in 1779, and served in Pritchard's Company until its disbandment; see Watt, *Burgoyne's Auxiliaries*, 84, and Watt, *King's Rangers*. Also see Oscar E. Bredenberg, *Military Activities in the Champlain Valley after 1777* (Champlain, NY: Moorfield Press, 1962), 15. Bredenberg identifies him as Solomon Johns of Clarendon, but offers no source; **Sherwood's serjeant**: Two men are likely — Vermonter John Beach, whose property was confiscated in 1778 — he was a serjeant in Sherwood's Company on January 29, 1778 — or John Ward, who was returned as a serjeant in Sherwood's company in early 1778. See Watt, *Burgoyne's Auxiliaries*, 161, 163.
86. **McIntosh**: Washingtons, 23&24.
87. **Benedict**: most likely Private Benajah Benedict of Arlington, VT, who was recruited by Reuben Hawley for the 1777 campaign. He transferred to Jeremiah French's Company, QLR, and in January 1778 transferred to Captain Samuel Adams's Rangers. See Watt, *Burgoyne's Auxiliaries*, 166. Of further interest, the *Vermont Historical Gazetteer*, I, 11 notes that Benajah Benedict, who had sided with the Crown during the rebellion, returned to Addison afterwards, "took the oath of allegiance, and became a warm supporter of our free institutions."
88. A major reason for Carleton's success as a mixed-force commander

was his care to keep his Native auxiliaries fully informed, and to take their advice about how and when to proceed. He held this trait in common with other successful partisan leaders such as Johnson and Butler.

89. Alexander Webster to George Clinton, Black Creek, November 26, 1778 (hereafter Webster's report), *PPGC*, III, 308–10. **Webster**: b. Scotland; d. America, 1810. Immigrated 1772. Member of Committee of Safety for the Provincial Congress. In the state Senate, 1777–85 and 1789–94. Member of the Council of Appointment while a senator. An assemblyman, 1788–89. Judge of Washington County, 1786–88. Served as captain through to colonel in Charlotte County's militia during the war. Ibid., III, 310n, and *New York in the Revolution*, I, 133. Webster is listed as major.

90. "Carleton's Journal," 89; Washingtons, 40; *Enys*, 27.

91. **Crook**: Michael Barbieri research, "Pay Roll of Capt Jesse Safford's Company of Provenshial Troops From the Dates of their Seaveral Inlistment Untill charge Boath Days Included Commensing the 1st May and Ending 20th Novmb 1778," Revolutionary War Rolls, 1775–1783, National Archives and Records Administration, RG93, MG246, mf roll 91, folder 75, 2 and 3; Michael Barbieri research, pension deposition of Abraham Hawkins, S13255. Hawkins served under Jesse Safford at Fort Rutland and marched under him to White Hall (Skenesborough), "hunting indians and Tories," then returned to Rutland until his enlistment was up. Was this the excursion under Crook? See "Revolutionary War Pension and Bounty-Land Warrant Application Files," NARA, RG15, M804; **Whitcomb's account**: *Papers of the Continental Congress*, reel 52, f379, v10, Item 41. Hereafter Whitcomb's account.

92. Whitcomb's account; **Warren**: Gideon Warren resided in Sunderland, and commanded the men guarding the frontier, February 7, 1778. Appointed colonel, 5VMR, May 27, 1778.

93. **Andrew Ross**: b. Scotland, 1756; d. 1796. Ens, 31st, September 23, 1772. Lieut, 31st, January 18, 1775. Capt, 31st, March 9, 1776. Bvt Maj, November 18, 1790. Bvt LCol, March 1, 1794. LCol, 21st, September 1, 1795. See Houlding, *King's Service*. **Jones**: Carleton did not provide Jones's given name, but there was only one Provincial captain of that surname in Quebec at that time. Jonathon Jones was senior captain of the King's Loyal Americans, and had arrived in Quebec with the Jessup brothers in late 1776. "Served Genl Burgoynes Campaign With credit[,] was wounded & is esteemed an

Intelligent Officer." When the small Provincial units were combined in November 1781 into the Loyal Rangers, Jonathon became the 2nd senior captain. Watt, *Burgoyne's Auxiliaries*, 99. **Fraser brothers**: both gave good service during Burgoyne's expedition. William later commanded an Independent Company, with Thomas serving under him. The Independent Company was absorbed into the Loyal Rangers on November 12, 1781. Soon after, Thomas was given his own company in the battalion. Ibid., 244, 245; **Brown**: Richard Brown, 31st Regt. had been seconded to the KRRNY in 1776 and 1777 to assist in training, and temporarily commanded the Light Infantry Company before returning to his regiment on June 3, 1777. Brown served in the QID in 1778, and was repeatedly recommended for a captaincy in 2KRR by Sir John Johnson in 1780/81. Ernest A. Cruikshank and Gavin K. Watt, *The History and Master Roll of The King's Royal Regiment of New York* (Campbellville, ON: Global Heritage Press, 2006), 180.

94. **Farquhar**: Francis William — b. England, 1757. Ens, 69th, December 25, 1775. Lieut, 29th, February 17, 1778. Capt, 39th, July 28, 1790. Bvt Maj, June 20, 1794. Maj, 29th, September 6, 1796. LCol, 2/17th Foot, August 5, 1799. Half-pay, September 25, 1802. Still on half-pay, 1807; **Dunlap**: Carleton spells this surname "Dunlop", but Houlding advises it was spelled "Dunlap" on the War Office lists. b. Scotland, 1744; d. Scotland, 1791. Lieut, 2/105th, October 24, 1761. Onto Ireland half-pay, March 31, 1763. Lieut, 53rd, October 2, 1765. Adjutant, October 8, 1767–May 24, 1775. As Quartermaster, May 24, 1775–March 29, 1776. Capt-Lieut, 53rd, April 30, 1771. Capt, 53rd, March 2, 1776. Bvt Maj, March 19, 1783. Half-pay, May 25, 1785. **Fireball**: there were several types of fireballs. The formula for the ball intended to burn buildings is found in Smith, *Dictionary*, 19. **Sherwood**: b. Connecticut, 1747; d. Quebec, 1798. Justus Sherwood, a former Green Mountain Boy, was the senior captain of the Queen's Loyal Rangers. He performed extensive services during Burgoyne's expedition. In 1781, he was appointed to command the Secret Service in Canada, and was the Crown's chief negotiator with Ethan Allen's clique for the return of Vermont to the British sphere. At disbandment, Sherwood was the Loyal Rangers' senior captain. Watt, *Burgoyne's Auxiliaries*, 157.
95. Webster's report, *PPGC*, III, 308.
96. Whitcomb's account.
97. Washingtons, 47; "Carleton's Journal," 91; *Enys*, 32.

98. *Enys*, 28, 29n31.
99. Ibid., 29, 30. **LaMothe**: Joseph Marie LaMothe was a Canadien officer stationed at Kanehsatake, the three villages at Lake of Two Mountains inhabited by Mohawks, Nipissings, and Algonquins. Mississaugas often served with them. In this particular instance, LaMothe was managing Ottawas, who also spoke an Algonkian dialect. Watt, *Burgoyne's Auxiliaries*, 328.
100. *Enys*, 31. **Arbuthnot**. b. Scotland, 1758; d. 1796. Ens, 40th, January 14, 1775. Lieut, 65th, May24, 1776. Lieut, 31st, September 10, 1776. Adjutant, July 22, 1782–April 2, 1788. Capt, 31st, February 27, 1788. Maj, 31st, after September 29, 1794. LCol, 31st, September 1, 1795. See Houlding, *King's Service*.
101. Webster's report, III, 308, 309.
102. "Carleton's Journal," 91.
103. Whitcomb's account.
104. *Enys*, 31, 32.
105. "Carleton's Journal," 92; *Enys*, 33. **Hoyt**: Carleton spells the name "Wintress Howick." On a list of the expedition's prisoners it is spelled "Herrick." In April 1775, Mohawk-speaking Winthrop Hoyt accompanied John Brown on a spy mission to Quebec with Peleg Sunderland, an Abenaki speaker. See John J. Duffy, Samuel B. Hand, and Ralph H. Orth, eds., *The Vermont Encyclopedia* (Lebanon, NH: University Press of New England, 2003), 68. Winthrop Hoyt was from Epping, NH, was captured during the Seven Years' War, and spent four years in Kahnawake, where he was adopted by a chief. Hoyt was a Green Mountain Boy, and in 1777 was one of the party that took thirteen Tories prisoner in south Monkton. See Washingtons, 25.
106. Washingtons, 54. Carleton's promised payment for cattle was repeatedly in default with the British Administration. The Natives claimed they had collected eighty head, but the administration argued that twenty of those were of people who had died on the stormy lake between Split Rock and Ile-aux-Noix. A year went by and no payment had been made, despite the major's intercessions. This led to great unrest and, later, an understandable lack of co-operation.
107. "Carleton's Journal," 92. Carleton described the *Lee* as a cutter; *Enys*, 33. He reports that the movement of cattle was not finished until four o'clock. **Gilliland's**: Washingtons, 60. **Lorimier**: originally, three Lorimier brothers served at Kahnawake. Claude-Nicholas-Guillaume (Chevalier de Lorimier) had his leg broken by a gunshot at

Walloomscoick, and was unable to serve actively until 1780. Jean-Claude-Chamilly de Lorimier was killed during the attack on Shelburne in March 1778. This left François-Marie-Thomas (Sieur de Verneuil), who was the man referred to by Carleton. Claude de Lorimier, *At War with the Americans* (Victoria, BC: Press Porcepic, n.d.), 66, 67, and Watt, *Burgoyne's Auxiliaries*, 327.
108. Whitcomb's account.
109. Webster's report, III, 309.
110. Washingtons, 60.
111. Claus to Haldimand, Montreal, December 5, 1778, LAC, HP, B114, 11 and 12.
112. *Almanac of American Military History*, Spencer Tucker, ed., 4 vols. (ABC-CLIO, 2012), I, 217.
113. Haldimand, London, April 14, 1778, HSGS, III, 44, ex CO, Series Q, V.15, 9.
114. Mintz, 230, 231; Washington to the President of Congress, November 11, 1778, and Washington to Henry Laurens, November 14, 1778.
115. An English translation was published in the *Massachusetts Spy* at Worcester, Massachusetts, December 10, 1778. *Magazine of American History*, xxii.4 (October): 257–59. For the original French and an English translation, see HSGS, III, 75–78.
116. A year later, Haldimand's anxieties were increased when a dispatch was received from Lieutenant-Governor Richard Hughes in Halifax.

> About six weeks ago a Spanish Pacquet under the care of an officer was brought into New York by a Privateer belonging to that place and by a very clever behavior on the part of the Master of that Vessel, the Mail and other papers were secured and I am informed that upon examination of its contents an authentic copy of a Treaty was found which had lately been signed at Paris between the courts of France and Spain, and Franklin, the American Agent on the part of Congress. And by one of the articles of this Treaty, the Congress binds themselves to deliver up by June 20th, 1780, the two Floridas into the hands of Spain and the Provinces of Canada and Nova Scotia to the French King.

117. Further, Hughes reported that the French fleet under d'Estaing, consisting of twenty-six ships of the line and fourteen frigates, was

set to attack Nova Scotia and Quebec, but fortunately had run afoul of horrific weather off the coast of Georgia. Hughes to Haldimand, Halifax, November 19, 1779, transcribed in HSGS, III, 138.
118. Williamson, 91.

Chapter Two: Mohawk Region

1. **Butler**: John Butler's rank at this time is confusing. Within the Indian Department, he was ranked as major, but in his former role in the Tryon County militia, he was a lieutenant-colonel. Consequently, he is sometimes referred to as major and at other times as colonel.
2. Lieutenant-Colonel Daniel Claus, "Anecdotes of Captain Brant," from NAC, MG2, 46, found in William Clement Bryant, "Captain Brant and the Old King," *Publications of the Buffalo Historical Society*, IV (1896): 28. **Funds**: Claus's report of his accounts, December 2, 1777, LAC, HP, B114, 322, and cited in Isabel Thompson Kelsay, *Joseph Brant 1743–1807 — Man of Two Worlds* (Syracuse: Syracuse University Press, 1984), 208.
3. Stevens, "Allies," XXII, 1463; Butler to LeMaistre, January 28, 1778, Smy transcripts, HP, AddMss21756.
4. Claus to Knox, Montreal, October 16, 1777. *Documents Relating to the Colonial History of the State of New York* (hereafter *Colonial History*), edited by Berthold Fernow, XV, State Archives, vol. 1 (Albany: Weed, Parsons and Company, Printers, 1887), 718–23.
5. Claus to Knox, November 6, 1777, *Colonial History*, 724, 725.
6. Bolton to Carleton, Fort Niagara, September 9, 1777, Smy transcripts, LAC, MG11, CO, Q14.
7. Pollard to Butler, Fort Niagara, September 1777, Smy transcripts, LAC, CO42/37, 225.
8. The rates of pay set in Butler's beating warrant later haunted him, and were the source of unrest within and outside of his corps. See a memorandum requesting a levelling of the rates prepared by Capt Walter Butler, March 31, 1779, found in NAC, WO24/8.
9. Butler's Beating Order, Smy transcripts. HP, AddMss21700.
10. Carleton's instructions to Butler, September 15, 1777, Smy transcripts, HP, AddMss21700.
11. Claus to Knox, October 16, 1777, *Colonial History*, 722. When Butler later reported the exchange error, he was asked to credit the

government for the excess; Carleton declined to address Claus's expenses. See Carleton to Claus, Quebec, October 20, 1777, Smy transcripts, LAC, MG19, F1, Claus Papers, vol. 1. Bolton wrote to protest his inability to assess Claus's request for approval of his expenses. See Bolton to LeMaistre, Niagara, November 22, 1777, Smy transcripts, HP, AddMss21756.

12. While there is no doubt about Mary Brant's great influence within the confederacy and her dedication to the British connection, Claus's descriptions need to be weighed carefully because of his personal war with John Butler. Lois M. Huey and Bonnie Pulis, *Molly Brant: A Legacy of Her Own* (Youngstown, NY: Old Fort Niagara Association, 1997), 49, ex two letters from Claus to Haldimand, August 30, 1779, HP, AddMss21774, 57, 58, and Claus Papers, MG19, F1, 2:131–33.

13. Gavin K. Watt, *Rebellion in the Mohawk Valley, the St. Leger Expedition of 1777* (Toronto: Dundurn Press, 2002), 278.

14. Butler and Bolton to Henry Clinton, Niagara, November 23, 1777, *Colonial History*, V.VIII, 741; Butler to Carleton, Niagara, December 14, 1777, Smy transcripts, HP, AddMss21756; Barbara Graymont, *The Iroquois in the American Revolution* (Syracuse: Syracuse University Press, 1972), 161; and Ernest A. Cruikshank, *The Story of Butler's Rangers and the Settlement of Niagara* (Owen Sound, ON: Richardson, Bond & Wright Ltd., 1975; first published in 1893 by Lundy's Lane Historical Society), 39.

15. Butler to LeMaistre, Niagara, December 14, 1777, Smy transcripts, HP, AddMss21756. Butler was stretching his luck with Carleton. Giving the Rangers' first company to his absent son Walter, then recommending his absent son Thomas to command another company, could be viewed as pure nepotism, and quite irregular. **LeMaistre**: b. Jersey ca. 1743; d. Quebec, 1805. Lieut, 98Regt, 1760. Half-pay, 1763. Lieut, 7Regt, 1765. Adjt, 7Regt, 1767. BdeMaj Quebec, 1775 and 1776. Carleton's aide-de-camp, 1776. Capt, 8Regt, November 1776. Deputy Adjutant General, Canada, July 1777. Military secretary to Lord Dorchester (Carleton), 1786–94. Resigned from the army, August 1788. L/Gov, Gaspe, and inspector, Labrador fisheries, 1794. Col, Quebec City British Militia, 1794. David Lee, *Dictionary of Canadian Biography* (hereafter *DCB*), vol. V. **Depew/Depue**: paid as a senior ranger on a list of officers employed in the Indian Department, LAC, CO, MG11, Q series, vol. 13, 329.

16. NY pension deposition of William Hammill, S10794. James F. Morrison's note No. 3 addresses Herkimer's appointment as colonel of the Minute Men. See Maryly Penrose, ed., *Mohawk Valley in the Revolution, Committee of Safety Papers and Genealogical Compendium* (hereafter *Mohawk Valley*) (Franklin Park, NJ: Liberty Bell Associates, 1978), 127–38.
17. Hazel C. Mathews, *The Mark of Honour* (Toronto: University of Toronto Press, 1965), 48.
18. Schuyler to Laurens, Albany, March 15, 1778, Penrose, *Indian Affairs Papers*, 118.
19. George Clinton, *PPGC*, II, 271n, and Clinton to Hoornbeek, September 3, 1777, ibid., II, 272, 274.
20. Penrose, *Indian Affairs Papers*, 100.
21. Minutes of Indian Commissioners' meeting, January 9–10, 1778, and Commissioners to Laurens, Albany, January 12, 1778, Penrose, *Indian Affairs*, 101–04. **Wolcott**: b. Connecticut, 1726; d. Connecticut, 1797. Graduated Yale, 1747. Militia captain, 7YrsWar. Studied medicine; served as sheriff, Litchfield County, Connecticut, 1751–71. Judge of the common pleas. Appointed Indian Commissioner, 1775. Major-General, commanded fourteen regiments at New York City, summer 1776. Congressman, 1776 — signed Declaration of Independence. Fought Burgoyne, 1777. In 1785, established peace with Six Nations. 19th Governor of Connecticut, 1796–1797. http://en.wikipedia.org/wiki/Oliver_Wolcott. **Douw**: b. New York, 1720; d. New York, 1801. Ship captain, storekeeper, city councillor; alderman, 1748–58. Mayor of Albany, 1761–1770. Militia officer, 7YrsWar. Judge/Justice, 1757–75. Member Provincial Assembly, 1757–68. Indian commissioner during Revolution. State senator, 1786–93. See Stefan Bielinski, "Volkert P. Douw," http://exhibitions.nysm.nysed.gov//albany/bios/d/vopdouw2234.html.
22. Stevens, "Allies," XXIII, 1550, 1551; Dean to the Indian Commissioners, Fort Schuyler, February 5, 1778, Penrose, *Indian Affairs*, 109, 110, ex Schuyler Papers, M247, Roll 173:282–84.
23. Brant to Claus, Niagara, January 23, 1778, Penrose, *Indian Affairs*, 106, ex Claus Papers, MG19, F1, vol. 2, 1–2. **Cayo-Kwen**: this settlement has not been located, but as Mary Brant wintered at Cayuga, Joseph was likely nearby; see Stevens, "Allies," XXIII, 1547, 1548.
24. Stevens, "Allies," XXIII, 1532.

25. Schuyler to Greaton, January 24, 1778, Penrose, *Indian Affairs*, 107, ex Schuyler Letters, M247, Roll 173.272. **Greaton**: Greaton's 3MA was assigned to the Northern Department beginning July 1, 1777, and ending March 31, 1778. See Wright, *Continental Army*, 205. **Canadien desertions**: I have found no evidence that Schuyler's agent was successful in encouraging this level of desertion, but it is certainly true that Burgoyne was unable to fill his two Canadien fighting companies, nor able to maintain the number of carters, artificers, and boatmen he required. Might this fellow be Joseph Langlois dit Traversy from chapter one? **Spencer**: Joseph T. Glatthaar and James Kirby Martin, *Forgotten Allies — The Oneida Indians and the American Revolution* (New York: Hill & Wang, 2006), 194. These authors do not use the English name "Spencer," but rather employ "Sinavis," and in their index refer to his second Oneida name, "Sewajis." As my earlier book, *Rebellion in the Mohawk Valley*, referred to him as "Spencer," for the sake of consistency, I have used that surname.

26. **Onondagas**: this emphasis on the Onondagas was most unfortunate. Their recent decision to espouse the Crown's cause saw very little commitment during the 1778 campaign, but resulted in disaster in 1779, when Continentals razed their primary settlement and raped and killed many of their young women. See Schuyler to Laurens, Albany, February 8, 1778, transcribed in Penrose, *Indian Affairs*, 110–12, ex Schuyler Papers, M247, Roll 173:276–79.

27. Butler to LeMaistre, Niagara, January 28, 1778, Smy transcripts, HP, AddMss21756; and Cruikshank, *Butler's Rangers*, 40.

28. Bolton to Carleton, Niagara, January 31, 1778, Smy transcripts, HP, AddMss21756.

29. Butler to Carleton, Niagara, February 2, 1778, Smy transcripts, HP, AddMss21756.

30. Stevens, "Allies," XXIII, 1544.

31. Penrose, *Mohawk Valley*, 139–47.

32. Lafayette to Gansevoort, Johnstown, March 6, 1778, transcribed in William W. Campbell, Jr., *Annals of Tryon County; or the Border Warfare of New York* (Cherry Valley, NY: The Cherry Valley Gazette Print, 1880), 169, 170; and Jeptha R. Simms, *Frontiersman of New York...* (hereafter *Frontiersmen*), 2 vols. (Albany: Geo. C. Riggs, 1883), 144, 145.

33. Graymont, 163.

34. Minutes of the Johnstown Indian Council, March 8–10, 1778, Penrose, *Indian Affairs*, 112–17.
35. Schuyler to Laurens, Albany, March 15, 1778, Penrose, *Indian Affairs*, 117–20.
36. Glatthaar and Martin, 194, 195.
37. Ibid., 198–200; Penrose, *Indian Affairs*, 121–24, ex Papers of the Continental Congress, M247, Roll 173:298–303.
38. Nisseker and Minpelaer to Tryon Committee of Safety, Albany, May 17, 1778. Attempts to identify these two men have failed. Penrose, *Mohawk Valley*, 151, 152.
39. Robert Venables, "Tryon County, 1775–1783: A Frontier in Revolution" (Phd diss., Vanderbilt University, 1967), http://hortonsarticles.org/Timeline1778.htm.
40. Schenectady citizens' petition to Clinton, March 20, 1778, *PPGC*, III, 63.
41. Graymont, 177
42. Simms, *Frontiersmen*, II, 191.
43. Guy Johnson to Germain, New York City, March 12, 1778, *Colonial History*, XLVI, 740–41.
44. Claus, "Anecdotes." "Old King" refers to Old Smoke/Sayenqueraghta.
45. Nelson Greene, *The Story of Old Fort Plain and the Middle Mohawk Valley* (Fort Plain: O'Connor Brothers Publishers, 1915); *History of the Mohawk Valley: Gateway to the West 1614–1925*, Nelson Greene, ed., 4 vols. (Chicago: The S. J. Clarke Publishing Company, 1925), I, 885–901; Thomas Wood Clarke, *The Bloody Mohawk* (New York: The Macmillan Company, 1940), 238–40; Simms, *Frontiersmen*, II, 560.
46. Nine depositions taken at Palatine, April 20 and 21, 1778, transcribed in Penrose, *Indian Affairs*, 125–34.
47. Cruikshank, *Butler's Rangers*, 43; see Richard Cartwright, Sr.'s claim for war losses, Smy Transcripts, AO12/26/111; David A. Charters, "Walter Butler," *DCB*, IV. **Guard**: Alden's Massachusetts Regiment website: http://home.roadrunner.com/~nlecompte/regiment/regiment.html.
48. Glatthaar and Martin, 194–205.
49. Graymont, 165, and Stevens, "Allies," XXIII, 1555, 1556. **Barren Hill**: www.oneidaindiannation.com/history/28612644, and Glatthaar and Martin, 147, 138, 215–19; opposite 179 is an image of a plaque dedicated to the lost warriors. Re. the building of the fort and stockade, see ibid., 237. **McLane's Partisan Corps**: this unit had a

chequered career. See Wright, *The Continental Army*, 134, 147, 273, 323, 342, 343; and Colonel John Womack Wright, *Some Notes on the Continental Army* (Vails Gate, NY: National Temple Hill Association, 1963), 54. "A partisan corps is a body of light troops from one hundred to two hundred men, consisting of infantry and cavalry, separated from the army for the purpose of securing the march and protecting the camp of the main body, reconnaissance, attacking the hostile posts and convoys."

50. Ken D. Johnson, *The Bloodied Mohawk: The American Revolution in the Words of Fort Plank's Defenders and Other Mohawk Valley Partisans* (hereafter *Bloodied*) (Rockport, MA: Picton Press, 2000), 132.

51. Cruikshank, *Butler's Rangers*, 43; Stevens, "Allies," XXIV, 1712. **Strength of Butler's Rangers**: see a rather confusing return dated Niagara, February 3, 1778, and Roll of Caldwell's Company, February 3, 1778, Smy transcripts, HP, AddMss21765.

52. Dixon to Clinton, April 4, 1778, *PPGC*, III, 126, 127.

53. Stevens, "Allies," XXIII, 1571. Stevens believes that Bowen escaped with Walter Butler. See also Graymont, 165. William Bowen is not mentioned in her account. Whether he escaped at this time is a matter of debate; Bill Smy states Bowen was held until 1779. Lieutenant-Colonel William A. Smy, *An Annotated Nominal Roll of Butler's Rangers 1777–1784 with Documentary Sources* (hereafter *Annotated Roll*) (St. Catharines, ON: Friends of the Loyalist Collection at Brock University, 2004), 47; Kirkland to Schuyler, Fort Schuyler May 23, 1778, Penrose, *Indian Affairs*, 140. Kirkland adds the information about "a number of Tories."

54. Stevens, "Allies," XXIII, 1568, 1569.

55. Smy transcript. Richard McGinnis, "Journal of Occurrences Respecting Our Suffering in the Late Rebellion," edited by Carol Lind, *The New York Genealogical and Biographical Record* (New York: 1975), 106.1: 14–18 and 2: 18, 113, 114.

56. Stevens, "Allies," XXIII, 1542.

57. Marjory Barnum Hinman, *Onaquaga: Hub of the Border Wars of the American Revolution in New York State* (n.p.: 1975), 37; affidavit of Robert Jones, Minisink, July 10, 1778. Francis Whiting Halsey, *The Old New York Frontier, its Wars with Indians and Tories, its Missionary Schools, Pioneers and Land Titles* (hereafter *ONYF*) (New York: Charles Scribner's Sons, 1917), 214, 215.

58. Statement of Barnabus Kelly, German Flatts, June 26, 1778, *PPGC*, III, 504–6. Also found, with slightly different wording, in Halsey, *ONYF*,

212, 213. **Servos**: the claim that he was Sir John Johnson's uncle appears to be untrue. See http://archiver.rootsweb.ancestry.com/th/read/UNITED-EMPIRE-LOYALIST/2007-11/1195504930.

59. The relative timing of the killing of Wormwood and the attack on Cobleskill is a matter of debate. For example, Stevens, "Allies," XXIV, 1718. Stevens states that Brant and five warriors scouted Cherry Valley on June 2, at which time a militiaman was killed and another captured; Campbell, *Annals*, 109, 110; Jeptha R. Simms, *History of Schoharie County, and Border Wars of New York...* (Albany: Munsell & Tanner, 1845), 281; Johnson, *Bloodied*, 132; James F. Morrison, "Brigade, Regimental & Company Officers — 6Aug77," in Gavin K. Watt and James F. Morrison, *The British Campaign of 1777, Volume 1: The St. Leger Expedition. The Forces of the Crown and Congress*, 2nd ed. (Campbellville, ON: Global Heritage Press, 2003), 162; Kelsay, 216, 217. **Peter Sits**: a Peter Seats was brought to lower Canada on November 15, 1778. His age was given as 55, and it was recorded that he had been taken on the Mohawk River on June 3 while not in arms. He does not appear in the prisoner records again. Was this the same fellow, or a coincidence? See McHenry, 4.

60. Simms, *Frontiersmen*, II, 151–58.

61. **William Patrick**: this officer's given name was found at Wikipedia.org/wiki/Battle_of_Cobleskill. This website states that seven captives were about to be burned at the stake until Maynard gave a Masonic distress signal. It states further that they were marched to Quebec, frequently forced to run the gauntlet, and had their fingers burned in pipe bowls. The first contention is unlikely, as the Iroquois had abandoned stake burning by the time of the Revolution. Five of the prisoners did not arrive in Quebec until November 15, 1778, so it is unlikely they were marched there directly. However, the gauntlet running and finger burnings are entirely likely. **Freemoyer**: variously Freemire, Freemeyer. **Ones-yap**: Joseph's sister Mary reported the wounding of a Cayuga chief, and the death of a Schoharie Indian named Jacob. Was Jacob Ones-yap's English name, or was yet another Schoharie killed? Mary Brant to Claus, Niagara, June 23, 1777, Smy transcripts, LAC, Claus Papers, MG19, F1, V.2.

62. Simms was correct: a lieutenant named Jonah/John Maynard was held in Quebec until being paroled in 1780. McHenry, 3, 23.

63. **Fester brothers**: pension deposition of Jacob Fester R3520, transcribed in A.J. Berry and James F. Morrison, *Don't Shoot (Part One)*

Until You See the Whites of Their Eyes (Trafford Publishing, 2007), 165. The dogs were far more likely to have been owned by the Natives, as they often accompanied war parties and were trained to pursue fleeing enemies. Christina Norman supported Jacob Fester's application, and deposed that it was his brother who was caught by the dogs, and had his innards removed and wound around a stump. See the Deposition of David Freemoyer, transcribed in John C. Dann, *The Revolution Remembered: Eyewitness Accounts of the War for Independence* (Chicago: University of Chicago Press, 1980), 289–91; Simms, *Frontiersmen*, II, 151–58; Stevens, "Allies," IIIV, 1714; Willis T. Hanson, *A History of Schenectady During the Revolution*.... (printed by author, 1916), 85.

64. Stark to Gates, Albany, May 31, 1778, Stark to Ten Broeck, June 1, 1778, and Stark to Gates, June 2, 1778, *Stark Correspondence*, 156, 157.

65. Joseph/Joost Loucks was a serjeant. Peter/Petrus and George Loucks were privates, all in Duncan's Coy in 1777. No one named Lintz served in the KRR; the closest spelling is Link. Two men of that surname, Johannes and Matthias, enlisted on May 22, 1780. A Daniel Sweeny enlisted in December 1880. Cruikshank and Watt, *KRRNY*, Master Roll.

66. As slim evidence of Johnson's and Claus's involvement, see Sir John Johnson to Claus, Quebec, June 18, 1778, transcribed in John Watts DePeyster, *Miscellanies of an Officer* (New York: C.H. Ludwig, 1838), LI; Cruikshank and Watt, *KRRNY*, Master Roll.

67. Evidence of Hendrick Warmwood, June 5, 1778, *PPGC*, III, 415, 416.

68. Simms, *Frontiersmen*, II, 217–20. **Catrina**: Simms, ibid., 216 reports her name as Catharine Frey. See Penrose, *Mohawk Valley*, 321, where her name is reported as Catrina Fry. **Howell**: Cruikshank and Watt, *KRRNY*, 237.

69. Report of Visscher, Fonda, etc... to Albany, Caughnawaga, June 3, 1778, *PPGC*, III, 395, 396.

70. Visscher and Veeder to Ten Broeck, Caughnawaga, June 5, 1778, *PPGC*, III, 405, 406.

71. Simms, *Frontiersmen*, II, 221.

72. Fonda and Van Horne to Henry Glen, Caughnawaga, June 5, 1778, *PPGC*, III, 407, 408; James F. Morrison, *A History of Fulton County in the Revolution* (Gloversville: printed by author, 1977). See also http://fulton.nygenweb.net/military/FCinRev4.html.

73. Klock to Ten Broeck, Caughnawaga, June 6, 1778, *PPGC*, III, 414, 415.
74. Johnson to Claus, Quebec, June 18, 1778. DePeyster, *Miscellanies*, LI.
75. Simms, *Frontiersmen*, II, 224. Solomon Woodworth gained considerable notoriety for his vigorous defence of the Sacandaga blockhouse in the spring of 1780. In 1781, he was appointed captain of a select body of rangers. On their first outing, his company fell into an Onondaga/Cayuga ambush, and was destroyed. See Watt, *Dirty, Trifling*, 218–84; After the raid, Godfrey Shew's son John was adopted into the Fort Hunter's Lachine community, and, while out hunting, escaped south. He was retaken in October 1780, and, conformable with Native custom, was executed for betrayal of trust. See Watt, *Burning*, 123.
76. Duane to Clinton, Albany, June 6, 1778, *PPGC*, III, 418, 419.
77. Barclay to Clinton, Albany, June, 7, 1778. *PPGC*, III, 424, 425.
78. Clyde to Stark, Cherry Valley, June 5, 1778, Halsey, *ONYF*, 209, 210.
79. Schuyler to Laurens, Albany May 29, 1778, Penrose, *Indian Affairs*, 144, ex Schuyler Letters, Papers of the Continental Congress, National Archives, Washington, M247, Roll 173: 330–33; Stevens, "Allies," XXIII, 1567.
80. Stevens, "Allies," XXIII, 1562.
81. Pickering to Schuyler, War Office, York Town, June 16, 1778, Penrose, *Indian Affairs*, 146, ex Papers of the Continental Congress, M247, Roll 77: 184.
82. Stevens, "Allies," XXIII, 1539, 1540; "Return of the Officers & Rangers of the 5 Nations Indian Department in the Province of Quebec, together with their P/day, & arrears due to Each, Montreal March 30th 1778," LAC, WO28/10, 406.
83. Walter Butler's report to Carleton, Quebec, June 4, 1778, Smy transcripts, BL, HP, AddMss21756.
84. Bolton to Carleton, Niagara, June 5, 1778, Smy transcripts, HP, AddMss21756.
85. Resolution of Congress, June 11, 1777. Williams, 3-273, ex Worthington Chauncey Ford, ed., *Journals of the Continental Congress*, 11:588–90.
86. Governor Clinton to Brigadiers Ten Broeck and Stark, Poughkeepsie, June 11, 1778, *PPGC*, III, 447, 448.
87. General Orders, Albany Militia Brigade, June 12, 1778, *PPGC*, III, 515, 516.

88. Stark to Klock, Albany, June 14, 1778, and Stark to Tryon Committee, June 16, 1778, *Stark Correspondence*, 162, 163.
89. Citizens of Schenectady to Clinton, June 15 1778, Halsey, *ONYF*, 210, 211; for Governor Clinton's detailed answer to this letter, see *PPGC*, III, 467, 468.
90. Gates to Stark, Peekskill, June 17, 1778, *Stark Correspondence*, 163–64.
91. Dean to Schuyler, Fort Schuyler, June 15, 1778, *PPGC*, III, 457–59.
92. Lester E. and Anne Whitbeck Hendrix, *Sloughter's Instant History of Schoharie County 1700–1900* (Schoharie, NY: The Schoharie County Historical Society, 1988), 38. **Mattice**: Henrick, a farmer and miller on the Breakabeen, joined 2KRR on December 5, 1780. Watt, *KRRNY*, 255.
93. Conspiracy Commission to Albany County representatives, Albany, June 20, 1778. New York State Library, Revolutionary War Manuscripts, Document #6752; Thomas Garnett, "A Journal of the Proceedings of Thomas Garnett appointed Senior Captain in a Battalion raiseing by Mr. James Howetson by order of Governor Tryon to serve under Sir John Johnson," (hereafter Garnett Journal), AO, HP, MS622, reel 109.
94. Ten Broeck to Clinton, Albany, June 20, 1778, *PPGC*, III, 473, 474.
95. Ten Broeck to Clinton, Albany, June 30, 1778, *PPGC*, III, 504.
96. Meeting of field officers, Albany, June 24, 1778, *PPGC*, III, 516; Ten Broeck to Clinton, Albany, July 1, 1778, ibid., 513, 514; Clinton to Ten Broeck, Poughkeepsie, July 2, 1778, ibid., 517, 518.
97. Stark to Gates, July 1, 1778, *Stark Correspondence*, 174.
98. Mathews, *Mark of Honour*, 51.
99. McGinnis, "Journal of Occurrences."
100. Quotation from Stevens, "Allies," XXIV, 1719, 1720.

Chapter Three: The Wyoming and Wyalusing Campaigns

1. Robert S. Grumet, *The Munsee Indians, A History* (Norman, OK: University of Oklahoma Press, 2009), 251–65; http://luzernehistory.org/?page_id=573
2. Thomas Verenna, "They were with the Continental Army in 1778," http://allthingsliberty.com/2014/02/connecticut-yankees-in-a-pennamites-fort.

3. See wikipedia.org/wiki/Paxton_Boys; wikipedia.org/wiki/Lazarus_Stewart.
4. "History of the 24th Connecticut Regiment of Militia," www.24thcmr.org/page2.php.
5. Ibid.
6. Joseph Doddridge, *Notes on the Settlement and Indian Wars of the Western Parts of Virginia & Pennsylvania, from the Year 1763 Until the Year 1783 Inclusive, Together with a View of the Western Country* (Albany: Joel Munsell, 1876).
7. Oscar Jewell Harvey and Ernest Gray Smith, *A History of Wilkes-Barré, Luzerne County, Pennsylvania: From Its First Beginnings to the Present Time, Including Chapters of Newly-discovered Early Wyoming Valley History, Together with Many Biographical Sketches and Much Genealogical Material*, 6 vols. (Wilkes-Barre, PA: Raeder Press, 1909), vol. V, 888–90.
8. Harvey and Smith, 889.
9. Stevens, "Allies," XXIII, 1547, 1549.
10. J. Kelsey Jones, "Loyalist Plantations on the Susquehanna," www.beth-website.net. Jones's article has a good analysis of the Up-the-River loyalists.
11. Wesley Johnson, ed., *Wyoming: A Record of the One Hundredth Year Commemorative Observance of the Battle and Massacre, July 3, 1778–July 3, 1878* (hereafter *Wyoming Commemorative*) (Wilkes-Barre, PA: Wyoming Commemorative Association, 1899), found in http://durkeesmenofwyoming.tripod.com/id20.htm.
12. Mathews, *Mark of Honour*, 49, 50. James Secord was a senior ranger in Butler's Indian Department contingent at Stanwix. He ranked as an Indian Department lieutenant in 1778 and 1779. See Watt and Morrison, *St. Leger Expedition*, 77–79. **Secord and Showers**: James Secord and Michael Showers were among the first settlers on the Canadian shore of the Niagara River. Alun Hughes, "John Butler and Early Settlement on the West Bank of the Niagara River," in *The Butler Bicentenary: Commemorating the 200th Anniversary of the Death of Colonel John Butler* (Niagara, ON: UEL Association of Canada, Colonel John Butler Branch), 67.
13. Stevens, "Allies," XXIII, 1546.
14. Stephen C. Young, "Identifying Loyalists on the Frontier — The Wyoming Valley Massacre," *Pennsylvania Genealogical Magazine* 43 (March 26, 2005): 296–98.

15. William Leete Stone, *The Poetry and History of Wyoming* (New York: Wiley and Putnam, 1841), 181n, cited in Young, 298.
16. Journals of Congress, vol. IV, 113.
17. *Wyoming Commemorative.*
18. Stevens, "Allies," XXIII, 1549.
19. Harvey and Smith; *Wyoming Commemorative.*
20. Stevens, "Allies," XXIII, 1558, 1559; Butler to Carleton, Niagara, April 10, 1778, Smy transcripts, HP, AddMss21756.
21. Cruikshank, 45.
22. *Wyoming Commemorative.*
23. Ibid.
24. John F. Meginness, ed., *History of Lycoming County, Pennsylvania* (Chicago: Brown, Runk & Co., 1892), chap. VII, www.usgennet.org/usa/pa/county/lycoming/history/lyco-history-01.html.
25. Cruikshank, 46; "Narrative of Lt. Col. Butler's Services in America, London May 1785," NAC, HP, B215, 196–202.
26. For Butler's report on the Wyoming expedition, see John Butler to Bolton, Lacawanack, July 8, 1778, HP, AddMss21760. In this report, Butler included the terms accepted at Forts Wintermoot and Jenkins, and the three forts at Lacawanack (presumably Pittstown) and Westmoreland (Forty Fort); Graymont, 168; Thomas S. Abler, *Cornplanter: Chief Warrior of the Allegany Senecas* (Syracuse: Syracuse University Press, 2007), 45.
27. Terms of surrender, Fort Wintermoot, Westmoreland, July 5, 1778, *PPGC*, III, 520, 521. This source also lists the animals taken from Scovell's Company, and spells Wintermoote as "Waindemuth"; Graymont, 168. She lists the terms as follows: "1. That Lieut. Elisha Scowell surrender the Fort with all the Stores, Arms, and ammunition that are in said Fort as well as Publick as private to Major John Butler. 2. That the Garrison shall not bear Arms during the present contest, And Major Butler promises that the men, women and Children shall not be hurt either by Indians or Rangers."
28. Young, 321–23; see list of animals taken noted above.
29. *Wyoming Commemorative.*
30. Smy transcripts. LCol Wm H. Zierdt, *Narrative History of the 109th Field Artillery, Pennsylvania National Guard* (Wilkes-Barre, 1932), 28; *Wyoming commemorative.* This source names each company and their captains and size, and gives a slightly different distribution.

31. *Wyoming Commemorative.*
32. Graymont, 168; Abler, *Cornplanter*, 45.
33. *Wyoming Commemorative.*
34. Graymont, 169.
35. Cruikshank, 47.
36. **Single rank**: this was a questionable decision, as fire production is limited to the front and rear only, and flanks are 'in the air," i.e. entirely unprotected.
37. Graymont, 169. The author gives no source for Zeb Butler's instructions.
38. *New York Journal*, July 20, 1778. Among a great many inaccurate assertions and exaggerations, this newspaper places the size of the Crown force at 1,600, in an effort to explain away the rebel defeat. However, rebel newspapers were not the only source for misinformation and exaggeration. *The Royal Gazette*, August 1, 1778, reports that John Butler marched from Detroit with "about 2,000 men, consisting of 200 regulars, a number of Tories, the rest Indians...." Of course, there were no Regulars with Butler, and the total is absurd.
39. Adam Crysler, "The Journal of Adam Crysler," in *Loyalist Narratives From Upper Canada*, edited by James J. Talman (Toronto: Champlain Society, 1946), 56–61.
40. Cruikshank, 47; Graymont, 171; *Wyoming Commemorative.*
41. Thomas S. Abler, ed., *Chainbreaker: The Revolutionary War Memoirs of Governor Blacksnake As told to Benjamin Williams* (Lincoln, NE: University of Nebraska Press, 1989), 98; Graymont, 172; Abler, *Cornplanter*, 46.
42. Cruikshank, 48; Graymont, 171.
43. For Butler's report of the Wyoming expedition, see John Butler to Bolton, Lacawanack, July 8, 1778, HP, AddMss21760; *Wyoming Commemorative* gives the name as Dr. Lemuel Gustin. I was unable to identify Beech. John Johnson is Captain John Johnston, Six Nations Indian Department, and William Caldwell is a captain of Butler's Rangers.
44. Cruikshank, 48; "Narrative of Lt. Col. Butler's Services in America," NAC, HP, B215, 196–202.
45. *Wyoming Commemorative.*
46. Ibid.
47. Ibid.; Butler's report.
48. Cruikshank, 50.

49. Frederic A. Godcharles, "Massacre at Wyoming Followed by 'The Great Runaway' on July 5, 1778: Luzerne (then Northumberland) Co, PA," *Daily Stories of Pennsylvania* (Milton, PA: 1924).
50. *Wyoming Commemorative.*
51. Meginness, *Lycoming County.*
52. Butler to Haldimand, Niagara, September 17, 1778, Smy transcript, LAC, HP, AddMss21756.
53. Edward G. Williams, "Fort Pitt and the Revolution on the Western Frontier," *The Western Pennsylvania Historical Magazine*, 59.3 (July 1976): 3-276; Godcharles.
54. During the American Revolution, committees of safety, also called committees of observation and committees of inspection, were local committees of Patriots that became a shadow government that took actual control of the Thirteen Colonies away from royal officials who became increasingly helpless. https://en.wikipedia.org/wiki/Committees_of_safety_(American_Revolution).
55. John W. Jordan, "Biographical Sketch of Colonel Thomas Hartley, of the Pennsylvania Line," http://archive.org/stream/jstor-20085978/20085978_djvu.txt; http://famousamericans.net/thomashartley.

> Washington appointed Thomas Hartley as colonel of an "additional" regiment. Hartley was the former lieutenant-colonel of the 6th Pennsylvania Battalion. Hartley had broad authority to select his own officers. Accordingly, Hartley chose as his lieutenant-colonel Morgan Connor, major of the 1st Pennsylvania Regiment. Hartley recruited eight companies from eastern Pennsylvania, eastern Maryland, and Delaware. Hartley's Regiment included a grenadier company, which was unusual for an American unit. The troops assembled at Philadelphia in the spring of 1777. On 22 May 1777 the regiment became part of the 1st Pennsylvania Brigade in Washington's main army. On 8 January 1778, Hartley's Regiment was assigned to the Middle Department and in March it became part of the Pennsylvania Line. Captain William Scott's company from Thruston's Additional Continental Regiment was absorbed on 4 April 1778.

> https://en.wikipedia.org/wiki/Hartley%27s_Additional_Continental_Regiment.

56. John B. B. Trussell, Jr., "The Battle of Wyoming and Hartley's Expedition," *Historic Pennsylvania Leaflet No. 40* (Harrisburg: Pennsylvania Historical and Museum Commission, 1976). **Walker**: http://pasocietyofthecincinnati.org/Names/AndrewWalker.html. **Fort Muncy**: www.accessgenealogy.com/pennsylvania/fort-muncy-lycoming-county-pennsylvania.htm.
57. Butler to Hartley, Camp Westmoreland, August 5, 1778, James B. Miller, *Curse of the Tomahawk: Colonel Hartley's 1778 Expedition against the Six Nations Indians* (CreateSpace Independent Publishing Platform, 2009).
58. Hartley to State Council, September 1, 1778, *Pennsylvania Archives*, Samuel Hazard, ed. (Philadelphia, 1853), VI, 730.
59. Hartley to Zebulon Butler, Westmoreland, September 10, 1778, Miller, 117, 118.
60. Bolton to Haldimand, Niagara, September 18, 1778, Smy transcript, HP, AddMss21765.
61. Hartley to Congress, October 8, 1778, *Pennsylvania Archives*, 1858, VII, 5–7.
62. Hartley to the Honorable Executive Council of Pensilvania, October 8, 1778. *Pennsylvania Archives*, vol. VII, 3. **Morgan**: Hartley refers here to Daniel Morgan, who had commanded a regiment of riflemen that had been recently disbanded. Hartley assumed that Morgan was with the two companies of the regiment sent north to Schoharie with Colonel William Butler, 4PA.
63. Captain Henry Carberry was retired by January, 1781. In June, 1783, he was implicated in a Pennsylvania Line riot, and fled to Maryland. In 1817, he applied for admission into the State Society of the Cincinnati of Pennsylvania, but his name does not appear on the records. John b. Linn and William H. Egle, eds., *Pennsylvania Archives*, Second Series (Harrisburg: 1896), V.XI, 48.
64. Rebel accounts were not the only ones to report ridiculous numbers, as Cruikshank notes that Hartley's force was estimated at 1,400. See Cruikshank, 54.
65. *The Royal Gazette*, November 7, 1778.
66. Deane to Schuyler, Fort Schuyler, October 10, 1778, Penrose, *Indian Affairs*, 156, 157.
67. John Franklin Meginness, *Otzinachson: Or, A History of the West Branch Valley of the Susquehanna; Embracing a Full Account of Its Settlement … Full Accounts of the Indian Wars … Together with an Account of the Fair Play System; and the Trying Scenes of the Big*

Runaway; Interspersed with Biographical Sketches of Some of the Leading Settlers, Families, Etc ... (Philadelphia: H.B. Ashmead, 1857), 230.

68. A variation of buck and ball, i.e., slightly smaller swanshot was substituted for buckshot.
69. Trussell, "The Battle of Wyoming and Hartley's Expedition."
70. Colonel Samuel Hunter, Lieutenant of Northumberland County (March 1777–March 1784) to Vice President George Bryan, Supreme Executive Council, Fort Augusta, October 7, 1778. Louise Welles Murray, *A History of Old Tioga Point and Early Athens* (London: Forgotten Books, 2013; first published in 1908), 142, 143; Miller, 361.
71. Letters and Papers Relating to Canadian Affairs, Sullivan Expedition, and the Northern Indians; 1775–1779. National Archives and Records Administration. M247, vol.166.
72. Graymont, 180, 181.
73. Cruikshank, 54; Bolton to Haldimand, Niagara, November 11, 1778, Smy transcript, HP, AddMss21756.
74. Bolton to Haldimand, Niagara, October 12, 1778, Smy transcript, HP, AddMss21756.
75. Abler, *Cornplanter*, 47; Abler, *Blacksnake*, 137–39; Graymont, 180.
76. John Durkee, "The Battle and Massacre of Wyoming," http://durkeesmenofwyoming.tripod.com/id20.htm.

Chapter Four: New York's Midwestern Frontier

1. Bruce G. Trigger, ed., *Handbook of North American Indians, Vol. 15: Northeast* (Washington: Smithsonian Institution, 1978); George F.G. Stanley, *Canada Invaded, 1775–1776* (Toronto: Samuel Stevens Hakkert & Company, 1977), 32.
2. As an example of the divided loyalties in these areas, on the Delaware's East Branch at Pepacton (Papacunck), there were twenty-seven white families prior to 1778 that had migrated from around Kingston and Great Shandaken. Of the heads of those families, by the war's end, four had seen service under Brant and then transferred to the Royal Yorkers to join eight others, and another four had served in Butler's Rangers. So, 59 percent of the twenty-seven males had remained loyal to the Crown. John D. Monroe, *Chapters*

in the History of Delaware County New York (Delhi, NY: Delaware County Historical Association, 1949), 31, and Cruikshank and Watt, *KRRNY*, Master Roll, and Smy, *Nominal Roll*.

3. Monroe, 42–48.
4. A deposition of Nicholas Conklin sent to Clinton, Minisink, May 28, 1778, including the letter written by Charles Smith dated May 27, 1778, *PPGC*, III, 367–69.
5. Wisner, Tusten, Hatfield, and Nicoll to Clinton, Goshen, July 5, 1778, and Clinton's reply to same, July 6, 1778, *PPGC*, III, 522–25; Benson to Lasher, Poughkeepsie, July 7, 1778, *PPGC*, III, 530.
6. Deposition of James Armitage to Ten Broeck, July 6, 1778, *PPGC*, III, 525–28.
7. **Jacobs**: Mathews, *Mark of Honour*, 48, 57, 58, 136. Mathews says this is Captain Jacob Lewis, an Oquaga Mohawk. **Pawling**: Levi Pawling resigned as colonel of the 1st Ulster militia regiment on February 21, 1778, as he had been appointed the county's First Judge of the Common Pleas. He was replaced by John Cantine. Alphonso T. Clearwater, *The History of Ulster County, New York*, 2 vols. (1907), I, 168; Dumond's statement to Pawling, July 10, 1778, *PPGC*, III, 544, 554; Jones's statement to Wisner, July 10, 1778, ibid, III, 542–44.
8. Tusten, Wisner, and Newkirk to Clinton, Minisink, July 10, 1778, *PPGC*, III, 539–41; Cuddeback's statement, Minisink, July 10, 1778, ibid, III, 541, 542; Clinton to Cantine and Pawling, Poughkeepsie, July 11, 1778, ibid, III, 538, 539.
9. Cruikshank, *Butler's Rangers*, 50; John Butler to Caldwell, Tioga, July 12, 1778, Smy transcript, HP, AddMss21771.
10. Cruikshank, *Butler's Rangers*, 52; Smy, *Nominal Roll*, 111; McGinnis, "Journal of Occurrences"; Jones, "Loyalist Plantations."
11. Smy, *Annotated Roll*, 111. Entry for Jacob Hutsinger.
12. Scott to Clinton, Hurley, July 12, 1778, *PPGC*, III, 546, 547. **Graham**: Colonel Morris Graham's regiment of State Levies.
13. John Brodhead and others petition Clinton, July 12, 1778, *PPGC*, III, 548, 549.
14. Vrooman to Ten Broeck, Schoharie, July 17, 1778, and Ten Broeck to Clinton, Albany, July 19, 1778, *PPGC*, III, 557, 558.
15. Cantine to Clinton, Nepenagh (Napanoch), July 30, 1778, *PPGC*, III, 597; Monroe, 50.
16. Claim of John Burch [Buck], late of Ulster County, in *Second Report of the Bureau of Archives for the Province of Ontario 1904*,

17. Cantine to Clinton, Hunk, August 11, 1778, *PPGC*, III, 634–36.
18. **Buyker and Avery**: Silas Bowker and Peter Avery, both of Pepacton. **John and Stephen Middagh**: the brothers joined 1KRR on February 1, 1780. **Hendrick Bush, Jr.**: Henry first served in Brant's volunteers, and on August 25, 1781, joined 2KRR. See Watt, *KRRNY*, Master Roll. **Nathan Parks**: Nathaniel joined 1KRR on December 23, 1779. **George Barnhart**: he joined 2KRR on May 22, 1780. Cantine to Van Keuren and Nicoll, August 12, 1778, *PPGC*, III, 626.
19. **Tylar**: possibly Captain Bezaleel Tyler III of the Cochecton militia company, whose preemptory discharge of his firelock prompted the 1779 Battle of Minisink. Vernon Leslie, *The Battle of Minisink* (Middletown, NY: T. Emmett Henderson, 1976), 83, 84. **Fort Penn**: located at Stroudsburg, PA. See www.monroehistorical.org/articles/files/f65142657e45365566da8639bf73c845-98.html. **Van Atten**: possibly Captain Johannes/John Van Etten, 4th Company, 5th Battalion, Northampton County PA militia. See www.portal.state.pa.us/portal/server.pt/community/revolutionary_war_militia_overview/4125/northampton_co__revolutionary_war_militia/435890.
20. Robert Benson, ADC to Van Keuren and Nicoll, Poughkeepsie, August 26, 1778, *PPGC*, III, 693. Cantine to Clinton, Marbletown, August 28, 1778, ibid., III, 698.
21. Cantine to Clinton, Rochester, August 19, 1778, *PPGC*, III, 664–66; Clinton to Cantine, Poughkeepsie, August 19, 1778, ibid, III, 666, 667; Cantine to Clinton, Hunk, August 21, 1778, ibid, III, 681.
22. Newkirk to Cantine, Peenpack, August 21, 1778, *PPGC*, III, 678, 679; Cantine to Clinton, August 21, 1778, ibid., III, 680, 681.
23. Monroe, 51–53.
24. Peter Hendricks's report mentioned in Cantine to Clinton, Marbletown, August 28, 1778, *PPGC*, III, 697.
25. Cantine to Clinton, Marbletown, September 4, 1778, *PPGC*, III, 728–30.
26. Wm Butler to Clinton, Schoharie, August 31, 1778, *PPGC*, III, 710, 711; Commissioners of Sequestration to Clinton, September 1, 1778, ibid, III, 714.

27. Regarding the events of August 26 and various testimonies concerning same, see Monroe, 53–55.
28. Levi Pawling to Clinton, Marbletown, September 5, 1778, *PPGC*, III, 738; Clinton to Wm Butler, Poughkeepsie, September 6, 1778, Ibid, III, 739, 740; Posey to Clinton, Schoharie, September 23, 1778, ibid, III, 139, 140; Clinton to Butler, Poughkeepsie, October 5, 1778, ibid, III, 140, 141.
29. Cantine to Clinton, Marbletown, September 4, 1778, *PPGC*, III, 728–30. **Cummings**: Thomas Cummings served in Butler's Rangers' sixth company, and was listed on a roll of August 1, 1778. He settled at Chippewa. Smy, *Nominal Roll*, 75.
30. Clinton to Cantine, Poughkeepsie, September 6, 1778, *PPGC*, III, 741, 742.
31. Tom Arne Midtrod, *The Memory of All Ancient Customs: Native American Diplomacy in the Colonial Hudson Valley* (Cornell University Press, 2012), 200, 201.
32. **Graham**: listed with the Exempts of Hanover, Colonel Hasbrouck's Regiment, Ulster County. *PPGC*, IV, 125.
33. Cantine to Clinton, Marbletown, September 9, 1781, *PPGC*, IV, 16–19; Monroe, 61.
34. Cantine to Clinton, Hunk, September 18, 1778, *PPGC*, IV, 64, 65; Clinton to Cantine, September 21, 1778, ibid, IV, 65, 66.
35. Sworn statement by Robert McGinnis, Marbletown, September 17, 1778, included with Cantine to Clinton, Marbletown, September 18, 1778, *PPGC*, IV, 113–16.
36. Phillips to Clinton, Walkill, September 19, 1778, *PPGC*, IV, 121, 122; Clinton to Phillips, Poughkeepsie, September 30, 1778, ibid, IV, 122, 123.
37. **Westbrook:** Doug Massey, "Anthony and Andrew Westbrook: A Fascinating Narrative of Disunity" (unpublished manuscript, May 2015); Taylor and Forsythe to Claus, Niagara, November 15, 1778, Smy transcript, LAC, Claus Papers, MG19, F1; Leslie, *Minisink*, 4, 5; Hardenburgh to Clinton, New Hurly, October 16, 1778, *PPGC*, IV, 166; Clinton to the New York legislature, Poughkeepsie, October 17, 1778, ibid., IV, 167.
38. Clinton to Washington, Poughkeepsie, October 15 and 17, 1778, *PPGC*, IV, 163, 164, 167–69.
39. Clinton to Cantine, Poughkeepsie, October 21, 1778, *PPGC*, IV, 181, 182.
40. Schoonmaker to Clinton, October 22, 1778, *PPGC*, IV, 185.

41. Clinton to Van Cortlandt, October 17, 1778, *PPGC*, IV, 210.
42. Kingston trustees to Clinton, October 17, 1778, and Clinton to the trustees, *PPGC*, IV, 211.
43. Ten Broeck to Clinton, Albany, November 23, 1778, *PPGC*, IV, 266, 267.
44. Clinton to Jay, Poughkeepsie, November 17, 1778, *PPGC*, IV, 289, 290.
45. Captain William Johnson, Mohawk chief, Joseph Ceskwrora, chief, Captain John, chief, and William George, chief to Colonel John Cantine, Mormeltown [Marbletown, Ulster Cty, NY] December 13, 1778, *PPGC*, IV, 364. Is this William Johnson of Canajoharie, son of Sir William? **Equinunk**: located on the PA/NY state line east of modern Binghamton and west of Kingston, northeast of Wyoming. Probably a Munsee community.

CHAPTER FIVE: BACK IN THE MOHAWK REGION

1. SJJ to Claus, Quebec, July 2, 1778, transcribed in DePeyster, *Miscellanies*, LII and III.
2. Cruikshank and Watt, *KRR NY*, 22, 133, 134. See LAC, HP, WO28/9, 147–56.
3. Stevens, "Allies," XXIV, 1740.
4. Stevens, "Allies," XXIV, 1742–44; William L. Stone, *Life of Joseph Brant–Thayendanegea: Including the Indian Wars of the American Revolution*. 2 vols. (New York: Alexander V. Blake, 1838), I, 358.
5. SJJ to Claus, Quebec, July 16, 1778, Smy transcript, LAC, Claus Papers, MG 19, FI, V.2.
6. Claus to SJJ, Montreal, July 20, 1778, LAC, Claus Papers, MG 19, FI, V.25.
7. Stevens, "Allies," XXIV, 1748. Henry White to William Knox, New York, August 14, 1778.
8. Brant to Carr, [July 1778], Smy transcript; Halsey, *ONYF*, 214.
9. Ten Broeck to Clinton, Albany, July 11, 1778, *PPGC*, III, 536, 537.
10. Washington to Stark, HQ Haverstraw, July 18, 1778, Stark Correspondence, 178.
11. Simms, *Frontiersmen*, 170. Simms places these incidents after Brant's attacks on Springfield and Andrewstown, but that does not

354 | FIRE & DESOLATION

make sense, as in his account there were intact buildings at the settlement; LCol Ford to Ten Broeck, Cherry Valley, July 18, 1778, *PPGC*, III, 555–57.

12. Klock to Clinton, Canajoharie, July 22, 1778 (misdated June 22), *PPGC*, III, 475; Graymont, 174–75; Ford's report to Ten Broeck, Cherry Valley, July 18, 1778, *PPGC*, III, 555–57.
13. Kelsay, 194; Halsey, *ONYF*, 123.
14. Stone, *Life of Brant*, I, 363. **Young**: Adam Young was a prosperous individual, owning six hundred acres in Young's Patent and two thousand in Livingston's Patent. He had a sawmill, potash works, and dry goods store, and traded with the local Natives. He had been convicted of supplying loyalists making their way to Niagara. By August 1778, he was a private in Butler's Rangers. He had three, perhaps four, sons in Butler's, two of them sergeants. Smy, *Nominal Roll*.
15. Klock to Clinton, Canajoharie, July 22, 1778 (misdated June 22), *PPGC*, III, 475. See also Klock to Ten Broeck, Palatine, July 19, 1778, *PPGC*, III, 559, 560.
16. Schuyler to Clinton, Albany, July 20, 1778, *PPGC*, III, 565.
17. Vrooman to Ten Broeck, Schoharie, July 17, 1778, and Ten Broeck to Clinton, Albany, July 1778, *PPGC*, III, 557, 558.
18. Clinton to Schuyler, Poughkeepsie, July 21, 1778, *PPGC*, III, 565, 566.
19. Return of detachment for Schoharie and Cherry Valley, July 20, 1778, *PPGC*, III, 562; Ten Broeck to Clinton, Albany, July 20, 1778, ibid., 562–64.
20. Peter Bellinger, Friederick Fox, Justice, Willem Deygert, Justice, Michael Ittick, Capt., and Henrich Hercheimer, Justice to Gov Clinton, German Flatts, July 22, 1778, *PPGC*, III, 581–83.
21. Halsey, *ONYF*, 223, 224. Includes excerpts from Captain Warren's diary.
22. Clyde to Clinton, Canajoharie, January 8, 1779, Simms, *Frontiersmen*, II, 210–11.
23. Stark to Washington, Albany, July 24, 1778. This date appears to be incorrect, as it mentions the arrival of the Continentals on July 27. Stark Correspondence, 182.
24. Richard B. LaCrosse, *Revolutionary Rangers: Daniel Morgan's Riflemen and Their Role on the Northern Frontier, 1778–1783* (Bowie, MD: Heritage Books, Inc., 2002), 19–21.
25. Fryer, *King's Men,* 82; Robert Malcomson, *Warships of the Great Lakes 1754–1834* (Annapolis: Naval Institute Press, 2001), 37.

The choice of Deer Island is explained to the American secretary in Haldimand to Germain, Sorel, October 14, 1778, HP, AddMss21714.
26. G.P. Browne, Biography of Guy Carleton, *DCB*, vol. 5; Stevens, "Allies," XXV, 1836, 1837.
27. Haldimand to Bolton, Quebec, July 31, 1778, Smy transcript, HP, AddMss21756; Guthrie's appointment in General Orders, July 24, 1778, HP, AddMss21743.
28. Smith to Walter Butler, Harpersfield, July 27, 1778, and Smith to Brant, July 27, 1778. *PPGC*, III, 617, 618.
29. John Taylor to Clinton, Albany, August 9, 1778, *PPGC*, III, 616, 617; William Butler to Clinton, Middle Fort, Schoharie, August 13, 1778, *PPGC*, III, 630–32; LaCrosse, 22 and 23, 27; Monroe, 70.
30. Mathews, *Mark*, 52; Stark to Alden, Albany, August 15, 1778, *Stark Correspondence*, 185.
31. Halsey, *ONYF*, 224, 225.
32. Clinton to Colonel Butler, Poughkeepsie, September 8, 1778, *PPGC*, IV, 12, 13.
33. McKenna — variously McKenzie. His deposition, Schoharie, August 29, 1778, *PPGC*, III, 711, 712.
34. LaCrosse, 28, 29.
35. Gansevoort to Washington, Fort Schuyler, August 13, 1778. Stone, *Life of Brant*, I, 360, 361, 361n. Unrest at Fort Stanwix would continue as one regiment replaced another. It was not only the brutal isolation of the fort, but its proximity to Indian Territory, which resulted in constant danger. Parties sent on work details outside the walls were frequently attacked. There was a brief period of relief in 1779, when the garrison destroyed the Onondaga villages in support of the Sullivan-Clinton expeditions. Yet, as time dragged on, the worst factor wearing down the soldiers' morale was the realization of the futility of maintaining a garrison out on the limb of the frontier. Enemy war parties and expeditions simply sidestepped the fort to attack the settlements below — which was precisely what St. Leger should have done in 1777, but he lacked the imagination or courage to do so. Ironically, it was an accidental fire in 1781 that finally ended Stanwix's career, and the troops were withdrawn to the lower valley. Watt, *Dirty, Trifling*, 126, 127.
36. Glatthaar and Martin, 223, 224.
37. Garnett Journal and Memorial of Roelif Van De Car to Haldimand, LAC, HP, AddMss21874, 235–37.

38. Cruikshank, *Butler's Rangers*, 53; Thomas Garnett's expenses approval and Gilbert Tice's and SJJ's supporting evidence, HP, AddMss21749; Van De Car Memorial, 236.
39. Aubrey to Haldimand, Carleton Island, September 2, 1778, Smy transcript, HP, AddMss21787. **Adams**: variously spelled Adems.
40. Glatthaar and Martin, 224; Cruikshank, *Butler's Rangers*, 53. Cruikshank's account of the capture of these Oneidas indicates that Caldwell commanded this expedition. Other sources give the command to Brant.
41. The movie *Drums Along the Mohawk* portrays Helmer's run as a feat of great heroism, in which he outran several warriors who pursued him in relays; Cruikshank, *Butler's Rangers*, 53. Cruikshank states that the sole surviving scout "outran all his pursuers"; Bellinger to Klock, Palatine, September 16, 1778, *PPGC*, IV, 39.
42. Halsey, *ONYF*, 226; Cruikshank, *Butler's Rangers*, 53; Ten Broeck to Clinton, Albany, September 18, 1778, *PPGC*, IV, 53; Stone, *Life of Brant*, I, 365n, ex The Remembrancer, Or Impartial Repository of Public Events.
43. Stone, *Life of Brant*, I, 366. **Carr family**: Halsey, *ONYF*, 226. **Whiting**: William Whiting is listed as the colonel of the 17th Albany County Militia. See *New York in the Revolution as Colony and State*, I, 132; Morrison advises that the inhabitants who took shelter at Fort Herkimer lived in that installation for the rest of the war. Berry and Morrison, *Don't Shoot*, 259. They must have worked their farms under militia guards, as reports of excellent harvests were frequently heard in later years.
44. Clinton to Ten Broeck, Poughkeepsie, September 19, 1778, *PPGC*, IV, 54, 55; Clinton to Washington, Poughkeepsie, September 24, 1778, ibid., IV, 78, 79.
45. McGinnis Journal.
46. Stone, *Life of Brant*, I, 366, 367.
47. Glaathaar and Martin, 225; Cochran's account of the Oneidas' and Tuscaroras' speech, Fort Schuyler, September 28, 1778, *PPGC*, IV, 131–33.
48. Return of Albany County militia at Schoharie, September 20, 1778, *PPGC*, IV, 59.
49. Jacob Klock, Samuel Campbell, Samuel Clyde, et al. to Clinton, Canajoharie, September 18, 1778, *PPGC*, IV, 117–19; Clinton to Klock, October 12, 1778, ibid, IV, 153–55.
50. "A Return of the Detachment of Foot Commanded by Wm. Butler

Esqr. Lt. Col. Comm'dt at Schoharry, October, 1778," *PPGC*, IV, 229–31(?); Lacrosse, 31. LaCrosse details Butler's force.

51. Monroe, 71. This historian writes that William Butler's intelligence prior to September 21 was that Brant had seven hundred men at these two locations, and that around October 1, spies advised that Brant had left both places, but other sources state that Brant left Oquaga to go to Cookoze on October 7. Whatever the case, considering that William Butler had such excellent information about the size of the loyalist force, was it likely that he would set out on a deep-penetration raid into hostile country with only two hundred men to take on four hundred on their home ground if he had not already known that they were gone?

52. Extracts from *William Butler's Journal*, *PPGC*, IV, 223–28. The colonel states that Stevens was sent specifically to collect Glasford, suggesting he had earlier been identified. **Glasford**: this was John Glasford, Sr., who likely served with Brant after this incident, and in 1783, was a private in Munro's Company, 1KRR NY. Cruikshank and Watt, *KRR NY*, 223; Monroe, 72. Monroe says that the expedition arrived at Unadilla on October 6, and took two white men captive, one being John Glasford.

53. It appears that William Butler became convinced that his prompt manoeuvre had driven off Brant's force, as his force was undisturbed during its retreat. In my opinion, he simply became inventive when his raid was at no time seriously opposed. **Killed children, raped women**: Helen Caister Robinson, *Joseph Brant: A Man for His People* (Don Mills, ON: Longman Canada, 1971), 81. Although Robinson provides a bibliography, she does not footnote her sources. Hers is the only reference to rape among the several sources I have consulted, so her contention is suspect. However, it is known that rebel troops raped and then killed Onondaga women during the destruction of their castle in 1779.

54. **Tuscarora**: the burning of two Tuscarora villages is a mystery. Were these villagers allied with Brant? He certainly had several Tuscaroras operating with him. Or had the villagers moved north, to the Tuscarora settlement of Ganaghsaraga on Lake Oneida, to be close to their Oneida allies? If so, the villages could have been harbouring those of Brant's men who were not Tuscaroras.

55. Monroe, 72, 73; LaCrosse, 30–33; *William Butler's Journal*, *PPGC*, IV, 223–28; Douglas Massey, "Benjamin Becraft UEL (Part 3)," *Loyalist Trails*, UELAC Newsletter, August 2014.

56. William Butler to Clinton, Schoharie, October 18, 1778, *PPGC*, IV, 222, 223.
57. Glatthaar and Martin, 226; Lieutenant-Colonel Van Dyck's report of Good Peter's visit to Fort Stanwix, and James Clinton to George Clinton, Albany, December 30, 1778, *PPGC*, IV, 418, 437.
58. Washington to James Clinton, October 17 1778, T.W. Egly, Jr., *History of the First New York Regiment* (Hampton, NH: Peter E. Randall, 1981), 108.
59. Simms, *Frontiersmen*, II, 212–14. In a typically macabre frontier manner, Flat Kop adopted the girls, and they were brought up as Native children. When reunited with their people after the war, the girls spoke no German and had a very difficult time adjusting. **Christian Sharrer**: Gavin K. Watt and James F. Morrison, *The British Campaign of 1777, Volume 1*, 180. Sharrer served in 4TCM.
60. Twiss report, September 1778, HP, AddMss21814; Haldimand to Germain, Quebec City, October 13, 1778.
61. Ray Ostiguy research. Deposition of William Byrne, Montreal, November 3, 1787, Records of Notary John Gerbrand Beek, Minute No. 330. BAnQ Vieux Montreal, CN601, 529. Fonds Cour supérieure, District judiciare de Montréal, Greffes de notaires. Oddly, Byrne deposed that this foray took place in September 1779.
62. Cruikshank and Watt, *KRRNY*, 24, 134. In 1984, in this book, I conflated Crawford and Byrne's little expedition with Major Carleton's on Lake Champlain, as Carleton's force was reported to include an officer and thirty men of "Sr. J. Johnson." However, I have now determined that Carleton's officer and thirty men were from the remnant units of Burgoyne's expedition, who had been assigned to Johnson's 1st battalion for administration.
63. Garnett journal, 286, 287.
64. Crysler, 56–61; Abler, *Chainbreaker*, 104.
65. Kelsay, 228, 229.
66. Hand to Washington, Albany, October 19, 1778, National Archives, http://founders.archives.gov/documents/Washington/03-17-02-0648#GEWN-03-17-02-0648-fn-0003.
67. Egly, 108.
68. Ten Broeck to Clinton, Albany November 8, 1778, *PPGC*, IV, 254.
69. Alden to Washington, Cherry Valley, November 4, 1778, National Archives, http://founders.archives.gov/documents/Washington/03-18-02-0037; Glatthaar and Martin, 230.

70. Gansevoort to Alden, Fort Schuyler, November 6, 1778, Johnson, *Bloodied*, 101, ex Gansevoort Papers, 356; Alden to Gansevoort, November 8, 1778, *Gansevoort Papers*, 357.
71. Clyde to Clinton, Canajoharie, January 8, 1779; "Cherry Valley—November 11, 1778," https://web.archive.org/web/20120918113253/http://home.roadrunner.com/~nlecompte/regiment/cherryvalley.html; Campbell, *Annals*, 117.
72. Hand to Clinton, Albany, November 10, 1778, Johnson, *Bloodied*, 102, ex General Edward Hand Papers, NYPL.
73. Hand to P.V. Van Rensselaer, Albany, November 10, 1778, Johnson, *Bloodied*, 103, ex Hand Papers, NYPL.
74. Kelsay, 230. **Serjeant**: it is a mystery why a latent Tory would be permitted to hold the rank of serjeant and be put at the head of a patrol away from the fort where he could possibly persuade his men to desert; Walter Butler to John Butler, Unadilla, November 17, 1778 (hereafter Walter Butler's account), Smy transcript, LAC, CO, Series Q, V.16-1.
75. Taylor and Duffin to Claus, Niagara, December 1, 1778, Smy transcript, LAC, Claus Papers, MG19, F1, V.25. Information about the 6MA officers being at mess was brought to Niagara by Lieutenant Peter Hare of Butler's Rangers.
76. Pension deposition of Henry Scott, W20049, excerpted in Johnson, *Bloodied*, 106.
77. Johnson, *Bloodied*, 112.
78. **Give warning**: Campbell, 125. **Hamlin**: spelled Hamble in Simms, *Frontiersmen*, II, 204, and Campbell, 118. See also Stone, *Life of Brant*, II, 373. He does not name the rider; Lieutenant McKendry, 6MA Quartermaster, credits Hammell with giving Alden the alarm. Johnson, *Bloodied*, 105; pension depositions of James Dickson, S22208, and Robert Dickson, R13762. James gave evidence that his brother Robert was the individual who alerted the garrison. As no other source agrees with this contention, I have not used this information in the text. See Johnson, *Bloodied*, 106. **Wounded woodcutter**: Kelsay, 230. **Alden's death**: Simms, *Frontiersmen*, II, 204. Simms claims that Brant killed Alden. **Little Aaron**: Campbell, 120; Stone, *Life of Brant*, II, 374; Simms, *Frontiersmen*, II, 205; and Kelsay, 232. Kelsay credits Lieutenant Peter Hare of Caldwell's Company with saving Dunlop and his daughter. **Newberry**: listed twice, first as a serjeant in Ten Broeck's Company and then as a private in Caldwell's. Pay List of Butler's Rangers, December 24,

1777–October 24, 1778, HP, AddMss21765. **Clyde family**: Simms, *Frontiersmen*, II, 207. **Totem**: Campbell, 124.

79. Halsey, *ONYF*, 244, 245.
80. Captain Benjamin Warren's account transcribed in Halsey, *ONYF*, 242; "Diary of Captain Benjamin Warren" (hereafter Warren's account), transcribed from Jared Sparks MSS Collection, Harvard University Library, posted at www.newrivernotes.com/historical_revolutionary_1778_cherry_hill_massacre_ny.htm.
81. *The New Jersey Gazette*, December 31, 1778, Smy transcript. **Rebel strength**: surely there could not have been 150 1TCM militiamen available locally.
82. John Dain's Journal, http://home.roadrunner.com/~nlecompte/regiment/cherryvalley.html.
83. Walter Butler's account.
84. Halsey, *ONYF*, 243.
85. One never knows whether to credit these accounts of men being saved by fellow Masons. I repeat this here for what it is worth. **Masonic emblems**: the wearing of trade silver masonic emblems was common and popular among the Iroquois. N. Jaye Frederickson, *The Covenant Chain: Indian Ceremonial and Trade Silver* (Ottawa: National Museums of Canada, 1980), 53, plate 25.
86. Fisher (Visscher) to Hand, November 11, 1778, Johnson, *Bloodied*, 106, ex Draper Collection 20F:14; Warren's account. No Lieutenant Debe appears in Warren's arrangement of officers, but a Lieutenant Parker is in a company without a captain, so he may have been acting in that rank.
87. Walter Butler's account; Campbell, 126, 127.
88. William McKendry, "Lieutenant William McKendry's Journal," http://archive.org/stream/sullivansexped00mckerich/sullivansexped00mckerich_djvu.txt.
89. Campbell, 123; **Butler's relatives**: the rebels were holding his mother, Catherine/Catalyntje, his brothers William Johnson and Andrew/Andreas, and sister, Deborah and also his aunt, Mrs. Walter Butler Sheehan, and her son, and his cousin, Mrs. Deborah Wall, wife of Edward. William A. Smy, "The Butlers Before the Revolution," *Butler Bicentenary*, 49–52. Genealogical charts.
90. Taylor and Duffin to Claus, Niagara, December 1, 1778, Smy transcript, LAC, Claus Papers, MG19, F1, V.25.
91. Warren's account.
92. Egly, 110.

93. Walter Butler's account.
94. **John Moore**: Moore had been a committeeman for Canajoharie District from the very first, and was elected a Provincial Congress delegate for Tryon County on September 13, 1775. See Penrose, *Mohawk Valley*, 7–43, 46.
95. Walter Butler to Schuyler, Cherry Valley, November 12, 1778. Stone, *Life of Brant*, II, 377, 378.
96. Simms, *Frontiersmen*, II, 210.
97. A letter written by M.R. published in the *Pennsylvania Packett*, January 7, 1779. Johnson, *Bloodied*, 119.
98. Campbell, 128; Morrison, *Fulton County*, 32. Morrison reports their arrival in Cherry Valley on November 12. He states that they gathered the bodies of the slain inhabitants and performed a mass burial.
99. Klock to Hand, Moore's place, November 12, 1778, Johnson, *Bloodied*, 107 ex Continental Congress Papers, Reel 168, Item 252, vol. 6, 512. **The Moores**: Klock's letter was dated at John Moore's place, yet Mrs. Moore and her children had been captured on the morning of the 11th. The family must have been staying in the village for safety, rather than at their farm, which lay four miles outside the settlement.
100. Pension deposition of Nathaniel Potter, R8377, Johnson, *Bloodied*, 108. **Gordon**: Lieutenant-Colonel James Gordon, 12th (Half Moon & Ballstown) Albany County Militia, *New York in the Revolution*, I, 120.
101. "William McKendry's Journal."
102. Pension depositions of George Feeter, S13013, and Daybold Moyer, W15789. Johnson, *Bloodied*, 109.
103. Morrison, *Fulton County*, 22, 23.
104. Johnson, *Bloodied*, 133; Simms, *Frontiersman*, II, 209.
105. Halsey, *ONYF*, 245.
106. Warren's account.
107. Harper to Clinton, December 2, 1778, and same to same, February 16, 1779, Halsey, *ONYF*, 246.
108. Warren's account.
109. Whiting to Hand, Cherry Valley, November 13, 1778, *PPGC*, IV, 286, 287.
110. Ten Broeck to Clinton, Albany, November 1, 1778, *PPGC*, IV, 266–67.
111. Campbell, 127.
112. Warren's account.

113. "The Victims at Cherry Valley," James Clinton to George Clinton, Albany, November 28, 1778. *PPGC*, IV, 338.
114. Gordon to Van Schaick, Fort Plank, November 14, 1778, Fonda to Van Schaick, [Johnstown,] November 14, 1778, and Hand to Clinton, Schenectady, November 15, 1778, *PPGC*, IV, 287–89.
115. **Buxton**: Stone, *Life of Brant*, II, 378. Stone points out that the killing of the Buxtons may have been the work of the rebel Oneidas who had earlier struck the Butternut settlement. If so, this act would have been contrary to the account given by their headmen to Major Cochran at Fort Stanwix.
116. Halsey, *ONYF*, 250.
117. Taylor and Duffin to Claus, Niagara, December 1 1778, Smy transcript, LAC, Claus Papers, MG19, F1, V.25; Klock to Vischer and Klock to Hand, Palatine, November 23, 1778, Johnson, *Bloodied*, 117, 118. **Chyle/Kyle**: the chyle was a sinkhole or sunken creek not far from Springfield that gave its name to a small group of houses burned at this time. The three prisoners were the brothers John, Sebastian, and Matthias Shaul. Pension deposition of John Shaul, W11441. Re. the destruction of the settlement, see William Harper to Clinton, Mohawk District, Tryon City, December 2, 1778, *PPGC*, IV, 414; A. Ross Eckler, "The McNeil Patent," http://herkimer.nygenweb.net/stark/mcneilpatent.html.
118. Warren's account.
119. Clyde to Fisher (Visscher), November 15, 1778, Johnson, *Bloodied*, 116; pension deposition of Azor Cole, S10473. Cole stated that the firing was the result of a returning patrol discharging their muskets before entering the fort.
120. Taylor and Duffin to Claus, Niagara, December 1, 1778, Smy transcript, LAC, Claus Papers, MG19, F1, V.25.
121. Walter Butler to John Butler, Unadilla, November 17, 1778, Smy transcript, LAC, CO, Series Q, V.16-1. **Surgeon's Mate**: Francis deBeviere, appointed August 26, 1778. He was kept a prisoner until the end of the war. James F. Morrison's notes to the pension application of Alexander Thompson, R22005.
122. Stone, *Life of Brant*, II, 379.
123. Walter Butler to John Butler, Unadilla, November 17, 1778, Smy transcript, LAC, CO, Series Q, V.16-1.
124. Egly, 110.
125. Clinton to John Jay, Poughkeepsie, November 17, 1778, *PPGC*, IV, 289, 290.

126. Hand to Washington, Albany, November 18, 1778. Johnson, *Bloodied*, 115, 116. **Sacandaga Blockhouse**: for details of the planning and building of this installation, see ibid., 117, 118.
127. Yates to George Clinton, Albany, November 18, 1778, James Clinton to George Clinton, Albany, November 28, 1778, and George Clinton to Yates, Poughkeepsie, December 3, 1778, *PPGC*, IV, 334–37.
128. Glatthaar and Martin, 233; Van Dyck's summary of Good Peter's visit, December 23, 1778, *PPGC*, IV, 417–19.
129. Bolton to Haldimand, Niagara, November 11, 1778, Smy transcript, HP, AddMss21756.
130. Claus to Haldimand, Montreal, November 19, 1778, LAC, B114, 13, 14.
131. Haldimand to Bolton, Quebec City, December 25, 1778, Smy transcript, LAC, HP, AddMss21756.
132. Haldimand to Butler, Quebec City December 25, 1778, Smy transcript, LAC, HP, AddMss21756.
133. James Clinton to Walter Butler, Albany, January 2, 1779, Smy transcript, LAC, HP, AddMss21765 and *PPGC*, IV, 457–59; **Campbell**: Morrison indicates that Samuel Campbell moved to Schenectady and spent the remainder of his war attempting to gain the release of his family. Oddly enough, he did not resign his commission as colonel. Consequently, 1TCM was led by Samuel Clyde as lieutenant-colonel. Berry and Morrison, *Don't Shoot*, 215.
134. Walter Butler to James Clinton, Niagara, February 18, 1779, Smy transcript, LAC, HP, AddMss21765.

BIBLIOGRAPHY

PRIMARY SOURCES — ARCHIVAL

Archives of Ontario
Ms622, an obsolete, miscellaneous selection of the Haldimand Papers.

British Library
Haldimand Papers
AddMss21700, Register of Letters from Carleton to Various Persons, 1776–77.
AddMss21714, Letters to the Ministry, vol. 1, 1778–80.
AddMss21743, General Orders issued by Carleton and Haldimand, 1776–83.
AddMss21749, Warrants for Extraordinary Service of the Army, 1779–84.
AddMss21756, Correspondence with officers Commanding at Mackinac & Niagara, 1777–82.
AddMss21760, Letters from Officers commanding at Niagara, vol. 1, n.d., 1777–80.
AddMss21765, Correspondence with officers at Niagara, 1777–84.
AddMss21771, Letters from LCol J. Campbell & others, 1778–81, vol. 1.
AddMss21787, Letters from officers Commanding at Carleton Is., 1778–84.
AddMss21814, Correspondence with Officers of the Engineers, n.d., 1777–83.
AddMss21874, V.1, Memorials from Prov Corps and Loyalists, n.d. and 1777–82.

Library of Congress
George Washington Papers. Series 4. General Correspondence: George Washington. 1741–99.

Library and Archives Canada
Claus Family fonds, MG 19, F1, vols. 25 & 26.

Haldimand Papers
MG 21
B62, Register of Letters to Various Persons.
B114, Correspondence with LCol D. Claus, 1777–84.
B215, Memorials from the Provincial Corps and Loyalists, vol. 2.

Colonial Office Records
42/37 (Q14), 1777, Burgoyne's expedition & Surrender.

War Office Records
24/8, Warrants authorizing the establishment of regiments.
28/9, Headquarters records & returns, America, 1775–95.
28/10, Records of Military Headquarters, America.

New York State Library
Revolutionary War Manuscripts, Document #6752.

Pennsylvania
Pennsylvania Archives
Samuel Hazard, ed. Philadelphia, 1853. Volume 6; 1858 Volume 7; John B. Linn & William H. Egle, eds. Second Series, 1896 Volume 11.

U.S. National Archives and Records Administration
Letters and Papers Relating to Canadian Affairs, Sullivan Expedition, and the Northern Indians, 1775–79. M247, vol. 166.
"Revolutionary War Rolls 1775–83." Microfilm reel 78, RG96, series M246.
"Revolutionary War Pension and Bounty-Land Warrant Application Files." NARA, RG15, M804.
"To George Washington from Colonel Ichabod Alden, 4 November 1778." *Founders Online.* Last modified December 28, 2016. http://founders.

archives.gov/documents/Washington/03-18-02-0037.

"To George Washington from Brigadier General Edward Hand, 29 October 1778." *Founders Online*. Last modified December 28, 2016. http://founders.archives.gov/documents/Washington/03-17-02-0648.

U.S. *Papers of the Continental Congress, Journals of Congress, 1777–78*. Vols. 3 & 4.

Primary Sources — Published

Newspapers
New Jersey Gazette, December 31, 1778.
New York Journal, July 20, 1778.
Pennsylvania Packet, January 7, 1779.
Quebec Gazette, June 4, 1778.
Quebec Gazette, June 27, 1778.
Royal Gazette of New York, August 1, 1778.
Royal Gazette of New York, November 7, 1778.
Toronto Globe, July 16, 1877.

Published Documents, Maps, and Contemporary Works

Clinton, George, Hugh Hastings, and James A. Holden. *Public Papers of George Clinton, First Governor of New York, 1777–1795, 1801–1804*. 6 Vols. New York & Albany: State of New York, 1902.

Dann, John C. *The Revolution Remembered: Eyewitness Accounts of the War for Independence*. Chicago: The University of Chicago Press, 1980.

Documents Relative to the Colonial History of the State of New York. O'Callaghan, E.B., ed. Albany: Weed, Parson, 1854. London Documents, XLVI.

Fernow, Berthold, ed. *Documents Relating to the Colonial History of the State of New York*. Vol. XV. Albany: Weed, Parsons and Company, Printers, 1887. State Archives, V.1.

Fraser, Alexander, ed. *Second Report of the Bureau of Archives for the Province of Ontario*. Baltimore: Genealogical Publishing Co., Inc., 1994. First published in two parts in 1904 by the Legislative Assembly of Ontario.

Frederickson, N. Jaye. *The Covenant Chain: Indian Ceremonial and Trade Silver.* Ottawa: National Museums of Canada, 1980.

Gazetteer and Business Directory of Windsor County, Vt., for 1883–84. Vol.1.

General Staff, Historical Section, ed. "The War of the American Revolution, The Province of Quebec Under the Administration of Governor Sir Guy Carleton, 1775–1778." Vol. 2 of *A History of the Organization, Development and Services of the Military and Naval Forces of Canada from the Peace of Paris in 1763 to the Present Time: With Illustrative Documents.* Canada: n.d.

General Staff, Historical Section, ed. "The War of the American Revolution, The Province of Quebec under the Administration of Governor Frederic Haldimand, 1778–1784." Vol. 3 of *A History of the Organization, Development and Services of the Military and Naval Forces of Canada from the Peace of Paris in 1763 to the Present Time: With Illustrative Documents.* Canada, King's Printer, n.d.

McHenry, Chris, compiler. *Rebel Prisoners at Quebec 1778–1783. Being a List of American Prisoners Held by the British During the Revolutionary War.* Lawrenceburg, IN: printed by author, 1981.

Penrose, Maryly, ed. *Mohawk Valley in the Revolution: Committee of Safety Papers & Genealogical Compendium.* Franklin Park, NJ: Liberty Bell Associates, 1978.

Roberts, James A. *New York in the Revolution as Colony and State.* 2 vols. Albany: State of New York, 1904. First published 1897.

Smith, George. *An Universal Military Dictionary, A Copious Explanation of the Technical Terms &c. — Used in the Equipment, Machinery, Movements, and Military Operations of an Army.* Ottawa: Museum Restoration Service, 1969. First published 1779 by J. Millan.

Stark, Caleb, trans. and ed. *Memoir and Official Correspondence of Gen. John Stark, with Notices of Several Other Officers of the Revolution. Also, a Biography of Capt. Phinehas Stevens, and of Col. Robert Rogers.* Concord, NH: G. Parker Lyon, 1860.

Walton, E.P., ed. *Records of the Council of Safety and Governor and Council of the State of Vermont, to Which are Prefixed the Records of the General Conventions from July 1775 to December 1777.* Montpelier: Steam Press of J. & J.M. Poland, 1873.

Washington George. *The Writings of George Washington from the Original Manuscript Sources, 1745–1799.* Edited by John C. Fizpatrick. 20 vols. Washington: US Govt Printing Office, 1937.

Primary Sources — Unpublished

Transcripts, Letters, Documents and Journals

Gansevoort, Peter. "Military Papers." Transcribed by the State Historian. NY State Archives: submitted 1906.

Smy, William A., trans. and ed. "The Butler Papers: Documents and Papers Relating to Colonel John Butler and his Corps of Rangers 1711–1977." n.p., 1994.

Published Memoirs, Depositions, Diaries, Journals & Correspondence

American

Butler, William. *William Butler's Journal.* PPGC, IV, 223–28.

"Cherry Valley — November 11, 1778." https://web.archive.org/web/20120918113253/http://home.roadrunner.com/~nlecompte/regiment/cherryvalley.html.

Dain, John. "John Dain's Journal." https://web.archive.org/web/20120918113253/http://home.roadrunner.com/~nlecompte/regiment/cherryvalley.html.

Dickson, James. Pension Deposition, S22208.

Dickson, Robert. Pension Deposition, R13762.

Eckler, A. Ross. "The McNeil Patent." http://herkimer.nygenweb.net/stark/mcneilpatent.html.

Fitzpatrick, John. C., ed. *The Writings of George Washington from the Original Manuscript Sources, 1745—1799.* 20 Vols. Washington: US Govt Printing Office, 1937.

Ford, Worthington Chauncey, ed. Vol. 11 of *Journals of the Continental Congress.* 34 volumes. Washington: Government Printing Office, 1908.

Hawkins, Abraham. Pension Deposition, S13255.

"James Clinton to George Clinton — Victims at Cherry Valley." Albany, November 28, 1778. PPGC, IV, 338.

McKendry, William. "Lieutenant William McKendry's Journal." http://archive.org/stream/sullivansexped00mckerich/sullivansexped00mckerich_djvu.txt.

Warren, Benjamin. "Diary of Captain Benjamin Warren." Jared Sparks MSS Collection, Harvard University Library. www.newrivernotes.com/historical_revolutionary_1778_cherry_hill_massacre_ny.htm.

British, German, and Canadian

Butler, John. "Major John Butler's report of the Wyoming Expedition." Butler to Bolton, Lacawanack, July 8, 1778. HP, AddMss2, 1760.

———. "Narrative of Lt. Col. Butler's Services in America, London May 1785." NAC, HP, B215, 196–202.

Claus, Daniel. "Anecdotes of Captain Brant." In William Clement Bryant. "Captain Brant and the Old King." Vol. 6. Publications of the Buffalo Historical Society, 1896.

Crysler, Adam. "The Journal of Adam Crysler." In *Loyalist Narratives from Upper Canada*. Ed. James J. Talman, n.p. Toronto: The Champlain Society, 1946.

De Lorimier, Claude-Nicolas-Guillaume. *At War with the Americans: The Journal of Claude-Nicolas-Guillaume de Lorimier*. Trans. and ed. by Peter Aichinger. Victoria: Press Porcepic, n.d.

Enys, John. *The American Journals of Lt John Enys*. Ed. Elizabeth Cometti. Syracuse: Adirondack Museum and Syracuse University Press, 1976.

Garnett, Thomas. "A Journal of the Proceedings of Thomas Garnett Appointed Senior Captain in a Battalion Raiseing by Mr James Howetson by Order of Governor Tryon to Serve Under Sir John Johnson." OA, HP, MS 622, Reel 109.

Hadden, Lieut. James M. *A Journal Kept in Canada and Upon Burgoyne's Campaign in 1776 and 1777*. Ed. Horatio Rogers. Albany: Joel Munsell's Sons, 1884.

McGinnis, Richard. "Journal of Occurrences Respecting our Suffering in the Late Rebellion." In *The New York Genealogical and Biographical Record*, vol. 106, nos. 1 & 2. Ed. Carol Lind. New York: n.p., 1975.

Penrose, Maryly B., ed. *Indian Affairs Papers, American Revolution*. Franklin Park, NJ: Liberty Bell Associates, 1981.

Peters, John. "A Narrative of John Peters, Lieutenant-Colonel in the Queen's Loyal Rangers in Canada Drawn by Himself in a Letter to a Friend in London." *Toronto Globe*, July 16, 1877.

Stevens, Paul L. *Louis Lorimier in the American Revolution, 1777–1782: A Mémoire by an Ohio Indian Trader and British Partisan*. Naperville, IL: The Center for French Colonial Studies, Inc., 1997.

Secondary Sources — Books

Abler, Thomas S., ed. *Chainbreaker: The Revolutionary War Memoirs of Governor Blacksnake As told to Benjamin Williams.* Lincoln, NE: University of Nebraska Press, 1989.
———. *Cornplanter: Chief Warrior of the Allegany Senecas.* Syracuse: Syracuse University Press, 2007.
Berry, A. Joyce, and James F. Morrison. *Don't Shoot (Part One) Until You See the Whites of Their Eyes.* Trafford Publishing, 2007.
Bredenberg, Oscar E. *Military Activities in the Champlain Valley after 1777.* Champlain, NY: Moorfield Press, 1962.
Campbell, William W., Jr. *Annals of Tryon County; or the Border Warfare of New York.* Cherry Valley, NY: The Cherry Valley Gazette Print, 1880.
Clarke, Thomas Wood. *The Bloody Mohawk.* New York: Macmillan, 1940.
Clearwater, Alphonso T. *The History of Ulster County, New York.* 2 vols. n.p., 1907.
Cruikshank, Ernest A. *The Story of Butler's Rangers and the Settlement of Niagara.* Owen Sound, ON: Richardson, Bond & Wright Ltd., 1975. First published 1893 by Lundy's Lane Historical Society.
Cruikshank, Ernest A., and Gavin K. Watt. *The History and Master Roll of The King's Royal Regiment of New York.* Revised ed. Campbellville, ON: Global Heritage Press, 2006.
DePeyster, John Watts. *Miscellanies of an Officer.* New York: C.H. Ludwig, 1838.
Dictionary of Canadian Biography. Toronto: University of Toronto Press.
Doddridge, Joseph. *Notes on the Settlement and Indian Wars of the Western Parts of Virginia & Pennsylvania, from the Year 1763 Until the Year 1783 Inclusive, Together with a View of the Western Country.* 1876, republished Pittsburgh: 1912.
Duffy, John J., Samuel B. Hand, and Ralph H. Orth, eds. *The Vermont Encyclopedia.* Lebanon, NH: University Press of New England, 2003.
Egly, T.W., Jr. *History of the First New York Regiment.* Hampton, NH: Peter E. Randall, 1981.
Everard, Major H. *History of Thos. Farrington's Regiment Subsequently Designated The 29th (Worcestershire) Foot 1694 to 1891.* Worcester: Littleby & Company, Worcester Press, 1891.
Fryer, Mary Beacock. *King's Men: The Soldier Founders of Ontario.* Toronto: Dundurn Press, 1980.
Glatthaar, Joseph T., and Martin, James Kirby. *Forgotten Allies: The*

Oneida Indians and the American Revolution. New York: Hill and Wang, 2006.

Graymont, Barbara. *The Iroquois in the American Revolution.* Syracuse: Syracuse University Press, 1972.

Greene, Nelson, *The Story of Old Fort Plain and the Middle Mohawk Valley.* Fort Plain, NY: O'Connor Brothers Publishers, 1915.

Greene, Nelson, ed. *History of the Mohawk Valley: Gateway to the West 1614–1925.* 4 vols. Chicago: S.J. Clarke, 1925.

Grumet, Robert S. *The Munsee Indians: A History.* Norman, OK: University of Oklahoma Press, 2009.

Halsey, Francis Whiting. *The Old New York Frontier, Its Wars with Indians and Tories, Its Missionary Schools, Pioneers and Land Titles.* New York: Charles Scribner's Sons, 1917.

Hanson, Willis T. *A History of Schenectady During the Revolution to Which is Appended a Contribution to the Individual Records of the Inhabitants of the Schenectady District During that Period.* n.p., 1916.

Harvey, Oscar Jewell, and Ernest Gray Smith. *A History of Wilkes-Barré, Luzerne County, Pennsylvania: From Its First Beginnings to the Present Time, Including Chapters of Newly-Discovered Early Wyoming Valley History, Together with Many Biographical Sketches and Much Genealogical Material.* 6 Vols. Wilkes-Barre, PA: Raeder Press, 1909.

Hemenway, Abby Maria, ed. *The Vermont Historical Gazetteer.* Vol. 3. Claremont, NH: Claremont Manufacturing Co, 1877.

Hendrix, Lester E., and Anne W. *Sloughter's Instant History of Schoharie County 1700–1900.* Schoharie, NY: The Schoharie County Historical Society, 1988.

Hinman, Marjory Barnum. *Onaquaga: Hub of the Border Wars of the American Revolution in New York State.* n.p., 1975.

Houlding, J.A. "The King's Service: The Officers of the British Army, 1735–1792." n.p.

Huey, Lois M., and Bonnie Pulis. *Molly Brant: A Legacy of Her Own.* Youngstown, NY: Old Fort Niagara Association, 1997.

Johnson, Ken D. *The Bloodied Mohawk: The American Revolution in the Words of Fort Plank's Defenders and Other Mohawk Valley Partisans.* Rockport, MA: Picton Press, 2000.

Kelsay, Isabel Thompson. *Joseph Brant, 1743–1807: Man of Two Worlds.* Syracuse: Syracuse University Press, 1984.

LaCrosse, Richard B. *Revolutionary Rangers: Daniel Morgan's Riflemen and Their Role on the Northern Frontier, 1778–1783.* Bowie, MD: Heritage Books, Inc., 2002.

Lanctot, Gustave, and Margaret M. Cameron, trans. *Canada and the American Revolution, 1774–1783.* Toronto: George G. Harrap & Co. Ltd, 1967.

Leslie, Vernon. *The Battle of Minisink.* Middletown, NY: T. Emmett Henderson, 1976.

Mack, Ebenezer, and Jules Cloquet. *The Life of Gilbert Motier de Lafayette, etc.* https://books.google.ca/books/about/The_Life_of_Gilbert_Motier_de_Lafayette.html?id=Zx0RAAAAYAAJ&redir_esc=y.

Malcomson, Robert. *Warships of the Great Lakes 1754—1834.* Annapolis: Naval Institute Press, 2001.

Mathews, Hazel C. *The Mark of Honour.* Toronto: University of Toronto Press, 1965.

Meginness, John F., ed. *History of Lycoming County, Pennsylvania.* Chicago: Brown, Runk & Co., 1892. www.usgennet.org/usa/pa/county/lycoming/history/lyco-history-01.html.

———. *Otzinachson: Or, A History of the West Branch Valley of the Susquehanna, etc.* Philadelphia: H.B. Ashmead, 1857.

Midtrod, Tom Arne. *The Memory of All Ancient Customs: Native American Diplomacy in the Colonial Hudson Valley.* Ithaca, NY: Cornell University Press, 2012.

Miller, James B. *Curse of the Tomahawk: Colonel Hartley's 1778 Expedition Against the Six Nations.* n.p.: CreateSpace Independent Publishing Platform, 2009.

Mintz, Max M. *The Generals of Saratoga: John Burgoyne & Horatio Gates.* New Haven: Yale University Press, 1990.

Monroe, John D. *Chapters in the History of Delaware County, New York.* Delhi, NY: Delaware County Historical Association, 1949.

Morrison, James F. *A History of Fulton County in the Revolution.* Gloversville, NY: printed by author, 1977.

Murray, Louise Welles. *A History of Old Tioga Point and Early Athens.* London: Forgotten Books, 2013. First published 1908.

Robinson, Helen Caister. *Joseph Brant: A Man for His People.* Don Mills, ON: Longman Canada, 1971.

Simms, Jeptha R. *Frontiersman of New York Showing Customs of the Indians, Vicissitudes of the Pioneer White Settlers and Border Strife in Two Wars with a Great Variety of Romantic and Thrilling Stories Never Before Published.* 2 vols. Albany: Geo. C. Riggs, 1883.

———. *History of Schoharie County, and Border Wars of New York; Containing also a Sketch of the Causes Which Led to the American Revolution; etc.* Albany: Munsell & Tanner, 1845.

Smy, William A. *An Annotated Nominal Roll of Butler's Rangers 1777–1784 with Documentary Sources.* St. Catharines, ON: Friends of the Loyalist Collection at Brock University, 2004.
Stanley, George F.G. *Canada Invaded, 1775–1776.* Toronto: Samuel Stevens Hakkert & Company, 1977.
Stone, William Leete. *Life of Joseph Brant — Thayendanegea: Including the Indian Wars of the American Revolution.* 2 vols. St. Clair Shores, MI: Scholarly Press, 1970. First published 1838 by Alexander V. Blake.
———. *The Poetry and History of Wyoming.* New York: Wiley and Putnam, 1841.
Trigger, Bruce G., ed. *Handbook of North American Indians, Volume 15: Northeast.* Washington: Smithsonian Institution, 1978.
Tucker, Spencer, ed. *Almanac of American Military History.* 4 vols. Santa Barbara, CA: ABC-CLIO, 2012.
Washington, Ida H., and Paul A. Washington. *Carleton's Raid.* Canaan, NH: Phoenix Publishing, 1977.
Watt, Gavin K. *A Dirty, Trifling Piece of Business, Volume I: The Revolutionary War as Waged from Canada in 1781.* Toronto: Dundurn Press, 2009.
———. *Poisoned by Lies and Hypocrisy: America's First Attempt to Bring Liberty to Canada, 1775–1776.* Toronto: Dundurn Press, 2014.
———. *Rebellion in the Mohawk Valley: The St. Leger Expedition of 1777.* Toronto: Dundurn Press, 2002.
———. *A Short Service History and Master Roll of James Rogers' 2nd Battalion, King's Rangers.* Milton, ON: Global Heritage Press, 2015.
Watt, Gavin K., and James F. Morrison. *The British Campaign of 1777, Volume 1: The St. Leger Expedition. The Forces of the Crown and Congress.* King City, ON: Gavin K. Watt, 2001.
———. *The British Campaign of 1777, Volume 2: The Burgoyne Expedition — Burgoyne's Native and Loyalist Auxiliaries.* Milton, ON: Global Heritage Press, 2013.
Watt, Gavin K., with James F. Morrison. *The Burning of the Valleys: Daring Raids from Canada Against the New York Frontier in the Fall of 1780.* Toronto: Dundurn Press, 1997.
Williamson, Chilton. *Vermont in Quandary: 1763–1825.* Montpelier, VT: Vermont Historical Society, 1949.
Wright, John Womack. *Some Notes on the Continental Army.* Vails Gate, NY: National Temple Hill Association, 1963.
Wright, Robert K., Jr. *The Continental Army.* Washington, DC: Army Lineage Series, Centre of Military History, United States Army, 1989.
Zierdt, William H. *Narrative History of the 109th Field Artillery, Pennsylvania National Guard.* n.p.: Wilkes-Barre, PA, 1932.

Secondary Sources — Articles, Monographs, Booklets, Newsletters, Catalogues & Theses

Barbieri, Michael. "Living History." *Rutland Historical Society Quarterly* 8.4 (Fall 1978): https://archive.org/stream/RutlandHistoricalSociety QuarterlyVol.8No.41978/RhsqVol.8No.41978_djvu.txt.

Bryant, William Clement. *Captain Brant and the Old King: The Tragedy of Wyoming.* Publications of the Buffalo Historical Society, Vol. IV, 1896.

Burleigh, H.C. *The Bones of David Redding.* Burleigh, n.d.

Calloway, Colin G. *The American Revolution in Indian Country: Crisis and Diversity in Native American Communities.* Cambridge, U.K.: Cambridge University Press, 1995.

Durkee, John, "The Battle and Massacre of Wyoming." http://durkeesmenofwyoming.tripod.com/id20.htm.accessed.

Fenton, Walter S. "Seth Warner." *Proceedings of the Vermont Historical Society.* New Series. 8.4 (1940).

Fort Penn. www.monroehistorical.org/articles/files/f65142657e45365566da8639bf73c845-98.html.

Godcharles, Frederic A. "Massacre at Wyoming Followed by 'The Great Runaway' on July 5, 1778: Luzerne (then Northumberland) Co, PA." *Daily Stories of Pennsylvania.* Milton, PA: 1924.

Johnson, Wesley, ed. *Wyoming: A Record of the One Hundredth Year Commemorative Observance of the Battle and Massacre, July 3, 1778–July 3, 1878.* Wilkes-Barre, PA Wyoming Commemorative Association, 1899. http://durkeesmenofwyoming.tripod.com/id20.htm, and https://catalog.hathitrust.org/Record/008957733.

Jones, J. Kelsey. "Loyalist Plantations on the Susquehanna." *Magazine of American History* xxii.4 (October). www.beth-website.net/LOYALIST-PLANTATIONS-ON-THE-SUSQUEHANNA.html.

Hughes, Alun. "John Butler and Early Settlement on the West Bank of the Niagara River." In *The Butler Bicentenary, Commemorating the 200th Anniversary of the Death of Colonel John Butler.* UEL Assoc. of Canada, Colonel John Butler Branch, 1997.

Massey, Douglas. "Anthony and Andrew Westbrook: A Fascinating Narrative of Disunity." Unpublished manuscript, May 2015.

———. "Benjamin Becraft UEL (Part 3)." *Loyalist Trails*, UELAC Newsletter, August 2014.

Rhicard, Flora J. "The Road That Never Was." *Rovers, Rebels and Royalists*, Missisquoi Historical Society Reports 18 (1984): 81–89.

Smy, William A. "The Butlers Before the Revolution." In *The Butler Bicentenary: Commemorating the 200th Anniversary of the Death of Colonel John Butler.* UEL Assoc. of Canada, Colonel John Butler Branch, 1997.

Spargo, John. *The Story of David Redding Who Was Hanged.* Bennington, NY: Bennington Historical Museum, 1945.

Stacy, Kim. "No One Harms Me with Impunity — The History, Organization, and Biographies of the 84th Regiment of Foot (Royal Highland Emigrants) and Young Royal Highlanders, During the Revolutionary War 1775–1784." Manuscript in progress, 1994.

Stevens, Paul L. "His Majesty's 'Savage' Allies: British Policy and the Northern Indians During the Revolutionary War — The Carleton Years, 1774–1778." Ph.D. diss., State University of New York at Buffalo, 1984.

Trussell, John B.B., Jr. "The Battle of Wyoming and Hartley's Expedition." *Historic Pennsylvania Leaflet No. 40.* Harrisburg, PA: Pennsylvania Historical and Museum Commission, 1976.

Venables, Robert. "Tryon County, 1775–1783: A Frontier in Revolution." Ph.D. diss., Vanderbilt University, 1967. http://hortonsarticles.org/Timeline1778.htm, www.worldcat.org/title/tryon-county-1775-1783-a-frontier-in-revolution/oclc/5123219&referer-brief_results.

Verenna, Thomas. "They Were with the Continental Army in 1778." allthingsliberty.com/2014/02/connecticut-yankees-in-a-pennamites-fort.

Williams, Edward G. "Fort Pitt and the Revolution on the Western Frontier." *The Western Pennsylvania Historical Magazine* 59.3 (July 1976): 251–87.

Young, Stephen C. "Identifying Loyalists on the Frontier — The Wyoming Valley Massacre." *Pennsylvania Genealogical Magazine* 43 (March 26, 2005)."

Secondary Websites

Alden's Massachusetts Regiment. http://home.roadrunner.com/~nlecompte/regiment/regiment.html.

Barren Hill Skirmish. www.oneidaindiannation.com/history/28612644.

Battle of Cobleskill. Wikipedia.org/wiki/Battle_of_Cobleskill.

Bayley, Jacob. www.rootsweb.com/~vermont/HistoryHazenMilitaryRoad.html.

Bedel, Timothy. http://en.wikipedia.org/wiki/Timothy_Bedel.

———. http://davidlibraryar.blogspot.ca/2010/11/timothy-bedel-papers-and-andrew-park.html.

———. www.nhhistory.org/finding_aids/finding_aids/Bedel_Timothy_Papers_1880.001.pdf.

Conway cabal. http://en.wikipedia.org/wiki/Conway_Cabal.
d'Estaing. www.britannica.com/EBchecked/topic/193274/Charles-Hector-count-dEstaing.
Dictionary of Canadian Biography. www.biographi.ca.
Douw, Volkert and Stefan Bielinski. "Volkert P. Douw." http://exhibitions.nysed.gov//albany/bios/d/vopdouw2234.html.
Fletcher, Samuel. "History of Eastern Vermont." www.rootsweb.ancestry.com/~vtwindha/hev/hevbio632.htm.
Fort Muncy. www.accessgenealogy.com/pennsylvania/fort-muncy-lycoming-county-pennsylvania.htm.
Fulton County. http://fulton.nygenweb.net/military/FCinRev4.html.
Hartley, Thomas, and John W. Jordan. "Biographical Sketch of Colonel Thomas Hartley, of the Pennsylvania Line." http://archive.org/stream/jstor-20085978/20085978_djvu.txt.
———. http://famousamericans.net/thomashartley.
Hartley's Additional Regiment. https://en.wikipedia.org/wiki/Hartley%27s_Additional_Continental_Regiment.
"History." 24th Connecticut Regiment of Militia. www.24thcmr.org/page2.php.
Lafayette, Gilbert du Motier, Marquis de. www.ushistory.org/valleyforge/served/lafayette.html.
Paxton Boys. http://en.wikipedia.org/wiki/Paxton_Boys.
Payne, Elisha. http://en.wikipedia.org/wiki/Elisha_Payne.
Stacy [Stacey], Lieutenant-Colonel. http://home.roadrunner.com/~nle-compte/regiment/. Website inactive as of October 8, 2015.
Stewart, Lazarus. http://en.wikipedia.org/wiki/Lazarus_Stewart.
Traversy. "Joseph Langlois dit Traversy (1728—1806) — Un agent secret au service des Américains." www.familleslanglois.com/deja-parus/Joseph%20Langlois%20dit%20Traversy%20-%20Un%20agent%20secret.pdf.
Walker, Andrew. http://pasocietyofthecincinnati.org/Names/AndrewWalker.html.
Wolcott, Oliver. http://en.wikipedia.org/wiki/Oliver_Wolcott.

Image Credits

6	*Gavin K. Watt, 2015.*
19	*Courtesy of the New York Public Library Digital Gallery.*
23	*© McCord Museum, M966.62.3.*
37	*ClipArt ETC.*
41	*ClipArt ETC.*
50	*Morges Chateau Military Museum, Switzerland.*
53	*ClipArt ETC.*
55	*Courtesy of the New York Public Library Digital Gallery.*
61	*ClipArt ETC.*
76	*Map by Michael Barbieri of Whitcomb's Rangers, 2015.*
92	*ClipArt ETC.*
97	*ClipArt ETC.*
107	*ClipArt ETC.*
113	*Courtesy of Metropolitan Toronto Library.*
119	*New York Public Library Digital Gallery.*
136	*ClipArt ETC.*
143	*Courtesy of James Kochan Fine Art & Antiques.*
147	(Top) *ClipArt ETC.*
157	*Wikimedia.*
173	*Canadian Museum of History, III-I-1216, IMG2009-0166-0025-Dm.*
175	*Courtesy of the Library of Congress Geography and Map Division, Washington.*

178	*Gavin K. Watt, 2015.*
179	*https://en.wikipedia.org/wiki/File:Chainbreaker.jpg#/media/File:Chainbreaker.jpg.*
181	*ClipArt ETC.*
190	*Pencil drawing, Scott D. Paterson, 1996.*
197	*Courtesy of Tioga Point Museum.*
223	*ClipArt ETC.*
231	*Canadian Museum of History, III-I-1325, S81-4349.*
260	*Courtesy of the Crown Point Foundation.*
294	*Courtesy of Otto E. Nelson photography.*
299	*Courtesy of the National Museums of Canada.*

Index

All page entries in bold indicate that the subject is in an image or on a map.

A Native person's affiliation is designated by a two- or three-letter abbreviation after his/her name, e.g., Abenaki (Ab); Delaware (De); Kahnawake (Kah); Tuscarora (Tu).

The abbreviation *en* indicates note numbers.

Abeel, John. *See* Cornplanter
Adams, Jacob, 202, 272, 314
Adams, Martha, 30
Adams, Samuel, 30
Addison, VT, 36, 69
Albany City, NY, 9, 24, 25, 33, 39, 40, 42, 44–49, 51, 52, 54, 56, 60, 61, 85, 96, 106, 110, 122, 123, 128, 149, 151, 152, 156, 160, 161, 173, 230, 254, 259, 260, 262, 267, 270, 281, 282, 286, 288, 291, 299, 301, 310, 312
   British hospital in, 41
Albany County, 40, 113, 148, 155, 158, 159, **219**, 313
     Committee of Sequestration, 235
Alden, Ichabod, 53, 261, 262, 267, 277, 289, 290, 293, 300, 305, 309
   killed, 294
Alder, Lieutenant, 68, 82
Allegheny River, 172
Allen, Ebenezer, 24, 33, 35, 37, 38
Allen, Ethan, **41**–44, 46, 47, 54, 91
Allen, Ira, 31, 44, 54, 322en15
Allen, Parmalee, 24, 81
American Army. *See* U.S. Army
Anderson, George, 223, 230, 231, 233
Anguish, Jacob, 177
Arbuthnot, Robert, 80, 332en100
Arlington, VT, 36
Arnold, Benedict, 25, 26, 28
Atayataghronghta. *See* Colonel Louis
Atskeorax (Se), 151, 152
Aubrey, Thomas, 202, 263, 272

Austin, Joel, 230

Ballard, William, 267, 297
Barclay, John, 40, 117, 149
Barnhart, George, 232
Barnum, Barnabus, 33
Barrow, John, 236, 237
Batavia, NY, **222**
Battles/skirmishes
   Barren Hill, PA, 1778, 10, 130, 131
   Bennington (Walloomscoick), VT, 1777, 18, 22, 43, 69
   Cedars, The, QC, 1776, 16
   Concord, MA, 1775, 166
   Hubbardton, VT, 1777, 69, 142
   Oriskany, IT, 1777, 94, 103, 105, 107, 111, 112, 118, 124, 129, 138, 155, 156, 183, 189, 249, 283, 313
   Plumtree Massacre, 1778, 176
   Rampart Rocks, PA, 167, **178**
   Saratoga, NY, 1777, 15, 17
   Valcour Island, NY, 1775, 83
   Wyoming Valley, PA, 1778, 10, 162–93, 221, 226, 317, 318
   Casualties, 189
Bay of Quinte, QC, 126
Bayley, Jacob, 31, 44, 57
Beaver Dam, NY, 265
Becker, Jost, 262
Bedel, Timothy, 16, 18, 20, 26, 39, 40, 42, 47, 48, 85
Beech, Zarah, 191
Belknap, James, 141
Bellinger, Christian, 283
Bellinger, Lucinda, 283
Bellinger, Col. Peter, 115, 116, 256–57
Bellinger, Peter, 283
Bennington, VT, 33, 45, 54
Bennington County, VT, 63
"Bennington Mob," 44
Big Tree Kaoundowana (Se), 151, 152, 158, 168, 173, 204
Blacks, 115, 140, 158, 271, 283, 295
Blacksnake Thaonawyuthe (Chainbreaker) (Se), **179**, 189, 216
Blatcop Tonyentagoyon (One), 129
Blodget, Asa, 78
Bolton, Mason, 42, 96, 97, 114, 124, 133, 134, 154, 201, 216, 264, 314, 315, 318
Boone, Captain, 208
Borst, Jacob, 137
Borst, Joseph, 137
Boston, MA, 27, 91
Bouck, William, 158
Bounty, 24, 25, 33, 314
Bowen, Luke, 126, 143
Bowen, West, 126, 143
Bowen, William, Jr., 126, 143, 145
Bowen, William Ryer, 101, 128, 133, 339en53
Bowman, Adam, 170
Bowman, Elizabeth, 170
Bowman, Jacob, 170
Bowman, Peter, 170
Bowman's Creek/Kill, 150, 170, 304
Boyden, Josiah, 24
Brady, Captain, 208
Brant, Joseph Thayendanegea (Mo), 94, 102, 109, 110, 114, 115, 123, 124, 132, **136**, 137, 139, 141, 149, 150, 158, 162, 196, 201, 219, 224, 226–28, 236, 237, 239, 242, 243, 245, 249, 252–53, 254, 256, 257, 260, 265, 266–68, 271, 273–76, 278, 285, 286, 290, 293–96, 299–301, 308, 310
Brant, Mary/Molly Wary Gonwatsijayenni (Mo), 100, 127, 141, 252
Bridport, VT, 36, 38
British, 94
   8th (King's) Regt, 42, 216, 264, 286, 297, 310

Light Coy, 134
29th Regt, 64, 68, 72, 75
  Rangers, 65, 328en80
31st Regt, 65, 73, 74, 80, 83
34th Regt, 23, 64, 143
  Grenadiers, 142
47th, 263
53rd Regt, 58, 65, 73, 75, 77
60th (Royal Americans) Regt, 59
84th (RHE), 264
Dragoons, 130, 131
Royal Artillery, 65, 66
Brisco, Isaac, 30
Brodhead, Daniel, 196
Brooks family, 233
Brown, Christian, 137, 138, 142
Brown, Richard, 74, 84, 331en93
Brownson, Gideon, 38, 39, 324en30
Bryan, Vice-President, 210
Buck, Philip, 170
Bulwagga Bay, NY, 68, 74, **76**
Burch, John, 230, 240
Burgoyne, John, 58, 65, 95, 96, 100, 220
Burrows, John, 234
Bush, Captain, 200, 201
Bush, Hendrik, Jr., 232, 233, 240, 241
Butler, Catherine, 301, 317, 318
Butler, John, 10, 42, 59, 93, 97–103, 108, 109, **113**, 115, 118, 124, 132, 134, 135, 151–53, 155, 162, 168, 170–85, 189–**90**–93, 196, 222, 225, 226, 230, 232, 236, 237, 239, 242, 250–52, 260, 266, 272, 293, 302, 313–18, 334en1
  poor health, 195
Butler, Richard, 261
Butler, Thomas, 103
Butler, Walter, 10, 101, 103, 128, 133, 153, 196, 202, 204, 206, 216, 232, 251, 264, 265, 269, 273, 286, 288, 291, 298–301, 309, 310, 315, 316
  arrogance of, 285, 286

Butler, William, 199, 203, 205, 235, 240, 242–45, 254, 259, 262, 265, 266, 268, 278, 280, 281, 290, 291, 293, 305
Butler, Zebulon, 165–68, 171, 172, 177, 178, 181–83, 189, 197, 200
Butternut Creek, NY, 308
Butternuts, NY, 135, 274, 275, 290
Button Mould Bay, NY, 75, 78
Buxton family, 308, 362en115

Caldwell, William, 180, 183, 191, 196, 201, 226, 228, 271, 272, 285, 286
Cameron, John, 69
Campbell, Jane, 295, 306
Campbell, John, 22, 23, 59, 84, 110, 153
Campbell, Mr., 66, 328en82
Campbell, Samuel, 123, 131, 136, 295, 301, 312, 316, 363en133
Campbell, William, 295
Campbell family, 301
Camplen, Mr., 207
Canadians (Anglophones), 8, 20, 21
Canadiens (Francophones), 8, 11, 18, 22, 28, 62, 87–91, 111, 154
Canajoharie, NY, 126, 258, **260,** 277, 290
Cannon, Mr., 306
Cannon, Mrs., 296
Cantine, John, 223, 225, 230, 231, 232, 235, 237, 240–46
Captain Bull (De), 165
Captain Jacob (Oq), 224
Captain Jacobs (Oqu), 301, 310
Captain Johnson Navondigwanok (Se), 168
Captain Mounsh (Mu), 226
Carberry, Henry, 203, 206, 348en63
Cardigan, NH, 36
Carleton (schooner), 66, 68, 83
Carleton, Christopher, 11, 64, 66, 67, 70–72, 74, 77, 78, 81, 83, 84, 85,

116, 327en74
Carleton, Sir Guy, 17, 22, 23, 32, 42, 50, 59, 64, 94–96, 98, 102, 110, 114–16, 133, 134, 143, 152, 216, 248–51, 314
  departs Canada, 263
Carleton Island, 202, 263, 272, 283, 310, 314. *See also* Deer Island
Carpenter, Benjamin, 31
Carr, Parsefor, 135, 253, 254, 256, 273
Cartwright, Richard, Sr., 128
Casselman, Severinus, 126
Castleton, VT, 36
Cataraqui, QC, 126, 248, 249, 263
Catskill/Katskill, NY, **219**, 222
Catskill Mountains, 218, 220, 265, 271
Caughnawaga, NY, 146, 148, 308, 310
Caughnawaga Church, 146, **147**
Chambers, William, 64, 327en76
Charles II, King, 163
Charlotte County, NY, 75
Charlotte River, NY, 150
Château Frontenac, QC, 49
Chemung River, IT, 95
Cherry Valley, NY, 11, 123, 132, 135–37, 146, 150, 151, 161, 202, 203, 222, 224, 247, 254, 259, **260**, 261–62, 266–68, 273, 286, 289, 291, 301–05, 309, 310, 312, 313, 316–19
Chimney Point, NY, 71, 72, 75
Chittenden, Thomas, 31, **37**, 38–40, 44, 45, 60, 62
Church, Major, 266, 280
Chyle/Kyle Settlement, NY, 308, 362en117
Clarendon, VT, 32
Clark, Isaac, 30, 35, 37, 38
Clark, Jeremiah, 31
Clark, Nathan, 31

Clark, Samuel, 241, 242
Claus, Ann, 110
Claus, Daniel, 59, 85, 93–96, 98, 100, 109, 110, 115, 124, 131, 144, 148, 154, 218, 248, 249–51, 284, 285, 314
Clinton, Governor George, 25, 54, **55**, 60, 106, 122, 132, 149, 155–57, 160, 220, 221, 224, 229, 232, 233, 240–45, 258, 260, 265, 268, 273, 274, 277, 278, 281, 290, 304, 310, 312
Clinton, Henry, 91, **92**, 102, 124, 220, 270
Clinton, James, 85, 245, 282, 307, 312, 316
Clyde, Catharine, 295, 300
Clyde, Samuel, 123, 150, 261, 295, 300, 307, 309, 310
Cobleskill (Cobus), NY, 10, 137, 142, 146, 149, 151, 158, 222, **260**
Cochecton (Cushetunk), NY, 9, **219**, 220–21, 232, 242, 245, 285
Cochran, Robert, 271, 276
Cole, Widow, 230
Colonel Louis Atayataghronghta (Kah), 35
Connecticut River, 44, 45, 57, 110
Connecticut (Colony) State, 114, 163–71
  General Assembly, 166
  Westmoreland County (Wyoming), 166, 167, 169, 171–74, 179, 190, 191, 193, 196
Continental Congress, 9, 18–21, 27–29, 35, 36, 43, 47, 48, 56, 60, 62, 82, 85–87, 91, 107, 111, 116, 117, 119, 151, 152, 155, 167–69, 171, 197, 202, 206, 212, 213, 310, 312
  Board of War, 19, 20, 25, 155
  Declaration of Independence, 30
Continental Village, 288

Conway, Thomas, 18, 19, 25, 39, 43, 117
Cook. *See* Crook
Cooper, Polly (One), 129, 130
Cöos Region, VT, 16, 48, 55, 56, 57
Cooyeman's, NY, 159
Cornelius, Henry (One), 129
Cornplanter Gayentwahga (Se), 124, 178, 182, 216, 286, 305, 308
Cottner, 199
Counties, New York
   Albany
      Schoharie Valley. *See separate listing*
      Charlotte, 71
   Tryon
      Canajoharie District, 121, 126, 170
      Kingsland & German Flatts District, 260
      Mohawk District, 312
      Palatine District, 126, 127
   Cumberland, 36, 324en26
Countryman, Jacob, 126
Covenhoven, Robert, 194
Crawford, William Redford, 32, 125, 143, 284
Crine, Hans (Mo), 146
Crofts, Wills, 23
Crook, William, 71, 72, 74, 77, 78, 81, 330en91
Crown Point, NY, 37, 40, 45, 62, 63, 67–69, 71, 76, 81, 291
Crown Point Road, VT, 75
Crysler, Adam, 105, 189, 286
Cuddeback, Abraham, 224, 243
Cumming, Thomas, 240, 352en29

Dahgonwasha (Twenty Canoes) (Se), 179
Dain, John, 297
Danby, VT, 63
De Kalb, Baron Johan, 19

Deacon Thomas (One), 129
Dead Creek, VT, 76, 81, 82
Dean, James, 48, 108, 111, 112, 118, 151, 158, 245
Debe, Lieutenant, 299
Deer Island, QC, 101, 114, 134, 248, 250, 263
Delaware River, 135, 152, 164, 193, 201, 218, 220, 227, 229, 238, 243, 278, 286
Denison, Nathan, 166, 169–71, 173, 178, 181, 183, 188–92, 201, 217, 293, 319
Depew, John, 103, 133, 171, 216
Deserontyon, John (Mo), 124, 144
d'Estaing, Charles-Hector Comte, 11, **53**, 326en51
   Proclamation of, 87–91
Deygart, Peter S., 104, 116, 123, 127
Dietz, William, 278
Dixon, Hugh, 72, 75, 77
Docksteder, John, 95
Donnegeosha (Jack Berry) (Se), 179
Dorrance, George, 171, 178, 183, 188, 192
Dorset, VT, 63
Douw, Volckert, 101, 107, 116, 336en21
Duane, James, **107**, 117, 149
Dumond, (Demong) Harmanus, 222, 223, 225, 234–39, 269
Dunlap, Hutchinson, 75, 77, 331en94
Dunlap family, 295
Dunlop, Reverend, 303
Dunmore, Lord, 35, 36
Durkee, John, 165
Durkee, Robert, 167, 168, 172, 182, 184
Dygert/Tygert, William, 275, 276

East Bay, 81
Eastern Union. *See* Vermont
Easton, PA, 165, 168

Eden, William, 91
Edmeston settlement, 273
Edmeston, William, 135
Edwards, Timothy, 107, 111, 116
Enys, John, 65, 69, 79, 82, 84, 328en79
Esopus, NY, 159, **219**, 220, 237, 242
Eton College, 65
Everest, Benjamin, 69, 70
Expeditions/Raids
  Andrewstown, NY, destroyed, 10, 255, 257, 258, 260, 277
  Braddock's 1755, 164
  Burgoyne's 1777, 15, 22, 24, 31, 56, 65, 98, 101, 102, 159
  Canada, Invasion 1775, 31
  Carleton's repulse of rebels, 1776, 64
  Carleton's Otter Creek raid, 1778, 63–85, 245
    Complement of, 65, 66
    Field days, 66, 67
  Cherry Valley, NY, 1778, 12, 246, 286, 290, 291, 315–19
    Raiders' and defender's casualties, 309
    force composition, 286
  Cobleskill, NY, destroyed, 1778, 10, 40, 51, 137–42, 151
  Ephratah, NY, attacked, 1778, 10
  Fairfield, NY, destroyed, 1778, 9, 125, 126
  Fonda's Bush, NY, 1778, 10
  Hartley's Wyalusing Expedition, 1778, 11, 202–15
  Kiskiminetas Creek, PA, attacked, 1778, 172
  German Flatts, NY, destroyed, 1778, 11, 101, 272–74, 277
  Lackawack, NY, struck, 1778, 11, 222–25, 230, 232, 233, 241
  LaFayette's Invasion of Canada, 1778, 9, 16, 19–29, 41–43, 50, 60, 116
    proposes new attempt, 1778, 85
  Mayfield, NY, 1778, 10
  Oneidas raid Butternuts and Unadilla, NY, 1778, 11, 267, 274, 276, 278, 280
  Oquaga, IT, Continentals destroy, 1778, 11, 278–81, 291, 293, 302
  Otter Creek/River, Carleton's expedition, 1778, 11, 64–85
    force composition, 64, 65
  Peenpack, NY, raided, 1778, 10, 224, 230, 233, 242–44
  Peters' Onion River raid, VT, 1778, 11, 55, 56, 58, 59, 63, 64
  Philadelphia Bush, NY, 1778, 10
  Recovery of Sir John's Papers, 1778, 284, 285
  Ross Raid, Mohawk Valley, 1778, 64, 142–49, 265, 312
  St. Leger's 1777, 15, 93, 103, 110, 131, 261
  Salisbury attacked, 1778, 127
  Schoharie Uprising, 1777, 105, 159
  Shelburne, VT, attacked, 1778, 9, 32, 33, 35, 45, 323en21
  Snydersbush, NY, destroyed, 1778, 9
  Springfield, NY, destroyed, 1778, 10, 254, 255, 257, 258, 260, 277
  Sullivan-Clinton Expedition, 1779, 246
  Tilleborough, NY, attacked, 1778, 10, 148, 158
  Unadilla, IT, Continentals destroy, 1778, 11, 160, 278–81, 291
  Wyalusing Expedition. *See* Hartley's Wyalusing
  Wyoming Valley, 1778, 178, 215, 226, 249
    force composition, 178

INDEX | 385

Execution. *See* Hanging

Fall Hill, 275
Farquhar, William, 75, 77, 331en94
Fay, Jonas, 31, 36
Fay, Joseph, 31
Feeter, William, 304
Fester brothers, 139
Finch, Samuel, 191
Fireball, 75
First Yankee-Pennamite War, 167, 171
Fish Carrier (Ca), 178, 179
Fish House, NY, 144, 147
Fisher. *See* Visscher
Fishkill, NY, 39–41, 44, 142, 158, 213
Flags of Truce (a flag), 62, 63, 182, 183, 300, 309, 316
Flat Kop (Tu), 283
Flat Rock Point, NY, 66
Fletcher, Samuel, 45
Fonda, Jelles, 146, 148, 307
Forbes Road, PA, 172
Ford, Jacob, 160, 254, 255, 259
Fort Hunter, NY, 104, 158. *See also* Forts
Forts (Blockhouses)
  Alden, NY, 261, 289–93, 296–98, 300, 304, 307, 308, 311
  Antes, PA, 193
  Augusta, PA, 194, 196
  Camp Westmoreland, PA, 197, 217
  Chambly, QC, 17, 21, 56
  Dayton, NY, 11, 115, 116, 131, 273, 313
  Detroit (Fort Lernoult), IT, 114, 134, 155
  DeWitt, NY, 243
  Duquesne. *See* Pitt
  Durkee, PA, 165, 166, **178**
  Edward, NY, 66, 70–72, 80, 291
  Fort Mott, VT, 37
  Fort No. 4, NH, 75
  Forty Fort, PA, 165, **178**, 180–**81**–82, 188–89, 191–93, 217
  Gumaer, NY, 243
  Haldimand, QC, 263, 283, 284
  Herkimer, NY, 255, **260**, 273, 283
  Jenkins, PA, 176–**78**, 180, 183, 184, 190
  Johnstown, NY, 146
  Île-aux-Noix, QC, 21, 42, 82, 83
  Middle Fort, NY, 262, 269, 280
  Middlebury blockhouse, **76**
  Mill Creek blockhouse, 165
  Muncy, PA, **175**, 176, **178**, 194, 196–200, 201, 215
  New Haven Fort, VT, 33, 34, **76**
  Niagara, IT, 24, 42, 94, 96, 97, 101–03, 105, 107, 108, 114, 134, 169, 171, 172, 195, 206, 216, 224, 226, 242, 250, 272, 275, 285, 314
    Ranger barracks, 314
  Ogden, PA, 165, **177**, **178**, 180
  Oswego, IT, 114, 118, 134
    Native demand for occupation, 98, 250
  Oswegatchie, IT, 24, 52, 54, 134, 225, 249, 263
  Pitt, PA, 164, 196, 202
  Pittstown, PA, 181
  Plank, NY, 10, 131, 295, 304, 307, 308
  Pointe-au-Fer, QC, 25, 83
  Ranger, VT, 31, 38, 74, **76**, 81
  Sacandaga blockhouse, 312
  St. John's, QC, 17, 21, 27, 40, 42
  Schuyler. *See* Stanwix
  Shelburne blockhouse, VT, 34, **76**
  Stanwix, IT, 29, 52, 54, 94, 96, 97, 104–06, 111, 112, 116, 120, 121, 128, 149, 152, 158, 170, 202, 220, 225, 230, 245, 261, 270, 271–74, 282, 286, 313, 314, 317, 355en35

Ticonderoga, NY, 37, 43, 63, 69–72, **76**
Tory House, 241
Upper Fort, NY, 158
Wilkes-Barre, PA, 165, **178**, 180, 181, 217
William, VT, 35
Wintermoot, PA, **178**, 181–87, 217
  Surrender terms, 180, 345en27
Wyoming, PA, 165, 166, **175**, 197, 212
Fowles (One), 275
France, 111, 119, 154, 164, 165
  enters war, 24, 85
Frank, John, 257
Fraser, Alexander, 22, 64, 65, 70, 72, 74, 81, 84
Fraser, Thomas, 74, 331en93
Fraser, William, 74, 331en93
Freemeyer, David, 138–40
Freemeyer, Jacob, 142
Frey, Barent, 132, 162
Frey, Henry, 104
Frey, John, 104

Gahgeote (Half Town) (Se), 179
Gahkoondenoiya (Ono), 178
Gallup, William, 36
Ganiodaio (Handsome Lake) (Se), 179
Gansevoort, Peter, 52, 104, 111, 116, 225, 270, 282, 288
Gardner, John, 192
Garnett, Thomas, 159, 160, 271, 272, 285
Garrett, Ensign, 297
Gates, Horatio, 16, 18, 19, 22, 26, 29, 38–42, 46–49, 53, 54, 57, 60, 61, 141, 142, 155, **157**, 158, 258, 259
George III, King, 24, 101, 104, 135, 191, 196, 214, 220, 236, 239, 252, 257, 316
Germain, Lord George, 22, 32, 56, 63, 124, 252

German Flatts, NY, 96, 112, 146, 202, 205, 242, 256–**60**, 268, 270, 272–74, 276, 277, 283, 307, 312
Gerritsen, Abraham, 121
Gilliland's Creek, **76**, 83, 149
Glasford, John, 279, 280, 357en52
Good Peter Agorondajats (One), 281, **282**, 313
Gordon, James, 307
Gouvion, Jean Baptiste, 120, 128
Graham, John, 241
Grande-Île, QC, 83
Grasshopper Ojistalale (One), 118, 129, 277
Great Runaway, The, 10, 193, 195
Greaton, John, 110
Green Mountains, 30
Gustin, Samuel, 191
Guthrie, Robert, 264

Haldimand, General & Governor Frederick, 57–60, 63, 64, 85, 91, 201, 248–50, 263, 264, 283, 284, 314, 315
  assumes command, 10, 50
Hamlin, Mr., 293
Hand, Edward, 85, 286, 289, 291, 299, 304, 305, 306, 308, 312
Hanging, 43, 46, 47, 51, 325en41
Hanson, Peter, 288
Hanyery (Sch), 137, 138
Hard, Philo, 30
Hardenburgh, Johannes, 244
Harding, Benjamin, 177–79, 192
Harding, Stephen, 177–79, 192
Harding, Stukley, 177–79, 192
Hare, Lieutenant, 309
Harper, Alexander, 105, 159, 235, 236, 237, 304
Harpersfield, NY, 262, 264
Hartford, VT, 35, 57
Hartley, Thomas, 196–97–200, 202–04, 206, 209–17, 245, 293,

318, 319, 347en55
Hasbrouck, Joseph, 244
Haverhill, NH, 16
Hazen, Moses, 17, 20, 24–27, 56–58
Hazen's (Bayley-Hazen) Road, 50, 57
Hellebergh, NY, 265
Helmer, John, Adam, 272, 273
Henderson, Caleb, 30
Hendrik (One), 116
Hendricks, Peter, 234
Hepburn, William, 194
Herkimer, NY, 126, 131
Herkimer, George, 104, 116
Herkimer, Johan/Han Jost, 104, 116
Herkimer, Nicholas, 104, 107, 111, 138, 183, 308
Herrick, Samuel, 24, 33, 41, 45, 63
Hewetson, James, 159
Hewitt, Detrick, 171, 177, 180
Hiakatoo (Se), 179
Hicks, Whitehead, 35, 36
Hill, Aaron Kanonraron (Mo), 114, 124, 145
Hill, David Karaghgunty (Mo), 124, 145
Hill, Isaac Onoghsokete (Mo), 124, 144
Hillyard, Nicholas, 149
Holden, Lieutenant, 297
Honeyewus (Farmer's Brother) (Se), 179
Houghton, Richard, 58, 65, 70, 74, 78
Howe, Sir William, 24, 98, 102, 120, 124, 154, 220, 293
  recalled, 91
Howell, John, 146
Howell, Warren, 145
Hoyt, Winthrop, 82, 332en105
Hudman, Charles, 297
Hudson River, 96, 157, 222, 282
Hudson Valley, 110
Hunk, NY, 230, 231
Hunter, Samuel, 194, 195, 210

Hurley, NY, **219**, 229
Hutsinger, Jacob, 228

Île-la-Motte, QC, 66
Indian castles and towns
  Akwesasne (Mo, Ab), 32, 131, 144, 153
  Canadesaga (Se), 95, 100, 108, 133, 204, 227, 250
  Canajoharie (Mo/One), 96, 100, 125, 127, 136, 153, **260**
  Cayo-Kwen (Ca?), 109, 132
  Cayuga (Ca), 95, 100, 101, 152
  Chemung (Shemong) (Se), **175**, 200, 201, 204–06, 210, 211, 214, 216, 245, 269
  Chenango, **175**
  Chucknut (Choconut), **175**
  Cookoze, (Mu), 220, 226, 243, 245
  Cunahunta (Tu), 280
  Fort Hunter (Mo), 59, 60, 106, 109, 125, 127, 146, **260**
  French Catherine's Town (Se), 161
  Genesee (Se), 108, 204
  Indian Castle. *See* Canajoharie and Fort Hunter
  Kahnawake (Mo), 16, 32, 35, 58, 83, 277
  Kanaghsaws (Se), 151
  Kanehsatake (Mo), 284
  Kanowalohale (One), 108, 110, 128, 129, 131, 132, 151, 154, 204, 245, 281, 313, 317
    Request fort at, 120
  Kendaia (Se), 178
  Lachine. *See* Fort Hunter
  Odanak, 23, 48
  Onanquage. *See* Oquaga
  Onondaga (Ono), 117, 118, 152
  Oquaga (Mo, On, Stock, Mah), 95, 105, 106, 109, 110, 132, 135, 137, **175**, 196, 201, 202, 217, 219, 220, 224, 226, 228, 230,

233, 241, 242, 243, 244, 247,
256, 266, 268, 271, 285, 293,
313
village described, 279
Oriska (One), 100, 111, 127, 258
Owego, **175**, 293
Queen Esther's Town (Se, De), 161,
206, 216
Sheshequin (De), **175**, 205, 210,
216
Tioga Point, (De) 10, 161, 162,
169, 170, **175**, 195, 199,
203–06, 210, 214, 216, 224,
226, 228, 285, 286, 289, 291
Unadilla, 109, 132, 134, 135, 153,
155, 161, 217, 224, 236, 244,
254, 257, 266, 268, 269, 274,
276, 278, 279, 290, 310, 313
Indian Departments
British
Six Nations (6NID), 22, 35, 42,
93, 95, 97, 98, 103, 104,
107, 113–15, 117, 123,
132, 133, 153–55, 170,
176, 189, 201, 202, 218,
230, 247, 250, 272, 286,
301, 314
Brant's volunteers (BV), 95,
96, 132, 158, 218, 244,
265, 272
Yellow lace, 123, 286
Department rangers, 152,
271
Quebec (QID), 22, 32, 34, 59,
64, 74, 78, 94, 110, 125,
126
United States, 35, 127, 152
Commissioners, 93, 107, 111,
116, 117, 118, 158, 161,
281
Indian Joseph (Ono), 168
Indian Nations
Six (Five) Nations Iroquois

Confederacy, 9, 10, 34, 93,
100, 102, 125, 158, 163–65,
168, 180, 195, 216, 217, 227,
249–52, 313, 314
Eastern and Western Doors of
the Longhouse, 162
Cayugas, 9, 94, 95, 102, 107,
108, 111–15, 117, 118,
124, 125, 128, 141, 152,
158, 162, 168, 172, 189,
204, 226, 313
Mohawks, 58, 59, 94, 102, 106,
109, 110, 114, 115, 117,
118, 121, 124, 125, 137,
142–46, 148, 153, 224,
226, 230, 254, 276, 284,
295, 296
Canajoharies, 271
Oneidas, 10, 100, 101, 106,
108–12, 118, 120, 121,
125, 128, 131, 132, 152,
203, 242, 258, 271–74,
276, 280, 281, 313, 314,
317
Onondagas, 101, 102, 108, 112,
117, 118, 128, 151, 158,
168, 189, 219
Senecas, 9, 46, 94, 95, 96, 97, 101,
102, 107, 111–15, 117, 118,
125, 128, 151, 152, 158, 162,
168, 172, 173, 178, 180, 189,
203, 215, 224, 226, 245, 246,
247, 250, 285, 292–96, 299,
301, 305, 337en26
Alleghany (Upper), 125, 172, 202
Tuscaroras, 101, 102, 108, 110,
112, 118, 120, 125, 129,
152, 270, 276, 280, 281
Affiliates of Six Nations
Nanticokes, 132, 163, 168
Oquagas, 227, 258, 295
Schoharie Mohawks, 132, 138,
141

Allies of Six Nations
  Canada Indians (Seven Nations of Canada), 59, 60, 64, 94, 110, 164, 219
    Abenakis, 17, 23, 48
    Akwesasnes, 32, 271
    Kahnawakes, 23, 32, 35, 65, 66
    Kanehsatakes, 12, 84, 126
    Oswegatchies, 272, 314
  Lakes' Nations, 155, 172
    Ojibways, 112
    Ottawas, 81, 82, 112
    Wyandots, 112
  Conoys, 132, 168
  Creeks, 118
  Delawares, 132, 162, 164, 165, 215, 216, 226, 251
    Esopuses, 218, 219, 242, 247
    Minisinks, 218, 219
  Mahicans, 132
  Maliseets, 48
  Mi'kmaqs, 48
  Mississaugas, 96, 114, 125, 126, 135, 272, 314
  Mohegans, 163
  Munsees, 163, 164, 168, 218, 226
  Ohio Nations, 96, 155, 226
    Mingoes, 112
    Shawnees, 162, 163, 165
  Stockbridges, 129
Indian Territory (Country), 105, 109, 115, 118, 125, 127, 130, 134, 135, 151, 153, 155, 204, 220, 244, 246, 251, 271, 293, 310
Ingersoll, Daniel, 181
Ittig, Michael, 103

Jay, John, 246, 310
Jenkins, John, 151, 152, 169, 173, 174, 182, 193, 217

Jenkins, Judge, 173
Jeskaka (Little Billy) (Se), 179
Johns, Solomon, 67, 68, 70, 329en85
Johnson, Guy, 59, 100, 102, 110, 115, 124, 153, 162, 168, 218
Johnson, Sir John, 23, 56, 59, 110, 135, 144, 146, 148, 159, 219, 248–50, 284, 285, 314
Johnson, Peter (Ca), 313
Johnson, Sir William, 59, 94, 100, 101, 144, 165
Johnson Hall, Johnstown, NY, 12, 125, 284
Johnston, Hugh, 296
Johnston, John, 95, 191, 202, 250, 286, 301
Johnston, William, 95
Johnstown, NY, 9, 107, 108, 116, 118, 149, 151, 284, 291, 299
Jones, Jonathon, 74, 82, 83, 330en93
Jones, Robert, 223, 224
Judd, William, 166, 167

Kayashuta (Guyasuta) (Se), 125
Kelly, Barnabus, 135
Kelly, Mrs., 148
Kennedy, 145
Kenney, Captain, 200, 201
Kennyetto Creek, NY, 145
King, Lieutenant, 208
Kingston, NY, **219**, 220, 225, 229
Kirkland, Samuel, 129
Klock, Jacob, 128, 136, 148, 155, 156, 255, 256, 257, 259, 278, 290, 303, 304
Knickerbacker, John, 259
Knouts, George, 123
Knox, William, 252
Kring, Lodowick, 304

Lachine, QC, 59, 114, 125
Lackawack, NY, 11, 223–25, 230, 233

Lackawana, PA, 181
Lackawana River, PA, **178**, 190, 225, 226
LaFayette, Marquis de, 9, 11, 18, **19**, 20, 25–30, 39, 42, 43, 116, 117, 120, 128–30
Lake Champlain, 18, 64, 75, **76**, 86, 245
Lake George, 71, **76**
Lake Memphremagog, 57
Lake Ontario, 248, 263
Lake Otsego, 254, 259, **260**, 267
LaMothe, Joseph Marie, 78, 81, 82, 332en99
Lancaster, PA, 172
Langlois, Joseph dit Traversy, 56, 57
Languedoc (ship), 91
Larraway family, 171
Laurens, Henry, 86, 111, 118, **119**, 130, 151
Lawyer, Lawrence, 141
Lee (sloop), 83
LeMaistre, Francis, 102, 103, 113, 335en15
Lincoln, Benjamin, 25, 26
Lintz, 143
Little Aaron (Mo), 295
Little, John, 148
Livingston Manor, NY, 48
Livingston, James, 19
Livingston, Peter R., 160, 161
London, England, 22, 85
Long, Gabriel, 262
Long, Reuben, 278, 280
Lord Dunmore's War, 226
Lorimier, Jean-Claude-Chamilly de, 23, 33
  killed, 34
Lorimier, Verneuil de, 66, 83, 332en107
Loucks, 143, 145
Louis XVI, King, 24
Loyal Provincial Army
  American Volunteers (McAlpin's), 59, 74
  Butler's Rangers (BR), 9, 42, 105, 113, 114, 132–34, 153, 162, 171, 177, 178, 180, 184–87, 189, 201, 202, 216, 219, 220, 226, 227, 228, 235, 242, 245, 250, 252, 264, 271, 272, 286, 292, 295, 297, 298, 299, 300, 302, 310, 315
    Beating Order, 98–100, 315
    belt plate, **228**
      Caldwell's Coy, 132
      Musket, **185**
  King's Loyal Americans (Jessup's) (KLA), 59, 74
  King's Royal Regt of New York (1st Bn) (1KRR), 12, 32, 65, 66, 126, 144, 149, 219, 249, 263, 271
    Light Infantry Coy, 284
  King's Royal Regt of New York (2nd Bn) (2KRR), 146
  'Loyal Volunteers' (Leake's), 59
  Quebec Militia (Milice de Québec), 23, 32, 49
  Queen's Loyal Rangers (Peters') (QLR), 43, 50, 51, 56, 67, 75
Loyalsock Creek, PA, 174, **175**
Lurenkill, NY, 230
Lycoming Creek, PA, 174, 176
Lyon, Matthew, 31

Mabee, Cobus, 126
MacBean, Forbes, 65
McDonald, 233
McDonell, John (Aberchalder), 264, 286, 292, 299–301, 310
McDonell, John (Scotus), 105
McGinnis (McGinn), George, 95, 230
McGinnis, John, 275
McGinnis, Richard, 134, 162, 226, 228, 242, 275

McGinnis, Robert (father), 242, 275, 276
McGinnis, Sarah Kast, 95, 101
McIntosh, Daniel, 68, 69, 82
McKean, Robert, 254
McKenna, John, 269
McKendry, Lieutenant, 300, 304
McLane, Allen, 130
Maclay, William, 194, 195
McMicking, Thomas, 105
Mamakating, NY, 244
Manchester, VT, 63
Mantlet, 65
Marbletown, NY, 242, 244
Maria (schooner), 66, 68, 83
Marsh, Joseph, 36, 38, 63
Martel, Captain, 199
Martin, Robert, 144
Masonic Order
  distress sign, 139, 299, 340en61
  emblems, trade silver, 299
Mathews, Robert, 264, 314
Mattice, Henrick, 159, 343en92
Mayfield district, NY, 145, 146
Maynard, Lieutenant, 139, 299
Middagh, John, 223, 231–33, 241, 242
Middagh, Stephen, 223, 231–33, 242
Middleburgh, NY, 137, 141
Middlebury, VT, 78
Mill Creek, PA, 165
Miller, Captain, 138
Miller, Hannah, 194
Miller, Jacob, 104
Mills, 75, 77, 83, 148, 190. 193, 200, 245, 273
  grist, 134, 148, 166, 280
  saw, 31, 69, 70, 280
    Moore's, **73**, 75, 77, 81
Minisink, NY, 171, 201, 220, 221, 224–26, 230, 232, 243, 245, 246
Missisquoi Bay, QC, 57, 58
Mitchell, 295

Mohawk District, NY, 148
Mohawk Valley, NY, 9, 32, 64, 93, 110, 126–28, 249, 254, 301, 313
Mompesson, John, 134, 135, 314
Monkton, VT, 34, **76**, 82
Montour, Esther (Se), 161
Montour, Madame (Se), 161
Montreal, QC, 17, 20–22, 32, 42, 56, 59, 65, 86, 134, 142, 152, 153, 172, 218, 249
Montreal (frigate), 49, 50
Moore, John, 301, 303, 312, 361en94
Moore, Paul, 75
Moore's Sawmill. *See* mills
Morgan, Daniel, 205, 235, 254
Morristown, NJ, 167
Moss, Timothy, 45
Mount Independence, VT, 72
Moyer, Daybold, 304
M.R., 302, 303
Murphy, Timothy, 266
Murray, James, 211, 212
Murrow, Captain, 207, 209

Nanticoke, William (Na-Co), 168
Napanoch, NY, 229
Navy, French, 53, 85, 86, 119
  Royal, ocean, 86, 159, 222
  Royal Provincial, 18, 26, 27, 37, 40, 62, 64, 66, 81, 82, 83, 105, 119, 263
Neversink River, 243
New Dorlach, NY, 104
New Hampshire Grants, NY, 17, 30, 42, 60, 163, 274. *See also* Vermont
New Hampshire State, 44, 47, 56, 59, 69, 163
New Jersey State, 153, 176, 206, 219
New York City, NY, 35, 54, 60, 124, 154, 158, 159, 204, 206, 216, 219, 226, 248, 249, 251, 252, 269, 311
New York State, 44, 54, 55, 59, 60, 91, 107, 112, 115, 125, 153, 163,

206, 246, 310
Albany County. *See separate listing*
Commission for Detecting and
   Defeating Conspiracies, 122,
   159, 160
Legislature, 122
Hudson Highlands, 225
Orange County, 218, **219**, 244, 246
Tryon County. *See separate listing*
Ulster County, 218, 219, 225, 242,
   244, 246, 254, 259
Newberry, William, 104, 295
Newbury, VT, 57
Newkirk, Jacob, 221, 224, 232, 244
Newtown Martin, NY, 150
Niagara, IT, 59, 86, 108, 111, 114,
   116, 133, 153, 154, 162, 168, 170,
   172, 230, 314. *See also* forts
Nicolet River, 23
Nicoll, Leonard D., 231–33
Nixon, John, 19
No. 4 Township, NH, 51
North-West Bay, NY, 68
Northern Department U.S., 61, 85,
   157
Norwich, VT, 38
Nova Scotia, 48

Ogden, Captain, 166
Ogden, Mrs., 296
Olcott, Peter, 38
Old Smoke Sayengaraghta (Se), 100,
   101, 108, 115, 124, 132, 135, 151,
   152, 158, 161, 162, 178, 183–86,
   216, 224, 285, 286
Ones-Yap (Sch), 137, 138, 141,
   340en61
Onion River, VT, 33, 40, 41, 45, 55,
   56, 58, **76**
Oswegatchie. *See* Forts
Oswego, IT, 62, 93, 95–97, **98**, 116,
   218, 316–18
Oteronyente, John Hill (Mo), **109**,

110, 124
Otter Creek, VT, 31–37, 63, 67, 68,
   72, 74, **76**, 78, 81, 83, 245
first falls of, **76**
McIntosh farm, **76**
Ousterhout, Jacob, 223, 230, 231

Pakatakan (Paghkatakean, Pakatagkan),
   NY, 11, **219**, 222, 230, 233, 234,
   235, 269
Panton, VT, 36
Papaconck, NY, 231
Parker, Lieutenant, 299
Parks, Nathan, 232, 241, 242
Parliament, British, 24
Parr, James, 262, 269, 280
Pasink, NY, 159
Patrick, William, 137, 138, 142,
   340en61
Pawling, Benjamin, 202
Pawling, Levi, 222, 225, 237, 240,
   242, 350en7
Pawling family, 171
Paxton Boys, 165, 166, 183
Payne, Elisha, 36
Peacham, VT, 57
Peekskill, NY, 245, 288
Peenpack, NY, 225, 233, 243, 286
Penn, William, 163
Pennamites, 165–67, 171, 200
Pennsylvania (Colony) State, 93, 102,
   112, 115, 125, 151, 153, 163,
   165–68, 171, 175, 206, 219, 246,
   250, 286
   Northumberland County, 193, 194,
      196, 210
   State Executive Council, 198, 203,
      213
Pepacton, NY, **219**, 220, 222, 230,
   231–33, 241, 242, 349en2
Peters, John, 43, 50, 55–59, 64
Phelps, Elijah, 177
Phelps, Joel, 177

Philadelphia, PA, 120, 130, 131, 216, 220
Phillips, Moses, 243
Philo, 34, 323en21
Pierson, Moses, 32, 34
Pierson, Mrs., 34
Pittsburg, PA, 85
Pittsford, VT, 36, 37, 70, **76**
Pittstown, PA, **178**, 190
Plunkett, William, 167
Pollard, Edward, 97, 98
Pontiac Uprising 1763, 166
Posey, Thomas, 235, 236, 238–40, 262, 269
Potter, Nathaniel, 303
Potts, William, 134
Poughkeepsie, NY, 159, 161
Powell, Henry Watson, 32, 56, 66, 249
Powell, John, 133, 201
Proctor, Samuel, 297

Quebec City, 18, 32, 55, 65, 96, 97, 153, 248, 263, 285
Quebec Gazette, 42, 49
Quebec, Province of, 47, 57, 63, 85, 93, 148, 277, 314
    Legislative Council, 49
    surrender predicted, 53
Queen Esther (Se), 229

Raids. *See* expeditions
Ransom, Samuel, 167, 172, 182, 183
Raymond's Mills, NY, 75, **76**, 77
Redding, David, 43
Reed, Jacob (One), 129
Reid, Colonel, 69
Rhode Island State, 85
Richelieu River, 18
Rinepee, John (Es), 240
Rivingston's *Royal Gazette*, 204, 206
Robinson, Moses, 31
Robinson, Samuel, 45, 46

Rochester, NY, **219**, 223, 242, 245, 246
Ross, Andrew, 74, 78, 81–83, 330en93
Ross, John, 64, 142, **143**, 149, 265, 312
Rouville, Jean-Baptiste-Melchior Hertel de, **23**
Rupert, VT, 63
Rutland, VT, 31, 36, 38, 39, 45, 46, 51, 66, 70, 72, **76**, 78, 81

Sacandaga River, NY, 144, 148, 149
Sagwarithra (Tu), 178
Saint-François du Lac, QC, 56
St. John's, QC, 16, 18, 20, 31, 35, 57, 58, 60
St. Lawrence River, 16, 23, 35, 86, 134, 148
St. Leger, Barry, 94–97, 103, 113, 154, 170, 220, 249
Sandgate, VT, 63
Saratoga, NY, 18, 21, 95, 143, 220
Sawyer, Jesse, 24
Sawyer, Thomas, 32, 34
Schank, John, 263, 327en76
Schenectady, NY, 122, 157, 290, 308, 312
Schoharie Kill/River, NY, 266
Schoharie Valley, NY, 9, 140–42, 158–60, 199, 201, 222, 229, 234, 235, 239, 245, 254, 258, 259, 262, 265, 266, 269, 277, 290, 291, 299, 306
Schuyler, (Jacob?), 268
Schuyler, Philip, 9, 25, 26, 34, 35, 97, 106–08, 110–12, 116, 119, 120, 151, 258, 301
    U.S. Indian Commissioner, 96, 101, 121
Schuyler's Lake, NY, 268
Scott, Henry, 294
Scott, John Morin, 229
Scovell, Elisha, 180

Scribner, Thaddeus, 304
Sealey, Abner, 24
Secord, James, 95, 170, 171
Secord, John, 176
Secord family, 171
Secret Service, Quebec, 23, 92, 144
Seneca Lake, IT, 161
Sequidonquee (Little Beard) (Se), 179, 292, 293
Servos, Christopher, 135, 265, 266
Servos, Clara, 266
Seven Nations of Canada. *See* Canada Indians
Seven Years' War, 97, 166
Shandaken, Great and Little, 230, 234, 242, 245, 247
Shanks, Ben (Es), 230, 240, 241
Sharrar, Margaret, 283
Sharrar, Nancy, 283
Shawnee, PA, 174, 206
Sheehan, Mrs., 318
Shelburne, VT, 9, 32
Sherwood, Justus, 67, 75, 77, 78, 331en94
Shew, Catrina, 145
Shew, Godfrey, 144, 145, **147**, 148
Shew, Jacob, 145, **147**
Shew, John, 144, 145, **147**
Shew, Stephen, **147**
Shoemaker's Tavern (Rudolph), 273
Showers, Michael, 170, 177
Simmons, Peter, 228
Simon, James, 300
Sits, Peter, 136, 340en59
Skenesborough, NY, 72, 80, 81, 83, 84
Sleeper, John, 308
Sleeper, Mrs., 308
Sleeper's Mills, NY, 308
Smith, Charles, 220, 222, 226, 235, 264, 265
    killed, 266
Smith (gunner), 66

Smith, Joseph, 297
Smith, Nathan, 38
Smyth, 71, 72
Snow, John, 223, 230
Snyder, Johannes, 245
Snydersbush, NY, 9
Spaulding, Simon, 172, 182, 183, 193, 207, 209
Spencer, Thomas (One), 110, 129, 131, 337en25
Split Rock, NY, 68, 83
Spooner, Paul, 31
Springfield, NY, 150, 151
Stacey, William, 267, 268, 294, 299, 319
Stacy Brook, NY, 75
Stanwix Treaty Line, 1768, 105, 135, 256
Stark, John, 18–20, 25, 33, 38, 40, 44, 46–52, 54, 60–**61**–62, 85, 123, 141, 142, 148, 150, 155, 156, 160, 161, 235, 260, 261, 266, 267, 286, 287, 291
    criticized, 268, 269, 274
Stevens, Asa, 169
Stevens, Ebenezer, 53
Stevens, William, 278, 279
Stewart, Lazarus, 165–67, 184, 201
Stoddard/Stoddert, Captain, 207–09
Stone Arabia, NY, **260**
Summer House Point, NY, 145
Sunbury, PA, **175**, 194, 195
Susquehanna River, 95, 109, 134, 153, 164, 167, 168, 172, **178**, 193, 202, 203, 256, 279, 280, 289, 290, 313
    east and west branches of, **175**
Swartout, Philip, Sr., 243
Sweeny, 143
Sweeny, Lieutenant, 207, 208

Tayojaronsere, John (Oq Mo), 110
Teedyuscung (De), 165
Telford, William, 241

Ten Broeck, Abraham, 40, 117, 141, 142, 148, 155, 156, 160, 161, 222, 229, 230, 245, 254, 258, 273, 277, 306
Ten Broeck, Peter, 101, 127
Tenhoghskweaghta (Ono), 117, 118
Tewahangarahken, Han Yerry (One), 129
Thahoswagwat, Han Jost (One), 129
Thompson, Archibald, 105, 265
Tice, Christiana, 103
Tice, Gilbert, 103, 152–54, 271, 272, 285
Tousard, Louis de, 120, 128–31
Treaty of Alliance, France & United States, 1778, 50, 85
Tribes Hill, NY, 126, 288
Trois-Rivières, QC, 32
Tryon County, NY, 45, 113, 123, 131, 142, 143, 155, 156, 158, 160, 218, 277
  Commission of Forfeiture and Sequestration, 104, 105, 267
  Committee of Safety, 103, 104, 115
    dissolved, 121
Tunkhannock, PA, 174, 176, 177
Tunnicliff, John, 123, 256, 267, 268
Tunnicliff, William, 123, 267
Turney, John, 180, 228, 300
Tusten, Benjamin, 224
Twiss, William, 263, 264, 283
Tylar, Mr., 232, 351en19
Tyorhansere, Abraham (Mo), 106, 107

Unadilla (Creek) River, 242, 272, 276
United States Army
  Continental, 15, 24, 40, 41, 51, 52, 120, 123, 129, 158, 225, 230, 243, 256, 258, 261, 262, 267, 274, 288
    Artillery, 53, 54
    McLane's Independent Partisan Corps, 130, 339en49
    Morgan's 2nd Rifle Corps, 254, 261, 262
      Long's Coy, 262, 266
      Parr's Coy, 262, 269, 278
    Pulaski's Legion, 246
    Stevens' Artillery, 39
    Steven's artillery maintenance Coy, 53, 54
    Thomas Lee's Ranging Coy, 31
  Massachusetts, Brigade, 19
    Alden's 6th Regt (6MA), 11, 39–41, 52, 137, 141, 142, 155, 160, 261, 262, 267, 274, 277, 287, 288, 291, 296, 297, 301, 305, 309, 312
    Greaton's 3rd Regt (3MA), 39
  Connecticut
    3rd Regiment, 171, 177
    6th Brigade, 167
    24th (Westmoreland) Militia Regt, 166, 178, 179, 180, 181, 183
    Westmoreland Independent Coys, 167, 168, 172, 182
      Hewitt's Coy, 171, 180, 181, 182, 183
      Spaulding's Coy, 172, 182, 184, 193, 194, 205, 207
  New Hampshire, 130
    Bedel's Rangers, 17
    Bedel's Regt, 20, 26, 38, 41, 42, 44, 46, 47, 260
    Whitcomb's Rangers, 17, 20, 31, 62, 71, 75, 77
    Safford's Coy, 72
  New York, 111
    1st Regt (1NY), 19, 245, 282, 288, 290, 301, 307, 310

2nd Regt (2NY), 230, 245, 246
3rd Regt (3NY), 104, 161, 282
    desertions from, 270, 271, 282, 355en35
Brigade, 245, 282, 316
Hazen's 2nd Canadian Regt, 17, 19, 20, 56
Livingston's 1st Canadian Regt, 19, 20
Warner's Additional Regt, 19, 31, 37–39, 41, 44, 51, 69, 72, 75

Levies & State Troops
  New York, Graham's, 229

Militia, 15
  Massachusetts, 42, 259, 287
    Berkshire, 40, 41, 46, 48, 52, 54, 160, 259
    Hampshire, 40, 41, 46, 48, 54, 259
  New York
    Albany County, 40, 156, 160, 222, 230, 259, 274, 277
      1st Regt (1ACM), 51, 52, 123
      2nd Regt (2ACM), 259
      9th Regt (9ACM), 254
      14th Regt (14ACM), 259
      15th Regt (15ACM), 40, 41, 51, 137, 141, 259, 277, 278
      17th Regt (17ACM), 273, 303
      Dietz's Ranging Coy, 278
    Charlotte County, 71, 75, 80
    Tryon County Brigade, 94, 103, 104, 111, 112, 120, 127, 128, 145, 149, 152, 160, 183, 249, 259, 273, 274, 278, 291, 303, 306, 310
      Exempts Coy, 146
      Ranging companies, 156, 278
      1st Regt (1TCM), 123, 131, 257, 291, 297, 301
        4th, 5th & 6th Coys, 131
        Coapman's 5th Coy, 132
      2nd Regt (2TCM), 257, 304
        Hess's Coy, 136
      3rd Regt (3TCM), 146, 288, 299, 305
      4th Regt (4TCM), 104, 115, 126, 257
      Minutemen Battalion, 104
    Orange County Brigade, 230, 240, 242, 243, 245
      2nd Regt (2OCM) 224
      3rd Regt (3OCM) 224, 225
      4th Regt (4OCM), 224, 243, 244
    Ulster County Brigade, 105, 106, 230–32, 240, 242, 243, 245
      1st Regt (1UCM), 245
      2nd Regt (2UCM), 222, 224, 225, 231, 241, 243, 244
      3rd Regt (3UCM), 223
      4th Regt (4UCM), 230, 244
      Clark's Independent Coy, 241
      Hanover Exempts Coy, 241
  Pennsylvania, 130, 167, 232

4th Regt (4PA), 199, 203, 235, 254, 261, 262, 266
  Grenadiers, 280
8th Regt (8PA), 196
Carberry's Light Horse, 203, 205–07, 209
Hartley's Additional Regt, 196, 293, 347en55
Vermont, 24, 31, 33, 37, 38
  Cumberland County Regts, 45, 63
  Green Mountain Boys, 41, 69
  Herrick's Second Regt (2VMR), 24, 30, 38, 45, 81
    Arlington Coy, 36
    Bennington's Coy, 45
  Warren's Fifth Regt (5VMR), 38, 45, 74
Up-the-River District, 168, 170, 171, 174

Valley Forge, PA, 30, 120, 129, 168
Van Cortlandt, Philip, 245, 246
Van De Car, Roeleff, 271
Van Deusen, Melchart, 121
Van Dyck, Cornelius, 313
Van Keuren, Henry, 231–33
Van Schaick, Goose, 19, 282, 288, 301, 307, 308, 310
Van Schaick, Jacob, 160
Van Waggenen, Catherine, 235–37
Van Waggenen, Simeon, 235
Varick, Richard, 42
Veeder, Volkert, 146
Vermont, Republic of, 36, 47, 54, 55, 57, 63, 91, 245, 246, 274
  Board of War, 31
  Council of Safety, 30, 32, 34, 35, 36, 39, 43
  Eastern Union, 43, 44, 47, 91
  General Assembly, 31, 35, 39, 44
  Governing Council, 24, 30, 36, 41, 43, 54, 56, 63

  Negotiations/Talks, 47, 91, 92
Virginia (Colony) State, 36, 102, 108, 112, 164
Visscher, Frederick, 146, 288, 299, 305, 309
Vrooman, 302
Vrooman, Lieutenant, 159
Vrooman, Peter, 158, 229, 258

Wait, Benjamin, 24, 30
Walker, Andrew, 197, 198
Wall, Deborah, 318
Wallace, Ebenezer, 36
Walloomscoick, VT, 22
Warmwood, Hendrick, 144
Warner, George, 138, 139, 142
Warner, Seth, 20, 31, 52, 66, 80, 322en15
Warren, Benjamin, 261, 296, 300, 303, 306, 308
Warren, Gideon, 38, 63, 74, 81, 83
Washington, General George, 19, 25, 28, 60–62, 85, 86, 120, 128, 129, 152, 203, 254, 261, 274, 282, 286, 289, 312
  precipitates war, 164
Washington, Martha, 130
Wawarsing, NY, 229, 254, 259
Weare, Meshech, 47, 50, 51
Webster, Alexander, 71, 75, 77, 80, 330en89
Welch, David, 51, 52
Wells, Robert, 293, 294
Wells, VT, 45
Wells family, 294, 295
Wells House, Cherry Valley, 292
West Canada Creek, NY, 126
Westbrook, Anthony, 244
Westbrook, Frederick, 230
Wheelock, Officer, 267
Whitcomb, Benjamin, 16, 20, 30, 31, 62, 66, 70, 71, 74, 77, 81, 83, 84
  description of, 17

White Plains, NY, 52
Whiting, Daniel, 294, 305, 306
Whiting, William, 273
Wilkes-Barre, PA, 165, 166, 168, 174, 193, 197
Willett, Marinus, 112, 120, 121, 161, 254
Williams, Joseph, 34
Wintermoot family, 171, 180
Wisner, Henry, 224
Wolcott, Oliver, 107, 111, 336en21
Wood, Ebenezer, 24
Woodsum, Samuel, 297
Woodworth, Jacob, 144
Woodworth, Solomon, 144, 148, 342en75
Wormwood, Mathias, 136, 290
Wright, Zadock, 50
Wyalusing, PA, 168, 169, 172, **175**, **178**, 202, 206, 207, 211
Wynkoop, Adrian, 245
Wyoming Valley, PA, 103, 109, 114, 125, 151, 162, 163–69, **175**, 200, 202, 205, 210, 213, 215, 216, 224, 226, 250

Yamaska River, 23
Yates, Abraham, Jr., 312
Yates, Lieutenant-Colonel, 142
York Town, PA, 152, 172
Young, Adam, 104, 170, 257, 354en14
Young, John, 135, 170, 202

- dundurn.com
- @dundurnpress
- dundurnpress
- dundurnpress
- dundurnpress
- info@dundurn.com

FIND US ON NETGALLEY & GOODREADS TOO!

DUNDURN